AMATEURS, TO ARMS!

MAJOR BATTLES AND CAMPAIGNS

John S. D. Eisenhower, General Editor

MAJOR BATTLES AND CAMPAIGNS

AMATEURS, TO ARMS!

A MILITARY HISTORY OF
THE WAR OF
1812

By John R. Elting
Colonel, United States Army (Ret.)

DA CAPO PRESS • NEW YORK

Library of Congress Cataloging in Publication Data

Elting, John Robert.
  Amateurs, to arms!: a military history of the War of 1812 / by John R. Elting.—
1st Da Capo Press ed.
      p.   cm.—(Major battles and campaigns)
  Includes bibliographical references and index.
  ISBN 0-306-80653-3 (alk. paper)
  1. United States—History—War of 1812—Campaigns. I. Title. II. Series.
[E355.E48   1995]
973.5′2—dc20   95-16004
                                                                             CIP

First Da Capo Press edition 1995

This Da Capo Press paperback edition of *Amateurs, To Arms!* is an unabridged republication, with minor textual emendations, of the edition originally published in Chapel Hill, North Carolina in 1991. It is reprinted by arrangement with Algonquin Books of Chapel Hill.

Published by Da Capo Press, Inc.
A Subsidiary of Plenum Publishing Corporation
233 Spring Street, New York, N.Y. 10013

Manufactured in the United States of America

CONTENTS

LIST OF ILLUSTRATIONS

LIST OF MAPS

ACKNOWLEDGMENTS

TO ANN, MY WIFE AND GOOD COMRADE of fifty-five years, who typed and edited this "one more" book.

To friends who shared their own research and knowledge with me: Alan C. Aimone, Gerard T. Altoff, René Chartrand, Brian L. Dunnigan, Donald E. Graves, Jack Meyer, Patrick A. Wilder, and Thomas P. Williams.

To other friends who helped me assemble the illustrations: Major Leonid Kondratiuk, USNG; Michael E. Moss, USMA Museum; Brigadier General Edwin H. Simmons, USMC; Don A. Troiani; Colonel Charles H. Waterhouse, USMCR; Eric I. Manders; Liliane and Fred Funcken; and H. Charles McBarron, Jr.

And to my friend Edward J. Krasnoborski, master cartographer of the History Department, USMA, who did the maps.

PROLOGUE

I very much doubt if a parallel can be found for the state of things existing on this frontier. A gallant little army struggling with the enemies of their country and devoting their lives to its honor and safety, left by that country to struggle alone . . .

—Jacob Brown [1]

THE ARMIES THAT THE UNITED STATES MUSTERED for the War of 1812 were truly amateurs at arms. No other national conflict, even our War of Independence, found us so unready and so ill-prepared. In 1775 the embryo United States could muster hundreds of men—still in their prime of life—who were veterans of the long French and Indian War [2] and Pontiac's Rebellion. Far more important, it had George Washington, who was both a competent military commander and a dedicated national leader of unflinching courage, character, and patriotism. Neither of these resources was available in 1812. The Revolution had ended twenty-seven years before; its surviving veterans were mostly old in body, mind, and spirit and out of touch with all things military. There was no effective national leader; the national government's direction of the war was limp-wristed, erratic, and sometimes altogether lacking.

The war's causes were tangled. One was the constant interference with American shipping resulting from the British blockade of Napoleon's European empire. This had involved the total derangement of American trade overseas, seizure of American ships and cargoes, impressment of American seamen into the brutally disciplined Royal Navy, interference

1. Adams, *The War of 1812*, p. 256.
2. Europe's Seven Years' War, 1756–63, which actually began in North America in 1754.

with American coastal traffic, and even attacks on United States naval vessels—all of it carried through with galling arrogance.

The other major cause was the unappeasable land hunger of the westerning American frontier—shiftless squatter and big-scale land speculator together. They wanted Indian tribal territories, Florida, and Canada, and felt a God-given right to whatever they could grab. Most of this period's frontier clashes were sparked by their constant encroachments on Indian lands and their disregard for Indian rights. Westerners bitterly resented the fact that those Indians got arms and ammunition from British traders; they accused the British of encouraging and arming the Indians to resist American expansion, of setting "the ruthless savages to tomahawk our women and children."[3]

There was much self-righteous exaggeration in such charges, and yet also a certain core of fact: English traders, operating well within American territory, did arm the hostile tribes. And behind them were the shadowy maneuverings of the great Anglo-Canadian fur companies, intent on maintaining their control of the North American trade and seldom boggling at any measure essential to that end. The frontier also had long memories of British-inspired raids and massacres through the Revolution, of rewards given for American scalps at Detroit; of English-Canadian rangers who still ran with English-supplied war parties thereafter, until Anthony Wayne broke the tribes at Fallen Timbers in 1795. Now the westerners were certain, and with good reason, that both English traders and officials supported Tecumseh's efforts to form a league of Indian tribes. In 1811 representatives from the western and southern states—soon to be dubbed "War Hawks"—got control of the House of Representatives and elected Henry Clay as its Speaker. Mostly young, ardent, and ambitious, they shared two common characteristics: they were eager for war with England, and they knew nothing whatever about war.

Desperately engaged with Napoleon, England did not wish war with the United States. The Duke of Wellington's army in Spain was largely dependent on American foodstuffs and shipping for its daily rations. (On the 4th of July, 1811, Bandmaster John Westcott of the Cameronians/ 26th Foot saw some 200 American vessels in Lisbon harbor, all bright with flags in honor of the date.) At the same time, England neither anticipated nor feared conflict. Then as always, England at war dealt harshly

---

3. Homer C. Hockett, *Political and Social Growth of the United States, 1492–1852* (New York: Macmillan, 1936), p. 393.

with neutrals, expecting them to favor England's interests and to make all sacrifices that might be required. Up until 1810 the United States had appeared sufficiently cowed. President Jefferson had responded to British highhandedness only with words and suicidal trade policies that crippled American commerce without troubling England. His successor, James Madison, was no more aggressive. Moreover, the powerful New England commercial interests could be relied on to seek peace and whatever profits England would allow them, no matter what the attendant humiliations.

By late 1810, however, with Napoleon again victorious over Austria and Wellington penned up around Lisbon,[4] England became conscious of swelling American hostility. Relations grew tighter: on May 16, 1811, the United States frigate *President*, hunting the British frigate *Guerrière*, which had impressed an American citizen from a merchant vessel, clashed by night with the English sloop-of-war *Little Belt* and swiftly wrecked her—and Madison proved unexpectedly unresponsive to British protests.[5] By June 23, 1812, England at last thought it wise to voluntarily revoke most of her restrictions on American commerce—only to learn that the United States had declared war on June 18.[6]

THIS BOOK IS AN ATTEMPT TO PRESENT the military character of the ensuing war, its strategy, logistics, and tactics. In so doing, it is necessary to deal bluntly with two of present-day America's favorite figures, the American Indian and Thomas Jefferson and his disciples, by presenting them as many of their contemporaries saw them. Americans of 1812–15 lived and died by what they knew: the gentler, reasoned visions that many of this generation cherish would have been meaningless in those desperate years when the war whoop rang at your cabin door, and flame and smoke along our coasts signaled the coming of George Cockburn or Alexander Cochrane.

---

4. He had been driven into a fortified camp he had previously built around Lisbon, the famous "Lines of Torres Verdes."

5. *Little Belt* fired first when challenged to identify herself. Her captain's report is that of a desperately shocked man. Losing his ship was tragic enough, but losing it to an American—!

6. Had England acted several weeks earlier the war probably could have been at least postponed. But England would not renounce her practice of impressment, and the West's land hunger would have remained unappeased. It must be noted that Napoleon too had been seizing American ships. However, we could not get at Napoleon, and he had no possessions we wanted.

AMATEURS, TO ARMS!

ONE

Of Arms and Men, Bad Roads and Short Rations

This is no field for a military man above the rank of a Colonel of Riflemen.
—General Frederick P. Robinson [1]

THE UNITED STATES SWAGGERED INTO the War of 1812 like a Kansas farm boy entering his first saloon. And, like that same innocent, wretchedly gagging down his first drink, the new nation was totally unprepared for the raw impact of all-out war.

Beginning with President Thomas Jefferson's inauguration in 1801, the armed forces of the United States had been the object of not-so-benign neglect. Jefferson and the leading figures of his Republican party [2] —from scholarly James Madison to poker-playing Henry Clay—were gentlemen and patriots, willing to expend their time and fortunes in the service of the United States. They were not pacifists: they would squelch the Barbary pirate states, commandeer West Florida from a prostrate Spain in 1810, and plan to ingest the rest of Florida and as much of Canada as possible. But they were lawyers, scholars, and politicians— men of words and theories, and too often impractical. Very few had served in the Revolution, and those few had learned little from that service. The rest were blissfully ignorant of everything military, and thoroughly content with their ignorance. Also, most of them were careless, sloven administrators.

Jefferson found an Army of approximately 4,000 officers and men; he

---

1. Robinson had served under Wellington before coming to Canada in 1814. He was not prepared for North America.
2. The direct lineal and doctrinal ancestor of the present Democratic party.

promptly cut it to 3,200, leaving two regiments of infantry, one of "artillerists," and a "corps of engineers" consisting of seven officers and ten cadets.[3] This last was to be stationed at West Point "and shall constitute a military academy." Almost a third of the Army's officers were dismissed; the one general retained was James Wilkinson, confidence man in uniform and traitor extraordinaire, who called himself "a scientific soldier."

Having so reduced the Army, Jefferson paid little attention to what remained of it except to employ it on various explorations. Pay remained low, medical supplies ran short, rations and clothing frequently were skimpy. By 1807 the Army's strength had fallen below 2,400 men. When the *Leopard-Chesapeake* incident in June that year caused an explosion of anti-British sentiment, Jefferson did secure authorization from Congress for five new regiments of infantry and one each of riflemen, light dragoons, and light artillery to serve for five years, unless sooner released by Congress. More money was appropriated for coastal defenses, and an annual appropriation of $200,000 was authorized for distribution among the states to arm and equip their militia.

Recruiting these additional regiments went slowly. By 1812 the Army could muster only some 6,750 men out of an intended 10,000. Jefferson and his successor Madison took little interest in them, except to make certain that they were officered by deserving Republicans. On the whole, these appointees deserved the famous condemnation that Winfield Scott (one of them, until trouble brought out his basic good sense) loosed upon them: "swaggerers, dependents, decayed gentlemen and others fit for nothing else" who always turned out to be utterly "unfit for any military purpose whatever." Everything else was done equally on the cheap—in part because Abraham Gallatin, secretary of the treasury and the one truly able cabinet member in both administrations, was insistent on paying off the national debt and did not like soldiers. Though cavalry required the longest time of any arm to train and equip, the light dragoon regiment was never completely organized and had to serve dismounted as light infantry. The Regiment of Light Artillery did not get a lieutenant colonel until 1811, or a colonel until 1812; meanwhile—like the Regiment of Artillerists—it too served as infantry.

Jefferson's secretary of war was Henry Dearborn, who had fought his way up to colonel during the Revolution by good and gallant service. Since then he had turned Republican politician, a somewhat rare thing

---

3. This reduction abolished one artillery and two infantry regiments and the Army's small force of cavalry.

in his native Massachusetts. He did much to modernize American ordnance, and made an honest effort to get the Light Artillery Regiment properly equipped as horse artillery—succeeding to the extent of one company, which Captain George Peter organized in 1808–9.[4] However, he was too unquestioningly loyal to Jefferson to champion the Army against the President's indifference. Also, he supported the government's cheese-paring stinginess. No post or unit commander could make an expenditure of over $50 without first obtaining Dearborn's consent. An officer in an isolated frontier station, needing medicines and proper food for sick soldiers, could either wait for the several months that such correspondence might require or make the necessary purchases and hunch his shoulders against Dearborn's wrath.

When Madison succeeded Jefferson in 1809, things went from bad to worse. Dearborn's replacement was one William Eustis, who had served faithfully as a surgeon through the Revolution, but now was a miserly detail chaser with neither administrative ability nor foresight. He promptly sold the Army's few horses to save the cost of their feed. When Wilkinson held a large portion of the Army in the pesthole swamp of Terre aux Boeufs, south of New Orleans, from June 9 to September 10, 1809—while he courted a Creole belle and cheated his men out of their proper rations—Eustis would not allow the purchase of mosquito nets or chickens, eggs, and wine for the hospital.[5] Out of some 2,000 soldiers there, approximately 900 died and 166 deserted; 40 officers died or resigned. The Army's morale was badly dented.

War with England appearing inevitable, Madison called Congress to an early session in November 1811 and recommended some sensible preparations, such as recruiting the Army up to strength. In January, Congress accordingly authorized ten new regiments of infantry, two of artillery, and another of light dragoons.[6] Madison also requested authority to enroll 50,000 "volunteers" (best described as temporary regulars) and $3 million with which to do it; in February, Congress gave him 30,000 and $1 million.

---

4. Dearborn equipped the Army with iron, rather than bronze, cannon. (The United States had plenty of excellent iron ore, but would have to import copper and tin.) He also ruled that artillerymen would serve as drivers for their gun teams, a great improvement over the European practice of forming separate units of artillery drivers.

5. Eustis had ordered Wilkinson to move north to a more healthful site, but failed to enforce his orders.

6. Also six companies of rangers for frontier duty.

The officers for the new regiments were once again commissioned according to their political purity. With considerable justice they were described as "coarse and ignorant. . . . Young men of dissipated habits . . . or political brawlers who had recommended themselves to the Government by their noisy patriotism." Few Federalists [7] were accepted, though many were willing to serve, and this had the side effect of dampening the already weak war spirit in New York and New England. Only a few experienced officers could be spared from the older regiments to organize the new ones; in fact, really competent officers were relatively scarce. Repeated reorganizations and reductions since the Revolution had made the Army an unattractive career; aside from a dedicated handful such as Alexander Macomb, Zebulon M. Pike, Edmund P. Gaines, Winfield Scott, and Henry Atkinson, few able men considered it a rewarding profession. Most of the senior officers were relics of the Revolution, often physically unfit but hanging on to their positions because there was no system of retirement for age or length of service. Years of duty in isolated posts had left most of them indifferent, contentious, and ignorant; few had experience in handling a whole regiment or had even seen one.

Once appointed, the new officers had to recruit their units. This proved slow, frustrating work. The new 16th Infantry Regiment was activated in Philadelphia on February 11; recruiting began in May; in September several companies were grouped into a temporary battalion and sent to the northern frontier. The remainder of the regiment was not completely recruited until January, 1813.

The 2d Light Dragoons had a truly woeful history. Their Colonel James Burn was not appointed until April 30; Eustis permitted no recruiting for almost a month, and then initially for only three companies out of twelve. Recruits came in, but no clothing or equipment appeared until September and October; it was December before the regiment (then shivering in northern New York) received all its cloaks. Purchase of horses was ordered in March; it was September before half the regiment was actually mounted—and then many of its mounts proved unfit for service. Eustis proceeded to scatter the regiment from the Ohio River to Vermont; one company simply vanished from the War Department's records.

By 1812 that new military academy at West Point had produced seventy-

7. The Federalist party was the political opponent of the Republicans, and especially strong in New England.

one graduates, of whom twenty-three had died or resigned.[8] It was a school without definite entrance requirements—until Eustis established some in 1810—or standard curriculum. Cadets were of all ages and conditions. They learned some artillery and infantry drill and a smattering of military engineering, but this little was far more knowledge than most regular and practically all militia officers possessed. They were useful, but most of them too junior to have much influence. Twelve of them would die in action or of wounds or disease. In 1812 Eustis ordered all military instructors to the field armies.[9] The Academy limped along thereafter, the average cadet being rushed off to the front after a year's hasty instruction by the civilian staff and Captain Alden Partridge, professor of engineering. One of them, Second Lieutenant Thomas Childs, was cited for valor before he was eighteen.

In March, 1812, Congress finally considered the problem of a staff for the Army it had authorized. It refused to enlarge the War Department, where Eustis and eight clerks struggled to handle the Army, Indian affairs, and pensions, but it did authorize a quartermaster general, a commissary general of purchases, and a commissary general of ordnance—and gave them conflicting and overlapping responsibilities. (Some cynic referred to this establishment as "an act for the speedy enrichment of contractors and the periodical starvation of the troops of the United States.") Morgan Lewis, the quartermaster general, was honest but lacked self-confidence and initiative. Somehow Madison did not appoint a commissary general of purchases until two months after war had been declared. His choice, Callender Irvine, was competent but had everything to learn, while Madison's delay left Irvine too little time to provide sufficient winter uniforms. The inspector general was incompetent, the adjutant general a semi-invalid; their mutual inefficiency denied Eustis and Madison reliable information as to the strength of the Army, the progress of recruiting, or even the precise location of some units.

In the matter of appointing general officers, Madison faced the difficult choice of choosing between Revolutionary veterans now in their fifties and sixties, or untrained, untried politicians. None of the veterans had achieved a rank higher than that of colonel, and all were thoroughly out of practice. In the end, Madison achieved a definite consistency: with the

8. Several of those who had resigned returned to regular or militia service during the war.

9. Eustis disliked the Academy. For over a year he had refused to appoint new cadets.

possible exception of Brigadier General William H. Harrison, all of his initial appointments were bad.

To further exacerbate this situation, staffs had to be improvised for the field armies that were gradually forming. The necessary adjutant generals, quartermaster generals,[10] inspectors, engineers, and aides-de-camp could be procured only by commissioning civilians or detailing officers from the already weakly officered regiments. In the latter case, generals naturally took the most competent men available, thus draining combat units of their most-needed officers. Moreover, the American staff organization of that period could only be described as primitive by contemporary Napoleonic standards: it included neither equivalents of the modern G-2 (intelligence) or G-3 (plans and operations) officers to assist the commander in planning and conducting operations, nor a chief of staff to coordinate staff activities. The generals were on their own.

The nation's seacoast defenses—in addition to the Navy and Jefferson's pet gunboat flotillas [11]—consisted of a scattering of twenty-four forts and thirty-two batteries stretching from New Orleans to Maine. Work on them had proceeded in an on-again, off-again manner, construction done at great expense in periods of crisis being allowed to fall into decay in less troubled times. Until 1807 Jefferson too had neglected them. After that, work was pushed, especially once Congress realized that such expenditures made excellent pork-barrel items. These funds, however, were allocated more on a political than a strategic basis; the southern states, being Republican strongholds, were therefore much favored.

The design, construction, and siting of these defenses were often dubious. Fort McHenry, outside Baltimore, was one of the strongest, yet had neither a bombproof magazine nor casements. To fully arm and garrison the existing forts would have required some 750 cannon and 12,610 men. As it was, they were held by skeleton garrisons of regular artillery, manning an assortment of new and antiquated guns. In emergencies they supposedly would be reinforced by the local militia.

The militia was a broken reed. Under the Constitution and the Militia Act of 1792, it was to embody every free, white, able-bodied male citizen between eighteen and forty-five. Militiamen were to provide themselves with weapons and basic individual equipment; the states were to organize them into companies, battalions, regiments, brigades, and divisions "if

---

10. These two staff positions might be held by officers of any grade, even lieutenants and captains.

11. See chapter five.

convenient." Each state was to appoint an adjutant general to generally supervise its militia, assisted by as many "brigade-majors" as it had militia brigades. The federal government could summon the militia to active duty to enforce the laws of the United States, suppress insurrection, or repel invasion, but no militiaman could be required to serve the United States for more than three months in any one year. When in federal service, militia were subject to the same regulations as regulars, but if guilty of any military offense, they must be tried by courts-martial composed only of militia officers.

This "standing" militia was increasingly supplemented by units [12] of "volunteer" militia, made up of citizens with an interest in the military art and the time and money to learn something of it. These formed the militia's elite companies of riflemen, light infantry, cavalry, and artillery. Favoring smart (and sometimes amazing) uniforms, they often functioned as both military units and social clubs. They were better trained and disciplined than the standing militia, but they served under the same restrictions. Their cavalry was valuable as couriers and occasionally as scouts but, lacking the sustained, hard training of man and horse that professional cavalrymen required, they would be incapable of knee-to-knee, all-out charges against British infantry and guns. (For lack of proper officers, few regular light dragoons got such training, either.)

During their presidencies, Washington and John Adams had hoped to develop the amorphous standing militia into an effective force, in part by "classifying" it into age groups, and giving the men between eighteen and twenty-five special training so that they would form a ready reserve under federal control. Jefferson continued this effort, as a means of getting rid of the Regular Army. His vision of the future United States saw every citizen trained, armed, and organized to serve as a soldier in time of crisis—and instant-ready to do so. As it had done before, Congress went into instant opposition: there must be no federal interference in the states' control of their respective militias. Some politicians expressed the fear that allowing the federal government to help arm and equip the militia might subtly weaken its pristine democratic virtue.

In 1802 Dearborn called on the states for returns, as required by law, on the strength and organization of their militia. After eighteen months' correspondence, he acquired reports from all states except Maryland, Delaware, and Tennessee. The aggregate was some 525,000 militiamen,

12. Most volunteer militia units were company-size, but in thickly settled communities like the New York City area they might be battalions or even regiments.

more or less organized into units of amazingly varied strength. (The average governor seems to have been quite hazy about the whole business; North Carolina, Maryland, Delaware, and Tennessee did not even have adjutant generals.) To arm this force there was a total of 249,000 weapons, sabers and spontoons [13] included. The New England states were the best prepared; the Carolinas could arm possibly half their men, but Virginia had weapons only for two men out of ten and Georgia had even fewer. Camp equipment was even scarcer than weapons. Over 94 percent of the militia were infantry, 3.8 percent cavalry, only 1.5 percent artillery. Cavalrymen provided their own horses, but most artillery units had none and so had to rent gun teams for their drills.

There was some improvement in weapons by 1812, thanks to the federal subsidy. But the major weaknesses of the militia remained. They were state troops, under the command of their respective governors who chose not to share their authority. Several states had militia laws forbidding the movement of their troops beyond the state boundaries without the militiamen's consent. All states allowed a militiaman summoned to active duty to hire a substitute to go in his place. Most troublesome of all was the fact that the militia was inextricably entangled in state and congressional politics. The company officers—captains and lieutenants— were elected by their men; majors, lieutenant colonels, colonels, and generals were chosen by state authorities or by their subordinate officers. A militia commission became a convenient bit of political small change; the higher grades carried a definite prestige, and might open the way to high political office. Members of Congress, state officials, judges, and candidates for those offices often doubled in brass as militia officers. Their frequent indiscipline and ignorance was equaled only by their pretensions. Somewhat worse was the fact that the average militia officer had no idea how to take care of his men in the field, even by that period's rather primitive standards of military hygiene.

On April 10, 1812, Congress asked the governors to have 80,000 men ready for federal service. But when Madison called on the New England states for their quota the following June, the governors of Massachusetts, Connecticut, Rhode Island, New Hampshire, and Vermont refused— their major pretext being that their states' territory was not in danger of being invaded, and thus there was no legal reason for mobilizing their militia.

13. Spontoon—a short spear, carried by infantry officers up through the Revolution, but obsolete by 1804.

As for its housekeeping problems, the Army got its rations through contractors—business entrepreneurs who secured contracts to furnish the official ration to the troops through competitive bidding. The results were what might be expected from the "lowest possible bidder"—late deliveries, short weight, and inferior quality. This was complicated by the problems of storing and transporting large quantities of flour, salt meats, and whiskey. Surprisingly, the United States lacked sufficient supplies of wool cloth suitable for uniforms and blankets, especially cloth of regulation blue. There were no reserve supplies on hand; newly raised regulars were issued linen summer uniforms that could be rapidly produced. Some regiments, especially in the West, wore the ragged remains of these and ruined shoes through the winter of 1812–13. Naturally there was much sickness from lack of proper food and clothing. Those regiments that got woolen uniforms found themselves wearing black, brown, drab, or gray as well as blue.

Stocks of muskets and rifles proved generally adequate, thanks to the efficiency of the federal arsenal at Springfield, Massachusetts, and the somewhat less efficient one at Harpers Ferry, Virginia. (Had the Regular Army been recruited to its authorized strength—62,274 by 1814—there undoubtedly would have been shortages.) The "Model of 1795" musket was an excellent weapon, lighter and more accurate than the British musket, though of slightly smaller caliber.[14] American musket ammunition was commonly of the "buck and ball" type, each cartridge containing three buckshot in addition to the musket ball. (The British regarded its use as something of a minor atrocity, though most of the buckshot wounds proved to be slight.) The federal arsenals could not produce artillery, but sufficient private gun-foundries were available.

Before the war and during its early stages, the Army was definitely handicapped by the lack of both standard infantry drill regulations and capable sergeant instructors. The militia and some regular units still used Baron von Steuben's 1779 "Blue Book," but there was increasing reliance on adaptations or translations of the French 1791 *Reglement*.[15] Up into 1814, American infantry formed in three ranks; thereafter a two-rank formation such as the British used and Napoleon adopted in 1813 seems to have been introduced. In musketry training, the Americans

14. The rifle regiments (four by 1814) had the excellent Model 1803 rifle, a short-barreled .54-caliber weapon.

15. See the outstanding "Dry Books of Tactics: US Infantry Manuals of the War of 1812 and After" by Donald E. Graves, *Military Collector and Historian*, Vol. XXXVIII, No. 2 (Summer 1986) and No. 4 (Winter 1986).

emphasized accuracy, the British fire discipline and rate of fire. The 13th Infantry was taught to take aim by using rail fences as a substitute target for an enemy line of battle. As in the Revolution, Americans showed a distressing tendency to pick off enemy officers.

AT THE WAR'S BEGINNING, THE AVERAGE AMERICAN GENERAL had little knowledge as to the effective employment of his artillery and cavalry. The latter usually was detailed in small units as escorts, orderlies, and couriers. Poorly trained, mounted, and equipped, their understrength regiments had few chances to operate in true cavalry fashion. The artillery normally was employed as garrison artillery and infantry: of the twenty companies of Macomb's 3d Artillery Regiment, only one ever was equipped and used as field artillery. There was an everlasting shortage of vehicles and horses, and usually of forage for whatever horses were available. Nevertheless the few companies of field artillery that were properly employed gave an excellent account of themselves.

Madison had recommended preparation for war on November 5, 1811. The following June 4, the House of Representatives approved a declaration of war; the Senate followed on June 17. During the intervening seven months, Congress had orated endlessly, created a paper army, and shied violently from any serious financial preparations. Madison signed the declaration of war on June 18.

And so we went to war. There was little knowledge of the strength or location of the British forces. Since it would be risky to shift many of the older regular regiments from their frontier and seacoast forts— any such proposal brought frantic howls from southern and western congressmen—the planned conquest of Canada would have to be entrusted to the militia and partially raised regiments of "new" regulars. Swaddled in the insouciance of ignorance, however, the Republican leaders were unworried. Henry Clay thought that invading armies really would be unnecessary; it would be sufficient to send cadres of officers to organize and lead the Canadians against their British oppressors.

MEANWHILE, IN CANADA, LIEUTENANT GENERAL SIR GEORGE PREVOST held the offices of governor general and commander-in-chief, and had his own troubles. He was a competent administrator, with the political skills to gain the support of the French Canadians, and so could exploit Canada's limited resources far more effectively than Madison could manage the greater ones of the United States. Brave in action and capable of planning offensive operations, he was however hagridden by doubt and indecision. Possibly the chronic dropsy that would kill him in 1815 sapped him of essential energy.

At the outbreak of war Prevost commanded approximately 10,000 regular troops, British and Canadian. The latter were "fencible" units, raised for service only in North America, but equal to British regiments in training and equipment.[16] A more powerful regular force than the United States possessed at that time and far more ready for combat, it was scattered from Nova Scotia to the Great Lakes, and would require months to concentrate.

Canadian militia numbered some 86,000, and on the whole were as poorly organized and armed as their American counterparts. Out of 11,000 in Upper Canada (now the province of Ontario), only 4,000 were considered trustworthy, the rest being mostly recent immigrants from the United States who had come into Canada in search of cheap land. However, Canadian law placed no geographical restrictions on the employment of its militia, so that they could be used anywhere in Canada, or even across the United States frontier. Moreover, Prevost persuaded the legislature of Lower Canada (now Quebec province) to "embody" 2,000 unmarried militiamen between eighteen and twenty-five for three months' training in early 1812, and to extend this service for one year in case of an American invasion. Even in Upper Canada Major General Isaac Brock, who was also president of that province's civil administration, managed to organize and arm elite "flank companies" in each militia regiment and to give them six days' drill a month.[17]

Another major advantage that Prevost possessed was the Canadian Provincial Marine, an embryo navy with armed warships—the largest a 22-gun sloop-of-war—on Lake Erie and Lake Ontario. The Marine was not especially well officered or manned, and half of its ships needed repair, but it was building new ones and the Americans could not match it.[18] Consequently, the British had naval control of the lakes during the first vital months of the war.

Especially on the upper lakes, the Marine was supplemented by armed vessels of the North West Company, which controlled the vast fur trade of the Canadian backcountry and reached deep into modern Michigan,

16. The New Brunswick Fencibles had volunteered for unlimited service and so were designated the 104th Regiment of Foot in 1811. New Brunswick raised another regiment for garrison duty in 1813 to replace them.

17. Upper Canadians were practically all small-scale subsistence farmers who could not leave their holdings for protracted service.

18. See chapter six.

Minnesota, and Wisconsin. The "Nor' Westers" controlled hundreds of experienced, hard-case wilderness men under quasi-military discipline. Its principal officers were daring men, used to risk and quick decisions and determined to protect their trade empire. Even more than the British Indian Department, which handled official relations with the tribes, they had the Indians' trust. There could be no better auxiliaries for frontier warfare. Early in 1812 Brock was asking them to see what support they could provide him from among the western tribes.

The western tribes—Sioux, Winnebago, Menomini, Sac, Fox, and Kickapoo—were eager to join their British and Canadian friends against the steady western expansion of American settlements. Hunters and warriors from childhood, they were masters of the wide-ranging raid, surprise attacks, and ambush. These tactical skills, and the savagery with which they too often applied them—prisoners tortured; wounded, women, and children butchered; houses and crops burned—had a thoroughly demoralizing effect on green American troops, whether militia or regular. They were far more feared than British soldiers.

The Indian was hard to hold to any fixed plan, uncontrollable when drunk (which, with most, was as often as possible) or in the heat of combat. He went to war for excitement, loot, and fame. After a victory, he preferred to take his loot and go home. He was not interested in a glorious death; if such appeared possible, he went elsewhere. Only the greatest war chiefs such as Tecumseh could inspire him to stand and fight in a pitched battle, and he was of little use during sieges. Moreover, Indian allies presented unusual logistical problems: they always wanted presents as tokens of their English brothers' esteem, and the problem of feeding both the warrior and his extensive family grayed the hair of more than one of His Majesty's commissary officers.

With the British Army fully committed against the French in Spain, Prevost could not hope for immediate troop reinforcements from England. He could draw some troops from the West Indies, but otherwise would be mostly dependent on Canadian resources, and these were limited.

Canada was barely self-supporting in foodstuffs. Weather and crops were unpredictable; winter came earlier than in the United States, and in 1812 it was particularly early, catching the wheat and oats half-harvested in many areas. The addition of increasing numbers of British troops as the war went on and the necessity of feeding thousands of friendly Indians put an almost intolerable strain on Canadian agriculture. Had it not been for traitorous Americans who grew rich smuggling livestock and foodstuffs into Canada all through the war, the British forces would have gone hungry indeed.

With a population estimated at no more than 500,000, as compared to 7.5 million in the United States, Canada lacked manpower to meet all the war's requirements. The movement of troops and supplies required the services of thousands of Canadians in addition to those in the provincial regiments and embodied militia. These men were obtained under the semi-medieval "corvee" system whereby citizens could be called up with their teams and wagons or boats for transport service or to repair roads. This was very unpopular; men so summoned often slipped away. It also was a major drain on the Canadian economy, especially agriculture, and it was periodically intensified by calls for more militia for active field service.

The eventual arrival of British reinforcements further increased this problem. During late 1813 and early 1814 the legislature of Lower Canada was protesting that one male citizen out of every three was on active duty of some sort. In addition to the lack of manpower, there was a decided shortage of skilled artisans, especially in Upper Canada. Those that were available demanded astronomical wages—and often proved to be thirteen-thumbed incompetents.

THERE WOULD BE NUMEROUS OCCASIONS WHEN BOTH Americans and British would find North American geography a far more formidable problem than their mere human enemies. Most of the Canadian/American border ran through heavily wooded country, much of it practically primeval wilderness, without food for men and forage for horses. Except for settlements along the Ohio, Wabash, and Mississippi, Illinois was practically uninhabited; Chicago was only an isolated, fortified government trading post;[19] until around 1818 the interior of Michigan was considered an impenetrable morass, unfit for human habitation. Northern Ohio, Pennsylvania, and New York were lightly settled; between Plattsburg (also known as Plattsburgh) and Montreal were sixty miles of "barren, resourceless country." Northern Vermont, New Hampshire, and Maine were more of the same.

South of the Ohio River, settlements followed its south-bank tributaries. Tennessee and Kentucky now were relatively well populated, but

19. From 1795 to 1822 the United States maintained a number of government trading posts that were supposed to sell needed goods to the Indians at cost, thus protecting them from exploitation by private traders.

much of modern Georgia, Alabama, and Mississippi still was Indian territory. Along the coast of the Gulf of Mexico from Mobile west to New Orleans stretched a fringe of small towns and plantations; a similar line of them edged the banks of the Mississippi River from New Orleans upstream to beyond Baton Rouge. Yet the whole population, slaves included, of Louisiana was estimated at no more than 20,000—still more French or Spanish than American in composition and character.[20] North of Louisiana the Mississippi's west bank was unsettled debatable ground. St. Louis was a frontier town, facing the wilderness to the north and westward, sending out its traders and trappers to probe the newly explored lands "across the wide Missouri."

Roads were few. Once out of well-settled districts, "road" was only a general term for a clearing through the forest. Trees eighteen inches and under were sawed off at ground level, larger ones at the "usual height." Drainage problems were commonly ignored. The average "road" would be impassable for months in the winter and spring. In the backcountry the U.S. Mail depended largely on post riders and pack horses. The famous Zane's Road from Wheeling, Virginia, to Chillicothe, Ohio, supposedly was open all year round, but in 1814 was almost unusable, with ruts "deep enough to bury a horse." The settled portions of Ohio had a fairly good road net, but the roads themselves were fervently described as "intolerable, shocking wretched, and devilish" things that wrecked wagons and killed horses.

One major westward route was from Philadelphia to Pittsburgh—310 miles, much of it through mountains. Express riders could cover this in approximately three days, stagecoaches in six. Marching troops or convoys of heavy wagons might need four weeks. From Pittsburgh, southbound freight was sent by boat down the Ohio and Mississippi rivers. Cargo for the north and west was sent up the Allegheny River and French Creek to Erie, and there transshipped by lake boats to Detroit, Mackinaw, and Chicago, which were completely dependent on this navigation. Some shipments went east to Niagara. Another major route was from New York up the Hudson to Albany, then westward up the Mohawk River and its tributaries through Schenectady and Stanwix, across the portage to Wood Creek, Oneida Lake, and the Oswego River to Oswego on Lake Ontario. From there, you could turn east to Sackets Harbor and on down the St. Lawrence to Montreal and Quebec; if bound west, you took ship

20. They had been American citizens only since the 1803 Louisiana Purchase.

to Niagara, traveled on by land to Buffalo, and then waited for another ship—there were not many on Lake Erie—to take you to Detroit and the lakes beyond.[21] The route north went from Albany to the Hudson's head of navigation at Fort Edward, then overland to Lake George, and from Lake George by a steep three-mile portage to Lake Champlain and the Richelieu River with its ten-mile portage around its rapids.

Water navigation could be as rough as overland travel, and sometimes abruptly fatal. There were no navigational aids; rivers were full of snags, shifting sandbars, and sawyers. Autumn or dry years meant low water; winter brought ice; the lakes were subject to sudden, savage storms. Portages meant hard work in all weathers, unloading and reloading cargo with frequent damage to perishable items. Battered barrels soaked flour or drained away the brine from salt meats; apparently sound whiskey kegs developed inexplicable leaks.

For the British the situation was even worse. Canadian roads were few and often far between. The one established route was the old French road along the St. Lawrence from Quebec to Montreal. Lieutenant Colonel Cecil Bisshopp who traveled it in a cart in October 1812 defined it succinctly: "Pease porridge . . . Knocked and Jolted during the whole of the way first out of one hole into another and so into a third that my sides I believe are nearly Black & Blue." A road of sorts existed from Montreal to Kingston, but wheeled vehicles could use it only after the ground froze in winter. From Kingston west there were only sections of road between the larger towns, and those primitive. It might take as much as two weeks for troops to march the 160-odd miles from Kingston to York (now Toronto). The inadequacy of the Canadian roads was further complicated by the shortage of draft animals and wagons. Sleighs were relatively plentiful for winter travel, but had only small cargo capacity.

Men and supplies therefore had to move by water, and even here the British worked under serious handicaps. Reinforcements and essential military supplies had to come from England, a voyage requiring a minimum of six or seven weeks even with good ships and fair sailing weather. Neither was assured in the North Atlantic and, for all the Royal Navy's vigilance, American and French privateers and warships might pounce on lightly guarded convoys. Once safely into the St. Lawrence River, ships from England usually docked at Quebec or Sorel. Goods and men

21. At this time there were three low-powered steamboats on the Ohio and Mississippi, but none appeared on the lakes until after the war.

St. Joseph Island

Ft. Mackinac

GEORGIAN

LAKE HURON

Menominee R.

Fox R.   GREEN BAY

LAKE   MICHIGAN

M I C H I G A N

T E R R I T O R Y

Prairie du Chien

LAKE

Fort
Gratoit

Oxford

Thames R.

Moraviantown

Chatham

Detroit
Sandwich

Ft. Malden

Frenchtown

PUT-IN-BAY

L A K E   E R I E

Ft. Meigs

Maumee R.

Sandusky

Ft. Stephenson

Ft. Seneca

Ft. Wayne

(Miami)

Ft. Defiance

Prophet's Town

Wabash R.

I N D I A N A

O H I O

Urbana

N

Dayton

Miami R.

Scioto R.

Ohio R.

Ft. Harrison

Cincinnati

WAR OF 1812

NORTHERN THEATER

25   0   25   50   75

SCALE OF MILES

Ohio   R.

K E N T U C K Y

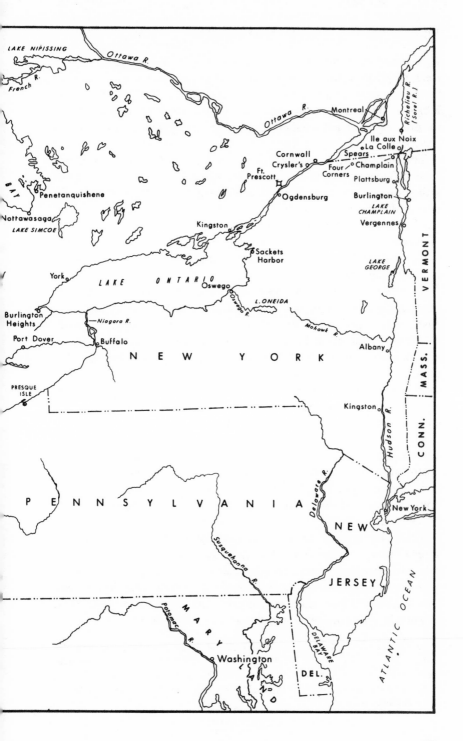

were transferred to river schooners that took them upstream to Montreal, where they were again shifted to bateaux,[22] which could be worked up the rapids at Lachine, Split Rock, Long Sault, and Mille Roches to Kingston. From Kingston a light lake vessel could reach Niagara in one to three days in good weather, for another transshipment to a vessel on Lake Erie.

The British, and especially their forces in Upper Canada, were almost entirely dependent on this St. Lawrence–Great Lakes supply route. (The skilled canoe men of the North West Company could move some freight during the summer through the network of streams and lakes farther north.)[23] Winter, however, came early in Canada, lasting from mid-November to late April or early May. The St. Lawrence froze over, isolating much of Canada, and harbor ice and storms made lake navigation normally impossible.

Thus North American geography and the lack of serviceable roads imposed a major limitation on both British and American strategy. Though hasty raids might be possible, no army, however small, could carry out sustained operations at any great distance from navigable water—river, lake, or ocean. And for all of their control of the sea, this factor hampered the British considerably more than the Americans: Canada lacked the resources to support an overland offensive, and England could never equip any of its expeditionary forces with enough draft animals and vehicles for such an operation.

These same geographical factors gave the War of 1812 a unique aspect. The St. Lawrence and the lakes formed the front line between the two hostile armies, which also depended on them for the movement of men and supplies—probably the only war in history in which both armies' lines of communications ran through the middle of the battle zone between them!

There also were the "bilious" fevers, dysentery, "fluxes," and diarrhea, spread through the general lack of camp sanitation. Few American officers and surgeons had any real appreciation of its importance. In winter a variety of pulmonary diseases ravaged the armies, intensified by the lack of proper winter clothing. For every man killed in battle or dead of wounds, approximately seven American soldiers died of disease—yet

22. Bateaux covered a great variety of small river craft. Properly, it was a double-ended, flat-bottomed rowboat, usually from twenty-eight to thirty-two feet long, with flaring sides.

23. The standard "North canoe" could carry eight men, their supplies, and one and a half tons of cargo.

even this was not as great a drain on the Army's combat efficiency as were the thousands of sick, whether hospitalized and requiring care or simply unable to do their duty efficiently. A sick commanding officer might even bring essential operations to a halt. Available medical treatment probably disabled as many patients as it cured: a favorite treatment for dysentery was massive doses of calomel, opium, castor oil, ipecacuanha, and then calomel again. Swarming mosquitoes and black flies were a major torture, and camps in the Niagara area were much troubled by rattlesnakes. A soldier might find two of them seeking warmth in his blankets when he awoke. Some scholar suggested Pliny's dictum that putting ash branches around the tents would keep serpents away; unfortunately, American rattlesnakes ignored the classics.

PREVOST'S PLANS WERE SIMPLE. On land, he would stand on the defensive; if possible he would seek to avoid hostilities. He had two principal points to protect—Quebec, the capital of Canada, and Halifax, the site of England's major naval base in the Western Hemisphere. Since the tiny American Navy was no threat to Halifax, he could shift most of its garrison westward. Meanwhile the Royal Navy would move to blockade the major American harbors, preventing sorties by American warships and snapping up homeward-bound American merchant vessels.

The United States' planning seemed equally simple, but it proceeded in the strategic vacuum provided by Madison, Eustis, and Dearborn. The last-named, called from his old politician's benefice as collector of customs at Boston to be the senior major general of the enlarged U.S. Army, probably was most to blame. The major American offensive, to include as many of the newly raised regulars as possible, would thrust up the old road of war along Lake Champlain and the Richelieu River to seize Montreal and block the St. Lawrence against British reinforcements from Quebec. This would isolate all British forces further west, cutting them off from all supplies except their scanty local resources. Two secondary offensives—one from Sackets Harbor across the eastern end of Lake Ontario, the other across the Niagara River—would pin down the British forces in those areas so that they could not be concentrated to defend Montreal. A third secondary offensive, from Detroit into Upper Canada, would overrun that province and overawe the western Indians. It would require careful coordination of the four offensives to prevent the British from concentrating against each American force in turn and defeating all four in detail. Once these initial objectives were secured, the Americans would regroup for an advance down the St. Lawrence against Quebec.

Completely overlooked was the strategic lesson of the French and Indian and Revolutionary wars: there could be no conquest of Canada without naval superiority on the St. Lawrence River—something beyond the United States' capabilities to achieve.

Although the general plan must have been settled by mid-April, 1812, little or no attention was given to the necessary preparations—in fact, there was no one in authority in the United States capable of comprehending what would have to be done before any offensive could be launched. Dearborn, who was to command the operations against Montreal, established his headquarters at Albany on May 3 and busied himself with the construction of a military base. Recruiting for the Regular Army was going very slowly—fewer than 300 men in New York during the previous six weeks—but he was not troubled. Having been saddled by Madison and Eustis with the additional, and distracting, responsibility for organizing the coastal defenses of the New England states, probably because they counted on his political influence in that area, on May 22 he proceeded with stately deliberation to Boston. There he found the New England states thoroughly recalcitrant about lending a hand to defend themselves.

Dearborn immersed himself in politics and detail-chasing. Informed on June 22 that war had been declared on the 18th, he continued at Boston. Even Eustis finally would become alarmed and, by repeated orders, get him back at last to Albany on July 26. Once there, Dearborn would plaintively ask who was to command the secondary offensive on the Niagara front. He was quite certain that "my command does not extend to that distant quarter."

Meanwhile out in the West, the war was in full swing and stumble.

TWO

Disaster in the West

The acquisition of Canada this year, as far as the neighborhood of Quebec, will be a mere matter of marching, and will give us experience for the attack of Halifax the next, and the final expulsion of England from the American continent.

—Thomas Jefferson

THERE HAD BEEN SMALL WARS AND RUMORS of greater ones in the West for several years. Tecumseh, a Shawnee chieftain and a truly great American, had worked for years to build a confederation of Indian tribes, from the Gulf of Mexico to the Great Lakes, that could confront the United States on equal terms and halt its acquisition of Indian lands. He was a man of intelligence, eloquence, courage, and character; a relentless enemy, but merciful to captives and respected by his opponents. His ugly, wry-witted brother Tenskwatawa,[1] called "the Prophet," was a shaman who reinforced Tecumseh's diplomacy by preaching a return to the Indians' ancestral way of life. The brothers had established a capital of sorts, called Prophet's Town, at the junction of the Wabash and Tippecanoe rivers in acknowledged Indian territory.[2]

Tecumseh's dream marched with British imperial strategy. England had never really accepted the loss of the Ohio Valley at the end of the American Revolution. It still hoped to establish a "neutral Indian state" to include most or all of the territory from the Ohio River north to the Canadian boundary; its western boundary apparently was to reach the

---

1. Also called "Lolawauchika" (Loud-Mouth).
2. Just north of modern Lafayette, Indiana.

Mississippi and Missouri rivers—a proposed grab of almost one-third of the territory of the United States. British traders supplied the tribes with weapons and ammunition as routine business, but Tecumseh also was in contact with bloody-minded old Matthew Elliott, superintendent of Indian affairs for Upper Canada, who was generous with gifts of weapons, blankets, and other warriors' gear, though he urged postponing any open warfare.

Tecumseh's principal adversary in this prewar period was William Henry Harrison, governor of the Indiana Territory, who had been energetic and expert in persuading Indians to sell their lands. The American frontier districts having become increasingly alarmed by the growing Indian concentration at Prophet's Town, Harrison obtained Madison's permission to deal with the situation as he saw fit. The 4th U.S. Infantry Regiment, commanded by Colonel John P. Boyd, who had been a mercenary officer in the army of the Nizam of Hyderabad in India from 1789 to 1808,[3] was ordered to assist him. To these regulars, Harrison added Indiana militiamen and a squadron of Indiana and Kentucky volunteer light dragoons to make up an "army" of approximately 900–1,000 men.[4] He had been a regular officer for seven years and had served on Anthony Wayne's staff during the successful Fallen Timbers campaign in 1794–95. Now he applied Wayne's tactics. Halting near Prophet's Town late November 6, 1811, he camped with his army in a hollow rectangle, horses and wagons in the center, covered by strong outposts. It was bitter cold, with a thin rain.

Tecumseh had gone south to urge the Creek and Cherokee to join his league. The silent menace of Harrison's encampment quickly put the Indians into an uproar that none of the minor chiefs then present could control. The unstable Prophet "made medicine," raising this excitement to a frenzy, promising that he had rendered the Americans weak, their bullets as harmless as water. Such claims have generally been considered evidence that he was a bare-breeched fraud. But the Prophet had seen plenty of fighting and was thoroughly familiar with the shortcomings of American militia. Undoubtedly he expected that Harrison's men would be huddled in their blankets, with only a few nodding sentries posted, and their ammunition damp from the rain.

3. Boyd had served during the Revolution, and had reentered the U.S. Army in 1808.

4. See Elting, *Military Uniforms in America, Vol. II: Years of Growth, 1796–1851*, pp. 10–11.

Certainly the Prophet's plan was well thought out. He attacked about 4:00 A.M., just before first light when human energy burns lowest, first sending in a wave of black-painted picked warriors who were to crawl through the American lines and kill Harrison and his senior officers. Some were detected, but others slipped through; Harrison narrowly escaped, and there was desperate hand-to-hand killing through the center of the camp. Behind the infiltrators came the rush of the Prophet's main body. Three successive times the warriors surged up into point-blank range, soldiers and Indians firing at each other's musket flashes in the dark. With dawn, the attacks dwindled. The light dragoons, who had been fighting dismounted, mounted up and led Harrison's counterattack, hunting the disheartened warriors into a nearby swamp. Harrison burned Prophet's Town and the stores it contained—he reported numbers of new English muskets. He had lost 37 officers and men killed and 151 wounded, of whom 29 died in the jolting wagons on the march home, and 2 men missing. Thirty-eight of the Prophet's warriors were found dead on the field.[5]

Tippecanoe, as the battle was named, had been a costly victory, and some historians have considered it an inconsequential one. On the contrary, Harrison had won an important success: Tecumseh's capital was destroyed; the warriors who had concentrated there were scattered and discouraged. More important, the Prophet's mystical authority had been completely shattered; Indians who had revered him now mocked his pretensions. Tecumseh also lost prestige; balked in his efforts to form his Indian confederation, he would lead only a small band of faithful warriors to join the British in early 1812.

In 1812 the West was held, in theory, by a thin screen of stockaded forts, most of which also were government trading posts, or "factories." Their tiny, often sickly garrisons were merely symbols of the United States' territorial claims, pushed out into the far reaches of the frontier to fend for themselves. Detroit, the key post of the "Old Northwest," had a garrison of some 120 regulars; Fort Mackinac (known to Indians as "Michilimackinac," to traders as "Mackinaw") had 62; Fort Dearborn (modern Chicago) 50-odd. Another 50 men or so garrisoned Fort Madison, on the west bank of the Mississippi, near the site of the mod-

---

5. Reports of Indian casualties were never certain. Indian accounts were incomplete at best; a body count was seldom exact because of the Indian custom of carrying off their dead whenever possible. If they left dead on the battleground, they had been thoroughly defeated.

ern Fort Madison, Iowa, periodically heckled by the Fox and Sac tribes, which claimed the fort had been built on their land. Further east, Fort Wayne—another frontier post that would become a city—had approximately 85 regulars to patrol the nine-mile portage between the Maumee and Wabash rivers. Fort Harrison, built by Harrison in 1811 near modern Terre Haute on his way to Tippecanoe, might have had 50 more.

Illinois, Indiana, and Michigan being very thinly settled, there were practically no militia available to reinforce the garrisons of these frontier posts. Moreover, much of their population consisted of French Canadians and half-breeds, shiftless subsistence farmers and part-time hunters and trappers. Most of them cared little who ruled them. William Hull had attempted to organize a Michigan militia during 1805–12, but had only scant success—some "French gentlemen officers" he appointed would not even provide themselves with uniforms, let alone drill. Since Congress had decreed that American "factories" must handle only American-manufactured trade goods, which were often poorly made, the Indians naturally preferred the English traders, who knew what goods they needed, visited their encampments, would grant credit, and dealt freely in alcohol. Consequently the North West Company was able to operate across much of the northwestern United States as if it were British territory. The few Americans who appeared at Prairie du Chien (now in southwest Wisconsin), the great inland center where Sioux, Sac, Fox, Winnebago, and Chippewa gathered to trade, had little prestige and less influence.

This weakness of the northwestern frontier and the probability of further Indian troubles made it essential that Detroit be rapidly and strongly reinforced. This would not only overawe the "savages" but would prepare for an invasion of Upper Canada, an event long anticipated by land-hungry American westerners. To President Madison, the logical commander of such a force was William Hull, governor of the newly established Michigan Territory since 1805.

Hull had served with the Continental Army from 1775 to 1784; a courageous, conscientious officer, he had distinguished himself at Trenton, Saratoga, Stony Point, and Morrissania, functioning equally well as a staff and combat officer. In February, 1812, he was in Washington, urging Madison to prepare for renewed Indian troubles in the Northwest. Madison offered him the military command there, but Hull refused; he was fifty-nine and had no desire for more soldiering. However Madison could find no other fit officer for that assignment; after repeated entreaties, Hull finally accepted it, and was commissioned a brigadier general in the

United States Army. On the basis of Revolutionary War service, he was the best qualified of all of Madison's generals.

Hull's orders were to muster his "army" at Urbana, Ohio, and to move north to Detroit, building his own road through the wilderness between the two towns for almost 200 miles. (This route would necessarily pass through the Black Swamp area of northwest Ohio, described as "treacherous enough in summertime, seemingly bottomless at other seasons.") The last sixty miles would run along the western shore of Lake Erie, exposed to raids by British warships. Before leaving Washington, Hull secured a promise—or so he later claimed—that he would be rapidly reinforced, and that an American naval force would be organized on Lake Erie to guard his communications. (The one U.S. warship there, the 14-gun brig *Adams*, was in the Detroit dockyard being slowly rebuilt, and would not be ready for service for several months.) However, in a careless moment, the general had written Secretary of War Eustis that a successful invasion of Canada would result in the capture of the British naval forces on Erie and Ontario, apparently by seizing their bases, and so save the United States the expense of building a naval force there. Such an economical method of making war appealed to Eustis and Madison. They gave no more thought to the matter, though Hull soon was again stressing the need for additional ships.[6]

On April 1 Governor Return J. Meigs of Ohio had summoned three regiments of militia, roughly 1,200 men, to report to Dayton for active duty.[7] Duncan McArthur, Lewis Cass, and James Findlay were their colonels. All three, especially Cass, would later have respectable careers, but at this time they were only small-town politicians in uniform. When Hull took command on May 25, he discovered that they had done little or nothing to prepare for a campaign. Some soldiers still lacked clothing and blankets, weapons and accoutrements were in poor repair, and there was no "powder fit for use" in the Ohio magazines. Worse, no contracts had been established to feed the troops during the coming campaign, or to make up the shortages in clothing and equipment.

Working rapidly, Hull bought powder from Kentucky mills, secured clothing and blankets locally, and hired armorers in Dayton and Cincinnati to put the militia's weapons into serviceable order. By June 1

6. They also may, as Henry Adams suggests, have been unwilling to postpone operations long enough to "create a fleet," but *some* ships could have been readied in the three or four months available.

7. These men were mostly volunteers from the standing militia, and so were referred to indifferently as "volunteers" and "militia."

he had the three regiments and a troop of Ohio cavalry ready to move out. Reaching Urbana on the 10th, he was joined by the 4th U.S. Infantry Regiment, approximately 300 men under Lieutenant Colonel James Miller, and completed his organization. Some of the militia were already semi-mutinous: frontier farm boys, accustomed to independent ways and working no harder than they chose to, they had turned out for adventure, only to discover that following the path of glory included humping mired wagons out of bog holes. At Urbana there was uproar and speechifying; one militia company rode its captain on a rail; personal quarrels in another ended with one soldier killed. Other militiamen refused to leave Urbana. However, the regulars—a "powerful argument," Hull termed them—restored enough order for the march to continue. (The fact that Miller was only a lieutenant colonel and thus was outranked by McArthur, Cass, and Findlay remained an awkward complication.)

From Urbana north, the army built its own road, including bridges and causeways over swampy ground. Four blockhouses were constructed along the way to cover important stream crossings. The militia was handy at such work, and Hull kept them working. He handled the movement efficiently: Sir George Prevost observed that he had exhibited "a more than ordinary character of enterprise." On June 26, approximately seventy-five miles into the wilderness, a special messenger overtook the column with a dispatch from Eustis dated June 18: war was imminent; Hull should "pursue your march to Detroit with all possible expedition."

Hull promptly abandoned his heavy baggage and pressed his march. Arriving at the Rapids of the Maumee River, near modern Toledo, on June 30 and finding his horses worn down by the constant marching, he further lightened his baggage by chartering the schooner *Cuyahoga*, which had come up the river to the foot of the rapids. Onto it he loaded his intrenching tools, medical supplies, officers' baggage, and headquarters records, along with his band and some thirty of his sick, with a surgeon's mate to care for them.

Pushing on, Hull reached the small settlement of Frenchtown on the River Raisin, approximately forty miles from Detroit, on July 2. There a second express rider caught up with him with another letter from Eustis, also written on June 18, announcing that war had been declared. Leaving twenty-five of his most seriously sick at Frenchtown, Hull hurried his weary command on to Detroit, arriving on the 5th. He was greeted with the stunning news that the Canadian Provincial Marine had seized the *Cuyahoga* as she passed Fort Malden at the mouth of the Detroit River.

Eustis had written his first dispatch on the morning of June 18 while awaiting Congress's vote as to the declaration of war, and his second that afternoon once the declaration had been approved. For reasons comprehensible only to his mouse-skinning mind, he sent it off by ordinary mail; it got to Cleveland on the 28th. Probably such carelessness shocked the Cleveland postmaster: he hired an express rider, who worked across northern Ohio through Sandusky to catch up with Hull.

By contrast, the British ambassador in Washington had acted swiftly. On June 24 both Prevost in Montreal and General Isaac Brock at Fort George on the Niagara learned that war had been declared. Brock sent the news on hot-spur to Fort Malden, where it arrived June 30. Consequently, when the *Cuyahoga* appeared on July 2, Lieutenant Frederic Rolette of the Provincial Marine put out in a long boat with a dozen sailors and hailed her. Unsuspectingly the *Cuyahoga* hove to, and was at once boarded and captured. (As an added insult, Rolette made the band play "God Save the King.") Brock also warned his westernmost garrison on St. Joseph's Island, in the strait between Lake Huron and Lake Superior.

Resting his weary men and horses at Detroit, Hull assessed his position. Detroit was still a largely French-Canadian village, dirty and unhealthy, of some 800 inhabitants, surrounded by a twelve-foot palisade. Fort Detroit, built on a slight rise behind the town, was a square, two-acre earth-and-wood structure, surrounded by a dry ditch. It had some forty guns, not all mounted, and an ample stock of ammunition, but its field of fire was partially blocked by the town, and it did not command the Detroit River. (This "river" was actually the twenty-seven-mile-long strait between Lake Erie and Lake St. Clair.) Both fort and town were short of provisions, a situation that rapidly worsened since Hull's troops had brought along nothing much but their appetites, and the area around Detroit produced little food. Reportedly the only plentiful items were soap and whiskey, and stocks of the latter went down rapidly after the army's arrival.

The army's sick list was growing, a problem compounded by the lack of medical supplies and personnel. The Michigan militia would not be of any appreciable use, its only reliable element being the 140-man Michigan Legionary Corps, which Hull had raised in 1805–6. Nevertheless the Ohio militia colonels, eager to begin the conquest of Canada, were already complaining about Hull's lack of enterprise. Hull preferred to await orders from Washington before launching an invasion. He was also writing Eustis and Meigs, demanding food for his men and reinforcements to guard his 200-mile line of communication from Urbana. Eustis's orders came on July 9: if Hull considered his force "equal to the enterprise, consistent with the safety of your own posts," he was to take Fort Malden and "extend your conquests as circumstances may justify." However, he was not to expect cooperation from Dearborn, since the latter did not yet have an "adequate force" to begin operations.

Hull believed that the British were preparing fortifications along the east bank of the Detroit River. Actually they had only a screen of scouts there but, the British-held east bank being higher than the west bank, it was difficult to determine what they were doing. Collecting small boats, Hull planned to cross into Canada on July 10, but was delayed for two days by a rumor of Indian attack on Detroit and the semi-mutiny of some of the Ohio militia, who suddenly developed conscientious scruples against crossing the river and thus taking part in a war of aggression. (Shakespeare had it just backwards when he wrote that "conscience does make cowards.") The crossing on the 12th went smoothly. Hull set up a lightly fortified base near the village of Sandwich, reconnoitered toward Fort Malden, sent McArthur north to overawe the countryside and collect supplies, and urged the local Indians to remain neutral. He also released a proclamation to the population of Upper Canada, assuring them of protection if they remained quietly in their homes, but stating flatly that no white man "fighting by the side of an Indian" could expect quarter.[8] McArthur returned on the 17th; his mounted patrols had gone deep into Canadian territory collecting cattle and 200 barrels of flour. A number of pro-American Canadians formed an irregular cavalry unit and joined Hull.

The British meanwhile had concentrated their available troops—300 men of the 41st Regiment of Foot, 400 Indians, and an indefinite number of militia—at Fort Malden with an outpost line along the Canard River, some twelve miles to the north. Cass drove the picket at the Canard River bridge back in a brief skirmish on the 16th, but was recalled by Hull, who wanted to postpone any attack on Fort Malden until he could get some heavy guns from Fort Detroit. When the Ohio colonels protested the delay, Hull gave them their choice: he would attack at once if they considered their men ready to storm the fort. Miller said his regulars were; McArthur, Cass, and Findlay decided that their militiamen were not. And then the troubles began.

Brock's warning to Captain Charles Roberts at Fort St. Joseph—recognizing that post's isolation—had told him to act according to his own

---

8. This undoubtedly was directed at "blue-eyed Indians"—white renegades or British agents who ran with Indian war parties and had an ill name for atrocities.

best judgment. Roberts received the message on July 8. He had a sergeant and two gunners from the Royal Artillery and forty-seven officers and men of the 10th Royal Veterans Battalion, noted as being so "debilitated and worn down by unconquerable drunkenness" that neither punishment nor patriotism could stimulate them.[9] Nevertheless, Roberts got them moving, and drew eager reinforcements from the North West Company, which mustered 400 Indians—Sioux, Menominee, Winnebago, Ottawa, and Chippewa—and 150 white and half-breed employees, as well as its armed schooner *Caledonia*.

Their target was Fort Mackinac on Mackinac Island, in the strait between Lake Huron and Lake Michigan, since the mid-seventeenth century a center for the Indian trade. The nation that held it controlled a large share of that trade, and thereby influenced the western tribes who could no longer live without the white man's weapons, cloth, utensils, and tools. British traders bitterly resented its loss after the Revolution and were deadly eager to reclaim it.

Mackinac Island has a fine natural harbor on its south coast, commanded by the fort, which was built on an abrupt ridge several hundred feet inland. In turn the fort was commanded by a still higher ridge several hundred yards behind it, but this had been of no importance in Indian wars. The fort, held by Lieutenant Porter Hanks and sixty-one artillerymen, was in a rather rickety condition, but mounted seven guns and had supplies and ammunition enough. The civilian population of Mackinac Island included many former British subjects, all of them fur traders with the typical trader's lack of loyalties. Hanks had somehow picked up word of unusual British activity at St. Joseph (with Indians and traders always passing and repassing, even the empty frontier could be an oversized whispering gallery) and so had sent an American trader named Michael Dousman, who was also an officer in the Michigan militia, to investigate.

Moving by night, Roberts' fleet—the *Caledonia*, several bateaux, and a collection of Indian canoes—intercepted Dousman's boat and learned that the Americans were unaware there was a war on. (Dousman promptly switched sides.) The British landed on the north shore of Mackinac Island in the early morning of July 17, muscled a 6-pounder two miles through heavy timber (the North West voyageurs must have drawn that detail), and onto the ridge behind the fort. Firing one shot to wake everyone up, Roberts sent in a flag of truce with a demand for Hanks' surren-

9. This battalion was scattered in small garrisons across the length and breadth of Canada.

der. The flag was accompanied by three local citizens whom Roberts had swiftly collected; they blabbered at Hanks about Indians, bloody murder, and needless bloodshed. (Both sides understood that, once shooting started, the Indians would get joyfully out of hand. And, while a massacre of the Mackinac traders might have been a definite public improvement, there were their women and children to consider.) In any event, Hanks was no hero. Without firing even one round "for the honor of the flag," he capitulated immediately and unconditionally.[10] The garrison was to be released on parole, not to serve until the end of the war, but Roberts, as arrogantly acquisitive as he had been daring, seized three of them as deserters from the British forces and twenty more as alleged "British subjects." (Possibly they had French-Canadian names.) Civilians, Dousman excepted, were told they must swear allegiance to King George or leave within a month. Excited by this significant victory and avid for scalps and more loot, the western tribes sent their warriors south to join the war.

Worry over the fall of Mackinac (of which he learned on August 3), together with somewhat exaggerated reports of reinforcements reaching Fort Malden and his dwindling supplies and growing numbers of sick soldiers, began to sap Hull's resolution. Now that more Indians were becoming hostile, his line of communications would be increasingly vulnerable to British raids. Meigs had taken action to resupply Hull, mobilizing a militia company under Captain Henry Brush and sending it off with a drove of 300 cattle and 70 pack horses carrying flour. Brush reached the River Raisin, learned that Indians were between him and Detroit, and slipped a messenger through to Hull asking for a strong escort. On August 4 Hull dispatched Major Thomas Van Horne of the 2d Ohio Regiment with 200 infantry and some cavalry to join Brush and also to forward the army's accumulated reports and letters home.

Indians had kept the British advised of Hull's activities. The new commander at Fort Malden, Colonel Henry Procter, sent a Captain Muir with 100 men of the 41st Foot, 24 Indians under Tecumseh, and a few militia across the Detroit River to ambush Van Horne. Van Horne cooperated, marching carelessly, without scouts or advance guard. At the first burst of gunfire his command dissolved into a race back to Detroit. Initially, he reported 18 killed, 12 wounded, and 70 missing: 68 of the latter eventually straggled in. The other 2 were captured; to avenge the loss of a

10. Hull put Hanks before a court of inquiry, but he was killed during the August 15 British bombardment of Detroit. His men were captured again with Hull's surrender and sent as PWs into Canada.

chief killed in the clash, the Indians chopped them to death. The British collected the abandoned mail, which proved to be a collection of complaints against Hull, the war, and army life in general, as well as Hull's dispatches requesting reinforcements and supplies.

Meanwhile Dearborn had hopelessly compromised Hull. Despite repeated orders from Eustis to take the offensive against Niagara and Kingston in order to fix British forces that might move against Hull, it was August 3 before the idea that he really should do something on the Niagara front penetrated Dearborn's equanimity. Having no idea what American troops were available there, he could only ask that some militia be mustered. Then, on August 9, he entered into a truce on the Champlain/Niagara fronts with Prevost. This truce was to be extended to Hull, if Hull so willed; Prevost was even willing to leave him in occupation of whatever Canadian territory he held at that time. Dearborn wrote Hull, proposing his concurrence—but, like Eustis, sent his letter by ordinary mail.

Aware of this truce proposal, Brock decided to strike a quick blow to clear the Americans from Upper Canada. For some time he had been dribbling reinforcements westward to Procter. Now, at last getting the Upper Canada legislature and militia into some order, and having learned that there were only a few hundred undisciplined American militia "without tents, shoes, pay, or ammunition" along the American side of the Niagara River, he left Fort George on August 5 and sailed up Lake Erie, his somewhat ramshackle fleet pausing here and there for repairs or to pick up more militia. He reached Fort Malden on the 13th; Dearborn's letter to Hull concerning the proposed truce had not yet reached Buffalo.

Hull's first inkling of this situation had come on August 7 when letters from General Amos Hall and General Peter B. Porter, commanding New York militia at Niagara and Black Rock, warned him that considerable numbers of British troops and Indians were shifting westward. From intercepted British messages, Hull also was aware that large numbers of Indians were moving against him from the north. He therefore withdrew from Canada during August 7–8, though he left a garrison in a fortified bridgehead on the east bank of the Detroit River for several days more. He considered a prompt retreat behind the Maumee River, but was assured that the Ohio troops would disband if any such movement were attempted. To clear his communications, and if necessary his line of retreat, he sent Lieutenant Colonel Miller with 600 troops—the 4th Infantry, some picked militia, a company of artillery, and a company of cavalry—to establish contact with Brush.

Captain Muir had remained on the west bank of the Detroit River and now had approximately 250 men. Taking up a position across the road fourteen miles south of Detroit, he endeavored to trap Miller on August 9 as he had Van Horne. Miller, however, was marching with proper security; at the first clash, he deployed, peeled Muir out of his position,[11] and chased him two miles through the woods. In the confusion, British and Indians fired on each other. Thanks in part to a heavy rain that burst over the battlefield, Muir got back to his boats and escaped across the river.

Instead of pushing ahead, the Americans milled in place. Their casualties had been heavy, eighteen killed and sixty-four wounded (Procter admitted to six killed and twenty-one wounded, apparently not including Indians and militia), but Hull soon reinforced them. There were excuses that the rain had ruined the road, which had already been "ankle-deep" in mud, and the soldiers' rations were insufficient. Some correspondence suggests, however, that Miller was very ill and had practically collapsed; his subordinates lacked the drive to continue the march, and possibly face another ambush. Hull recalled the force the next day.

The lakeshore road being obviously unsafe because of the British control of Lake Erie, Hull decided to make a final attempt to reach Brush by opening a road along a roundabout back trail that ran some distance inland from the lake. Brush knew of its existence and was prepared to follow it toward Detroit, if given an escort. McArthur and Cass volunteered for this service and moved out on August 14 with the best 350 men in their regiments. Possibly Hull was glad to see them go: they had been actively working to develop an officers' mutiny to depose him and give his command to Miller, who gave them a flat rejection, or McArthur.

Brock's first concern on reaching Fort Malden had been to study the papers captured on the *Cuyahoga* and from Van Horne. His next was to hold a council with Tecumseh and the crowd of Indians assembling there. Except for the ability he had shown since 1802 in Canadian administration and politics, there had been nothing particularly outstanding in Brock's career. Like most other British officers he had purchased his first commission as an ensign and his promotions up to lieutenant colonel;[12] his only extensive combat service had been with the thoroughly defeated British army in Holland in 1799. But now he quickly saw and grasped

11. Miller reported that Muir had thrown up log breastworks.
12. His promotion to lieutenant may have been an exception. He actually was a colonel at this time, acting as "major general on the staff in America," a British technique for giving promising young officers a temporary grade in some unpopular outpost of empire.

his opportunity: Hull's army was weak, riddled with sickness, short of supplies, and wracked by internal dissension. Hull himself was obviously discouraged. On the 15th Brock sent a flag of truce across the Detroit River with a demand that Hull surrender, including the usual, sanctimoniously regretful British reminder that the Indians would be "beyond my control the moment the contest commences." It was a shrewd psychological thrust.

Brock had never seen Indian warfare; Hull had. Through the 1777 campaign, Burgoyne's Indian auxiliaries had harried the upper Hudson valley, and Hull—then a reliable officer who could hold a rear guard steady—had learned the look of a scalped child's sagging little face, of a flaming farm house and the mangled women's bodies scattered about it. His own daughter and her children were with him; the families of the citizens of Detroit, many of whom he knew from his years as governor, were his responsibility. He rejected Brock's summons—but in terms that betrayed his inner uncertainties—and sent a rider to recall McArthur and Cass. Those fire-eaters had reached a point some twenty-four miles south of Detroit; the messenger reached them about sundown and found them disinclined to risk a night march back to Hull's assistance.

Even before Brock had arrived at Fort Malden, Procter had emplaced a battery of heavy guns and mortars on the high east bank of the river opposite Detroit. As soon as Hull's refusal was received, the battery opened fire; two Provincial Marine warships, the *Queen Charlotte* (eighteen guns) and the *Hunter* (ten guns), joined in. Both the town and fort of Detroit were battered; American gunners replied as best they could against the higher-placed British battery.[13] The bombardment fell off during the night, but built up again in the morning. During the night, Tecumseh had slipped across the river with an estimated 600 Indians to surround the town on its south side. Just at dawn of August 16, Brock crossed the Detroit River about three miles below the town, with 330 regulars, 400 militia, and five light guns. (The militia had been issued the 41st's worn-out coats, which made them appear to be regulars.) A roughly equal force remained in reserve on the east bank.

Brock's initial purpose seems to have been to occupy a position across Hull's communications to force the Americans to sally out and fight in the open or starve. However, on learning that McArthur was loose somewhere south of the town, he decided to risk an assault and moved boldly

---

13. Reportedly Hull held down the American rate of fire because his long 24-pounder guns were rapidly using up his reserve ammunition.

to the attack. (McArthur had merely sent a few mounted scouts forward to discover what was going on.) As Brock's column moved up against the waiting American gunners, Hull suddenly surrendered.

There is little doubt that Hull could have repulsed Brock's assault; there is even less that he would have been eventually starved and bombarded into surrender, with great loss of life among the citizens of Detroit. He probably had fewer than 800 serviceable men; the Michigan militia charged with the defense of the town palisade had evaporated. Exhausted in mind, body, and spirit, certain that he had been sent on a hopeless mission and then abandoned, he quit.

His surrender included McArthur, Cass, and Brush, in order to protect them from attack by the Indians. The first two came in once the shooting was over. Brush, having been warned by some former British subjects who had been serving with Hull and now preferred to risk the Indian-haunted woods rather than be captured and hanged, promptly headed for Urbana and got away. Somewhat snidely, Brock refused to grant Hull the honors of war. The American regulars were carried off as prisoners of war, the Ohio militia paroled and told to find their own way home.

Brock's victory was a tremendous boost for British/Canadian morale, dampening the pro-American attitude that had been so marked in much of Upper Canada. Almost as important was the capture of some 2,500 muskets and their accoutrements, which were badly needed to arm the Canadian militia. American morale was correspondingly weakened. By popular acclamation Hull became the scapegoat. Thomas Jefferson— who had done more than any man to make the United States militarily impotent—led the denunciation of the "treason, or the cowardice, or both, of Hull," demanding that he be hanged or shot.[14]

Detroit lost, a tidal surge of war parties swept the northwest. Farms and small settlements went up in flame, their inhabitants butchered, herded into captivity, or sent fleeing in uncertain search of safety. The little frontier forts caught the full fury of the exultant tribes. Fortunately, Indian siegecraft was primitive. Their most effective tactic was a surprise attack,

14. Hull was brought before a stacked court-martial, headed by, of all people, Dearborn, and charged with treason and cowardice. He was refused access to War Department records needed for his defense. Van Horne, among others, testified to the cowardice. The court found him innocent of treason but guilty of cowardice and neglect of duty, sentenced him to be shot, but "earnestly" recommended him to the mercy of President Madison because of his age and prior service. Madison approved the sentence, but graciously remitted the penalty. Hull died in relative poverty. One of his sons was killed in action in 1814 at Lundy's Lane.

possibly disguised as a friendly visit or a parley. Failing to catch the garrison off-guard, they might attempt to draw them out of the fort and into ambush by a feigned withdrawal. Otherwise, they would try to wear the garrison down by sniping, or to set the fort on fire. But they practically never risked a mass assault, even when they had warriors enough to overwhelm a weak garrison in one determined rush.

Fort Dearborn was the first to go. Fort Mackinac's capitulation having cut its only practical supply line, Hull had promptly dispatched a well-known frontiersman named William Wells with thirty mounted Miami Indian scouts to order its garrison to withdraw across country to Fort Wayne. The post's store of trade goods was to be distributed among the neighboring Potawatomi tribe. These Potawatomi had been ostensibly friendly, but Tecumseh's agents and British traders had been among them. Several American traders who had been out with the tribes warned that they could not be trusted, that it might be safer to remain at Fort Dearborn rather than risk evacuating it.[15] Reportedly Wells soon shared their opinion. Captain Nathan Heald, the post commander, decided however to follow Hull's orders. All whiskey was poured into a nearby stream, and surplus weapons and ammunition destroyed. On August 15 the garrison moved out, Wells leading with half his Miami scouts, followed by Heald with fifty-five regulars, twelve male civilians, nine women, and eighteen children; the remaining Miami closed the column. (Legend has it that Wells, so long among Indians that he sometimes thought like one, rode out with black "death paint" on his face.) A column of Potawatomi escorted them for a little distance along the sandy shore of Lake Michigan before vanishing into the dunes farther inland.

A mile and a half from the fort some 500 Potawatomi burst out of ambush, trapping the forlorn little column against the lake. A few of the Miami quirted their horses and broke free. The rest of the command fought and was swamped by numbers.[16] Hazy reports claim that twenty-nine soldiers, seven women, and six children momentarily survived as prisoners. Then the Potawatomi knocked their seriously wounded captives on the head; later they used others as centerpieces for happy evenings of torture. Hardship and abuse killed more; only eighteen seem to have survived till the war's ending. The Potawatomi burned Fort Dearborn. It would not be rebuilt until 1816.

15. Indians being thoroughly individualistic, some Potawatomi warriors reportedly had joined Tecumseh and fought at Tippecanoe. Naturally, they would want revenge.

16. Muzzle-loading muskets simply did not have the rate of fire necessary to stop such an overwhelming rush.

Farther north at Prairie du Chien the few Americans present were driven away, lucky if they could save their shirts and scalps.

Fort Wayne came under siege on September 6. Fortunately, Kentucky already was responding to the emergency. A Kentucky congressman, Richard M. Johnson, hastily raised several hundred mounted riflemen and swept southern Indiana clear of war parties. Harrison[17] relieved Fort Wayne.

Fort Harrison had a rougher time. Its tiny garrison was mostly on the sick list when Tecumseh led a strong band against it on September 4, and succeeded in burning down one of its blockhouses. Nevertheless, inspired by their commander, Captain Zachary Taylor, the garrison fought off all attacks until the arrival of a column of Kentucky militia broke the siege.

Fort Madison was kept under sporadic harassment. Its crisis came a year later, on September 3, 1813, when the Sac made a major attack. The garrison held firm, but its provisions were almost exhausted and there was no hope of reinforcement. That night, therefore, a detail quietly dug a trench from one corner blockhouse to the riverbank where their boats were moored. Another prepared the fort for burning. When all was ready, the garrison crept down the trench and embarked, the last soldier setting the post afire behind him to cheat the Sac of any booty. They got safely to St. Louis.

WITH ALL THE TRIBES OF THE UPPER MISSISSIPPI RIVER up in arms in alliance with the British, and the American frontier pushed back to the line of the Maumee and Wabash rivers, St. Louis became the crucial western outpost. An almost unremembered war, one of few records and those largely lost, flared and ebbed along the Missouri River, the one area in which American traders had held an edge ever since the 1804–6 expedition of Captain Meriwether Lewis and Lieutenant William Clark. British traders and agents had been working for several years to turn the Sioux and even the Mandan against the Americans; one of the agents had married the sister of the principal chief of the Yanktonai Sioux to gain their support. (Possibly it was not entirely stern duty—an early American missionary noted that Sioux squaws were "less pendulous" than those of other tribes.)

William Clark was now commissioner for Indian affairs of the Louisiana Territory—which meant generally everything farther west to Spanish-held territory—and a general of the Louisiana militia. His right-hand

17. See chapter four.

man was Manuel Lisa, born of an old New Orleans Spanish family and long the most daring and successful of the Missouri traders. When Lisa reported the British maneuvers in 1811, Clark had scraped together men and money to send him back up the river to build a fortified trading post from which the tribes might be brought back under American influence. Lisa already had established a small temporary post at the junction of the Yellowstone and Little Big Horn. By October, 1812, he had enlarged and strengthened it, but a combination of North West Company influence with the surrounding tribes and the Blackfeet's inherent hostility to Americans forced him out the next March with the loss of fifteen men. Dropping back downriver to Cedar Island, near modern Pierre, South Dakota, he reestablished his post [18] and managed to keep the Sioux bands of the lower Missouri friendly for the rest of the war.

One final blow remained. In 1811 John Jacob Astor's newly established Pacific Fur Company had built Fort Astoria, the present-day Astoria, Oregon, at the mouth of the Columbia River, thus reinforcing Lewis and Clark's claim of United States sovereignty over the Oregon area. News of the declaration of war did not reach Fort Astoria until January 15, 1813, and then through employees of the North West Company, which had been pushing from the north to gain control of the Columbia area. After a period of truce, Astor's representatives (who were mostly former North West Company men) learned through letters from Canada that a British warship was en route to seize their fort. If that happened, the Royal Navy would confiscate the fort's valuable holdings of furs as a prize, a fate equally distasteful to Pacific Fur and North West traders. On October 16 the former therefore sold out to the latter at a fair profit, though not enough to satisfy Astor. Equally disappointed was the commander of the British sloop-of-war *Racoon*, who arrived on December 13 to find the North West Company in full and legal possession of his anticipated loot. However, he did raise the British flag over Fort George (as he renamed Astoria), and proclaimed the Oregon territory a British possession. Except for a few wandering trappers, the United States now had no presence west of the Black Hills.

18. This was probably the little-known Fort Recovery.

THREE

Champlain and Niagara

*Alarm pervades the country, and distrust among the troops. They are inces-
santly pressing for furloughs under every possible pretext. Many are without
shoes; all clamorous for pay; many are sick. . . . I receive no reinforcements of
men, no ordnance or munitions of war.*
—Major General Stephen Van Rensselaer, August 31, 1812

WHEN, ON AUGUST 3, 1812, Major General Henry Dearborn at long
last had comprehended that his area of responsibility included the Niagara frontier as well as Lake Champlain, his solution was to request that
1,000 New York militia be mobilized, and then to thrust the problem of
launching an invasion upon Major General Stephen Van Rensselaer. Van
Rensselaer was head of a great patroon family, rich, proud, and fully conscious of his public responsibilities.[1] A strictly amateur militia general,
he did have the assistance of his adjutant general (and cousin) Lieutenant
Colonel Solomon Van Rensselaer, an officer of some combat experience.[2]

Van Rensselaer's mission was to force a crossing of the Niagara River,
in order to cut the main west-bank Portage Road between Lake Ontario
and Lake Erie. This would have the double strategic effect of largely isolating Upper Canada, and also of attracting and then fixing British forces
that otherwise would be available to oppose the major American offen-

1. He was a promoter of the Erie Canal and an expert agriculturist. He paid the
costs of New York's first geological survey and established the present Rensselaer
Polytechnic Institute.

2. Solomon had served competently with regular light dragoons during 1792–
1800, and had been wounded at Fallen Timbers.

sive, Dearborn's advance down Lake Champlain and the St. Lawrence against Montreal.

Like earnest small boys sent to do a job requiring several grown men, the two Van Rensselaers labored to make an army out of dubious militiamen, some of whom showed up with nothing much except ragged working clothes, native dirt, and large appetites. Like practically all other states, New York had neither the staff organization nor the necessary matériel (camp equipage, vehicles) to supply its militia on active duty. Short of supplies himself and lacking energy and interest in the matter, Dearborn was of little help. So, with less than 1,000 men, only a few light cannon, and no trained artillerymen, and faced by superior British forces (especially after Brock returned to Fort George on August 23), Van Rensselaer reluctantly concluded that, should the British move against him, his only possible course of action would be a rapid retreat.

Dearborn's acceptance of Sir George Prevost's proposal for a suspension of military operations on the northern frontier relieved Van Rensselaer's immediate apprehensions.[3] Both sides used this truce to hustle supplies and reinforcements forward. Undoubtedly the Americans got the larger profit from it, since the British had far more and better troops available, and were capable of—as at Detroit—limited offensive action. (Brock had wanted to make a spoiling attack to capture Sackets Harbor, the only good port on the American side of Lake Ontario.) On August 9 Dearborn himself still had only some 1,700 men—half militia and all untrained—between Albany and Plattsburg. Though Madison and Eustis demanded that he forthwith denounce the armistice and proceed to capture Kingston and the British posts on the Niagara frontier, he continued to observe it until August 19 and, even after terminating it, remained strictly on the defensive, much to Prevost's satisfaction.

By early October, however, the American position had considerably improved, though Dearborn continued pessimistic. Troops and supplies had at last appeared in quantity; American naval squadrons were organizing at Sackets Harbor and at Presque Isle.[4] Van Rensselaer's "Army of the Center," encamped behind the villages of Lewiston and Grand

3. The British government, belatedly anxious to avoid war with the United States, the source of much of the supplies for Wellington's army in Spain, proposed new negotiations, based on the repeal of its "Orders in Council," which had strangled American overseas trade. Pending American reaction, Prevost was to stand on the defensive. Madison refused to consider the British offer.

4. See chapter six.

Niagara, had increased to approximately 2,650 militia; there were some 1,300 regulars around Fort Niagara, at the junction of the Niagara River and Lake Ontario, and 1,650 more at Buffalo under Brigadier General Alexander Smyth. Van Rensselaer had carefully reconnoitered the British dispositions. (Fleeing American sympathizers undoubtedly were a major source of information.) His militia were in good spirits but threatening to disband unless he launched an offensive. A Federalist who had opposed the declaration of war, Van Rensselaer was regarded with increasingly loud distrust by some of his Republican subordinates, as well as by rabid Republican newspapers.

His initial plan was sound, if somewhat ambitious for the troops he commanded. One part of his army would attack directly across the Niagara River to seize Queenston, cutting the Portage Road between Lake Ontario and Lake Erie; a strong force of regulars meanwhile would move by boat from Fort Niagara westward along the shore of Lake Ontario, land in the rear of Fort George, and storm its weaker inland front. To anchor his right flank, Van Rensselaer pushed the strengthening of Fort Niagara. Unfortunately, the place had been built to resist an attack by land from the south and east; its lake front was completely dominated by the guns of Fort George across the river. (Here, as at Detroit, the British bank was considerably higher than the American.) Considering Fort Niagara's commanding officer, Lieutenant Colonel John R. Fenwick, of the Regiment of Light Artillery, to be more interested in emptying bottles than building up his ramparts, Solomon Van Rensselaer took hold and made some amateurish improvements.

The arrival of Alexander Smyth, however, converted the Niagara campaign into a costly three-month farce. Born in Ireland and brought to America as a child, Smyth had become a successful Virginia lawyer and Republican politician. In 1808 Jefferson had rewarded his services in the latter capacity by commissioning him colonel of the new Regiment of Riflemen; four years later Madison had promoted him to brigadier general and made him the Army's inspector general. If Smyth showed any occasional competence in any of these military assignments, it remains undiscovered. Once he had arrived at Buffalo (and still magnificently ignorant of the Niagara terrain), instead of reporting in person to Van Rensselaer as Dearborn had ordered, Smyth merely sent him a condescending letter proclaiming that the "interests of the service" required that any crossing of the Niagara River be made at its upper (southern) end, between Fort Erie and Chippewa. He did close this singular epistle with an offer to wait for any "instructions or better information" Van

Rensselaer might have, but thereafter evaded Van Rensselaer's attempts to confer with him. Van Rensselaer therefore decided to make a direct attack on Queenston during the night of October 10, using only the troops he had under his direct command around Lewiston. Amid a driving rainstorm that turned dirt roads into bogs, he brought his men down to the crossing site [5]—to find no boats ready for them! Either a coward or a traitor, the officer in charge of the boats—a Lieutenant Sim—had slipped away downstream through the dark and rain in one of them, taking with him the oars for all the others and so vanishing from military history. After vainly waiting in the storm for several hours, the troops splashed back uphill to their tents.

By now Van Rensselaer's men were in the mood later described as "browned off"—still willing to fight, but completely fed up with delays. So definite was their attitude that Van Rensselaer decided against calling his senior officers to a council of war to work out a detailed plan for another offensive. Instead, setting the night of October 12 as the date of his next effort, he made what hasty improvements were possible in the time available. A 300-man detachment of the 13th Infantry Regiment was brought down from Fort Niagara, moving along a new-cut road through the woods some distance east of the river to avoid being detected by the British outposts. Smyth, told to furnish what help he could, dispatched Lieutenant Colonel Winfield Scott with two companies of the 2d Artillery Regiment from Black Rock.[6] Scott almost arrived too late. The roads were so bad from constant rain that, with no vehicle heavier than the carriages of his four 6-pounders (the guns themselves had to be brought down by boats), it took him two days to reach Fort Schlosser the evening of October 12. Learning of the impending action from a passing militia staff officer, he forced his march through the night, arriving around 4:00 A.M. to add his guns to those already emplaced on Lewiston Heights to cover the crossing.

The first wave of the assault was to consist of 300 regulars and 300 volunteers from the militia [7] under Lieutenant Colonel Solomon Van Rens-

---

5. In time of peace there was a regular ferry service between Queenston and Lewiston. Van Rensselaer planned to use the ferry landings to embark and disembark his troops.

6. Van Rensselaer had ordered Smyth north to exploit the crossing he had planned for the 10th, but canceled that order once it was obvious no crossing was possible.

7. The regulars were from the 6th and 13th infantry regiments, with some officer volunteers from the Light Artillery Regiment. The militia came from the 16th through the 20th regiments of New York detached militia.

selaer. Men and guns would be fed in behind them once they established a beachhead on the west bank. General Van Rensselaer's selection of his cousin to command this force brought protests from the three regular lieutenant colonels present—Scott, Fenwick, and John Chrystie of the 13th Infantry—but to no avail. Solomon Rensselaer had seen at least as much regular service and combat as any of the three, and the militiamen knew and trusted him. At the end of the argument, Fenwick waived his rank and went as another volunteer; Chrystie agreed to go, under Solomon's overall authority, as commander of the regulars involved. Scott refused—correctly according to regulations—to serve under a militia officer of his own grade, and so was left with the supporting artillery.

In sad fact all these gallant gentlemen, regulars and militiamen together, were amateurs at war. For most of them it would be their first experience facing the proverbial "shot fired in anger" that makes soldiers out of mere men wearing uniforms; even the few combat veterans among them had never faced regular European troops. Eager to get at their enemy, they overlooked too many practical aspects of their business. To begin with, there were not enough boats—a mere thirteen, though thirty would not have been too many and close to a hundred were available at Fort Niagara and Fort Schlosser. The boatmen would prove to be a timid lot. Although Van Rensselaer might have borrowed a detail of tough seamen from the new Navy base at Black Rock to keep them to their duty, it never occurred to him to do so. No single officer seems to have been directly responsible for the management and loading of the boats; urgently needed entrenching tools and extra ammunition piled up on the east bank but were never sent across. Similarly, the plan to send over Captain James Gibson's company of the Light Artillery Regiment[8] collapsed when it was discovered—after the action had begun—that none of the available boats could accommodate his 6-pounders. None of the artillery officers had thought to mass guns so as to smother the British battery on Vrooman's Point. But the major flaw in the American plan was its lack of any clearly stated objective once the troops reached the west bank. Solomon Van Rensselaer may have had definite ideas, but he did not tell his subordinates specifically what they were to do.

Across the Niagara River, Brock had approximately 2,000 men, including most of the British 41st and 49th regiments of Foot, between his headquarters at Fort George and Fort Erie. His victory at Detroit had

8. One of that regiment's few companies actually equipped and employed as artillery.

brought many of the reluctant Canadian militia and also the warriors of the Six Nations[9] to join him wholeheartedly. In and around Queenston, he had some 300 infantry, the elite grenadier and light infantry companies of the 49th Foot and some Lincoln County militia. The river here was commanded by two British batteries: partway up the steep slope of the heights (called Queenston Heights), just south of that village, was a single 18-pounder; at Vrooman's Point, a mile to the north, were two 24-pounders. Two 3-pounders were emplaced in Queenston. The river here was a serious obstacle, swift and rough in normal times and now running in full spate from days of rain. Expecting an attack, Brock kept his forces on the alert behind it. He had noted Van Rensselaer's collection of boats, but that had been done so openly that Brock considered it a mere demonstration, to draw his attention away from the intended point of attack, which he suspected would be Fort George. Consequently, he kept most of his British troops concentrated in that area.

"Hurry up and wait" is an ancient principle of civilized warfare. The Americans began forming at their embarkation point just after midnight on October 13, hunching their shoulders against chill winds until 3:00 A.M., when the order came to embark. Chrystie and his regulars were ready; there was some confusion with the militia.[10] By some accounts, the thirteen boats could not take all 600 of the first wave, but possibly 500 officers and men did get off into the darkness and racing waters. Partway across, Chrystie's boat lost an oarlock and was swept downstream, fortunately ending up on the American bank. Two other boats, less fortunate, were carried down against the west bank and were captured by an outpost of Canadian militia. The remaining ten hit the intended landing point, the ferry terminal just south of Queenston. Stumbling in the darkness, the troops piled ashore and began forming up while the boats pulled away to pick up the second wave.

Almost at once a British sentry on the high bank above the terminal gave the alarm. Captain James Dennis's grenadier company were light sleepers; Dennis brought them up to the edge of the bank and began blazing into the dimly seen mass of Americans below him. For a few minutes it was like shooting fish in a barrel: Solomon Van Rensselaer took six bullets and went down; eight more officers and forty-five enlisted men

9. Elements of the six Iroquois tribes that had fled into Canada after the Revolution. Initially, they had declared themselves neutral in this white man's war.

10. Being volunteers from different militia regiments, they would require some time to organize into temporary units.

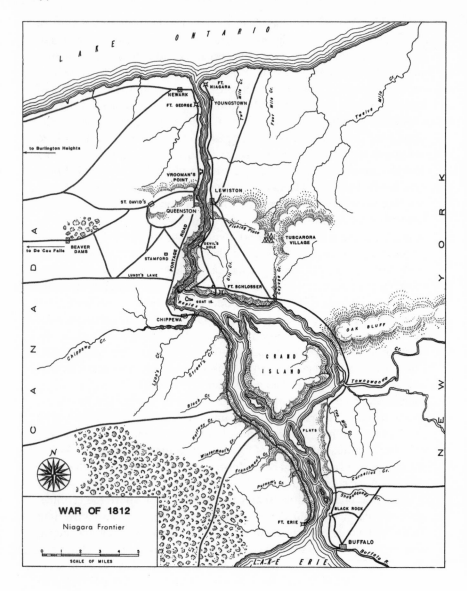

WAR OF 1812

Niagara Frontier

SCALE OF MILES

were hit; British artillerymen roused and began blazing at the crossing. Then little Captain John E. Wool of the 13th Infantry, newly commissioned,[11] shot through both buttocks, took over. Swinging his raw troops into a ragged line, he slugged Dennis back into Queenston.

Wool's new-won beachhead, however, was a hot place, under fire from the 18-pounder on the heights above him and from Vrooman's Point. He found Van Rensselaer still faintly conscious and asked for his orders. Van Rensselaer told him to take the high ground—Queenston Heights— directly to his front. A direct assault up the open slope against the 18-pounder and the 49th's light infantry company, with Dennis firing into his right flank, promised to be costly. An enveloping attack to his left appeared impossible, since Queenston Heights curved to the river there, forming an almost precipitous escarpment. Fortunately, Lieutenant John Gansevoort of the Light Artillery Regiment, present as a volunteer, had heard of a little-known fisherman's path along the face of those cliffs. Wool at once decided to risk it. Leaving 100 men to keep Dennis fixed, he worked to his left, found the path, and followed it easily to the top of the heights, emerging above and to the rear of the 18-pounder battery— and of General Brock!

Brock had been asleep in his quarters at Fort George, approximately six miles north of Queenston. Brought awake by the rumbling of artillery fire, he got to horse and galloped south along the river, ordering the troops at Fort George, and the various detachments he passed, to follow as soon as possible. Reaching Queenston around 5:00 A.M., he rode up to the 18-pounder battery, apparently to get a better view of the situation. Wool's sudden appearance sent Brock and the artillerymen fleeing downhill for shelter in Queenston—but not before they did a thorough job of spiking their gun.

Brock was, instinctively, a fighter. Rather than wait for reinforcements he gathered what men he could and sent them uphill against Wool. The odds were against them; the Americans shot fast and fairly effectively. As their charge recoiled, Brock rallied them, shouting that he never before had seen the 49th run; then, on foot, he led them once more up the hill. An American rifleman picked him off, and the charge ebbed back to Queenston. There Brock's aide-de-camp, Lieutenant Colonel John Macdonell, gathered some fifty men and made a rush to avenge Brock. His handful came on in fury, breaking into the battery, but could

11. Commissioned from civil life March, 1812. Retired 1863 as a major general.

not maintain their drive. Macdonell and his horse went down together; Dennis and Captain John Williams of the 49th's light infantry company were wounded. Dennis got the survivors back toward Vrooman's Point, rallying what men he could collect in several stone buildings along the edge of Queenston.

Meanwhile more Americans came ashore, though not in the best order. As the sky grew lighter, the accuracy of the Vrooman Point battery improved. Several boats were smashed; few of their passengers survived. One of those lost carried Lieutenant Colonel Fenwick; badly wounded, he was captured when the wrecked craft grounded on the west bank. Chrystie arrived about 7:00 A.M. and found complete confusion around the landing. Some Americans had pushed into Queenston, rescuing Fenwick and others, but—without artillery—could not dislodge Dennis from his strong point, from which the 3-pounders were pot-shooting at the boats. Unable to accomplish anything, Chrystie went back and reported the situation to General Van Rensselaer. The general sent Smyth orders to march for Lewiston, at once and "with dispatch." Then, possibly thinking that Chrystie lacked firmness, he told Scott to take command on Queenston Heights, following himself about 10:00 A.M. with Chrystie and Captain Joseph G. Totten of the Engineers. Brigadier General William Wadsworth of the New York militia meanwhile had gone across on his own hook as a volunteer, in civilian clothes but armed with a sword and an astounding talent for speaking "profane."

Taking a quick survey of the situation, Van Rensselaer sent Chrystie and Totten to join Scott, with word that he would get reinforcements, ammunition, and entrenching tools across to them as quickly as possible. Captain Gibson, by some feat of improvisation, did get one of his 6-pounders to the west bank, but with only a limited supply of ammunition.

On Queenston Heights, Scott and Totten roughed out a defensive position for the approximately 600 Americans there. Wool, weak from loss of blood, and other wounded men were sent down to the boats. The crisis of the battle obviously was at hand. A long column of redcoat infantry—Major General Roger H. Sheaffe with the Fort George garrison—was coming deliberately down from the north. The Americans had been on the move or fighting since before midnight; hungry, thirsty, their cartridge boxes emptying, they waited for the promised reinforcements—which did not come. Men sent to the rear with the wounded did not return; despite Wadsworth's freely bestowed expletives, groups of militiamen seeped away from the crest of the hill, hiding or slipping down to the landing to crowd aboard whatever boats might put in.

On his return to the east bank, Van Rensselaer found that much of his militia army had dissolved into a crowd of spectators, watching the distant battle as if it were waged solely for their entertainment. Most of the returning wounded had had the usual terrible tales to tell. (By another amateur staff bobble, these wounded had been brought back through the militia, thus giving them a shocking introduction to some of the horrors of war.) Nothing would move a single company to cross the river; Van Rensselaer ordered, begged, damned, and exhorted, but the militia, their former ferocity quite evaporated, had suddenly developed constitutional scruples against invading Canada. In disgust and shame, Van Rensselaer sent Wadsworth a hasty note: there would be no help from the east bank. He must decide whether to stay and fight or to withdraw while he still had a chance; the boats would be sent over to pick up his men.

That last promise, too, fell false; weary and frightened, the boatmen on the east bank refused to risk another trip. As soon as the first war whoops echoed from the Heights above them, those at the west-bank landing pushed off and rowed frantically for home, bringing only a few malingering militiamen.

Sheaffe was the antithesis of Brock in everything but courage; prudent and calculating where Brock had been impetuous, he would not attack until he had all possible odds in his favor. By now, after calling in all nearby detachments, he had much of the 41st and 49th Foot, several companies of militia, one of black pioneers,[12] and something over 100 Indians, mostly Mohawk—in all, at least 1,000 men, the greater part of them British regulars. Reaching Vrooman's Point, he swung his column inland along back roads to reach the Queenston Heights at a point west of the American position. (An advance straight on through Queenston might have cut the Americans off from the river, but also would have exposed his troops to a hammering by the American artillery on Lewiston Heights.)[13] To cover his deployment, he sent his Indian contingent forward under John Brant, Captain Jacob, and the half-breed Captain John Norton. Yelling furiously, they burst out of the timber along the crest of the Heights, but were sent promptly right about by American volleys and a limited counterattack led by Scott and Chrystie. Beyond them, how-

12. Captain Robert Runchy's "Company of Colored Men," some twenty-five blacks, by tradition mostly fugitive slaves from the United States, and "expert axemen."

13. Also, there must have been some Americans, mostly militia, squabbling with Dennis in and around Queenston, and, possibly, looking more formidable than they were.

ever, Sheaffe, just then joined by another detachment of the 49th Foot
and militia from Chippewa, was getting his men into attack formation.
Both the Vrooman's Point battery and Dennis's two 3-pounders were
firing into the American right rear, while the Indians were rallying and
attempting to get around the American left flank along the river.

Amid such uncomfortable conditions, Wadsworth received Van Rensselaer's message and called together the senior regular and militia officers
for a hasty consultation. Along the Heights there still were 125 infantry and 14 artillerymen from the regulars (Scott had just counted noses)
with 296 militia, almost half of them young officers who either had come
over as volunteers or stayed in line when their men faded off to the rear.
Gibson's lone gun had only a few rounds left. Agreement was quick and
general: get out while there still was a chance of escaping!

The withdrawal began in some order, with Scott attempting a rear
guard action with the regulars, but the pressure was too heavy and his
men too raw. A general stampede toward the ferry site developed, sweeping the officers along with it. Some Americans, missing their footing or
wild with panic, went over the edge of the escarpment into the racing
river. (One English officer, obviously possessed of an elastic imagination,
reported the river "filled with poor wretches.") Most ended in a huddled
crowd around the landing, searching for boats that were not there while
enemy fire lashed at them. Surrender was the only possible course of
action, but the first two officers sent out with white flags were murdered
by the Mohawk. Scott then went himself, accompanied by Totten and
Gibson; for lack of another white flag, he carried Totten's white cravat on
the point of his sword. The three of them also were close to being killed
before British soldiers drove the Indians away. Even after Sheaffe had
formally accepted the American surrender it took him considerable time
and effort to get the Indians to stop shooting.

Across the river the New York militia watched their comrades' defeat
with exemplary fortitude.

When all the American prisoners were gathered in, they reached the
surprising total of 958. Many were stragglers, skulkers, and deserters who
had hidden out during the fighting, but others must have been engaged
in the apparently unrecorded hole-and-corner fighting around Queenston. One militia national color and Gibson's 6-pounder were additional
trophies. Other American losses remain uncertain; militia records were
incomplete, and a good many men could not be accounted for—men
drowned when their boat was wrecked, or deserters who simply took off
for home without notice or permission. The best estimate was 90 men

killed and 150 wounded, of whom some 30 later died. The British had only 14 killed and 77 wounded among their regulars and militia; of the Indians, 5 were reported killed and 9 wounded.[14] There were further losses during the artillery duel between Fort Niagara and Fort George during the day. The raw, poorly prepared Americans literally took a beating, finally abandoning the fort, apparently in disorder. Late in the day the better officers rallied enough of them to reoccupy the place.

Thinking the battle over afterward, Scott decided that its loss was chiefly due to the American failure to clear Queenston and organize it for defense as soon as Wool had carried the Heights, thus covering the right flank and rear of that position. But he had to admit that no one, himself included, had thought of doing that.

Once the firing had ceased, Sheaffe proposed a truce. He had prisoners and the wounded of both armies to collect and get off the field, and his own forces were in some disorder. The Indians were still dangerously excited. Brant and Jacobs attempted to kill Scott in the hallway of Sheaffe's temporary headquarters that evening. In fact, a good part of the British and Canadian enlisted men went on a five-day, drunk-and-disorderly spree to celebrate their victory. Sheaffe and Van Rensselaer carried out their truce, the dispatch of American surgeons to assist in the British hospital, and arrangements for the exchange of prisoners with professional courtesy. When Brock was buried on October 16 at Fort George, American artillery fired minute guns to echo the British salute. (This mutual respect was ruffled later when Prevost attempted to seize all Irishmen among the captured regulars for trial as traitors.)

Three days after the battle, Van Rensselaer sent Dearborn his resignation. He had made a hash of his attempt at invading Canada, but he had done his honest best, according to his lights, with the poor tools his government had given him. Being a Federalist, he got no sympathy from the administration. Jefferson, who never had heard that shot fired in anger, wanted Van Rensselaer "broke for cowardice and incapacity." Dearborn complained that Van Rensselaer had been a mere militiaman, too jealous of the greater military talents of Smyth and other regular officers to take their advice. Still comfortably ensconced in his Albany headquarters, he then ordered Smyth to take command of the Army of the Center and proceed with the invasion of Canada. By way of encouragement, he

14. There also is the odd fact that one "chief" was captured by New York riflemen and sent across the river. As Charles W. Elliott points out in his excellent *Winfield Scott*, the "marksmanship on both sides was shockingly bad."

promised a diversionary attack on the Lake Champlain front, and expressed the hope that Harrison already would have recovered Detroit. (He made no attack, and Harrison was far from Detroit and hip-deep in his own troubles.)

SMYTH AT ONCE ATTEMPTED TO SET HIMSELF up as an independent commander. Writing directly to Eustis, he requested that his force be increased to 8,000 men, plus some additional cavalry and twenty field guns. He also wanted 130 boats of various types, money, and better provisions—"and I will retrieve your affairs or perish." Eustis reminded him that he was subordinate to Dearborn, but did find him more troops, building up the Army of the Center to almost 4,000 regulars. Smyth's militia, however, were going home in droves, and those who remained were semi-mutinous. Also, the political sound and fury of a presidential election was working among them, with Brigadier General Peter B. Porter and other Republican militia officers quarreling with Federalists. The regulars, mostly half-trained and partially disciplined, were restless over lack of pay, proper rations, and winter uniforms. As might be expected under such conditions, sickness soon reached epidemic proportions; by late November scarcely half the regulars were fit for active service.

Smyth disregarded such things. Taking command on October 24, he bombarded his army, the citizens of New York State, and the enemy with a series of proclamations in an amazingly *miles gloriosus* style, replete with perorations such as "Shame, where is thy blush! No!" One intent of this rhetoric was to secure volunteers. Some did respond; Porter may, or may not, have helped by offering to lead any interested New Yorkers on a private invasion of Canada. Meanwhile the forts on either bank of the Niagara River occasionally shot at each other. (The Americans *did* show some improvement.)

With Dearborn's approval, Smyth planned to cross near the southern end of the Niagara. He insisted, certainly with reason, that he must have at least 3,000 men available for the attempt. In the first hours of November 28, he finally moved: two detachments embarked at Black Rock—one under Colonel William H. Winder to capture the British batteries directly across the river; the other under Lieutenant Colonel Charles G. Boerstler to destroy the bridge over Frenchman's Creek and thus block any British reinforcements moving south from Chippewa and Fort George. Meanwhile Smyth's main force would embark at the Buffalo Navy Yard and move north to occupy the bridgehead Winder and Boerstler were to establish.

Sheaffe had expected a renewed American offensive, and had guessed that it would strike in the vicinity of either Fort Erie or Fort George. He had called up additional militia, thickened his outpost line along the river and the lakeshores west of both forts, and prepared to shift his reserves rapidly in any direction.

Coming in out of the darkness, Winder's men landed, outflanked and took the batteries opposite Black Rock, and mopped up the adjacent English outposts and local reserves. One detachment then pushed too close to Fort Erie and was in turn overwhelmed by a larger British force. Boerstler's approach was detected by Canadian sentries: he lost two boats to British artillery fire, quickly lost interest in the war, and retired to the east bank. Sometime later Winder withdrew. This tangle of small unit actions cost each army approximately 100 men, killed, wounded, and captured. Meanwhile Smyth had begun embarking about sunrise, but things went very slowly. By noon he had only some 1,200 men and a few guns afloat. With them he went downriver to Black Rock, where he ordered the troops to "disembark and dine" while he summoned all his field grade officers to a council of war as to whether to continue the crossing. The council, doubtlessly studying the general out of the corners of their eyes, decided against it. By way of salving his battered ego, Smyth then sent Lieutenant Colonel Bisshopp, the commander at Fort Erie, a demand that he surrender immediately "to spare the effusion of blood"—and marched his own men back to camp, probably leaving Bisshopp more than a little bewildered.

On November 30 Smyth made one last attempt at a night attack but again preparations went too slowly and only 1,500 men were in the boats by sunrise. Smyth called another council, and decided to suspend offensive operations on the Niagara frontier for the winter. That produced something of a mutiny. Smyth was cursed and threatened. The militia went home. Porter denounced Smyth as a coward; Smyth challenged Porter to a duel; and the Republican heroes exchanged pistol shots. Unfortunately, both missed.[15]

The Niagara frontier thereupon went into hibernation, except for a brief false alarm in February when—Lake Erie having frozen over—the Canadian militia was turned out to meet an imaginary American attack across the ice.

15. Smyth next asked Dearborn's permission to visit his family; three months later, since he showed no further interest in a military career, Madison dropped him from the service. As might have been expected, however, he resurfaced after the war as a member of Congress and chairman of the Military Committee.

TO THE EAST ALONG THE ST. LAWRENCE RIVER, however, there had been a fairly lively "small war" of raids and outpost squabbles. A tentative venture by the Provincial Marine against Sackets Harbor on July 19 was beaten off with much shooting and few casualties, and there were occasional indecisive gunboat clashes along the river. The sector from Oswego east to Ogdensburg had been placed under Brigadier General Jacob J. Brown of the New York militia. A former Quaker and schoolteacher, Brown had become a magnate in the semi-frontier woodlands north of Watertown, New York, and both an energetic violator of Jefferson's Embargo and an effective militia officer. His only regular troops were a company of the green-uniformed Rifle Regiment under a Captain Benjamin Forsyth, whom a Canadian described as a "big, dashing daredevil from North Carolina." Short of ammunition, Brown sent Forsyth with eighty-two riflemen and thirteen militia on a raid against Gananoque, a British convoy staging post twenty miles down the St. Lawrence from Kingston, to capture some. Moving by boat through the maze of the Thousand Islands, Forsyth surprised Gananoque on September 21, routed a larger force of Canadian militia, burned a storehouse of provisions, and returned with eight prisoners and barrels of flints, cartridges, and gunpowder, having lost only one man killed and one wounded.

Deciding that Ogdensburg would make the best base for attacks against British convoys up and down the St. Lawrence, Brown then established himself there with a brigade of militia and Forsyth's company. This move sorely distressed Prevost, and also the local citizenry, who had been raking in profits from their illegal trade with Canada. Colonel Robert Lethbridge, commanding the British garrison at Fort Prescott, opposite Ogdensburg, mustered two gunboats and a considerable force of militia and regulars and attempted a boat attack to dislodge Brown. His planning was somewhat inferior to Van Rensselaer's. Brown let him get halfway across the river, then dosed him liberally with grapeshot until the assault collapsed. However the service obligation of Brown and his militia expired in December. They went home for Christmas, leaving Forsyth and the local militia to hold Ogdensburg. Dearborn seems to have ignored the whole business; Governor Daniel D. Tompkins of New York reportedly felt it impossible to replace Brown's brigade with another militia levy because troop movements down the St. Lawrence were too risky and the roads were impassable—though Brown's men seem to have encountered no outstanding difficulties on their homeward march.

The Champlain front had been almost peaceful, Dearborn being content to sit comfortably in Albany, accumulating troops and supplies and pampering his "rheumatic" attacks. His subordinate at Plattsburg, Brigadier General Joseph Bloomfield—an unnoticed major during the Revolution, but Republican governor of New Jersey for the past ten years —was equally inactive. Occasionally junior officers took action. On the St. Lawrence at the northern border of New York was the St. Regis Mohawk reservation. Hoping to keep the Mohawks out of the war, Governor Tompkins had declared it a neutral area, but the British had sent recruiters into the reservation, enlisted some eighty warriors,[16] and stationed a company of Canadian militia there to solidify their influence over the tribe. On October 12 Major Guilford D. Young, leading a force of volunteer militia from Troy and three companies of ordinary New York militia, surprised this post, killing five and capturing forty of its garrison, along with some sort of British flag. Young left one militia company to hold the captured outpost. Unfortunately, it was surprised and gobbled up in turn in late November by a company of the Glengarry Light Infantry Fencible Regiment.[17]

Finally, in early November, Dearborn plucked up the courage to risk an advance on Montreal while Smyth's jumblings were keeping the enemy forces on the Niagara frontier occupied. It was his intention to have Bloomfield lead this offensive, but Bloomfield was too sick to take the field. On November 19 Dearborn himself therefore ordered an advance. He had a strong force, probably 6,000 men including seven regiments of regular infantry and some regular artillery and light dragoons, as well as a contingent of militia. An advance of twenty miles brought him to the village of Champlain, a mile below the Canadian frontier, where Major Charles-Michel d'Irumberry de Salaberry had mustered a hasty collection of militia, Indians, and voyageurs. Some minor outpost bickering in the dark and fog next morning was sufficient to convert Dearborn's militia to pacifism. Though they refused to advance, Dearborn still had regulars enough to walk over de Salaberry. Instead, he dithered in place for two days more, then went back to Plattsburg. There he wrote Madison and Eustis wailing letters, offering his resignation, which they unfortunately chose not to accept.

16. Some of these St. Regis Indians lived in Canadian territory, on both sides of the St. Lawrence.

17. Organized in February, 1812, from the Macdonnells of Glengarry who had recently settled in Ontario. Many of their officers and men were veterans of earlier service in the British Army.

Begun far too late to assist Hull, the American operations along the Niagara River, crippled by amateur commanders and insufficient forces and supplies, had failed to win a beachhead on its west bank. They had, however, forced Prevost to dispatch additional troops from Lower Canada to reinforce his Niagara garrisons. But Dearborn's inertia and pusillanimity had made even this strategic gain meaningless.

Some American regimental officers were learning their new, hard, and dangerous profession. The repeated fiascos perpetrated by their generals however had wasted men and eroded popular support for the war. England would see Americans as contemptible opponents—not only cowardly but ridiculous.

FOUR

Marching, Mud, and Misery

Their appearance was miserable to the last degree. They had the air of men to whom cleanliness was a virtue unknown, and their squalid bodies were covered by habiliments that had evidently undergone every change of season, and were arrived at the last stage of repair. . . . It was the depth of winter; but scarcely an individual was in possession of a great coat or cloak, and few of them wore garments of wool of any description.

—Major John Richardson [1]

IN HIS INITIAL DISTRIBUTION OF BRIGADIER GENERAL commissions to deserving Republican politicians, Madison had included James Winchester of Tennessee. "Mild, generous, and rich," Winchester had been another minor officer during the Revolution, but later somehow had achieved a reputation as an Indian fighter in North Carolina. Now he was the senior regular officer in the West. He was not, however, capable of politically outmaneuvering William H. Harrison.

To Harrison in July and August, 1812, Hull's worsening predicament in Detroit was both a challenge and an opportunity. The hero of the West since Tippecanoe, he was the logical leader of a rescue expedition. Kentucky, the most heavily populated of the western states, would have to provide much of the manpower. A caucus of leading Kentucky citizens, including Henry Clay, was moved to make Harrison (then still governor of the Indiana Territory) a major general of Kentucky's militia and invest him with the command of a relief force that, when news of Hull's surrender arrived, swelled into something of a crusade to recover Detroit.

As a beginning, Harrison had browbeaten Winchester into letting him

1. Eyewitness description of Americans captured at River Raisin.

55

command the expedition to relieve Fort Wayne. Winchester countered by producing an order from Secretary of War William Eustis, specifically giving him command of a "North Western Army." Kentucky political influence made itself felt and Harrison received a regular brigadier general's commission, the command of the North Western Army, and a free hand in recovering Detroit.[2] Winchester was told that he could either serve under Harrison or be transferred to the Niagara frontier.

Harrison now found himself in the position of the man who—in Abraham Lincoln's homely parable—won a lottery and then discovered that the prize was a live rhinoceros. A veteran soldier, experienced in frontier warfare, he understood the problems he faced and the absolute need for careful preparation. An effective leader, he had inspired the West— and Madison and Eustis—to expect a quick, triumphant campaign. And, being at least as ambitious as he was able, he would not risk the loss of popularity that a deliberate, methodical campaign might entail. Consequently he went ahead with his crusade, hoping against all probabilities for what could only be called a lucky break—an unusually dry fall, the discovery of a new all-weather route through or around the Black Swamp, or unusual initiative by his subordinates.

Having a free hand, Harrison made liberal use of the West's resources to improvise an army, organizing three columns that were to converge on the Maumee Rapids, where an advance base with supplies for 10,000 men would be formed. Winchester's command of some 2,500 men, then at Fort Wayne, would form the left column, advancing along the Auglaize River to its junction with the Maumee and then down the Maumee to its rapids. The center column—1,200 Ohio militia and some regulars under Brigadier General Edward Tupper—would follow Hull's new road from Urbana while Brigadier General James Leftwick would lead the right column of 3,500 Virginia and Pennsylvania troops down the Sandusky River. To cover his left flank and rear, Harrison ordered Major General Samuel Hopkins of the Kentucky militia to march with 2,000 mounted volunteers to destroy the Indian villages along the Wabash and Illinois rivers.[3] If the weather stayed "very dry," Harrison promised Eustis, he

2. This intrigue naturally involved much political shuffling; at one point Secretary of State James Monroe was preparing to elbow Harrison aside and become the conquering hero of the West—of which he knew nothing. As a climax, Harrison did not accept the proffered brigadier general's commission, insisting that he should be a major general. In the meantime he operated under his Kentucky commission, thereby partially detaching himself from Eustis's control!

3. Harrison feared possible Indian raids on his communications so much that he

would take Detroit before winter. If there were "much rain," his army would have to wait at the Maumee Rapids until the rivers and the edges of Lake Erie froze solid enough to support its supply trains and artillery. Harrison would have to bring along some heavy guns to reduce Fort Detroit and (though he said nothing about it at that time) Malden, since it would be impossible to hold Detroit as long as the Provincial Marine could operate out of Malden against the American communications.

Harrison's four columns would be hopelessly out of mutual supporting distance, isolated targets for a British counteroffensive. He knew British Major General Isaac Brock and part of his troops had returned to the Niagara frontier after seizing Detroit; otherwise he seems to have been largely ignorant of the size and dispositions of the British force confronting him. Actually, the British were somewhat nearer than he realized. Probing south from Detroit, Colonel Henry Procter had occupied Brush's former camp at Frenchtown and established an outpost at the Maumee Rapids. Then, to encourage his Indian allies, he sent Muir (now a brevet major), up the Maumee River toward Fort Wayne with approximately 500 regulars and militia, 500 Indians, and a few light guns. The river was low at the end of summer, making boat handling difficult, but Muir reached the site of Fort Defiance (abandoned since 1797), at the junction of the Maumee and Auglaize. Leaving his boats, he continued overland, but on September 25 his Indians encountered five of Winchester's scouts. These Americans obviously were amateur frontiersmen; they accepted the Indians' protestations of friendship, told them the location and size of Winchester's column, and thereupon were expeditiously killed and scalped. Thus alerted, Muir hoped to draw Winchester into an ambush, but Winchester, warned in turn by finding the scouts' mangled bodies, took up a defensive positive. Clearly outnumbered, with his supplies dwindling, Muir finally retired.

Harrison pushed his preparations, but the whole offensive had to be organized from scratch—men levied, artillery located, contractors found to furnish and transport supplies. There was the usual lack of competent staff officers; Harrison's amateur command system performed in such a slipshod fashion that he never was certain how many men he had or where his supply trains were.

Then it rained. All through October and into November of 1812

---

also sent Colonel John B. Campbell with a force of mounted volunteers and regular light dragoons to raid the Miami Indian villages along the Mississiniway River. Campbell was successful, but lost heavily from cold, sickness, and hardship.

the downpour continued. Every stream was over its banks; roads dissolved; the bottom fell out of the Black Swamp. From the Auglaize to the Sandusky River, the country was one vast morass. Winchester's column reached the ruins of Fort Defiance and halted there in complete misery, slapping at occasional Indian war parties. Tupper could not get beyond Urbana; the Virginia/Pennsylvania column wallowed slowly toward the Sandusky River. Along the Wabash, Hopkins' column simply dissolved as its wet, weary militiamen gave up and headed home. Roads were littered with bogged wagons and broken-down pack horses.

Harrison did not spare himself, riding the entire front of his command, urging and encouraging, vainly seeking better routes. By October 23, however, he had to notify Eustis that there could be no advance, even to the Maumee Rapids, until the ground froze. Meanwhile, his army suffered. Tupper's men were the best off, Urbana being a supply depot, but even the most determined efforts could not get sufficient supplies to Winchester's men, who were lucky when they got half rations of beef from half-starved cattle, eked out with fish and edible roots.[4] The wet, increasingly chill weather, combined with the lack of proper food, clothing, and shelter and the usual militia neglect of military hygiene, soon brought on sickness, including typhus. Proper medical care, like everything else needed by Harrison's army, was in pitifully short supply. Sick soldiers went into improvised hospitals or dosed themselves with frontier home remedies. The death rate climbed rapidly; desertion increased.

Meanwhile, Eustis, increasingly browbeaten by Congress, the press, and public opinion, had resigned. (One of Congress's complaints was that he had commissioned too many Federalists.) Secretary of State James Monroe then temporarily took over the additional duties of secretary of war. He must have suddenly felt the real weight of these new responsibilities when he received the strange report Harrison sent off on December 12. Claiming that he believed it to be the Madison administration's urgent wish that he continue his campaign through the winter to recover Detroit as soon as possible, Harrison reported himself preparing to get on with it. However, he explained, Detroit would not be tenable so long as the British held Malden, which should be the objective of any American offensive, and he could not get at Malden unless the Detroit River was frozen hard. Therefore it would save vast sums of money if the administration would postpone his offensive until April or May of 1813

4. One welcome issue was several hundred razorback hogs, which had been driven through the woods to Winchester's camp.

and concentrate on building ships to secure the command of Lake Erie. That done, Malden could be taken and Detroit and Mackinac recovered "without difficulty." However Harrison also insisted that there was nothing wrong with his original plan, and blamed its failure on delays caused by the "imbecility and inexperience of the public agents [5] and the villainy of the contractors." There *had* been a plenitude of those three failings, but the first two were to be expected in any such hurriedly assembled army, and cheating contractors were a traditional feature in North American military operations.

Madison and Monroe recognized Harrison's ambiguous report for what it undoubtedly was—an attempt to shift the blame for his failing campaign onto their administration. They *could* order him to go over to the defensive, but the responsibility of explaining such an order to still-optimistic western leaders would be theirs. Harrison would appear an eager, faithful soldier, checked in midcareer by eastern politicians. As Monroe's successor, sardonic John Armstrong, later phrased it, the two Virginians decided "with less perhaps of patriotism than prudence" to leave the decision—and any ensuing blame—to Harrison. The North Western Army's casualty rate apparently was not considered. Thus rebuffed, Harrison admitted on January 6 that it would be sensible to suspend operations for the winter, but before Washington could receive, ponder over, and answer this letter, Harrison's situation had changed.

Some things had been accomplished. With great waste of lives, money, and suffering horses, supply depots had been built up at Urbana and Upper Sandusky. On December 20 Harrison had ordered Winchester to march down the Maumee River from Fort Defiance to the Rapids, and there establish a post and build sleds for a projected advance on Malden. He himself would arrive at the Rapids on January 20.

By early January, 1813, the ground was at last frozen hard enough to support wheeled traffic; troops, artillery, and supplies were hurried forward. Because sickness and desertion had whittled Harrison's forces away to a strength of approximately 6,300, and the service periods of most of the militia would end in February, prompt action was necessary if anything at all was to be accomplished.

Winchester reached the Rapids on January 10 and began constructing a poorly located fortified camp on the north bank of the Maumee. Hardship and disease had destroyed half of his command (the 1st and

5. Civilian representatives of the Commissary, Quartermaster, and Ordnance departments, responsible for supplies and transportation.

5th Kentucky infantry regiments, the Kentucky Rifle Regiment, and the 17th U.S. Infantry Regiment, recruited in Kentucky), so that it mustered only some 1,300 men. Practically all of them, both officers and enlisted men, were more than fed up with their commanding officer. The fact that Winchester was a Tennessean, imposed on them by Eustis, had not pleased the clannish Kentuckians to begin with; his ineptitude deepened their dislike. Isolated as he was, Winchester did not concern himself with the dangers of an English attack. On January 13 two civilians came into his camp to ask help for the citizens of Frenchtown, some thirty miles farther north. Procter had posted approximately 250 Canadian militia and Indians there with one 3-pounder; the inhabitants had found them discomforting visitors. The destruction of this detachment and the capture of its supplies would be a showy little victory; the Kentuckians—cold, hungry, bored, and soon to go home without having fired a shot—wanted a fight. It is doubtful that Winchester could have held them at the Rapids, had he wanted to do so. A council of war voted unanimously for an advance, and the next morning Colonel William Lewis marched with 450 men, followed a few hours later by Colonel John Allen with 110 more.[6] Moving on the windswept ice along the shore of Maumee Bay and Lake Erie, they reached Frenchtown at 2:00 P.M. on the 18th.

During cold weather Indians frequently were careless of their security, and often could be surprised in their camps. Coming in along the frozen River Raisin, the Kentuckians were on the edge of Frenchtown before the enemy saw them. The Canadian gunners got off a wild round or two but the Americans swarmed through the village, knocking over (and scalping) twelve warriors and losing only a few men wounded. Excited by their initial success they pursued their enemies into the woods beyond Frenchtown where the Canadians and Indians waged a stubborn, tree-to-tree bushwhacking withdrawal that cost the Kentuckians heavily. However, their superior numbers and drive carried them forward until dark, under cover of which the enemy broke contact and withdrew. American losses totaled twelve killed and fifty-five wounded. Those of the enemy during the woods fighting are unknown, but were undoubtedly fewer than they inflicted.

Informed of this success, Winchester ordered Frenchtown held. The Kentuckians still at the Rapids clamorously demanded that they too go

6. Lewis commanded the 5th Kentucky Regiment, Allen the Kentucky Rifle Regiment, but the men probably were volunteers from all three Kentucky regiments at the Rapids.

forward. Accordingly Winchester left the Rapids on the evening of January 19th, followed by the 17th U.S. Infantry under Colonel Samuel Wells. He did not think to bring ammunition to replace that expended on the 18th. At Frenchtown Winchester found total confusion. Frenchtown lay along the north bank of the Raisin (or Au Raisin) River; the other three sides of the town were covered by a slight palisade, little stronger than a picket fence. Lewis's and Allen's detachments had fumbled themselves into billets in the town in no sort of order whatever. There being no room left for the 17th Infantry, Wells was told to camp in an open field just outside the palisade. Not wanting to disturb the wounded (so he later reported), Winchester picked a comfortable house some distance south of the town for his headquarters. He supposedly considered withdrawing, but rejected that because he could think of no means of transporting the wounded. Though he knew that the palisade would be no protection against artillery fire, he postponed strengthening it until the "means for getting out timber might be had." (Since the Kentuckians had axes, and more tools would be available in Frenchtown, this alibi remains thoroughly opaque.) On December 21 he sent out a patrol that claimed to have reached Brownstown, eighteen miles farther north, without encountering any enemy forces.

That same day a friendly Canadian came in from Malden to warn that Procter was preparing to attack. Winchester dismissed his story as mere rumor, confident that Procter would need several days to collect sufficient troops. Meanwhile, Winchester took no interest in seeing that sentries were posted and patrols sent out after dark, leaving those details to his colonels. The Kentucky colonels did not bother. After getting a good look at the mess they and Winchester were making of the situation, Colonel Wells took the unheroic but practical action of getting himself ordered back to the Rapids, officially to hurry supplies forward, actually to report the state of affairs to Harrison.

Harrison was no help. En route to the Rapids he had received Winchester's report of the capture of Frenchtown. Arriving on January 20, he found a half-finished post held by some 300 Kentuckians, undoubtedly Winchester's lame, sick, and lazy. Though he believed that Procter had around 4,000 men in the Detroit/Malden area, he nevertheless approved of Winchester's advance, ordered him to hold Frenchtown, and began collecting reinforcements. The only explanation for such actions is that Harrison was unwilling to accept the onus of ordering a retreat after Winchester had proclaimed a victory.

General Procter—described as fat and haughty—had indeed marched out on January 21. Summoning militia to take over the garrison duty at Detroit and Malden, he collected all available regulars[7] and crossed the frozen head of Lake Erie on the ice from Malden to Brownstown, where he picked up troops from Detroit and the detachment driven out of Frenchtown. Five miles north of Frenchtown he halted for the night. His exact strength is uncertain, but did include between 500 and 600 regulars and militia, at least 450 Indians under a Wyandot chief named Roundhead, and six light cannon. Two hours before dawn Procter had his men up again and on the move, closing to within musket range of the Frenchtown palisade before the sun rose.

A quick rush would have carried the palisade and caught the Americans asleep. But Procter paused to form his troops into line and get his guns into position. This maneuvering created just enough noise to wake up an American sentry—and the Kentuckians came out of their blankets shooting.[8] They knew nothing much of war but were eager to learn; the palisade blazed with deadly fire. Caught ranked in the open, the British regulars were badly shot up; Procter had to pull them back into the shelter of the timber. The gun crews also were picked off: apparently only the guns on the left of the British line were able to stay in action, directing their fire at the unfortunate 17th Infantry, which also had had to form up in the open. Meanwhile the Indians poured past the town on both sides, getting across the River Raisin. Soon the already battered 17th Infantry, under fire from front, flank, and rear, began giving ground. Colonel Allen sortied from Frenchtown with two companies to support the 17th, but could not reestablish its line. Beaten back across the frozen river, these Americans finally panicked and broke. In Indian fighting this was fatal; floundering in the deep snow, the Americans were run down and butchered. Allen was killed and scalped; caught in the rout, Winchester was captured by Roundhead, who stripped him almost bare before turning him over to Procter. (Hence the legend he was wearing only his nightshirt.)

Some 384 Americans, commanded by Major Madison of the Kentucky Rifle Regiment, still held out in Frenchtown, definitely unwhipped but almost out of ammunition. Procter suggested that Winchester order them to surrender, and Winchester complied. Procter had won a com-

---

7. Most of Procter's regulars were from the 41st Foot, with two companies of the Royal Newfoundland Fencibles that had been serving with the Provincial Marine.

8. One Kentuckian recalled that their drums had just begun beating reveille when the sentry gave the alarm.

plete success, but he had bungled his tactics and so had been badly hurt. Twenty-four of his regulars and militia were dead and 161 wounded. Indian losses were as usual unknown, but must have been serious enough, for Madison's men had been picking them off.

With possibly a third of his command dead or wounded, and his Indians in their usual after-action disorder, Procter can be excused from the blame usually heaped upon him for not driving ahead to the Rapids and dealing with Harrison. But the man does seem to have been gripped by a sudden funk that sent him headlong back to Malden. Most of the captured Americans able to walk—approximately 500 men—were hustled northward. As a grim sequel, between 60 and 80 seriously wounded were left unguarded[9] in Frenchtown. Early on the morning of the 23d, a crowd of drunken, revenge-crazy warriors came down on Frenchtown, robbed the inhabitants, set fire to the houses used as hospitals, and fell upon the wounded with tomahawk and scalping knife. At least 30 were murdered or burned to death. Others were carried off by the Indians, to be held for ransom or entertainment; those who could not keep up with their captors were casually killed. In all, approximately 400 Americans died in action or by massacre.[10]

Some 30-odd survivors straggled into Harrison's position at the Rapids where he had collected 900 men, one gun, and some supplies. Harrison at once set fire to his post and supplies and retreated behind the Portage River, fifteen miles to the south. It was a rare incident in military history—two opposing armies running from each other as fast as they could.

Frenchtown—or "the River Raisin" as most Americans termed the debacle—brought Procter promotion to the grade of brigadier general. Winchester's report to the secretary of war, written from Malden the next day, remains an outstanding example of uncomprehending asininity: he conceded that his defeat *was* regrettable, but he was "flattered by the belief that no material error is chargeable upon myself."

HARRISON REMAINED BEHIND THE PORTAGE RIVER despite a letter (dated December 26) from Acting Secretary of War Monroe, rebuking him

---

9. Apparently two American surgeons and a British officer of some sort were left with them. A Canadian historian recently asserted in all seriousness that they were left "under an Indian guard." The English officer obviously could do nothing useful, even if he had been so inclined. Most Englishmen feared their savage allies as much as the Americans did, and were occasionally killed by them.

10. Figures for American losses here are horseback estimates at best.

for his lack of activity and ordering him to resume his offensive. Then on February 1, 1813, having collected 2,000 men, Harrison returned to the Rapids and began the construction of a strongly fortified base of operations, named Fort Meigs, on the south bank of the Maumee. Well situated and carefully planned, this work was one of the first large-scale achievements of a West Point graduate, Harrison's engineer officer, Major Eleazer D. Wood.[11] During the next week, Harrison massed 4,000 men at this point. Still hoping to achieve some success that would justify his waste of men, money, and material during the past five months, he moved out on February 11 for a hit-and-run raid across frozen Lake Erie against Malden. Reaching the lake he found that the ice was breaking up and so marched back to Fort Meigs, reluctantly reporting that his campaign had ended for the winter.

WHILE HARRISON FOUNDERED IN MUD AND INDECISION, beyond his left flank renewed Indian raiding raked the Illinois Territory. The Kickapoo there were a conservative tribe, deeply attached to their own culture and lands; they disliked white men in general and Americans in particular. They had supported Tecumseh, and a good many of them had been at Tippecanoe. Harrison considered their warriors the best among the northwestern tribes. The disintegration of Hopkins' force left them free to take the warpath whenever they chose. Their autumn harvests and hunting done, they began stalking the outlying settlements, striking suddenly, and vanishing with fresh scalps, loot, and an occasional stumbling captive. Settlers fled to the riverbank towns or even back across the Ohio River into Kentucky.

In October, 1812, the territorial governor, Ninian Edwards, had mustered a small army of volunteers and moved north. To make certain he could have supplies enough for a prolonged raid, he took a wagon train, the first wheeled vehicles ever used in central Illinois. This slowed his march; when he reached Kickapoo Town, the tribe's major settlement (near modern Bloomington), he found it empty. Forty-odd miles to the northwest, at Peoria, was another large village. Leaving the wagons behind and marching hard, Edwards surprised it, killing twenty-four warriors. Most of the Kickapoo escaped into a nearby swamp, one warrior walking away through American rifle fire with a typical Indian scatologi-

---

11. Class of 1806; a brevet lieutenant colonel in 1814, he was killed in action at Fort Erie.

cal sign of derision. Both towns were burned, leaving their inhabitants with no shelter and scant supplies for the winter.

MEANWHILE POLITICAL SHIFTS IN WASHINGTON were changing the whole American strategy. Monroe was another Virginian, a better administrator than most of his fellows, but so innocently convinced of his superior abilities and republican virtue that he felt obliged to advise and meddle in other men's responsibilities. He had shown bravery during the Revolution, being wounded at Trenton and winning promotion to major, but had dropped out of the army before the war's end to study law. Anxious for high military command, he also yearned to be secretary of war. This was too much Virginian ambition for many northern Republicans to swallow.[12] In his search for a permanent replacement for Eustis, Madison thus had to pass over Monroe; Senator William H. Crawford of Georgia and Dearborn both refused his offer of the post. John Armstrong of New York finally was chosen.

Armstrong was the first secretary of war to comprehend strategy, army organization, and the sad fact that politicians seldom make good combat officers. Likewise a Revolutionary major, he had fought with credit through the whole war. (His service as aide-de-camp to conniving Horatio Gates, which involved him in the "Newburgh Address" troubles of 1783, may have taught him something of army administration as well as polishing his tendency to bold intrigue.) Son of a Pennsylvania frontier hero, he knew something of western problems; as ambassador to France during 1804–10 he had seen Napoleon's *Grande Armée* at the peak of its efficiency. He had studied the art of war and written sensibly about it. In 1812 he was made another of Madison's political brigadier generals and charged with the defense of New York City. Intelligent, outspoken and rough-spoken, a man of strong opinions who welcomed responsibility, his efficiency was flawed by erratic periods of negligence and indolence and a headlong, sometimes perverse self-will. Appointed reluctantly by Madison, confirmed unwillingly by the Senate, his work would be clogged by the animosity of the rest of the Madison administration—which he in turn regarded with considerable contempt. Monroe was especially hostile, behaving as if Armstrong had swindled him out of his rightful heri-

12. Monroe apparently wanted to become the commanding general of the Army in Dearborn's place *and* to secure the appointment of a secretary of war who would back him completely.

tage, and constantly warning Madison—by his own lights, with perfect sincerity—that Armstrong was a menace to both the United States and the Republican party.

Taking office on January 13, Armstrong found everything in a muddle, especially in the West. A year earlier, six months before the declaration of war while he still was a civilian, he had warned Eustis that the proper objective for any American offensive was to cut British communications along the St. Lawrence River, thus throttling Upper Canada. As for the West, he quickly determined that Harrison's offensives had merely expended thousands of men and millions of dollars without regaining any lost territory, and that Harrison seemed eager to continue more such campaigning as long as the administration would let him. It was March 1 before he received Harrison's report of February 11, confessing the failure of his raid on Malden. On the 5th he sent Harrison new orders: remain on the defensive, reorganize your army, and wait until our Lake Erie squadron is built and gains command of the lake.

Meanwhile, the West counted its dead and nursed its wounds. The massacre at Frenchtown had been a small affair but an especially brutal one. Its story was told and retold; exaggerations and inventions embellished it. Through the winter and all across the West, a sullen, frustrated fury against Procter and the Indians was ripening. And a slogan grew with it—"Remember the River Raisin!"

FIVE

Handful of Fir-Built Frigates

It must be superfluous to observe that this species of naval armament [gunboats] cannot become an excitement to engage in offensive maritime war, toward which it will furnish no means.

—Thomas Jefferson

THE ARMY HAD DR. EUSTIS. The U.S. Navy was in even worse condition, being headed by Secretary Paul Hamilton, who seldom was sober enough to attend to business in the afternoon—and hardly competent even when sober. At 1812's end he was replaced by a William Jones, who *was* reasonably sober after lunch and knew something about ships, but was hardly equal to his responsibilities.

In 1801 Jefferson had inherited the first-class little navy that had battered the French through the West Indies and had ended their piratical privateering in American waters. There were thirty-four frigates, sloops, brigs, and schooners, with six great ships of the line under construction, and a well-thought-out system of naval yards to support them.

Jefferson did not mistrust naval power to quite the same degree that he disliked a regular army. But he wanted no more than an irreducible minimum of it, and the Republican majority of his Congress considered even that a danger to the Republic. The government sold off all vessels except for thirteen frigates and one fast schooner (the "lucky little *Enterprise*"), which was kept only because of public clamor.[1] Seven of the frigates were to be "laid up in ordinary" (the nineteenth-century version of "mothballing"), anchored in some backwater, stripped of their gear, and left with

---

1. *Enterprise*'s various feats had made her a popular ship; the decision to sell her brought protests from every American seaport.

only a caretaker or two for a crew. The crews of the seven ships retained in service were reduced to two-thirds of their normal strength. Navy pay was cut, most of the senior naval officers and all the naval constructors discharged. Work on the ships of the line was halted; the timber collected for their completion was carelessly stored. To save money, repairs and maintenance on all ships, whether in commission or in ordinary, were postponed and neglected.

Jefferson did move to put the fear of justice into the North African pirate states of Algeria, Tripoli, and Tunis. It was an affair of many gallant exploits and a good deal of bumbling, especially in the handling of the final peace treaties. The American frigates could not operate effectively in the shallow North African coastal waters (the *Philadelphia* was lost attempting it), so Jefferson was forced to buy or build a few brigs and schooners for inshore operations. Meanwhile, the Navy borrowed some gunboats and mortar boats[2] from the Kingdom of Naples for attacks on Tripoli's harbor. These proved useful and so may have been the inspiration that set Jefferson off on his gunboat mania. Between 1803 and 1808, he pushed the construction of some 278 of them—small craft armed with one or two heavy guns. To Jefferson, these would form the ideal Navy—suitable only for coast defense or operations on inland lakes and rivers. Also, they were cheap to build. The fact that most of them proved too unseaworthy to operate in open waters—or that their small crews (twenty-five to thirty men) could not fight off an enemy boat attack[3]— never occurred to him. If it came to war, he theorized, the enemy's merchant shipping could be harried by American privateers, which would take the place of a deep-sea navy. And if a British fleet should bombard New York, Boston, or other American seaports, Jefferson would retaliate by hiring arsonists to set fires in London!

Except for completing Jefferson's gunboat program when he took office in 1809, Madison ignored the Navy. By 1812 two of the three frigates in ordinary at Washington Navy Yard had been allowed to rot beyond any chance of repair; the third had been disarmed and converted into

2. Mortar boats—known variously as "bomb ketches," "bombards," or "bombs" —were small warships mounting one or two heavy mortars and several light cannon. The Navy bought two and built two; being a new type of vessel to Americans, none were properly designed or equipped. One was soon sold; the others were militarily useless and apparently used as receiving ships.

3. In boat attacks large warships launched their various boats, loaded with sailors and marines, for attacks on becalmed enemy ships or coast fortifications. The larger boats had cannon at their bows.

a sheer hulk. Three more—*John Adams, Constellation,* and *Chesapeake*—
needed extensive work to be seaworthy. The *Constitution* was refitting but
had neither crew nor stores aboard; the *Essex* was having its foremast replaced; the light frigate *Adams* was being slowly converted into a sloop-of-
war.[4] The remaining three—*President, Congress,* and *United States*—were
manned and ready for service though all, especially *Congress,* were in less
than perfect condition. The sloop-of-war *Hornet* and the brig *Argus* were
in American waters; the sloop *Wasp* and the brigs *Enterprise, Vixen, Syren,*
and *Viper* at sea. Most of the gunboats were laid up, without weapons,
equipment, or crews. Only the Washington Navy Yard was active, and it
was ruled by Captain Thomas Tingey, an officious, persuasive dry-land
sailor, who once had served in the Royal Navy and so did not approve
of most American innovations—such as fast schooners—in naval construction. There was no reserve of ammunition or ordinary naval stores
and the Navy Department's tiny staff had barely been able to handle its
peacetime responsibilities.

Against this "handful of fir-built frigates . . . manned by bastards and
outlaws" (so the London *Times* described them), the Royal Navy could
muster more than 640 warships in commission, including some 124 ships
of the line and 116 frigates. Much of this strength was tied down in
the blockade of French ports, but there always were strong squadrons
in North American waters and the West Indies. For years they had held
the American coast under a semi-blockade, halting and searching merchant ships—and, on two occasions, United States naval vessels[5]—and
impressing American sailors into the British service.[6] All this was done
with a self-righteous arrogance, as if dealing with an inferior species,
which was not the less infuriating for being perfectly sincere. Royal Navy

4. A frigate was a ship-rigged vessel carrying guns on two decks. A sloop was
properly a small, one-masted craft, but a sloop-of-war was a ship-rigged vessel, next
in size to a frigate, carrying guns on its upper deck only. Europeans often termed this
class of warships "corvettes."

5. In 1798, USS *Baltimore,* fifty-five men seized; 1807, USS *Chesapeake,* four men.
The story of one man being seized from the bomb ketch USS *Spitfire* in 1811 seems
to have resulted from a confusion of names. One citizen was taken from an American
coastal vessel of the same, or similar, name.

6. The basic pretext was that these men were deserters from the Royal Navy, as
indeed some of them were, or else British subjects. (England did not recognize their
right to become naturalized American citizens.) By 1812 there were over 6,000 officially established cases of such impressment of Americans. Probably there were more
Americans in the Royal Navy than in the United States' service—and practically none
of them happy about it.

morale was high from years of victories over the French, Spanish, Dutch, and Danes. Fighting desperately to bring down Napoleon, the British naturally considered their cause that of all virtuous humanity. When the United States finally declared war, the British would somehow consider it an act of deep ingratitude, undoubtedly the result of dastardly strategic plotting between Madison and Napoleon.

The long blockade of French ports, however, with no major naval actions to break the monotony, had resulted in a falling-off of the efficiency of many British ships, gunnery training being especially neglected. A few French sea captains had already discovered this, and had handed the Royal Navy's frigates some unexpected clobberings.[7] These scattered defeats, however, had not dented the English certainty in their national superiority at sea.

American naval strategy of this period was strongly influenced by several factors. To begin with, its sailing warships could remain at sea for long periods. What supplies they required could be found in most minor seaports; they could take on water at any handy river's mouth. A resourceful captain such as David Porter of the *Essex* could even find an isolated island where he could careen his ship to scrape and recaulk her bottom. Consequently, commerce raiders could make long, destructive cruises, ranging widely from one choice "hunting ground" to another to avoid avenging British warships, resupplying themselves and even picking up new seamen from the ships they captured.

Communications, however, were a different, difficult matter. While all navies had effective systems of flag signals for messages between their ships, once a vessel put to sea and dropped below the horizon it was practically beyond recall or control. The captain had his orders, but must depend on his own skill and judgment to carry them out. He might receive information as to the war's general progress from prisoners, chance-met neutral ships, or American vessels that had sailed later, but generally it was an isolated existence, always alert for first sight of another vessel and the decision whether to fight or run. Captains might leave messages with American consuls or merchants in neutral ports, but there were few of those, and the Royal Navy was apt to regard neutral waters as part of its world-wide combat zone, whenever that suited its lordly convenience.

Once safely back in port, the captain of an American warship had another set of problems. His crew had "signed on" for the length of whatever cruise he had made, not for a definite period of enlistment. Some

7. Most of these were in the Indian Ocean, 1808–10, and so got little publicity.

of them would sign and go again, but many would leave for a prolonged spree or—increasingly—to join the crew of some privateer that offered shorter cruises, easier discipline, less fighting, and a better chance at prize money. The captain might be held in harbor for weeks, even months, seeking men to replace them, then put to sea with an uncombed new crew, strangers to the ship and to one another.

It was the ancient custom of prize money that often tripped up the best-planned naval strategies. Every sailor, regardless of grade and rank, had hopes of capturing a richly laden enemy ship; British admirals dreamed of seizing enemy seaports with full warehouses and scores of ships at anchor, like Admiral George Rodney's capture of St. Eustatius during the American Revolution. The British Army had complained (and would complain bitterly again before this war was over) that British admirals, anxious to build up their retirement funds, did not hesitate to involve it in impossible amphibious actions that killed off soldiers wholesale.[8]

Faced with the possibility of war with the United States, Vice Admiral Herbert Sawyer, commanding the British naval forces in North America, had planned to follow routine English strategy. He would drop one or two frigates off each major American harbor, penning in the Yankee warships while gathering up the American merchant ships that would come crowding home once war began. It would be a most satisfactory operation, with much profit and very little risk beyond the everyday chances of wind and weather. Once his blockade was established, English sea traffic could move freely in the Atlantic and Caribbean, safe from American raiders. American vessels still on the high seas would be hunted down, and the United States left unable to export goods or draw military supplies from Europe. (Of course, American ships smuggling foodstuffs to feed England's armies would be given safe-conducts, but any vessel without one would be lucky if it could sail from New York harbor to Staten Island without being intercepted.) The Yankee Navy just possibly might attempt some interference, but it had nothing except a few oversized

---

8. Prize money was the value of the captured ships and cargo, less legal fees. Of this, the government—or, for privateers, the owners—got half. The remaining half was split into twenty "shares," of which the captain got three, the lieutenants two, the marine and warrant officers two, midshipmen and chief petty officers three, and petty officers three. The remaining seven shares were divided among the rest of the crew. If the ship that made the capture was operating as part of a fleet, the admiral claimed a twentieth for himself, no matter how far away from the action he had been. No wonder one British common seaman prayed that God would distribute wounds in the same proportions as prize money!

frigates and waddling little brigs—no history, no traditions, no chance whatever against British ships and seamen.

President Madison and Secretary Hamilton were very much of the same opinion. To begin with, they did not know what to do with the few ships they had. Hamilton solicited suggestions from his captains,[9] who recommended that the frigates be sent by ones or twos on long-range raids against English shipping. Not specifically stated, but certainly implied, was their strategic aim: England was a mercantile nation—Napoleon's "nation of shopkeepers"—dependent on foreign trade for its prosperity and even much of its food supply. Destroy enough of the merchant ships that carried that trade and England's economy would totter; its great traders, manufacturers, and West Indies planters would howl for peace. (German submarines would apply the same strategy in World War I and World War II.) But this was too aggressive a concept for Hamilton; he ended by ordering all serviceable warships concentrated at New York under Commodore John Rogers.

According to old Navy legend, two captains, William Bainbridge and Charles Stewart, personally called on President Madison, winning his consent that those warships already in commission could put to sea. This was embodied in Hamilton's orders to Rogers on June 18: he was free to strike at any enemy ships off New York harbor but was to return immediately to port after having done so; there would be "more extensive and more particular orders" for him, once the secretary could make up his mind what those orders should be. At this point Secretary of the Treasury Gallatin provided the necessary stimulus, demanding that all available ships be ordered on coastwise cruises to protect returning American merchantmen. Accordingly, on June 22 Hamilton so ordered. Afterward the Navy could be used as floating batteries for harbor defense and for training sailors for service on Jefferson's little gunboats, which were being taken out of mothballs. After all, the Navy *was* weak and inexperienced; it would be a useless sacrifice of ships and men to pit it against the Royal Navy. But the Gallatin/Hamilton inspiration came a few days too late. The U.S. Navy had decided to fight its own war.

The Navy had excellent officers and seamen. It could draw on considerable numbers of experienced merchant officers and sailors who had

9. At this time, captain was the highest permanent grade in the U.S. Navy. (If a group of ships cruised together, the senior captain received the temporary title of "commodore.") Apparently John Rogers, Stephen Decatur, and William Bainbridge replied.

taken years of abuse from the Royal Navy and longed to get even for it. Also, an amazing temptation of prize money was dancing before Rogers' eyes: a major British convoy of richly laden ships from Jamaica was known to be homeward bound, just a few days' sailing time off the east coast. To eager, aggressive sea captains who had endured years of national humiliation and neglect, the possible combination of revenge and booty was irresistible.

Rogers received Hamilton's first orders on June 21, 1812. Within an hour he was outward bound with *President, United States, Congress, Hornet,* and *Argus.* Two days later he encountered the British frigate *Belvidera,* which had been making so great a nuisance of itself halting and searching American ships that even Secretary Hamilton hoped Rogers might catch her. He almost did, but after a long chase *Belvidera* got away by good seamanship and jettisoning boats, anchors, and drinking water to increase her speed.[10] Unable to take like measures, which would have left him unable to carry out a long cruise, Rogers gave up the chase and turned east and north after the Jamaica convoy. Three weeks' pursuit brought him within a day's sailing of the English Channel, without ever sighting it. Reluctantly he turned south toward the Canary Islands.

The banged-about *Belvidera*'s arrival at Halifax was Admiral Sawyer's first notification that he had a war on his hands—accompanied by the jarring news that Rogers was out and on the prowl. Abandoning his planned blockade, Sawyer sent his four readiest ships—three frigates and a small battleship under Captain Sir Philip Broke—south to New York in the hope of intercepting Rogers upon his return. En route, Broke picked up the British frigate *Guerrière* off Nantucket, where it had been busy bullying American shipping, and ran down and captured the American brig *Nautilus.* On June 17 he encountered the *Constitution* off Sandy Hook.

Following Hamilton's instructions for a concentration at New York, Captain Isaac Hull, nephew to General William Hull, then marching toward Detroit and disaster, had taken the *Constitution* to sea from Annapolis as soon as he could complete his crew. Initially, he thought Broke's squadron was Rogers' but once it did not answer his signals he quickly saw his danger and headed for open sea. Winds were light and infrequent; Broke pushed the pursuit doggedly for three days, yet never was quite able to match Hull's skill at ship handling. Slipping away, Hull headed for

10. *President,* the swiftest of the American squadron, was also handicapped by the explosion of one of her forward guns, which killed or wounded sixteen men, including Rogers, who sustained a broken leg.

Boston, hastily replenished his supplies, and put out again without waiting for orders from Washington. Late on August 18 he met an American privateer that reported having been chased by a British frigate.

Meanwhile the frustrated Broke had learned that a second Jamaica convoy was coming north along the American coast. With Rogers unaccounted for and the *Constitution* at large, he had no choice but to find and escort it. The *Guerrière* being in some need of refitting, Broke ordered it back to Halifax. On the morning of the 19th, it met the *Constitution* and gleefully bore in for what it considered an easy victory, its Captain James Dacres promising his crew a bonus of four months' pay if they took the American within fifteen minutes.

It was, however, hardly a fair match. The *Constitution*, like the other American heavy frigates, was a big ship, built expressedly to outgun any enemy ship of her own class and outrun any more powerful vessel.[11] In less than thirty minutes, the *Guerrière* was a complete wreck, her masts gone, her hull shattered, seventy-nine officers and men killed or wounded. Hull had only fourteen casualties.

The *Guerrière* had not been the first British warship taken. On July 3 the *Essex*'s repairs completed, Master Commandant David Porter had cleared New York with orders permitting him either to join Rogers or to cruise southward as far as St. Augustine, Florida. On the 11th he encountered seven British transports, en route from the West Indies to Halifax with a battalion of the 1st Regiment of Foot (the Royal Scots), under convoy of a small frigate. The British captain handled the situation expertly, but Porter did capture one transport with 197 officers and men aboard. (They were exchanged for American officers captured at Detroit and Queenston.) Originally a swift light frigate, the *Essex*, through the clumsy ministrations of Tingey and various earlier captains, had become something of a slug, armed with short-range carronades.[12] Porter therefore frequently disguised her as a sloppily handled merchantman to lure opponents into easy reach. In that guise, on August 13 she was attacked

---

11. *Constitution, United States*, and *President* were rated as 44-gun frigates but actually carried at least fifty-two; *Constellation, Chesapeake*, and *Congress* were officially 38-gun ships but carried over forty. (Both U.S. and British captains were apt to load extra guns onto their ships, thereby sometimes spoiling their sailing qualities.) *Guerrière*, rated a 38, had forty-eight guns, but over half of these were much lighter than *Constitution*'s.

12. Carronades were short-barreled weapons, very effective at short range since, being lighter than regular ships' guns, a 32-pounder carronade could replace a 12- or 18-pounder gun.

by the British 20-gun sloop-of-war *Alert*, which surrendered in most un-British haste after *Essex*'s first broadside. Having released the transport for $14,000 ransom, burned two merchant vessels, captured four others, and rescued a captured American ship, Porter brought his prizes home.

Rogers had come into harbor at Boston, having netted only two British privateers and six merchant vessels. His raid, however, had thrown Sawyer's plans into confusion. American ports had remained unblockaded; hundreds of merchantmen were safely home; and *Constitution* and *Essex* had been able to get to sea. Moreover, dozens of American privateers, mostly hastily outfitted small vessels, likewise had put out to snap up unsuspecting English ships, particularly in the nearby West Indies.

These Navy operations were a mighty stimulant to the American war effort, even in New England. Faced with such jubilant public enthusiasm, the administration decided to let its naval officers continue with their own brand of warfare, though it did nothing to set up an effective naval organization. It was January, 1813, before Congress decided to authorize three more heavy frigates and six sloops-of-war, and approximately a month of political agonizing passed before a shipbuilder of sufficiently pure Republican principles was chosen to serve as "naval constructor" at the Washington Navy Yard. This was William Doughty, fortunately a man of talent.

Meanwhile, the active warships were organized into three squadrons, each with one heavy and one light frigate and a sloop-of-war, with Rogers, Decatur, and Bainbridge as commodores. Rogers would operate in the North Atlantic; Decatur the Azores/Madeira Islands sector; Bainbridge the South Atlantic. Not all the designated ships were ready; the sloop-of-war *Wasp*, coming up from Norfolk to join Rogers, fell in with the British brig *Frolic* and completely wrecked it. Before the Americans could get their rigging repaired, however, a British battleship appeared and forced the *Wasp*'s surrender. The *Frolic* proved unrepairable; the *Wasp* was taken into the British Navy, but was wrecked in 1813. Eventually Rogers and Decatur sailed together on October 8 with *President, United States, Congress*, and *Argus*. Decatur, commanding the *United States*, left the squadron four days later; on October 25 off the Azores he met and captured the lighter British frigate *Macedonian*, which was thereafter added to the U.S. Navy. Rogers' cruise with *President* and *Congress* encountered only a few ships, though his captures included a whaler loaded with whale oil, whalebone, and ebony and a British mail packet with some $175,000 aboard.

Bainbridge got away late on October 25 with *Constitution* and the sloop-of-war *Hornet*. *Essex*, then in the Delaware River, was ordered to join him if possible at one of several South Atlantic ports. Cruising down the coast of Brazil, Bainbridge left the *Hornet* at San Salvador to blockade the British sloop *Bon Citoyenne*, which was carrying a shipment of coin. On December 29 he met and destroyed a slightly weaker British frigate *Java*, thereafter returning to Boston to refit. After vainly challenging the *Bon Citoyenne* to come out and fight, and being chased away from San Salvador by a British battleship, Master Commandant James Lawrence of the *Hornet* raided along the coast of British Guiana. While attempting to get at a small British warship, the *Espiegle*, anchored amid shoal waters at the mouth of the Demarara River, he was attacked by the English brig *Peacock*, which he sank in eleven minutes. The *Espiegle* failed to aid the *Peacock*; apparently it somehow was not aware of the battle. But Lawrence, an ardent young giant with a hot sense of personal and professional honor, concluded from his three recent experiences that the Royal Navy was officered by cowards and incompetents.

Meanwhile Porter and the *Essex* had missed the rendezvous with Bainbridge. A man of much energy and courage, though sometimes short of judgment, Porter decided to start a war of his own. Rounding Cape Horn, he came into the Pacific Ocean, cleaned out the British whaling fleet there, and refitted his ships in the Marquesas Islands. Then, learning that the British frigate *Phoebe* and two sloops had been sent to hunt him down, he sailed back to Valparaiso, Chile, in the hope of meeting them. There, the *Essex*'s rigging crippled by a squall, he was attacked in technically neutral waters[13] by the *Phoebe* and the sloop-of-war *Cherub* on March 28, 1814. Keeping out of range of the *Essex*'s carronades, the English ships methodically wrecked it by long-range fire, forcing Porter's surrender. A wiser captain would have sailed on westward into Chinese waters where his arrival would have been disastrous to British commerce.

England's response to the hammerings it had taken through 1812 was to press the establishment of its blockade of the American coast. For better control, all British naval forces from the Gulf of Mexico to Halifax were combined into a new "North American Naval Station," under Admiral John B. Warren. Warren may have been somewhat lacking in energy, but his mission was a really difficult one. Ships had to be dis-

13. Chile had not yet established its independence from Spain. Also, Captain James Hillyar, the British commander, had explicit orders to get Porter, regardless of how he did it.

engaged from their operations off Napoleon's Europe, refitted, and dispatched westward, a voyage that, depending on wind and weather, would take from one to three months and might end with storm-battered ships in urgent need of repair.

Therefore Warren applied his available forces piecemeal against what he thought the most important areas, the Chesapeake and Delaware bays, in November of 1812. Thereafter, as more ships dribbled in to join him, he extended his operations to cover Charleston, Port Royal, Savannah, New Orleans, and Long Island Sound. Except for its naval base at Boston, New England was left largely unblocked, in order to facilitate the treasonous and profitable trade in foodstuffs its merchants were carrying on with England and Canada. Not until May, 1814, was the whole United States seaboard closed down.

What with the innate perversity of North American weather, blockading could be dangerous duty. Moreover, because of the demonstrated superiority of the American frigates, British ships of that class had to operate in pairs or squadrons and had to be backed by ships of the line. And there was a crying need for swift small warships capable of running down American privateers and operating in shallow coastal waters.

Through 1812 and most of 1813, American raiders came and went. The light frigate *Chesapeake*, its repairs finally completed, cruised for four months with little success, though one of its six prizes reportedly was the richest capture of the war, the merchantman *Volunteer*, worth $350,000. Broke kept two frigates off Boston, where *Constitution*, *Congress*, *President*, and *Chesapeake* were gathered, hoping to coax one of them to come out and fight. Rogers regarded such heroics as pointless. Boston being a hard port to blockade, he simply went away on the night of April 30 with *President* and *Congress*, all unperceived by Broke. Once at sea the two American ships separated. Crossing to the Azores and then swinging northward of the British Isles, *President* replenished its water supply at Bergen—the first American warship to visit Norway. Being themselves much abused by the Royal Navy, the Norwegians made Rogers welcome. He came into Newport in September, having taken thirteen vessels, including a light warship. *Congress* cruised nearly eight months and made only four prizes. On her return to Boston, she was found so rotten from long prewar neglect that she was declared unfit for further service. Unaware of her true condition the British kept her under careful blockade.

Meanwhile, fearing another American frigate's escape from Boston, Broke had sent in a polite challenge to Lawrence, now a captain commanding the *Chesapeake*, to come out and fight him ship against ship. In size and fire power it would be an even match, but Broke had commanded his *Shannon* for seven years, training his crew carefully and developing an exceptional skill at naval gunnery. The *Chesapeake* had the old repute of being an unlucky ship; most of its seamen were new men, not yet shaken down into a functioning crew. Its first officer was also new to the ship; the third and fourth officers were young midshipmen, acting as lieutenants. Lawrence's orders were to sail as soon as possible for the Gulf of St. Lawrence, to intercept British ships and transports; the average captain would have tried, like Rogers, to run out of the harbor after dark and get about his mission: Lawrence went out in full daylight to meet the *Shannon*, like two gentlemen settling a private point of honor with "pistols for two, coffee for one." With the two ships running broadside to broadside at forty yards' range, Broke's skilled gunners swept the American quarterdeck, killing the sailing master and helmsman, mortally wounding Lawrence and his first and fourth officers. The third officer lost his head and helped carry Lawrence below deck instead of taking command. Out of control, the *Chesapeake* drifted into the *Shannon* end-on, unable to bring a single gun to bear, and was savagely raked. Lawrence called for his crew to board the *Shannon*, but his black bugler panicked under the merciless fire and forgot the proper call. Instead it was Broke who boarded the *Chesapeake*. Its second officer, Lieutenant George Budd, left his post on the lower gun deck and led what men he could rally on a counterattack. Broke took a saber cut that opened his skull, but once Budd was shot down the resistance collapsed. It had been a hot and messy fifteen minutes—sixty-two Americans and forty-three Englishmen dead or mortally hurt; seventy-three and thirty-four respectively wounded. The *Shannon* had been hulled repeatedly by *Chesapeake*'s fire, and had to pump to keep afloat on her return to Halifax, where *Chesapeake* was added to the Royal Navy. Lawrence died en route. His last command, variously reported, passed into history as "Don't give up the ship."

Broke's success was hailed in England with almost as much enthusiasm as Nelson's victory at Trafalgar. He was made a baronet and praised for having, in Warren's words, "restored to the British naval service the preeminence it has always preserved," but he never fully recovered from his head wound. The *Chesapeake* was an unlucky ship indeed for all concerned.

As the British blockade tightened, the American frigates found it next to impossible to get out to sea. By the end of 1813, the *Constitution* and the useless *Congress* were held at Boston, the *United States* and *Macedonian* at New London;[14] the *Adams* remained at Washington and the *Constellation* at Norfolk. *Essex* still was hunting British whalers in the Pacific, and Rogers had slipped the *President* out for a fourth cruise.

Admiral Warren meanwhile had been cleaning out the Chesapeake Bay area to make it a secure base for further British operations. His strategy was frankly one of terror, carried out zestfully by Vice Admiral George Cockburn, an expert and courageous sea captain, necessitous Scot, an enthusiastic arsonist and souvenir collector. Any American seaport that had a protective battery, usually an antique fieldpiece or two behind a primitive earthwork, was subject to bombardment and assault without warning. Any militiaman's home was the equivalent of a military barracks and so liable to be burned. Little Maryland villages such as Frenchtown, Havre de Grace, Fredericktown, Georgetown, and many more were plundered and burned along with their wharves, fishing boats, and ferries. (At Havre de Grace, Rogers' home went up with the others.) Plantations were raided for food to feed Warren's fleet. The weak, untrained local militia could make no effective resistance against Cockburn's vastly superior force; the few shots they fired Cockburn considered "useless rancor" and an excuse for additional devastations. Some British officers remembered such service with shame, but the Warren/Cockburn strategy did successfully terrorize much of the upper Chesapeake area into a humbled neutrality.

In this warfare the vaunted Jeffersonian gunboats proved completely worthless, their conduct being largely farcical, as when fifteen of them sortied from Norfolk on June 20 and shot at a becalmed British frigate for half an hour; hit her once, or maybe twice; and then had to run for it when a breeze came up. This incident apparently sharpened Warren's interest in Norfolk. He moved against it on June 22, hoping at least to burn its navy yard and the *Constellation*. The first stage of his attack was to pinch out an outlying American battery on Craney Island, at the mouth of the Elizabeth River, by landing a force farther up the coast to attack it from the rear, while another detachment made a boat attack on it from the bay. Things soon went awry. The land force literally bogged down in tidal creeks and marshes; the boat attack, pushed on recklessly anyhow, grounded in shoal water some 200-odd yards from the shore. Fortunately for the British, American gunnery was wild. In two hours the Americans

14. Decatur had sailed from New York with *United States*, *Macedonian*, and *Hornet* on June 1, but was intercepted by a strong British squadron and chased into New London.

hit only three boats, killing only three Englishmen and wounding sixteen more; twenty-two waded ashore to surrender and forty reportedly deserted from the land column. No American was even nicked. Warren reported a grave atrocity: allegedly, Americans had fired on men from the wrecked boats while they were foundering in the water. Since those men were among other British who were shooting at the Americans, the only sensible conclusion is that a thwarted admiral was enriching his alibi. However, if Norfolk was hard to get into, its narrow single entry made it equally difficult to leave. *Constellation* remained bottled up for the entire war, serving only to occupy two or three British warships in that task.

To refurbish his honor and reestablish his "preeminence," Warren turned on Hampton, Virginia, where a force of some 400 militia manned a battery on the shore of the James River. On June 25 he landed approximately 1,000 men two miles above that village to take it from the rear, while Cockburn threatened a boat attack to distract the Americans. After considerable shooting and some casualties on both sides, the militia extricated itself. Then the British literally took the place apart. Warren's land force included two companies of "Canadian Chasseurs," who actually were deserters from the French Army, enlisted voluntarily in the British service.[15] These added murder and rape to the general looting. Lieutenant Colonel Charles J. Napier of the 102d Foot and other British officers tried (not with entire success) to restrain their own men, but no Englishman made any real effort to beat the chasseurs from their screaming prey. Not one man was punished. Warren did later send the chasseurs to Halifax, where they instituted a major crime wave, but this was because he feared that their ferocious indiscipline would end in a mutiny aboard one of his own ships. Hampton capped the Warren/Cockburn maraudings. Like the River Raisin massacre, it hardened American hearts. Obviously it was no longer a gentleman's war.

Some of the small American brigs still kept the seas. "Lucky little *Enterprise*" took the British brig *Boxer* in a stubborn battle off Portland, in which both captains were killed. (*Enterprise* had been trying to check the illicit trade between New England and Halifax.) However, most of the

---

15. For a full story of these vicious yardbirds, see Albert W. Haarmann, "The Independent Companies of Foreigners at Hampton, Virginia, June 1813," *Military Collector and Historian*, Vol. XXXVIII, No. 4 (Winter, 1986), p. 178, and John R. Elting, "Those Independent Companies of Foreigners," *Military Collector and Historian*, Vol. XI, No. 3 (Fall, 1968), pp. 124–25. Napier's 102d Foot also was a hard lot, originally the New South Wales (or "Rum") Corps, formed from military criminals and deserters for service in Australia, and apparently including some Australians.

brigs were too small, slow, and weakly armed to resist the now-swarming British ships. During 1812–14 *Viper, Vixen, Syren, Rattlesnake,* and *Argus* were run down, *Syren* after a satisfactory raid off the West African coast. *Argus,* however, made her mark before being lost. Newly promoted Captain William H. Allen had taken her to France in June, 1813, to deliver a new American ambassador. That done, he followed his orders to cruise off the mouth of the English Channel where he sank twenty ships, to the consternation of London merchants and marine insurance underwriters. It was exhausting work for his small crew, and he pushed his luck too far. His twenty-first capture was loaded with Portuguese wines and some of his men seized the chance to get drunk. Allen recklessly set the prize on fire instead of scuttling her. The flames attracted the British brig *Pelican,* and Allen chose to fight rather than run from a ship no heavier than his own. But his luck was out: in five minutes he was mortally wounded; then his first lieutenant went down. His second lieutenant handled the *Argus* well enough, but her tipsy, weary gunners could not shoot straight, and *Pelican* won.

The tightening of the blockade also ended the first outbursts of American privateer activity that had cost England something over 400 merchantmen and kept Jamaica and other West Indies islands under semi-blockade for weeks. Those first improvised privateers, however, mostly lacked the speed and fire power to face the growing swarm of light English warships off the American coast. Privateering was also a highly speculative business—actually legalized piracy with a variable infusion of patriotism. Privateers looked for easy pickings and avoided combat; rather than destroying their more valuable prizes, they tried to send them back to the United States for sale, which meant that the British recaptured at least half of them en route. (One unhappy English sea captain had his vessel captured and recaptured three times in one voyage.) Privateering offered a gambler's chance at quick money for small risk; the average privateer's cruise was short and his discipline relaxed. Naturally seamen flocked to privateer service, and shipwrights to the construction of new privateers, while the Navy had trouble manning its active ships and getting its authorized new ones built. But privateering's greatest drawback was its inefficiency: of approximately 515 privateers and "letters of marque" [16] commissioned, 300 never succeeded in capturing a single English ship,

---

16. Properly a "letter of marque" was an armed merchant ship engaged in trade (usually for small quantities of especially valuable goods), which had authority to take prizes if chance offered. Privateers proper carried no cargo and hunted prizes.

and the British claimed the capture or destruction of some 250 of them.[17]

The new frigates authorized would take some two years to build, but the sloops-of-war were launched in less than a year. By early 1814 *Frolic*, *Peacock*, and *Wasp*,[18] all strong, swift 22-gun vessels, were at sea. *Frolic* took two prizes, then was caught between a British frigate and a captured privateer schooner that had been taken into the Royal Navy. *Peacock* defeated and brought in the British brig *Epervier*; then ran amuck down the Atlantic trade routes from the Faroes to the Canary Islands, making fourteen prizes and coming into New York at the end of October. *Wasp*, under Captain Johnston Blakeley, followed *Argus*'s track, raiding into the English Channel, snatching fifteen prizes in the teeth of the Royal Navy, taking and blowing up the British brig *Reindeer* after a gallant fight, then sinking the sloop-of-war *Avon* while two other British warships hovered bashfully nearby. (Their conduct seems to have created much high-level unhappiness in London.) Swinging south, Blakeley captured another merchantman[19] and—off the Cape Verde Islands on October 9—exchanged greetings with a Swedish vessel. Then the *Wasp* vanished without a trace. The *Adams*, her conversion to a powerful 27-gun sloop-of-war finally completed, slipped through Warren's blockade of Chesapeake Bay and went hunting. Often chased but never caught, she took nine prizes before an accident crippled her.[20] And somehow *Enterprise* survived, slow and unhandy but always in luck.

By contrast with the destruction dealt out by the sloops, the frigates accomplished very little. *Constitution* had gotten out on New Year's Day, but her three-month cruise netted only four merchantmen and one small British warship. *President* came back in mid-February, once more with only four small prizes to report. It was obvious that sloops-of-war were far better fitted for commerce raiding, being easier to build, man, and

17. Statistics are vague, but privateers seem to have taken over 2,000 British vessels, many very small. Approximately 600 of these may have been destroyed or released as "cartels" to carry the crews of other captured vessels into port. Some 750 more were recaptured.

18. The American system of naming warships during 1812–15 was confusing: *Wasp* was named after the sloop lost in 1812, the *Frolic* and *Peacock* apparently after defeated British ships of those names, a habit the English much resented as "rubbing our noses in it." Of the other three sloops authorized, one was burned when the British took Washington; two were built in Baltimore, but could not escape from Chesapeake Bay.

19. He sent this in under a prize crew to Savannah.

20. See chapter sixteen.

equip. Moreover their superior speed and maneuverability made it easier for them to evade blockaders, while they had enough fire power to handle English vessels of their class.

Privateer owners had come to much the same conclusion, if from the opposite direction. A new type of privateer, built specifically for that purpose, began harrying British trade in late 1813 and became a major menace through the following year. They could be built quickly in any small seaport—and there were so many of those along our Atlantic coast that the Royal Navy never could hope to blockade them all. The new ships were amazingly fast and maneuverable, and increasingly well armed. Some, like the *Prince de Neufchatel*, *Mammoth*, and *Young Wasp*, were almost as powerful as a Navy sloop-of-war, though far more lightly built, designed to strike and run rather than for heavy slugging.

Privateer captains learned their trade; only the expert, brave, and lucky could succeed. Most of them came to maintain Navy-style discipline; many of their sailors had served one or more cruises aboard warships and were ready and able to fight. These raiders were everywhere in the Atlantic. No matter how many the British captured, more appeared. Some of them sailed the long course into the Indian Ocean and China Sea, arriving all unexpected among the rich traffic there. (Word that war had been declared did not reach the East Indies until January, 1813!) Others raked the West Indies, the Mediterranean, and the Baltic;[21] a reckless few played tag with frustrated English warships off Halifax. But the most effective work was done by those captains who haunted the British Isles, making trade between England and Ireland, and often trade between two British ports, a highly risky business. One of the most galling was the *Chasseur*, a smallish schooner out of Baltimore, with sixteen guns and a cheerful captain named Thomas Boyle. Boyle captured some twenty ships off the south coast of England, fought and took a stronger British warship (ironically, a captured American privateer), and proclaimed the British Isles under a "strict and rigorous blockade." In fact, an informal blockade existed intermittently through much of 1814, bringing the bitter taste of unsuccessful war home to England as no foreign seamen had done since Michel de Ruyter took a Dutch fleet up the Thames in 1667 and burned or carried away England's finest ships.

By the end of 1814, the American Navy did not have one ship at sea,

21. The British were forced to build two martello towers to protect the assembly area for their Baltic convoys in the Sound of Longhope, a side pocket to Scapa Flow.

but this was the proverbial quiet before an intended storm. Through 1813 and 1814, in an inchoate, fumbling way, the United States was modifying its naval strategy. The process hardly could be called planning; instead it was an accretion of practical advice from sea captains and shipbuilders, political pressures, and general frustrations.

Circumstances had changed, and a different strategy was required. Napoleon's defeat and abdication in April, 1814, had freed the Royal Navy to give the United States its undivided and increasingly soreheaded attention. The American ships available, even when the two frigates under construction[22] were ready for action, would not have force enough to break up the British blockade. Privateers would be no help in that effort and, effective commerce destroyers though their best captains were, privateering had proven a wasteful way of making war. Too many of them did England little or no damage; too many of the most valuable prizes that successful privateers took were recaptured. They were bleeding England, but not fast enough.

Therefore the United States would build three very powerful line-of-battle ships, as superior to the average British ship of that class as our 44-gun heavy frigates had been to their English 38-gun opponents, to batter a way through the blockading squadrons. (A fourth battleship was authorized in 1814.) At the same time two squadrons of the swiftest brigs and schooners available, well armed and staunchly built, five of them under Porter and four under Oliver H. Perry, would be sent on raiding missions with the intent of destroying every vessel they captured. Decatur would take *President*, *Peacock*, and *Hornet* around the Cape of Good Hope to sweep the India trade routes. *Constitution* and the other frigates and sloops-of-war would strike out when ready. The resulting destruction would send large portions of the Royal Navy cruising frantically in all directions, and American privateers could run wild. English commerce, already badly hurt, would be ravaged from Halifax and the West Indies to Canton, from the Faroe Islands to Cape Horn.

In New York harbor a monstrous new sort of warship was being readied, the steam-propelled frigate *Demologus*, with sides five feet thick and thirty 32-pounder guns, designed by Robert Fulton for harbor defense and blockade breaking. A similar craft was under construction at Baltimore. Fulton also was involved with the dimly recorded *Mute*, which seems to have been an experimental submarine, and with the development of tor-

---

22. One had been destroyed with the Washington Navy Yard.

pedoes.[23] Many Englishmen were aware of his earlier work with both those exotic weapons, and some Royal Navy officers were wondering what sort of secret weapon might suddenly be used against them.

23. "Torpedo" at this time was a name given to a variety of explosive devices, usually what now would be called free-floating or drifting mines. Fulton reportedly was testing their use for what would be known during the Civil War as "spar torpedoes."

SIX

Battle for the Lakes

The Secretary of the Navy has honored me with a high destiny; we intend to seek and fight the enemy's fleet. This is the great purpose of the government in creating this fleet and I shall not be diverted in my efforts to effectuate it by any sinister attempt to render it subordinate to the army.
— Captain Isaac Chauncey, 1814

CAPTAIN ISAAC CHAUNCEY WAS A TALL MAN, increasingly portly-pompous, very certain of himself. Of approved skill and courage in storm, battle, and fire at sea, he had been noted particularly for the common-sense administrative efficiency and thoroughness with which he had handled every duty assigned him. When Madison and Hamilton named him commodore in command of the American naval forces on Lake Erie and Lake Ontario, they could credit themselves with having made the best possible selection.

In appointing him, however—as in just about everything else—they had dillydallied. It was August 31, 1812. The war was ten weeks old. Control of the lakes was vital to American operations on the Canadian frontier, and Hull had met disaster at Detroit for lack of it.

Nor had the war on the lakes waited for them. The Canadian Provincial Marine had had a major part in Hull's defeat, and its Lake Erie squadron had been strengthened by the capture of the *Adams*. (Completed and outfitted, *Adams* was now *Detroit*.) On Lake Ontario the Provincial Marine had six warships, the Americans one, the *Oneida*. *Oneida* had been authorized as a "gunboat" in 1809, but Jefferson's secretary of the navy Robert Smith had the unregenerate thought that she should be built strong enough to take on the biggest ship the Provincial Marine

86

had on Ontario. Consequently she emerged as a 14-gun brig, originally fast and handy, but now in need of repairs to her bottom and therefore slow. Moreover, half the Provincial Marine vessels mounted more guns, though possibly not as heavy.

On July 19 the whole Canadian Ontario squadron[1] struck at Sackets Harbor, the American base on Lake Ontario where Lieutenant Melancthon Woolsey, *Oneida*'s commander, had orders from Hamilton to organize an emergency squadron. An active, courageous officer, Woolsey had struck out as soon as he learned of the declaration of war, seizing three Canadian schooners.[2] Now he anchored *Oneida* across the mouth of Sackets Harbor, took out his inshore guns, and mounted them on a hill commanding the harbor's entrance. Local militia rallied to his support. For some reason the Canadians failed to push their attack. Getting something a little worse than they gave during a two-hour, long-range squabble, they finally hauled out for Kingston. Woolsey went back to his task of making warships out of his prizes and purchasing merchant vessels for conversion to fighting ships.

Naval warfare on the lakes had its peculiarities. Ontario was deep water, capable of taking large vessels, but because of ice was navigable for roughly only half the year. Lake merchant vessels therefore usually were lightly built schooners with large spreads of sail for swift, good-weather cruising. When armed as improvised warships, their guns made them top-heavy and tricky to handle.[3] A ship built specifically as a warship for lake service could have more cannon than a sea-going vessel of the same size, since it did not have to carry either fresh water for its crew or large quantities of food and other supplies. But such ships, whether British or American, would have to be hastily constructed from green timber, at the end of long and sometimes impossible supply lines.

Once appointed, Isaac Chauncey remained in New York getting his supply system organized, recruiting the necessary shipwrights, rope walkers, smiths, and other artificers. For the "constructor" to manage the Sackets Harbor shipyard he made an outstanding choice in Scottish-born

1. Sloop-of-war *Royal George* (twenty-two guns); brigs *Earl of Moira* (fourteen), *Prince Regent* (sixteen), and *Duke of Gloucester* (ten); schooners *Seneca* and *Simcoe* (both eight).

2. One of these, *Lord Nelson*, carried twelve guns and may have belonged to the Provincial Marine. (Apparently the Canadian captains did not yet know there was a war on, and so Woolsey was accused of "anticipating the outbreak of war.")

3. There are excellent pictures and descriptions of these vessels in "Ghost Ships of the War of 1812," *National Geographic*, Vol. 163, No. 3 (March, 1983), pp. 289–313.

Henry Eckford, who had helped to build *Oneida*. All these workmen and supplies, and drafts of seamen to man the new squadron, went north as rapidly as possible. Chauncey himself arrived in early November, with definite opinions as to how he would fight his war. First he would clear Lake Ontario of British shipping; then he would shift to Lake Erie and repeat the process. In the meantime, he dispatched Lieutenant Jesse D. Elliott to Lake Erie to begin assembling a squadron there. On November 8 he took *Oneida* and four schooners up to Kingston, chased *Royal George*, exchanged shots with shore batteries, and then sailed back to Sackets Harbor. Whether he could have done more is uncertain; the weather was turning bad, and his schooners were unchancy craft for autumn storms. Eckford had laid down the powerful sloop-of-war *Madison* and was pushing its construction.

Across the lake the Royal Navy had taken the Provincial Marine under its command, and sent a competent veteran, Sir James L. Yeo, to be Chauncey's opponent. Bringing in men and carpenters from British ships in the St. Lawrence, Yeo opened shipyards at both Kingston and York and began construction of a sloop-of-war at each place. He also purchased and armed a few small merchant vessels, though he appears to have had trouble finding enough suitable craft of that type.

The winter was bitter. On both sides men worked on ships in snow and biting cold, and at the same time hastily ran up huts, kitchens, hospitals, and storehouses for themselves. Food was rough and roughly prepared; disease flared among poorly clothed men living crowded together in chill, increasingly unsanitary quarters. Discontent was constant among civilians, sailors, and soldiers alike, but the work went on. Eckford was a leader as well as a talented shipbuilder, able to reassure and inspire his men. Through the worst weather he finished *Madison* and a fast dispatch boat, and had the heavy 26-gun *General Pike* and the large schooner *Sylph* well along.[4] By spring Chauncey could anticipate having command of Lake Ontario.

Lake Erie was a different problem, much shallower than Ontario, especially along the American shore, and in much more primitive surroundings. Lieutenant Elliott established an embryo naval base at Black Rock, on the Niagara River just north of Buffalo, and began purchasing and arming what vessels were available—small schooners capable of carry-

---

4. *General Pike* was variously described as a small frigate, sloop-of-war, or corvette. *Sylph* was soon rerigged as a brig.

ing only one or two guns. In choosing Black Rock, Elliott had contrived to shove his head into a sack: movement from that base into Lake Erie would have to buck the Niagara River's swift-moving current as it rushed toward its great falls ten miles on downstream. Moreover, the river was commanded by the guns of Fort Erie, across from Buffalo.

Even so, Elliott managed to get in one solid blow. On October 8 *Detroit* and *Caledonia* came down the lake from Malden to pick up rations for Colonel Henry Procter, and anchored under the guns of Fort Erie. Elliott proposed to take them by a night boat attack. He had a detachment of some fifty Navy seamen who had just arrived after a 500-mile hike from New York harbor. Colonel Winfield Scott's two companies of the 2d Artillery Regiment, then at Black Rock, provided fifty volunteers under Captain Nathan Towson, and some Buffalo citizens joined with two large boats. Just after midnight the Americans pushed off, Elliott heading for *Detroit*, Towson for the smaller *Caledonia*.

Elliott reached *Detroit* first and carried her in one rush before her crew realized what was happening. The resulting uproar woke *Caledonia*'s people, who put up a fight—thirteen against fifty—but were swiftly overwhelmed. Cutting the two vessels' anchor cables, the Americans tried to get them across the river by main strength and awkwardness, fighting the tug of the current while the aroused Fort Erie garrison blazed away at them. There was little or no wind, but Towson and his assistant, Sailing Master George Watts, finally brought *Caledonia* in. Elliott was less fortunate. Despite his best efforts, *Detroit* finally piled up on the western side of Squaw Island. British boat parties swarmed out to recover her; Scott brought reinforcements over to the island. After an extended donnybrook, the Americans burned what was left of the battered hulk.

Elliott's report, written to downplay everyone but Jesse Elliott, got him the thanks of Congress and a presentation sword. He reported only two killed and five wounded, which seems dubious.[5] But it had been a bold exploit that distressed both Brock and Procter—at least seventy-odd Englishmen killed or captured, forty American prisoners released, *Caledonia* to add to the American Lake Erie squadron, and two 12-pounder guns salvaged from *Detroit*. There even was some prize money, over $10,000 worth of North West Company furs in *Caledonia*'s hold. Elliott

5. Writing much later, Towson gave the losses for his boat alone as two killed and thirteen wounded. And there were more casualties on both sides in the seesaw fight for *Detroit*.

was a restless, darkly ambitious officer, entirely given to following his own conceits; to use Biblical phraseology, his horn now was mightily exalted.[6] In that mood, he learned that he had been replaced as a commander of the Lake Erie squadron.

Among the Americans who had escaped from Detroit had been one Daniel Dobbins, rated a master mariner on both Erie and Ontario. He came to Washington with extensive knowledge of the strength and condition of the Provincial Marine, and of the geography of the western lakes and rivers. Apparently he recommended the small port of Presque Isle (now Erie), Pennsylvania, as a useful base. Madison and Hamilton commissioned him a sailing master in the U.S. Navy, gave him the plans for one of Jefferson's fifty-foot gunboats and ordered him to Presque Isle to build four of them, and take his orders from Chauncey.[7] Dobbins left in September 1812.

In February the Navy Department also dispatched Noah Brown, a New York shipbuilder who had constructed a number of gunboats, to Presque Isle to build two 20-gun brigs. Taking a small crew of ship carpenters, Brown reached Presque Isle on February 24 to find himself in an almost complete wilderness. (Elliott had protested against trying to build ships there, reporting that it had only four occupied houses—two of which were taverns—and no supplies of any sort except standing timber.) Meanwhile Dobbins had the gunboats begun and had established possible sources of supply for ropes and ironwork in Pittsburgh, although Isaac Chauncey had completely ignored him. Like Eckford, Brown had to begin by building shelters, shops, and an office, plus a blockhouse for defense. More carpenters came in from New York and Philadelphia in April and May, bringing his total crew to 200 men. Presque Isle had communications of a sort, by turnpike from Philadelphia to Harrisburg, then by 200 miles of rough road (much of it through mountains) to Pittsburgh, then 130 miles north to Presque Isle by "common country tracks," which winter snows and spring thaws closed for days. Even food was in short supply; iron was procured by scavenging local farms and villages and by cannibalizing a Canadian schooner found frozen in the lake ice. Wooden pegs were used in place of spikes; trees were felled and sawed into beams and planks.[8]

6. After the war, sent with *Constitution* on a Mediterranean patrol, he brought that honored ship back full of Greek and Egyptian "antiquities" and Andalusian jacks and jennies, with midshipmen on stable detail and everything filthy as a pig-pen!

7. Sailing master was a senior warrant officer grade.

8. One observer remarked that as late as April 1 most of the squadron still was standing timber, awaiting cutting and sawing.

Oakum, to caulk the vessels' hulls, arrived in the late spring when roads were finally passable. In all, regardless of cold, foul weather, short rations, and chronic shortages of all essential materials, Brown and his civilians built the two brigs and three or four smaller vessels, including their gun carriages, and later rebuilt one of Elliott's little ships.

Madison, possibly disappointed by Elliott's unwillingness to base himself on Presque Isle, had named a new commander for the Lake Erie squadron, Master Commandant Oliver Hazard Perry, who had been commanding a gunboat flotilla at Providence, Rhode Island. One hundred and fifty officers and men from his gunboat crews volunteered to accompany him. Reporting to Chauncey at Sackets Harbor, he found his new commander still planning to clear Lake Ontario in the spring. However Chauncey held Perry at Sackets Harbor until mid-March, and then took most of Perry's seamen to man his own ships. Perry and Brown worked efficiently together, and Perry obtained a few more sailors from Black Rock to run up the rigging and make sails for the completed vessels.

They were working desperately against time. Once the ice on the lakes broke up, they would be vulnerable to attack by land and water. Local Pennsylvania militia proved unwilling to do guard duty; only seven privates out of two companies responded when ordered out. In early May a regiment of militia from central Pennsylvania began arriving. Their military value was dubious at best—when ordered to stand night guard aboard the ships, the "boys" refused to go—but they provided at least a simulacrum of a garrison that possibly might deceive Procter's spies.

Procter, then busy fumbling at Fort Meigs[9] was well aware that an American squadron was under construction at Presque Isle, and apprehensive of what would happen to his communications once that fleet was completed. Although the British squadron still controlled Lake Erie and was building a 19-gun sloop-of-war at Malden, Procter considered his forces too weak for an attack on Presque Isle. Meanwhile he wasted his regulars fruitlessly against such unimportant objectives as Fort Meigs and Fort Stephenson. Apparently Sir George Prevost also never grasped the situation: he sent Procter neither reinforcements nor explicit orders to mop up Presque Isle.

Perry's principal problem was Chauncey, who frequently did not answer his letters and gave him only dribbles of men. Chauncey's conduct remains inexplicable. His command included Lake Erie; in fact, on appointing him Hamilton had stressed that Erie was strategically more

9. See chapter seven.

important than Ontario. Chauncey could not help knowing that future American operations in the West hinged on the cooperation of the Lake Erie squadron, and also that the base at Presque Isle could be rubbed out anytime Prevost woke up and gave the necessary order. Yet he practically ignored Lake Erie to concentrate on making certain that his Lake Ontario squadron was strong, well equipped, and well manned. Probably Chauncey shared Dearborn's inability to think in strategic terms. Thus Perry remained grievously short-handed and in danger, even as William Henry Harrison was calling on him for assistance against Procter's forays into Ohio. As an additional problem, Perry's squadron was split: Elliott now had five small vessels ensconced at Black Rock, as useless to Perry as if they had been on the dark side of the moon.

The winter had gone quietly along Lake Ontario and the St. Lawrence, except at Ogdensburg where Benjamin Forsyth, now a major, continued to bedevil the British outposts, much to peaceable old Dearborn's distress. The night of February 7 he raided Elizabethtown some fifteen miles upstream, freeing a number of American sympathizers held in the local jail and taking fifty prisoners.[10] This exploit irked Lieutenant Colonel "Red George" MacDonnell of the Glengarry Light Infantry Fencibles beyond all respect for Prevost's orders to avoid offensive operations. On February 22 he led his 500-man command out onto the frozen-over St. Lawrence as if for a drill. This was not uncommon, and the Americans at first gave his evolutions only routine attention. Then MacDonnell suddenly converted his drill to an attack. Urged on by their officers—and encouraged from the rear by their chaplain, six-foot-four Father Alexander MacDonnell who used a heavy crucifix to stimulate laggards[11]— the tough Highlanders and Canadian militia swarmed over Ogdensburg's slight defenses despite a lively, if belated, resistance. Badly outnumbered, Forsyth got his men away. The Glengarries burned his barracks, two schooners, and two gunboats that were frozen in the ice, and carried off sixteen cannon and claimed 600 muskets (probably the weapons of the local militia), at a cost of seven men killed and sixty-three wounded. There is no clear statement of Forsyth's loss: British accounts put it at twenty-six men killed and wounded and between sixty and seventy-five captured (again, probably mostly local militia). In the sequence, Ogdens-

10. Some American commanders, like perfectly capable Alexander Macomb at Sackets Harbor, had worried that Forsyth's aggressiveness might some day lead him to bite off more than he could chew.

11. Legend has it that he had ecumenical cooperation from a Scots Presbyterian colleague swinging a large Bible!

burg suffered enthusiastic looting by both MacDonnell's men and Canadian civilians who crossed over from Prescott. (Like all upstanding Highlanders, the Glengarries had a talent for looting, long famous in Canada.)

Forsyth withdrew nine miles and asked for 300 reinforcements, pledging himself to retake Ogdensburg, and Prescott to boot. The citizens of Ogdensburg, however, demanded that their town be left ungarrisoned, claiming that Forsyth's return would only lead to further retaliation from the British. They naturally did not mention their major complaint—that Forsyth's presence had inhibited their supply of cattle and sheep to the British forces. Weak as ever, Dearborn gave in and ordered Forsyth to Sackets Harbor. Ogdensburg promptly became a major supply point for the enemy and so continued to the end of the war, to the vast enrichment of its patriotic citizens. In 1814 Prevost would boast that two-thirds of his army was eating beef provided by American contractors.

Secretary of War John Armstrong intended to shatter the Dearborn/Prevost stasis that gripped the Canadian frontier. His plans for 1813 centered on an offensive against Kingston, the major British base on Lake Ontario. Capturing Kingston would block the St. Lawrence, cut off supplies for Upper Canada, and provide an excellent base for a future offensive against Montreal. Armstrong wanted this attack launched with 4,000 men about April 1, when the ice in Lake Ontario had broken up but the St. Lawrence still was frozen, making any movement of British reinforcements very difficult and slow. (Originally, Armstrong thought of a surprise attack across the still-frozen lake in early March, but gave this up as too risky.) Once Kingston was secured, the Americans would turn westward to take York, then continue to the Niagara frontier where they would be joined by a force of some 3,000 men for a strike against Fort George. Capturing Kingston and York would leave the British squadron without a home, and also should bag quite a few of its ships. The remaining ones could be mopped up thereafter, while the Americans regrouped for the decisive drive on Montreal.

As always, Dearborn accepted his orders with apparent approval and zeal, and then looked about for some excuse for not further exerting himself. He quickly found a most sympathetic helpmate in Chauncey, whose pugnacity seemingly had dwindled during the winter. Here again, Chauncey's motivation is puzzling at best; possibly the common assumption that, having with vast labor created a fine new squadron, he was reluctant to take it any place where unfeeling Englishmen might shoot at it is at least partially correct. He much preferred—if he *must* do something—to move against York, where the British were building one ship and repairing another. Together these two gentlemen managed to completely obfuscate the existing strategic/tactical situation.

To begin with, Dearborn magnified the strength of the British forces in Kingston, reporting it to be 6,000 or 7,000 instead of the approximately 2,000 actually there—far too many, he insisted, for him to risk an attack. However, he *could* manage a small expedition against York. Chauncey had assured him that the capture or destruction of the British ships there would give the Americans complete control of Lake Ontario. They then would take Fort George and Fort Erie, after which all available troops and ships could be massed for an attack on Kingston. This whole plan was a piece of strategic imbecility—while the Americans were halloing after minor British posts at the western end of Lake Ontario, the St. Lawrence would be clear by mid-May and British reinforcements could move up from Quebec and Montreal. Moreover, such a move would uncover Sackets Harbor, the one good American base, to a counterstroke from Kingston. Nevertheless, believing that Dearborn, being on the frontier, would have better information as to Prevost's strength and disposition, Armstrong accepted it.

Sir James Yeo, now commanding the British Ontario squadron, has long been derided as merely another Chauncey, always getting ready to fight but never really fighting. In fact he was an efficient, if sometimes overcareful, officer who clearly understood his mission. As long as Prevost stood on the defensive, his duty was simply to prevent the Americans from gaining complete naval superiority on Lake Ontario for any significant length of time. His logistical problems were at least as great as Chauncey's and his local resources in men and materials far less. He had no shipbuilders to match Eckford and Brown; in fact, he finally had to have the framing for some of his ships made up in England and sent knocked-down to Kingston for completion. The provincial Marine ships he had taken over required much work to get them properly repaired, equipped, and manned. But being considerably more intelligent than Chauncey, he was able to do more with less.

The Dearborn/Chauncey expedition put forth on April 22; five days later it took York[12] and made a messy job of it. The almost-completed sloop-of-war *Sir Isaac Brock*, which Chauncey had hoped to capture, was burned by the retreating garrison. The Americans did gain the 10-gun brig *Duke of Gloucester*, but it was an old Provincial Marine vessel that

12. See chapter eight.

Chauncey disdained to add to his squadron. The expedition then moved up to the Niagara frontier, where reinforcements joined it, and took Fort George by a well-handled amphibious attack on May 27. Perry, whom Chauncey had summoned from Erie, had a major part in this, directing the light warships that gave close fire support to the landing.

Meanwhile, taking advantage of Dearborn's and Chauncey's concentration against Fort George, Sir George Prevost had sallied forth in person with Yeo (who had just completed the sloop-of-war *Wolfe* and so felt strong enough to meet Chauncey) to take Sackets Harbor. His attack on May 29 was a very near-run affair, with considerable damage to the shipyard, but ended in a costly repulse. Learning that Yeo was out, Chauncey became greatly concerned for the safety of the unfinished *General Pike*; gathering up his skirts, he dashed home to Sackets Harbor. With his opponent thus gone to earth, Yeo shifted to the west end of the lake and helped to thwart Dearborn's timid attempts to exploit the capture of Fort George.

However, the American advance on Niagara frontier had forced the British to evacuate Fort Erie, allowing Perry to get his five little ships out of Black Rock. They still had to be dragged upriver to Lake Erie, and Chauncey would give him only fifty-five men for that task. Had Dearborn not provided 200 soldiers under capable officers it would have been impossible, and even then over a week of brutal labor was needed to accomplish it. After finally arriving on Lake Erie, Perry had to get his flotilla to Presque Isle. Knowing his approximate route, the British squadron sailed to intercept him, but by some freak of winds and weather somehow missed him.

Back at Presque Isle on June 18, Perry found both brigs—to be named *Lawrence* and *Niagara*—launched, and busied himself getting them equipped and manned. The last was sheer frustration. Chauncey still would allow him only dribbles of men, and those "a motley set, blacks, Soldiers, and boys." Dearborn ordered his 200 soldiers back to Niagara. By mid-July, Perry had only 120 men fit for duty ("lake fever" was ravaging the American forces) out of the 740 that even Chauncey admitted the Lake Erie squadron required. Correspondence became heated: as an added irritant Chauncey ordered Perry to retake Fort Mackinac as soon as he had cleaned up the "business" at Detroit. Eventually Secretary of the Navy Jones prodded Chauncey. In the meantime Perry got some volunteers from the Pennsylvania militia, both as soldiers and as marines. (A Lieutenant John Brooks of the U.S. Marine Corps had joined him with a recruiting party, Brooks having been offered the alternative of service in the western wilderness or a court-martial for allegedly cheating at cards. He died gallantly at Put-in-Bay.)

In June Commodore Robert H. Barclay had taken command of the British naval forces on Lake Erie. While rushing his newest ship to completion, he kept Presque Isle under constant blockade, knowing that it would be difficult for Perry to come out to fight in good order. There was a large bar at the mouth of Presque Isle harbor where the water was only seven feet deep, undoubtedly too shallow for the American brigs. On July 31 the British suddenly withdrew. One popular story was that Barclay and his officers wanted to attend a banquet being given in their honor. More likely, tiring of his waiting game, he departed to resupply his ships, hoping that his absence would tempt Perry to come out, and intending to return in time to catch him trying to work the brigs across the bar.

If such was his intention, it almost worked. The brigs stuck on the bar, even after their guns and stores were taken out. But this danger had been foreseen; Brown had built a pair of "camels," large barges with one side shaped to fit closely under a brig's hull. These were submerged on either side of a brig and secured to her, then pumped out, lifting the brig as they rose. Driving himself and his skeleton crews for four days, Perry had his lighter vessels and *Lawrence* out in the lake and *Niagara* on the bar when Barclay reappeared. *Lawrence* had not yet been rearmed, but Perry formed line of battle on her with such an outward show of confidence that Barclay would not risk moving in close, none of his ships being powerful enough to stand up to Perry's brigs. Instead he retired on Malden. Perry got his squadron in order and followed.

The whole affair had been proof of the old proverb, "Fortune favors the brave"—or possibly of the Old Army quip that "God takes care of small children, idiots, drunkards, and the United States Navy!"

Failing to find Barclay, Perry returned to Presque Isle and discharged those militiamen who had volunteered for forty-eight hours' duty. These could be replaced by the arrival of Elliott with 102 Navy officers and men. With barely enough men to sail ten of his vessels, Perry went westward to Sandusky Bay, where he established contact with Harrison; who provided him with a mixed lot of volunteer seamen and marines from his army.[13]

13. I am much indebted to Mr. Gerard T. Altoff, supervisory park ranger of the Perry's Victory and International Peace Memorial at Put-in-Bay, Ohio, for permission to use his excellent draft research paper, "Deep Water Sailors—Shallow Draft

Perry then moved on to establish a new base at Put-in-Bay on South Bass Island in the southwestern corner of Lake Erie. Twice he cruised up to reconnoiter Fort Malden, but Barclay would not come out and fight, and the fort was too strong and the sailing conditions at the mouth of the Detroit River too tricky for even Perry to risk an unsupported naval attack.

Perry did, however, have command of the lake, and Procter's situation rapidly grew desperate. For weeks Procter's army had been living from hand to mouth, with those thousands of Indian families demanding more food. Barclay was in equally dire straits. His new ship, the 19-gun sloop-of-war *Detroit*, carried six different calibers of guns, scraped up from here and there, and her crew had to be made up of soldiers and Canadian recruits, both equally unhandy aboard ship. His men were eating their last days' rations, and scant rations at that. It was fight or starve, and on September 9, 1813, Barclay came out, "odds, bobs, hammer and tongs" in the old English way, to find and fight his enemy. *Lady Prevost* (thirteen guns) led his line, followed by Barclay himself in *Detroit*, then *Hunter* (ten), *Queen Charlotte* (seventeen), *Chippeway* (one), and *Little Belt* (three). Most of the British armament was relatively light long guns; apparently only the *Queen Charlotte* was armed sloop-of-war fashion with carronades.

Warned the next morning of Barclay's approach by the schooner *Ariel* (four guns), which had been on picket duty, Perry moved out with a light wind behind him. *Ariel* led, then *Scorpion* (two guns), Perry in *Lawrence*, *Caledonia* (three), Elliott in *Niagara*, *Somers* (two), *Tigress* (one), *Porcupine* (three), and *Trippe* (one). *Lawrence* and *Niagara* each had eighteen 32-pounder carronades, designed for close hammering and only two long 12-pounder guns, and so would have to fight at short range to be effective. The brig *Caledonia* and the schooners had mostly heavy long guns mounted on pivots, and were too lightly built to take much pounding. Perry's plan therefore was for *Lawrence* and *Niagara* to close in rapidly, *Lawrence* engaging *Detroit*, *Niagara* the *Queen Charlotte*, while his smaller ships took on the other British vessels at long range. Accordingly, he drove in through the pounding of Barclay's long guns, a special battle flag, blue with white lettering, "Don't give up the ship," tossing from *Lawrence*'s masthead. Swinging wide, *Ariel* and *Scorpion* began raking Barclay's line, but *Caledonia*, *Niagara*, and the four remaining schooners lagged behind. Getting into carronade range at last, *Lawrence* began de-

---

Soldiers," which demolishes the myth that the soldiers Harrison loaned Perry were all Kentucky sharpshooters.

molishing *Detroit*. But *Hunter* also engaged her, and the captain of *Queen Charlotte*, seeing *Niagara* hang back out of range, left his place in line and closed in on her. This bloody, point-blank hammering went on for over two hours, with Elliott ignoring all signals to close up. *Caledonia* finally got into action, but her three guns were small consolation. Barclay and *Detroit* were badly hurt, but *Lawrence* was a shattered wreck, only one gun still firing, over half her crew dead or out of action. By luck, however, one of her boats still was undamaged. Perry had it lowered and, taking his battle flag and commodore's pennant, had himself rowed to *Niagara*, after telling his lieutenant to surrender *Lawrence* once he was clear away.[14]

It took him almost a quarter-hour to reach *Niagara*. Wasting no words, Perry sent Elliott to bring up the four bashful schooners, hoisted his flags aboard *Niagara*, and drove into the center of the entangled British ships, firing double-shotted broadsides in both directions. Both *Detroit* and *Queen Charlotte* had been badly hurt in their fight with *Lawrence*. Unable to maneuver, they fell foul of each other and were crushed. *Caledonia*, *Ariel*, and *Scorpion* had done considerable damage with their heavy weapons; most of the British officers were down. In short order, all the British ships struck.

It had been a small clash on the edge of nowhere, between two improvised fleets with mostly greenhorn crews. These had been no inspired maneuvering—simply three hours of desperate broadside-to-broadside. No major sea battle was ever more sternly and valiantly fought, and few had greater strategic results. Perry's message to Harrison, "We have met the enemy and they are ours," signaled the end of the British threat to the old Northwest. His lake communications cut, Procter could only run for safety. Perry ferried Harrison's troops across Lake Erie, which remained securely under American control for the rest of the war.

OPERATIONS ON LAKE ONTARIO, MEANWHILE had developed into a pas de deux, and so would remain. Chauncey would not risk damage to his beautiful ships, while Yeo, entirely aware that the loss of his squadron meant the loss of Upper Canada, took no chances. As soon as *General Pike* had been readied, Chauncey had again ventured out, that ship's 24-pounder long guns giving it more fire power than any two of Yeo's ships. His first project was a raid on the British supply depot at Burlington Heights at the extreme western end of Lake Ontario. Picking up Winfield Scott and some 250 regulars at Fort George, he approached Burlington

14. This was to save the surviving members of her crew.

Heights on July 28 to find that the British had been warned of his coming and had called in enough regular troops, militia, and Indians to considerably outnumber Scott's men and the squadron's marines.[15] Also, the water offshore of the British position was so shallow that even Chauncey's schooners could not work in close enough to furnish fire support for a landing.

Deciding that any assault would be uselessly suicidal—and Scott never willingly avoided a fight—the Americans made a consolation landing at York. Its garrison having rushed to Burlington Heights, there was no opposition. The Americans gathered in a few prisoners, released a few captured Americans, burned or carried away whatever public property they could find, and went back to Fort Niagara.

There, American commanders planned a more powerful expedition, but on August 7 were interrupted by Yeo's appearance. The two squadrons sparred cautiously at long range. Chauncey's was somewhat unhandy, the top-heavy American schooners being, as his sailors put it, "tender" or, more bluntly, "coffins." In the first hours of August 8, two of the largest ones, *Scourge* (formerly *Lord Nelson*) and *Hamilton*, were caught by a sudden squall and capsized, taking down almost their entire crews.[16] On the 10th the small schooners *Julia* and *Growler* failed to obey Chauncey's signals and were captured. Chauncey then returned to Sackets Harbor, leaving the lake to Yeo.

Sylph being commissioned, Chauncey was out again in September, 1813, to aid General James Wilkinson in launching an offensive down the St. Lawrence against Montreal, but he did this carelessly, allowing several English gunboats to get into the St. Lawrence behind Wilkinson's flotilla.[17] Then, on September 28, with his men inspired by news of Perry's victory, Chauncey caught Yeo on the open lake. To give his schooners greater stability, Chauncey was towing them behind his heavier ships, slowing the latter considerably. At the first clash, *General Pike*'s long guns hurt *Wolfe* badly; Captain William Mulcaster, best of the British ship commanders, brought his *Royal George* forward to cover *Wolfe*'s withdrawal, but was considerably battered in turn as *Madison* and *Governor Tompkins* (six guns; the best of the schooners) drove into action. Clearly

15. Prevost and his subordinates had established an excellent intelligence net all across the northern United States, utilizing illegal traders and antiwar Federalists who hated Madison and the Republicans more than they did the British.

16. These ships are described in "Ghost Ships of the War of 1812," *National Geographic*, Vol. 163, No. 3 (March, 1983), pp. 289–313.

17. See chapter nine.

outgunned, Yeo turned and ran. Chauncey pursued but at a crawl, ob-
stinately refusing to order his schooners to cast off and follow as best
they could. Yeo got away into Burlington Bay, forming line there just offshore. Almost any other American captain would have gone in for a finish
fight. Chauncey looked Yeo over—and then sailed off to Niagara, reporting that the weather looked threatening and *General Pike* had suffered
some slight damage. Yeo slipped away; Chauncey pursued fruitlessly, but
did encounter seven British schooners, taking five (including *Growler* and
Julia) and sinking one.[18]

During the winter of 1813–14, Yeo built two frigates and began one
ship of the line at Kingston, thoroughly bamboozling Chauncey into
believing that the frigates were much heavier vessels than they actually were. Also, by renaming his old ships and converting his schooners
to brigs, he left the Americans bewildered as to the actual size of his
squadron. Chauncey should have been able to secure reliable information through spies, deserters, illegal traders, and American sympathizers
in the Kingston area, but he was taken in by Yeo's "disinformation," some
of which seems to have been planted by pretended deserters. (Possibly,
like George B. McClellan, Chauncey *wanted* to believe any bad news
that might come his way.) His own building program was producing two
heavy brigs, the 42-gun frigate *Mohawk* (built and launched in just thirty-
four days) and another of fifty-eight guns named *Superior*. Conditions
at Sackets Harbor remained disgraceful. For all his organizing ability,
Chauncey did not see to it that his men were properly sheltered or fed.
As one small example, in December 1813, out of 215 marines stationed
there, 32 were in the hospital, and there were many cases of scurvy. Considerable trouble was experienced in getting weapons and tackle for the
new ships.

In early 1814, his new frigates finished ahead of Chauncey's, Yeo took
command of the lake, striking shrewdly at the American line of communications. Supplies for Sackets Harbor had to come from Albany by way
of the Mohawk River, Oneida Lake, and the Oswego River. About twelve
miles up the latter, the Americans had established a depot where supplies
were held until they could be loaded on schooners and sent downriver
past Oswego and then eastward along the south shore of Lake Ontario to

18. The British were using these as transports and cargo boats. They had a number (variously reported) of troops aboard, but certainly not the entire regiment reported by Fletcher Pratt.

Sackets Harbor. (Oswego, being at the river's mouth, was too exposed to be utilized as a major supply point.)

Yeo came down on Oswego on May 5 with some 1,000 troops, including the Glengarries, marines, and the Regiment de Watteville (technically Swiss, actually a foreign legion). The fort guarding Oswego was well sited, but had been neglected; only 300 men were in garrison, plus an indeterminate number of local militia. Bad weather held off the attack until the 6th, however, giving the militia time to move a large quantity of supplies back into the woods. Coming ashore with gunfire support from Yeo's lighter ships, the British got a literally hot reception, one of their vessels being badly damaged by red-hot shot. Captain Mulcaster lost a leg. But numbers told: the American garrison withdrew in good order, leaving the British to gather in over 1,000 barrels of salt, flour, and pork (a most welcome addition to their scant commissariat), salvage a sunken schooner, and burn the fort and storehouses.[19] For this they paid 18 men killed and 73 wounded. Yeo made no effort to force his way up the George River to reach the American depot. Only his lightest ships could have gotten into the river and, as a subsequent action soon showed, they probably would have been trapped. Instead he moved on Sackets Harbor and established a tight blockade.

However, it was not tight enough. Captain Melancthon Woolsey organized a system of bringing supplies along the coast at night in bateaux from Oswego to Stony Creek, just west of Sackets Harbor, where wagons could pick up their loads. On May 20 a late-running convoy of nineteen bateaux were intercepted off the mouth of Big Sandy River, some eighteen miles short of its destination. One bateau was captured, but Woolsey took the rest up the Big Sandy and set up an ambuscade along its banks. Two British gunboats and some ships' boats with 200 sailors and marines recklessly followed him in. Woolsey bagged the lot. After that the Americans roughed out a wagon road from Rome to Sackets Harbor.

In July *Superior* and *Mohawk* were ready. After delaying long enough to insure the failure of General Jacob Brown's Niagara campaign, Chauncey came out. Yeo went back to Kingston, where he was building another frigate and two 120-gun ships. Chauncey puddled around the lake, picked up a small English brig, and put on a show of blockading Kingston, but

19. Figures vary greatly here. I have used Stanley's Canadian version. Adams cites 2,400 barrels and four schooners. I find no reliable listing of American losses, but they probably were less than the British.

he remained inexorably opposed to any attack on that base. In October, Yeo got his ship of the line, the 112-gun *Saint Lawrence*, ready. Chauncey promptly dived back into Sackets Harbor and feverishly strengthened its defenses. Some of his subordinates questioned his loyalty.

His own construction program was going all out. On learning of Yeo's new vessels, the Navy Department had sent Noah Brown and his brother Adam with 1,200 carpenters to supplement Eckford's work. During the winter of 1814–15, they labored on two great 130-gun ships and another 58-gun frigate. One or two more big frigates were to be laid down as soon as those vessels were launched, but both they and the two other British ships of the line remained unfinished when the war ended.

Yeo had won the battle for Lake Ontario, largely by default. Unwilling to fight a serious engagement, Chauncey had been content to pick up tactical pennies at York instead of going for the grand prize that was possible off Burlington. Both fleets had been a tremendous drain on their respective logistical systems, and had used up hundreds of men by hardship and disease. The whole business was hardly glorious.

SEVEN

Winter of Our Discontent:
Tribulation in the West

Remember the River Raisin!
—Popular slogan

THE ONE USEFUL ACTION JAMES MONROE attempted during his months as acting secretary of war was to increase the strength of the Regular Army. Eight additional infantry regiments had been authorized in June, 1812 as the war began; now Congress gave him twenty more, to serve for only one year.[1] This should have brought the Regular Army's strength to 57,351, but recruits were reluctant and few. (The Regiment of Sea Fencibles, which Congress established in July for local garrison duty only, had less trouble filling its ranks.)[2] On taking office, Secretary of War John Armstrong found a total of 18,945 regulars. William Henry Harrison had three infantry regiments; Armstrong assigned him three of the new ones, which, if all six could be fully recruited, would give him over 6,000 regulars.[3]

1. Because of the loss of records when the British burned the War Department building in 1814, the number of infantry regiments actually formed remains uncertain; also, the failure of some authorized regiments to secure recruits made renumbering necessary. Moreover, several regiments of one-year volunteers seem to have been redesignated as regulars. In January, 1815 forty-six regular infantry regiments, all understrength, were on War Department muster rolls.

2. The Sea Fencibles were stationed by companies in the coastal defenses of the major seaports. There were two at Fort McHenry in 1814.

3. Harrison had the 17th and 19th; the 24th was already scheduled to join him. The new regiments were the 26th, 27th, and 28th. In addition, Harrison had two companies of light dragoons and some regular artillery.

Harrison meanwhile had all but lost his army. His Ohio and Kentucky militia finished their six-month tour of duty in February 1813 and so went happily home. Harrison's new Fort Meigs was only partly finished. Designed for a garrison of approximately 2,000 men, it was held by a few hundred shivering regulars (Harrison reported the 17th and 19th regiments "nearly destroyed" for want of clothing) and Pennsylvania and Virginia militia—and the latter were soon to leave. (Instead of working on the fort, they had been using the wood cut for its palisades for their campfires.) Harrison doubted that the fort could be held against an attack, but evacuating it would mean the loss of the artillery and supplies he had accumulated there. He called for more militia from Ohio and Kentucky, but winter service had few attractions and such Ohio troops as appeared were "not to be depended on." Leaving Major Wood to finish Fort Meigs as best he could, Harrison headed for Cincinnati to try to raise more troops, see his family, and patch his political fences.

Fortunately, Procter could not or did not choose to strike at Fort Meigs during March and April. The same weather that had baffled Harrison's attempted raid on Malden would have clogged any effort he might have made; the spring weather also appears to have been wetter than usual. His own strategic situation was far weaker than the Americans realized: stationed at the far western end of Sir George Prevost's supply system, Procter had to largely subsist his men, and thousands of Indians, on whatever odds, ends, and leavings it could deliver. Between early bad weather and the militia call-ups that took hundreds of men from their farms, Upper Canada's 1812 harvest had been a poor one. Unless Procter could capture large quantities of supplies from the Americans, 1813 promised to be a hungry year.

At the same time, Procter obviously lacked the essential characteristic of a commanding officer—the ability (as George Patton would later phrase it) to "decide what will hurt the enemy most within the limits of your capabilities to harm him and then do it." Procter knew that the American ships being built at Presque Isle were the major threat to his position. He also knew, or certainly should have known, that they were defenseless, and that Harrison's sickly handful was incapable of any offensive action to protect them. He had command of Lake Erie and so could concentrate his whole strength of regular troops, militia, and ships against Presque Isle with little or no risk. Instead, he pleaded continuously that he must have more British troops and sailors before venturing such an operation. It is true that Procter got neither help nor sympathy from his immediate superior, Major General Francis de Rottenburg, the new military commander in Upper Canada, yet he had seen Isaac Brock go high-heartedly against far greater odds, and win. But Procter was not even Brock's shadow. Before long, Tecumseh would call him a coward.

Fearing to risk Presque Isle, Procter decided to attack Fort Meigs. Its capture would delay Harrison's preparations for a summer offensive and might gain valuable supplies. However, bad weather and various administrative woes delayed his departure long enough for Harrison to learn of his preparations. Hurrying forward with the approximately 300 men he had immediately available, and ordering a brigade of Kentucky militia to follow as quickly as possible, Harrison reached Fort Meigs on April 12. Sailing from Malden, Procter disembarked at the mouth of the Maumee River on the 26th with over 500 regulars, 450 militia, and approximately 1,500 Indians. He also had two 24-pounder guns that had been taken at Detroit, several lighter pieces, and two gunboats, each of which carried a 9-pounder gun. It took until May 1 to work the gunboats up the Maumee River, drag the cannon along the muddy river road, and construct battery positions. Meanwhile Tecumseh took most of the Indians across the river to close around the fort from the south.

Built of dirt and heavy logs on a bluff above the Maumee River, Fort Meigs commanded the best land route to Detroit. Its site was naturally strong, its north face protected by the Maumee and its east and west faces by deep-cut ravines. Its southern approaches had been completely logged off, leaving little cover even for Indians. The garrison numbered scarcely 1,100 men, but Brigadier General Green Clay's 1,200 Kentucky militia could be expected shortly.

On May 1 Procter's artillery and gunboats opened fire, banging away at the fort for four days without doing any appreciable damage. The Indians sniped, beat the woods for stray cattle, and generally enjoyed the war. They did not intercept the courier Harrison dispatched to Clay late on May 2 with orders to send 800 men downriver in flatboats to attack the British battery position on the north bank of the Maumee. The Kentuckians were to spike the guns (which included the 24-pounders), demolish their carriages, and then come into Fort Meigs. The rest of the brigade was to land on the south bank above the fort and force their way in through the Indians. Once his forces were all in hand, Harrison would sally out and attack Procter. Meanwhile, directed by Wood, the Americans quickly built a system of "traverses" (heavy embankments) inside the palisades as a second line of defense against the artillery fire.

Tecumseh's warriors also had failed to watch the river above the fort, though it was the obvious route reinforcements would take. Clay's leading regiments came driving and bobbing down the river early on the 5th, hit the north bank, swept over Procter's batteries, and began spiking their guns. It was a complete surprise. The artillerymen and some Indians who had been with them fled into the woods. Thereupon the American commander, Colonel William Dudley, lost control of himself, his men, and the battle. Leaving the captured guns half-spiked, the Kentuckians took after the fleeing Indians, vengeance and scalps very much in mind. Procter threw in part of the 41st Foot to recover the guns, and recalled Tecumseh to the north bank. A confused hole-and-corner brawl ended with Dudley and over 200 of his men dead and approximately 500 taken prisoner; only some 170 Kentuckians fought their way to their boats and escaped. The British had lost slightly over 50 killed and wounded, not counting Indian casualties.

On the south bank, however, Colonel John Miller of the 19th Infantry led a sudden sortie against a battery Procter had established to pound the northeastern angle of the fort. Scattering the Indians Tecumseh had left on the south bank, he overran the battery and brought back forty prisoners from the 41st Foot. Meanwhile Clay, aided by another sortie, reached the fort with little trouble.

Unfortunately, the bloodshed had only begun. Snatching captured Americans from the British troops supposedly guarding them (one English private reportedly was killed when he protested), the Indians drove them through a gauntlet and there beat them to death with war clubs, tomahawks, and gun butts. Procter did not interfere. At least twenty Americans had been killed and more mangled when Tecumseh learned what was happening and put an abrupt end to the butchery, bluntly offering to kill any warrior who dared disobey him.[4] Frontier tradition had it that he called Procter a squaw for permitting prisoners to be brutalized, and told him to go put on petticoats.

After two days of dickering over exchanging prisoners, Procter got some of his artillery back into action on May 7, but his offensive was already falling apart. Having won a battle and picked up satisfying quantities of scalps and loot, practically all the Indians faded off into the woods. The Canadian militiamen protested that they must be getting home to put in their crops; otherwise there would be scant harvests in the fall. It rained frequently, and more and more men came down with dysentery. On the 9th Procter gave up and embarked his troops. Harrison merely watched him go, not troubling him in the least.

4. All figures concerning losses in this action are approximate at best.

Back at Malden, Procter resumed his begging for reinforcements and supplies, but Rottenburg and Sir George Prevost had worries closer to home, with Isaac Chauncey lording it over Lake Ontario, York raided, and James Dearborn massing troops at Niagara. Perry's half-finished ships at Presque Isle were guarded only by a scattering of undisciplined Pennsylvania militia, yet Procter could never pucker up the courage for an assault on that strategically crucial objective. Meanwhile his supplies dwindled. The horde of Indians hanging around Malden—numbers are thoroughly doubtful, but there may have been 10,000 of them, of all ages and both sexes—grumbled over the smaller handouts that were all Procter's commissary could manage, and grew increasingly restless. He half-planned a raid on Sandusky in the hope of seizing supplies, but the Indians would not cooperate. Realizing that he should do something, in July, supposedly at Tecumseh's urging, he had another try at taking Fort Meigs, which now had no strategic importance.

Leaving General Clay in command at Fort Meigs, Harrison had shifted his headquarters to Cleveland and slowly begun organizing an army to cooperate with Perry, once Lake Erie was cleared. He continued stockpiling supplies in the Upper Sandusky area, forty-odd miles up the Sandusky River, whence they could be easily brought down to Lake Erie when required. This logistical base was protected by Fort Stephenson (now Fremont, Ohio), a strongly built log fortification, approximately one acre in extent, on the west bank of the Sandusky some ten miles from its mouth. Also, there were some troops undergoing organization and training at Upper Sandusky itself.

Procter again came up the Maumee River on July 20, this time without heavy artillery. He had some 400 regulars, possibly 100 militia, and approximately 1,000 Indians. His plan, apparently suggested by Tecumseh, was to stage a mock battle in the woods beyond the clearing south of the fort. Clay was supposed to leap to the conclusion that a column of American reinforcements on their way to join him was under attack, and sally out to rescue them. Once in the woods he could be ambushed; a force of British and Indians, held under cover as close as possible to the fort, would then rush its gates and overwhelm whatever Americans remained inside. This might have worked against a Dudley, but Clay had learned what rashness could cost. He also knew that no Americans were en route to Fort Meigs. Consequently he sat tight and let the enemy use up their ammunition. The fort was too strong to storm out of hand, and Procter's few 6-pounders could only dent its ramparts.

On July 28 the British again withdrew. A good many Indians drifted back to Malden; Tecumseh took others on a raid across the backwoods between the Maumee and Sandusky rivers. Procter shifted his troops by ship along the south shore of Lake Erie and up the Sandusky River; 200 or 300 warriors, more or less led by officers of the Indian Department, accompanied him. The multiplicity of alibis and accusations that clutter Procter's report make it difficult to determine his actual objective. He certainly hoped to seize supplies, and probably he had some idea of the existence of Harrison's depots; he mentioned that there were enough cattle in the Sandusky area to have fed his Indians for a considerable period. (How he was to get said cattle back to Malden remains another question.) Unwilling to risk bypassing Fort Stephenson, he emplaced his artillery around it and demanded its surrender.

Harrison had almost saved him that trouble. Rumor had mightily magnified the strength of Procter's command—Harrison reported it as 5,000 men—and pictured Tecumseh as leading 2,000 warriors directly from Fort Meigs against Upper Sandusky. Harrison had some 800 men, mostly raw recruits, around Upper Sandusky; Fort Stephenson was garrisoned by 160 regulars under a Major George Croghan. Thoroughly confused and three-fourths panicked by Tecumseh's imagined threat to his depots, Harrison ordered Croghan to burn Fort Stephenson and either join him or retreat to Sandusky, whichever offered the better chance of escape. Croghan insisted that he could hold Fort Stephenson. After some bickering, now considerably obscured by folklore, Harrison allowed him to try, moving his own available forces upstream to Fort Seneca[5] where cleared country would give his handful of cavalry a chance to charge effectively. (Indians dreaded being caught in the open by mounted men.) Here he was only some ten miles above Fort Stephenson, excellently placed, if he so wished, to move to Croghan's assistance.

Fearful that Harrison might do just that, Procter was in a tearing hurry. On Croghan's contemptuous refusal to surrender, Procter's artillery and gunboats began bombarding the fort, only to find its massive palisades practically impenetrable to 6-pounders' shot. The Indians were restless and bored; according to Procter they proposed that the fort be taken by storm and offered to join in the assault. Also, as he later claimed, the "gentlemen" of the Indian Department warned him that they would never be able to raise more Indian auxiliaries if Fort Stephenson were not

5. Fort Seneca was a large temporary stockade, enclosing several acres, used as a subsidiary supply depot. The site now is occupied by a village of that same name. (Some sources call it "Old Fort.")

quickly taken. An overnight bombardment having proven useless, late on the afternoon of August 2, Procter ordered an infantry attack. By some fatuity, he had not used the available time to improvise scaling ladders and fascines[6] to fill up the fort's ditch, or even ordered all axes sharpened. But his British, Canadians, and Indians surged forward with a will.

Croghan held his fire until the British were within fifty yards of the palisade, then opened with musketry and grapeshot from "Old Betsy," his one 6-pounder. At the first blast the Indians ran for cover. Their white comrades tried time after time; some got into the ditch and up against the stockade, but could go no farther, having no means of either climbing over it or chopping a gap in it. Procter finally halted the attack. After dark, Indians who had rallied once the shooting stopped crawled close to the fort to pick up some of the wounded left there. Even so, about thirty British were reported missing—men wounded or pinned down too close to the palisade to be retrieved and so taken prisoner. Twenty-six were killed and forty-one wounded.[7] (Croghan had one man killed and seven wounded.) Procter's reputation with his troops was another casualty; the 41st Foot knew that his tactical incompetence had wasted them again.

Harrison's reputation also had dimmed. All through the two days of Procter's siege he had remained at Fort Seneca, listening to the firing but showing no discernible interest in Croghan's fate. Had Fort Stephenson fallen he probably would have set fire to Fort Seneca and retreated to Upper Sandusky. As it was, a messenger from Croghan reached him during the night of August 2 to report that Procter was reembarking. To westerners such behavior was little short of cowardly; also it was plain that Harrison had missed an excellent chance to catch and destroy Procter's groggy command.

Meanwhile a new force had entered the western war. Armstrong had approved Richard Johnson's proposal to raise a volunteer regiment of mounted riflemen, to serve for four months and two more if the fortunes of war required it. Apparently Johnson had little trouble raising the requisite 1,000 officers and men; he was popular, had shown himself a good officer in the desperate days after Hull's surrender, and knew exactly what he wanted: a well-disciplined regiment, always fit and ready for combat. His men furnished their own horses, weapons, stripped-down equip-

---

6. Long bundles of sticks or brush bound together.

7. Procter's total casualties have been set as high as 150, not including whatever Indians stayed around long enough to get hit. One American claimed to have counted 27 dead in the fort's ditch.

ment, and red-fringed black hunting shirts. Going into the field about June 1, Johnson took over the sector between Fort Wayne and the River Raisin and put an end to Indian raiding there, moving mounted, fighting dismounted in traditional frontier style.

Though increasingly dubious of Harrison's ability, Armstrong left him in command, with instructions to push the organization of a 7,000-man army for the invasion of Canada. Armstrong had hoped that his force would be mostly regulars, but recruiting had been so slow that Harrison had fewer than 3,000 of them by September. Once more Kentucky came to the rescue. Harrison had asked that state for 2,000 militia; Governor Isaac Shelby offered 3,000 if Harrison would pay them all. The Pennsylvania militia regiment Harrison had summoned from Presque Isle having refused to serve outside their home state, he was delighted to accept any Kentucky "surplusage." Shelby marched to the wars with 3,000 of his constituents. Armstrong also added Johnson's regiment to Harrison's army. Perry's September 10 victory dispatch, which Harrison received at Fort Seneca on the 12th, found the North Western Army already concentrating to exploit his success. Getting his battered ships in order, Perry began a ferrying operation on September 20 by way of Bass Island to Middle Sister Island, twelve miles from the Canadian coast, while he and Harrison selected a landing place. On the 27th Perry put 4,500 infantry ashore at the mouth of the Detroit River, about three miles south of Malden. There was no opposition; Procter had gone elsewhere.

As soon as he heard of Commodore Robert Barclay's defeat, Procter began preparing to withdraw. Rottenburg had told him that if the Americans gained control of Lake Erie the British would have to evacuate most of Upper Canada; all troops on the Niagara front would be withdrawn to Kingston. Procter's command probably would have to retire northward along the lakes, to be picked up by the North West Company's canoe fleet. His supply situation had gone from bad to hopeless during the dry, still summer that followed the wet spring. Neither wind nor water mills could work for long periods, and harvested grain could not be ground. The thronging Indians ate the Malden commissary bare, and clamored for more.

Procter saw his situation starkly: if he remained at Malden he must fight; even if he fought and won against superior numbers, he would starve. Rottenburg's idea of retreating northward was equally unappealing; Procter had a considerable collection of army wives and children, artillery, reserve ammunition, miscellaneous baggage, a hastily collected beef herd, and a final reserve of bread and hardtack—all of which he

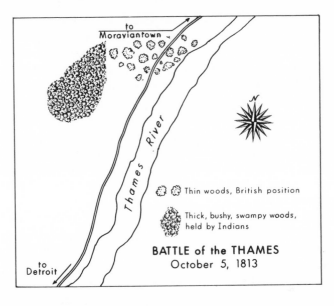

to
Moraviantown

Thames River

N

🌑 🌑 Thin woods, British position

🌑 Thick, bushy, swampy woods,
held by Indians

BATTLE of the THAMES
October 5, 1813

to
Detroit

intended to take with him. He therefore chose to retreat through Sandwich and along the south shore of Lake St. Clair to the Thames River; thereafter he would march up that river through Dolson's, Chatham, and Moraviantown. If necessary, he could continue on to the British base at Burlington Heights, at the western tip of Lake Ontario.

This decision angered Tecumseh and the other chiefs. Repeatedly the British had promised to never again abandon their "red brothers"—and now Procter was going to run away without fighting. By Tecumseh's lights this was cowardice, and he said so publicly. A good many Englishmen and Canadians quietly approved. After much wrangling Procter agreed to halt and give battle somewhere along the Thames; Tecumseh and other chiefs pledged to stand with him. Destroying what public property he could not take with him, Procter left Malden on September 24.

Harrison was slow to follow him. In part his reasons were valid; he had neither horses nor wagons to carry supplies, and he considered Johnson's mounted riflemen necessary for a successful pursuit. Coming overland through Detroit, Johnson did not get across the river to join Harrison until October 1. The next day Harrison moved out aggressively with 3,500 men, but felt "no probability" of overtaking Procter, who had had a week's head start.

Fortunately, for the Americans, Procter was even more incompetent at retreating than attacking. Moreover the roads were bad and the Thames

River was low; bateaux and gunboats with Procter's reserve ammunition and rations had to be muscled across shoals and around tight bends. Procter frequently rode with his wife and child well ahead of his troops, and paid little attention to their progress. Daily marches were short to allow the supply boats to keep abreast of the columns. The 41st Foot's morale dragged bottom, officers grew careless. Nobody thought to fell trees across the road or burn the numerous bridges behind them. By October 3 Johnson's troops began to catch up with Procter's weary column. Procter thought of standing to fight at Dolson's, and again at Chatham, where the Indians insisted on a battle but ran after a few shots. Procter lost his lagging boats, leaving his men only what ammunition remained in their cartridge boxes.

Hustled on by Harrison's pursuit, the drooping British finally halted on October 5 along the north bank of the Thames River, a mile and a half west of Moraviantown. That village still was jammed with their supply wagons, artillery, sick, and white and Indian women and children. To retreat further would be to abandon all of them. Procter himself had rejoined his troops the day before, much put out by their disorder. Now he hurriedly took up a position, posting the 41st in an open woods on the left, with its left flank resting on the river. Tecumseh's Indians were on the right along the edges of a deep swamp, their line slanting forward so as to threaten the flank of any attack against the 41st. The 41st was in two thin lines, 200 yards apart and so out of sight of each other, visibility in the woods being only some 20 yards. A single 6-pounder was emplaced in the road, just in front of the 41st, with a picket of twenty Canadian dragoons. Then came a two-hour wait while Harrison moved up into contact and Johnson's scouts felt out the enemy's position.

Harrison's plan was to send Lewis Cass's brigade of regulars[8] down the road against the 41st, while the Kentucky militia covered their left flank against the Indians; Johnson's mounted infantry would be held in reserve. Johnson, however, had grasped the weakness of Procter's line and asked permission to charge it. Harrison—whose knowledge of Napoleonic warfare must have been limited—said the idea was not "sanctioned by anything I had seen or heard of," but gave permission anyhow. Johnson sent his brother, James Johnson, with one battalion[9] against the

8. Since they were influential Republican politicians, who felt deeply that they had suffered grievous wrong in having had to serve under Hull, Madison had solaced Cass and McArthur with commissions as brigadier generals.

9. Johnson's mounted rifles were organized as a two-battalion infantry regiment, almost half again as large as a regular light dragoon regiment.

41st, wheeled his other battalion half-left, and went at Tecumseh. With a howled "Remember the River Raisin!" James Johnson's battalion burst forward, riding over the 6-pounder and over and through the 41st, then wheeled and rounded up the confused Englishmen. Casualties were not heavy: few Kentuckians had sabers, and few Englishmen had a chance to take aim before the black-clad riders were upon them. The 6-pounder did not get off a single round.[10]

Richard Johnson's charge stalled in dense underbrush along the swamp, which horses could not penetrate; dismounting, his men went forward in their usual way, fighting from tree to tree against furious opposition. Johnson was wounded, but pistoled the chief who shot him. (He remained convinced it was Tecumseh himself.) The rout of the 41st had left the Indians' left flank in the air. Getting around it, the riflemen forced the Indians westward until they came under the fire of the waiting Kentucky militia, and scattered into the swamp.

The battle had lasted barely a half-hour, possibly less. American losses reportedly were 15 killed and 30 wounded. The Indians left 33 dead on the field; 477 English were taken prisoner. During the whole campaign 28 British officers and 606 enlisted men had been killed or captured; only 200-odd escaped eastward, accompanied by about 400 warriors. Somewhere in the battle along the swamp, Tecumseh had gone down fighting. A body, identified as his by several British officers, was found among the dead. He had been a hero, and merciful—but several jubilant Kentuckians cut long strips of skin from his thighs for souvenir razor strops. Other frontiersmen honored him; a one-time Ohio militia officer, Charles Sherman, named his third son Tecumseh.[11]

Procter, his staff, and some Canadian dragoons got away, having left the field one jump ahead of James Johnson, but a little too soon for Procter's remaining military reputation. He tried to cover himself by blaming his defeat on the 41st Foot's alleged cowardice, but the facts soon became public knowledge. Procter was court-martialed and "suspended from rank and pay" for six months.

Harrison gathered in Procter's trains and artillery at Moraviantown, but made no effort whatever to run down Procter and the fleeting remnants of his command. Harrison's strategic position was excellent: an advance of slightly over 100 miles eastward would bring him to Burling-

---

10. By some accounts, its crew was surprised before they could fire. Others claim that they had no ammunition.

11. A devoutly Catholic foster mother later had "William," a good saint's name, tacked on in front of "Tecumseh," thus making him "William T."

ton Heights, which still was threatened from the east by the Americans around Fort George. Probably the mere threat of such an advance would have frightened Rottenburg into executing his planned withdrawal to Kingston. But the year's delays, especially those imposed by Chauncey on the readying of Perry's fleet, now took effect. Autumn rains were ruining the roads between Harrison and Detroit; soon it would be impossible to keep a force of any size supplied at Moraviantown. A determined general would at least have unleashed Johnson's mounted men to complete his victory and put a scare into the British high command. Harrison, however, promptly returned to Detroit. The Kentucky militia was discharged on October 14, Johnson's regiment shortly thereafter. The Americans retained the Sandwich/Malden area, which they used as a base for foraging expeditions. Most of the Indians drifted back to their tribal areas, although a great many remained around Detroit and Malden, drawing American rations.

Harrison and Perry next considered an attack on Mackinac, but had to abandon it because bad weather forced their supply vessels to jettison their cargo. Armstrong then summoned Harrison eastward. Originally he planned to use him for an attack on Burlington Heights; then, abruptly changing his mind, he ordered Harrison's troops to Sackets Harbor and gave Harrison himself a leave of absence.

Harrison went to Washington as a conquering hero and was generally acclaimed as such, his recovery of Detroit and defeat of Procter serving to obscure his previous fumblings, bumblings, and defeats. (That and Tippecanoe would make him the ninth President of the United States.) Armstrong, however, neither trusted nor liked Harrison. Though he left him in command of the northwest, he ignored him, sending orders directly to Harrison's subordinates without consulting or advising him. Such doubtless-calculated treatment enraged Harrison. In May, 1814, he resigned his major general's commission but—being Harrison—stirred up his Kentucky supporters to urge President Madison not to accept his resignation.[12] Madison, then resting at home, wished to consider this matter, but Armstrong, acting suddenly during the President's absence, accepted the resignation on his own authority, and transferred the vacant position to Andrew Jackson, whose promotion Madison had half-approved earlier.

The Americans had recovered Detroit, seized a bridgehead in Upper

12. He had received this promotion, for no visible military reason, in March, 1813.

Canada, and established control of Lake Erie. The Indians had been chastened and their one great leader killed; one British "army" had been destroyed. For 1813 the war in the West had ended in victory, however dearly bought.

EIGHT

Victories Wasted

I have doubts whether [Dearborn] will ever again be fit for service. He has been repeatedly in a state of convalescence, but relapses on the least agitation of mind.
—Morgan Lewis to John Armstrong, June 14, 1813

GENERAL HENRY DEARBORN'S PLANS for the raid on York were simple enough—he would send Brigadier General Zebulon M. Pike to carry it out, while he himself continued in rear-area comfort.

Pike was one of six new brigadier generals authorized by Congress in January, and certainly the most deserving of the lot.[1] An "Army brat" and frontier soldier, famous for his western explorations during 1805–7, he had been an efficient colonel and a proven leader. On April 22 he embarked with some 1,600 men aboard Commodore Isaac Chauncey's fleet of fourteen vessels, both warships and transports. Secretary of War Armstrong, however, had made one late change in Dearborn's plan; Dearborn himself must forsake his headquarters and take personal command of the expedition.

Though it was the capital of Upper Canada, York had no fortifications except for a large blockhouse and several batteries strung along the waterfront. Its only strategic importance was its shipyard, where the sloop-of-war *Sir Isaac Brock* was under construction and the old *Duke of Gloucester* was being repaired. The garrison numbered approximately 700 men: the York militia's flank companies, armed dockyard workers, one company of

---

1. The six were Pike, George Izard, William H. Winder, Duncan McArthur, Lewis Cass, and Benjamin Howard (governor of the Missouri Territory).

the Glengarries, two of the Newfoundland Regiment, some Indians, and two companies of the 8th (the King's) Regiment of Foot, which chanced to be passing through. York being the military headquarters for Upper Canada, Major General Roger H. Sheaffe was present and in command when Chauncey's squadron swept impressively into sight on April 27.

Supported by heavy naval gunfire, Pike sent his men ashore just to the west of the harbor entrance, thus avoiding the fire of the York batteries. Major Benjamin Forsyth's riflemen formed the first wave, engaging some Indians scattered along the shore.[2] Sheaffe attempted a counterattack, which promptly fell apart. The Indians had fled into the woods. The first British unit to reach Pike's growing beachhead, the grenadier company of the 8th Foot, went in with the bayonet without waiting for support, and was quickly used up. Coming into action just as the grenadiers broke, the Newfoundlanders were overwhelmed in their turn. The Glengarries, who had been ordered to support the grenadiers, somehow got lost on York's outskirts. Swinging to his right up the shoreline toward York, Pike took the batteries from the flank and rear, battering the militia and remnants of the regulars ahead of him, while Chauncey's ships pounded any British gun that opened fire. Pike was aided by an accidental explosion in the westernmost battery, where a fleeing British artilleryman, so the story goes, dropped his lighted portfire into an ammunition wagon.

Seeing his defenses crumbling, Sheaffe decided to get his regulars out of York before they were completely overwhelmed. Ordering the *Brock* and the shipyard burned and a major powder magazine on the western edge of York blown up, he abandoned the town. En route he told the senior militia officers to surrender York on the best terms they could get, undoubtedly intending that such negotiations would delay any American pursuit.

As the American advance probed into the western edge of York, some Englishman touched off the "Grand Magazine," which exploded with appalling uproar. Pike had halted only a few hundred yards away to interrogate a captured British soldier. The avalanche of falling debris crushed him, and scattered death, wounds, and confusion among advancing Americans and retreating British alike. Shortly afterward the militia officers appeared with their white flag. Negotiations were acrimo-

2. A Canadian account has them unable to land because of the accuracy of the Indians' fire, and so firing from their boats until the second wave outflanked the Indians.

nious from the start when the Americans, already furious over the explosion, discovered that the shipyard and *Brock* were being torched while they parlayed.

Pike's death left the Americans practically leaderless. Dearborn remained aboard ship and concerned himself as little as possible with developments ashore. For some reason it took over twenty-four hours to work out the terms of capitulation, which were merely those usually imposed in such a situation: all British and Canadian troops in York were to be prisoners of war, all military and naval stores were to be surrendered, and the citizens of York and their private property were not to be molested. Dearborn designated Forsyth's riflemen to preserve order in the town, regardless of the fact that they carried a grudge from Ogdensburg. The average American officer, Army or Navy, seems to have made little effort to keep his men from straggling into York; there was looting and vandalism (mostly of empty houses) in which some of York's inhabitants cheerfully joined, if no violence toward individual civilians. The climax came when some soldiers burned down the provincial legislative building.[3] Dearborn could only whimper that he had not ordered it done, and reimburse some citizens for property losses they had suffered.

By May 2 all captured stores and cannon had been shipped or destroyed. The action had hurt British prestige and wrecked Sheaffe's reputation. Besides the loss of the two ships, an indeterminate amount of scarce military stores and approximately 300 men were taken prisoner. Sheaffe had to report 62 killed and 94 wounded. Yet it had not been a profitable venture for the Americans. Their raid had cost them some 320 casualties; Pike would be sorely missed. And the burning of the legislative building set Sir George Prevost to baying for vengeance.[4]

Neither army came away in style. Sheaffe's draggled command spent fourteen sopping-wet days slogging the 160 miles of ruined roads into Kingston, half-frozen and hungry. Much of the population along the north shore of Lake Ontario was pro-American and gave them hard looks and little help. Even in Kingston conditions were spartan. There was a good deal of desertion; Indians were employed to bring deserters back dead or alive. Meanwhile adverse winds held Chauncey in York harbor until May 8; the numerous American wounded suffered from lack of proper accommodation and care. That same evening the squadron

---

3. A common story was that some Americans, exploring the vacant building, found the speaker's wig on a desk, mistook it for some unfortunate American's scalp, and so set fire to the building to avenge him.

4. See chapter twelve.

reached Fort Niagara where, naturally, nothing had been prepared to receive them: the wounded were huddled into the roofless "mess house"[5] where they lay in the cold and wet, many with their wounds not yet properly tended. Dearborn reported most of his command "sickly and debilitated," and proposed to give them time to recuperate while Chauncey went back to Sackets Harbor to pick up more troops. All available detachments from Oswego and northern New York were called in, troops being summoned from the Lake Champlain front to strengthen the Sackets Harbor garrison. Slowly the Army of the North, over 4,000 men, mostly regulars, was concentrated along the Niagara frontier. Dearborn organized them into three brigades under William H. Winder, John P. Boyd, and John Chandler,[6] and a reserve under Major General Morgan Lewis.[7]

To give Dearborn a high-ranking subordinate of more experience, one who could act in his place if necessary, Armstrong had summoned General James Wilkinson from New Orleans on March 10, ordering him to Sackets Harbor "with the least possible delay." Wilkinson and Armstrong had served together under Gates in 1777, but apparently the secretary had no recent acquaintance with the "scientific soldier," as Wilkinson loved to proclaim himself. (The fact that a number of southern senators considered New Orleans in danger as long as Wilkinson commanded there should have warned him.) On receipt of Armstrong's orders Wilkinson, recently promoted to major general, wrote at length of his burning desire to die if need be in the service of his country, then took his own sweet time getting under way. For Wilkinson official travel, no matter how urgent his orders, always had been a private triumphal procession, with frequent pauses for rest, recreation, and self-display. This time he left New Orleans only on June 10, taking his pregnant young wife with him; he finally honored Washington, D.C., with his presence on July 31.

Meanwhile the clutter of half-raw, half-strength regiments concentrat-

5. The "mess house" was the fort's major building, the stone "French Castle" completed in 1727, which still stands.

6. Chandler was a native of Maine, Revolutionary veteran, former congressman, and tavern keeper.

7. Lewis's command included the garrisons of Fort Niagara and other posts. Though he had been a failure as the Army quartermaster general, Madison had promoted him to major general early in 1813. Armstrong, however, relieved him of that assignment and sent him to troop duty. Brave and well meaning, he had no military instincts and was much concerned with his comfort. Porter acidly noted: "His own baggage moves in two stately wagons . . . carrying the various furniture of a Secretary of State's office, a lady's dressing chamber, an alderman's dining room and the contents of a grocer's shop."

ing at Niagara had received an unexpected shake-up. Armstrong could do little about Madison's political generals, except as defeat or public discontent made them vulnerable, but he could push forward an occasional deserving junior, as he had done with Pike. Now he designated Winfield Scott, twenty-seven years old and a fire-new colonel (once Madison had satisfied himself as to Scott's political views), as Dearborn's adjutant general, the equivalent of a modern chief of staff. Arriving on May 13 Scott found Dearborn half-sick, submerged in self-generated confusion, and only too glad to let Scott take over running the Army of the North. Drawing on his knowledge of the organization and operations of Napoleon's *Grande Armée*, Scott formed the Army of the North's first adequate staff, straightened out its administration, and began preparations for its next operation.[8] His general plan was very much like Van Rensselaer's original one: the Americans would land on the south shore of Lake Ontario to the west of Fort George, advance inland and strike the fort from the rear, bagging its garrison.

Scott's preparations were thorough. Chauncey, assisted by Oliver Perry who had arrived from Presque Isle, reconnoitered the shoreline after nightfall to select the best landing place and planted buoys to mark the stations of the larger warships during the attack. British batteries were located and ships designated to silence them before the landing began. More guns were emplaced in and around Fort Niagara.

Across the river, Brigadier General John Vincent knew that an American attack was building up, but could not be certain of its time and place. A veteran of service in the West Indies, Holland, and Denmark, he knew that he was seriously outnumbered. Most of his 1,200 regulars were concentrated near Fort George, with detachments at Queenston, Chippewa, and Fort Erie.[9] He had found his militia reluctant to turn out; Sheaffe's withdrawal from York had left them dubious of Prevost's determination to hold Upper Canada a feeling that the pro-American element among them was "indefatigable in spreading." Also, it was seeding time and most of them, anxious to get their crops in, resented the frequent calls for active service. Those called up frequently deserted. Even so, possibly 500 militia were then under arms, over half of them at Fort George.

8. Scott was becoming notable for his personal campaign library, which included the French 1791 infantry drill regulations and Thiebault's *Manuel* on headquarters organization and functioning.

9. These were parts of the 8th, 41st, 49th, Newfoundland, and Glengarry regiments.

Early on May 25 American batteries all along the Niagara River opened fire. The wide spread of this artillery preparation left Vincent still uncertain as to whether Dearborn's attack would come from the lake or across the river; accordingly he strengthened his outposts along the Niagara. The artillery hammering continued through the 26th; "hot shot" set parts of Fort George afire. By 4:00 A.M. the next morning the American assault force had embarked at the mouth of Four-Mile Creek. Most would go in boats and barges towed by Chauncey's ships, the rest aboard the larger vessels. Chauncey had planned the embarkation thoroughly; the boats for each unit had been designated and marked. It was a morning of dense fog and little wind; the schooners had to use their sweeps (long oars) as the fleet crept carefully westward.

Scott's plan provided for a quite modern-style amphibious attack in three waves. To make certain there would be no flinching at the crucial moment, he led the first wave—Forsyth's riflemen, the two flank companies of the 15th Infantry Regiment,[10] his own 2d Artillery Regiment serving as infantry, and one 3-pounder—which was to seize and hold the beachhead. It was to be followed immediately by the second wave, Boyd's brigade, with some light artillery and George McClure's Albany Volunteers to cover its flanks. The third wave was Winder's brigade, with Captain Nathan Towson's company of artillery; on landing, it was to form on Boyd's left flank. Chandler's brigade formed the reserve; it was to provide a detachment of 100 men to secure the landing site as soon as the first three waves had formed line and begun their advance.[11] Colonel Alexander Macomb with more artillery would land with the reserve, and thereafter go into action "as circumstances may require." Rank having its privileges, Major General Lewis would command this whole force. Dearborn, very sick and very apprehensive, had himself carried aboard the *Madison* to oversee the action.

Scott had added two subsidiary attacks. Colonel James Burn with the two mounted companies of his light dragoons was to cross the river five miles above Fort Niagara, to cut the road between Fort George and

10. Each infantry regiment supposedly had two, like the British, formed of picked men—variously termed grenadiers, light infantry, or riflemen. More study is needed.
11. Scott's "stacking" of the wave commanders is an interesting assessment of their respective capabilities. Boyd was a veteran, brave and a good soldier, if not particularly bright. Winder was a greenhorn but anxious to do well. Apparently nobody except Madison and Dearborn believed Chandler bright enough to take care of his natural functions without assistance.

Queenston and intercept any English fugitives from the fort. Another small force was to cross from Black Rock to occupy Fort Erie.

The assault began with a touch of high drama. Vincent had been visiting his outposts during the night and had ended his tour at a battery near the lighthouse that marked the mouth of the Niagara River. As he paused there, doubtlessly commenting unfavorably concerning the weather, a sudden breeze dispersed the fog to show him the two-mile-wide crescent of Chauncey's ships standing in. Next came the crash and bellow of naval gunfire as the schooners *Governor Tompkins, Conquest, Julia, Growler,* and *Ontario* swiftly knocked out the lakeshore batteries.[12] The warships cast loose their tows; the first wave formed and swept in for the beach, Perry in *Hamilton* guiding their formation. Behind it, Boyd's men took their places and poised their oars.

The assault came with such order and swiftness, covered by such a blaze of naval gunfire, that Vincent found himself in the same plight Sheaffe had experienced at York, without troops enough in hand to offer any effective resistance. Desperately he threw forward what men were available, some 108 Glengarries. Those stubborn Scots met the first wave as it scrambled out of its boats and up the bank, one of them almost bayoneting Scott, but the odds were too great. Within minutes more than half of them were down. The company of Newfoundlanders that followed them in took equal loss. Falling back, their survivors rallied in a ravine, out of the blast of grapeshot from the schooners' heavy guns. There five companies of the 8th Foot, some 100 militia, and the company of black pioneers joined them. Counterattacking, the British forced Scott back toward the beach, but the Americans held hard along a high bank inland from the shore, where Boyd's brigade already was spilling out of its boats and forming up. Quickly reorganizing, Scott again drove forward, the riflemen working past the British left flank, the schooners edging close to shore to keep up their supporting fire. Vincent brought up the 49th Foot, but quickly saw that he was hopelessly outnumbered and outgunned. Now Winder's brigade was pulling toward the beach, and American field artillery coming into action. Naval gunfire made it impossible for Vincent to anchor one flank on the lake, and the renewed American attack threatened to pocket him around Newark and Fort George with his back against the Niagara River. A retreat from Americans might seem inglorious, but it would save his army to fight another day. Ordering Fort George evacu-

---

12. Besides the one near the lighthouse, there was another at the mouth of Two-Mile Creek, close to the landing site.

ated, its guns spiked, and its magazines blown up,[13] Vincent withdrew southward across country, covered by an obstinate rear guard action.

Scott kept at his heels through the village of Newark, intercepting some of the British demolition party as they left Fort George. Learning that the fort's magazines were mined, he recklessly led two companies in a dash to save the ammunition. It was almost York all over again. One of the magazines went off; the shower of stones and wood fragments knocked Scott off the captured horse he was riding and broke his collarbone. Ignoring injuries, he left his artillerymen to save the other magazines and rejoined his main body, which was energetically chevying Vincent's column, sweeping up its stragglers and stray detachments. Some five miles south of Fort George, Scott met Colonel Burn with one company of light dragoons. Burn had been delayed in his crossing by a British battery; his second company was still crossing, and Burn was reluctant to advance without it. Lewis had already sent one aide-de-camp to Scott with orders to return to Fort George. A second aide appeared while Scott conferred with Burn and was told that once the dragoons were ready Vincent's whole force could be captured. But Scott agreed to wait for that second company. As it appeared, so did a disgusted General Boyd with Lewis's emphatic order to cease troubling the enemy.

It was undoubtedly the best-planned and best-fought engagement of the entire war. The one weakness in Scott's plan was his reliance on Burn to intercept Vincent's retreat, a mission better fitted for a strong force of infantry. (Scott clearly overestimated Burn's capabilities. Quite possibly he had been unconsciously influenced by memory of how in 1807, as a lance corporal of Virginia volunteer militia cavalry, he had led his squad out into a shallow inlet of the Chesapeake to capture a boatload of foragers from a British frigate.) Army/Navy coordination had been outstanding and greatly to Chauncey's credit. Soldiers and junior officers had fought with determination. Yet Lewis's timidity wasted this skill and bravery. Scott's command had fought (as Lewis would later state) "nine-tenths of the battle," and was still in lively contact with Vincent's rear guard. Boyd's brigade, only part of which had been actively engaged, was moving up to support Scott. Winder and Chandler had hardly fired a shot. Yet instead of piling in all these available troops to overwhelm Vincent, Lewis recalled Scott. Dearborn's share in Lewis's decision is unclear; he did express concern that his troops were too weary for further

13. These were small magazines in the bastions of the fort, not a large central one as at York.

combat, having been turned out at 1:00 A.M. that morning. Sick, worried, and feeble he must have judged his men's condition by his own.

And so Vincent got away. He had suffered heavy losses, 52 officers and men killed, 44 wounded, and 262 captured.[14] American losses had been 39 killed, 111 wounded. Retiring south to the Queenston/St. Davids road, Vincent turned westward, ordering the troops at Chippewa and Fort Erie to join him at Beaver Dam (now Thorold). Their arrival gave him approximately 1,600 men, but he chose to continue his withdrawal to Burlington, at the head of Lake Ontario, sending his militia home. Some 500 of these were subsequently picked up by the Americans; senior officers were sent back to the United States as prisoners of war, the rest released on parole.

At Burlington, Vincent held a strong defensive position, but still a risky one. If he attempted to withdraw toward Kingston, the Americans could intercept him by landing troops at York or elsewhere along the north shore of Lake Ontario. Also, such a withdrawal would leave Procter isolated whereas as long as the British held Burlington a bare sufficiency of supplies could be passed on to Procter by rough roads south to Turkey Point (now Charlottesville) on the north shore of Lake Erie, where British ships could pick them up, or, weather and available transportation permitting, by worse roads southwestward to the Thames River. Yet if Vincent held on too long at Burlington for Procter's sake, he might find himself overwhelmed by Dearborn's far larger forces and so lose both his own command and Procter's too. For Vincent, it was a choice of unpleasant possibilities—from which Dearborn and Chauncey promptly rescued him.

Quite bemused by his victory, Dearborn let himself be persuaded to send Lewis in pursuit the next day. Lewis used up the whole morning and afternoon in fussy preparations, finally marched at 5:00 P.M., and reached Queenston and St. Davids. Naturally he found no trace of Vincent. Equally naturally, the next morning a worried Dearborn recalled him. Much to the distress and growing anger of his subordinates, Dearborn thereafter coddled his personal "debilities" and did nothing useful, though urged "by all the considerations that decency would permit" as Porter phrased it, probably meaning everything short of a direct accusation of cowardice. Lewis supported Dearborn; it rained and rained, and the troops grew discouraged. Learning that Sir James Yeo had sallied out

14. Approximately half of those captured also had been wounded. The Glengarries lost 77 out of their 108.

from Kingston, Chauncey suddenly realized that his base at Sackets Harbor had been left feebly garrisoned. He sailed for home on May 31, taking with him Colonel Macomb and 200 soldiers, but refusing to leave even one small schooner with Dearborn or to allot Perry sufficient sailors to get his gunboats up the Niagara River into Lake Erie.[15]

Finally nerving himself into action, on June 2 Dearborn sent Winder with some 1,400 men[16] to find and fight Vincent. Advancing westward along the lakeshore road, Winder bethought himself that he had men enough to get into trouble, but hardly enough to overwhelm Vincent. He therefore halted some twenty miles west of Fort George and requested reinforcements. Dearborn sent Chandler[17] who, being senior, took command of the combined force and renewed the advance. Late on June 5 they encountered Vincent's outposts along Stony Creek, chased them away after a little miscellaneous shooting, and then encamped for the night.

Both Winder and Chandler were brigadier generals of the Regular Army, yet their carelessness would have startled even James Winchester, of River Raisin fame. Though only some ten miles from Vincent's position, they camped haphazardly, without setting up an outpost system. Reportedly only three sentries watched the western edge of their camp. This was begging for trouble, and Vincent was prompt to oblige. One or more British officers—Vincent's adjutant general, Lieutenant Colonel John Harvey, and a Captain H. B. O. Milnes are mentioned—reconnoitered the American camp. (One story had Milnes going into it as a Canadian farmer peddling potatoes for a closer look.) Shortly after midnight Vincent moved out with 700 men from the 8th and 49th, muskets unloaded and bayonets fixed. Thanks to an unusually dark night and a well-handled approach march, they reached the edge of the camp undetected, and quickly stalked and silenced two of the sentries. More alert, the third one challenged, then fired. He was instantly bayoneted, but some Americans must have been slumbering less confidently than their generals. Also, the British began cheering as they broke from march column into line. Then suddenly everyone was yelling; Americans started

15. See chapter six.

16. This was Winder's own brigade (5th, 13th, 14th, and 16th infantry regiments), two companies of artillery, one of riflemen, and a detachment of dragoons.

17. Chandler had the 9th, 23d, and 25th infantry regiments and a company of artillery—approximately 1,000 men. Dearborn's reasons for sending this pair of amateurs into the woods probably were his special liking for Chandler and his desire to give them the chance for glory they had missed on May 27.

shooting. The first rush of Vincent's attack drove in deeply, striking the American artillery, which had camped astride the road. The cannoneers mostly came up using anything that would shoot, stab, or smash; the British lost their formation, American infantry pitched in with gun butts and bayonets—and there were some 3,000 men packed into a few acres of rough woodland, lit only by lines of dying campfires, furiously applying the barroom tactical principle, "If you see a head, hit it!"

Chandler woke up, got to his horse, and rode into the melee. His horse tripped over a log, throwing him. Half-stunned, he attempted to rally a disorderly clump of passing soldiers—and found they were British. Winder also got himself captured. (The tale that he was discovered hiding under a gun and pulled out seems a later invention.) [18] Vincent simply vanished. The light dragoons had been camped behind the infantry and guns; those of them who could find their horses formed up and charged generally westward. One participant in the confusion complained that they cut their way through both the American 16th Infantry and the English 49th Foot. Eventually, the primitive fact that there were a lot more angry Americans than Englishmen threshing around in the smoke-choked woods took hold. Deciding that it was high time to get away from there, Lieutenant Colonel Harvey somehow got the leaderless English under control and off the field under heavy fire, marching back to Burlington with two captured guns and 113 American prisoners.

It had been a bold feat, but an expensive one: the English had 23 officers and men killed and 136 wounded, and had left 55 more in American hands. The Americans lost only 17 killed and 38 wounded, besides those taken captive. Vincent seems to have thought that the suddenness of his onslaught would stampede the Americans into panicked flight. When they refused to run, his gamble failed. His reasons for attacking with only 700 men are unclear; probably he did not wish, given the precariousness of his strategic position, to risk more. Still, though roughly repulsed, he had won a psychological victory.

Morning brought a hasty comparison of respective dates of rank among the American colonels in the battered Stony Creek camp, with Burn unfortunately proving to be the senior officer present. Actually the Americans had just won a smart little action and had put a definite nick in Vincent's troop strength. They had only to stand their ground and look determined. But Burn's endowments, mental and visceral alike, had been

18. It is one of the yarns told by Sergeant James Commins of the 8th Foot (see Lord, *The War on the Canadian Frontier, 1812–14*).

barely sufficient to handle a few light dragoons. He reported his "unpleasant dilemma" to Dearborn, then summoned his fellow field grade officers to a council of war. There was no surplus of heroes among them; they frightened themselves and each other into deciding on a ten-mile retreat to Forty-Mile Creek[19] and then went off in disgraceful haste, even leaving their dead unburied. Burn did find time to answer a letter Harvey sent in under a flag of truce, reporting Chandler and Winder in British hands, and asking if the Americans had Vincent. (Vincent had managed to mislay himself in the woods, losing his horse and hat, but finally limped back into his lines, footsore and empty-bellied.)

Dearborn responded promptly on the 6th to Burn's plea, ordering Lewis to take command of the "advanced army," giving him Boyd and Scott for assistants, and a special escort of light artillerymen equipped as cavalry. For good measure he threw in Brigadier General Robert Swartwout, the new quartermaster general, who was visiting the Niagara frontier. Lewis was to attack Vincent as soon as possible, making "every possible effort" to prevent his escape.

Lewis had not been long gone from Fort George, however, when a dispatch rider overtook him. Sentries had seen ships passing toward the head of the lake; Dearborn feared that they were Yeo's—Lewis had better get the advanced army back to Fort George as soon as possible. Some hours later a second rider pounded up: two British schooners had been reconnoitering the shore in the vicinity of the fort for several hours; Dearborn feared an attack before Lewis could return. Scott and Swartwout must rejoin him as soon as possible; the light dragoons and 500-odd infantry must follow with "all possible dispatch" to be at Fort George before noon of June 7.

EVEN SIR GEORGE PREVOST HAD BEEN ABLE to appreciate the strategic opportunity Chauncey and Dearborn had abandoned to him when they turned westward up Lake Ontario. The capture of Sackets Harbor (which his spies had reported very weakly garrisoned) would make instant orphans of Chauncey's ships and unhinge the whole American position on the lakes. Accordingly, Prevost mustered most of his available regulars—between 750 and 800 men from the 1st, 8th, 100th, 104th, Voltigeur, and Glengarry regiments[20] under the immediate command of

19. The creeks east and west of the Niagara River were generally named for their approximate distance from it.

20. For some reason both English and Americans frequently scattered their troops

Colonel Edward Baynes—and sailed with Yeo's whole squadron from Kingston on May 27. From the start, however, his expedition was bedeviled by calms and contrary winds. It had the good luck to accidentally encounter and capture several American bateaux carrying approximately 115 regulars en route from Oswego to Sackets Harbor, but Yeo's topsails were seen by the Americans late on the 26th, and his creeping progress gave them time to organize their defenses.

Before departing, Dearborn had asked Jacob Brown to take command of the Sackets Harbor area in the event of a British attack, and had outlined a sensible plan for its defense, devised by Colonel Macomb and other regular officers. Brown promptly rousted out some 500 militia. Sackets Harbor itself was reasonably well fortified. The harbor's entrance was flanked by Fort Pike on the east and Fort Tompkins to the west, both built on low bluffs and mounting several heavy guns, including 32-pounders. Tompkins was tied into an unfinished line of fortified log barracks, stockaded batteries, and felled trees that protected the western edge of the village and its shipyard.

The garrison consisted of approximately 400 regulars, mostly light dragoons with detachments and invalids from several infantry and artillery regiments, and 250 volunteers, the whole commanded by Lieutenant Colonel Electus Backus of the light dragoons. Dearborn (or Macomb) correctly guessed that the British would land on or near Horse Island, a good-sized islet a mile west of Sackets Harbor, connected to the mainland by a narrow 300-yard causeway. Brown accordingly stationed an outpost of Albany Volunteers on the island, and placed his militia with two 6-pounders to cover the inland end of the causeway and the adjacent shoreline. A second line, consisting of those regulars and volunteers who could be spared from the forts' garrisons, formed considerably to their rear.

Erratic winds had dogged Yeo again through May 28, but that evening the troops were put into boats almost two miles offshore, to row toward Horse Island for a landing at dawn on the 29th. Prevost and his personal staff accompanied them in a canoe. The light gunboats, which could move by means of their sweeps during calms, would support the landing. Yeo's heavier ships would give what help the morning wind would permit. The night was cold with a drizzling rain; some of the boats drifted out of for-

---

along the frontier by companies. The garrison of an important post might include elements of several regiments, and a colonel seldom had his whole regiment together.

mation, but Baynes got them together and into formation for a rush at the beach just as the day began.

Baynes' chosen landing point was just west of Horse Island, which would provide concealment and protection from the Sackets Harbor batteries. This, however, brought his boats into the fire of the militia's two 6-pounders. Recoiling in confusion, the British came round the eastern side of the island, right into the sights of an American 32-pounder. Its crew quickly got the range and began scoring hits. Hurt and disorganized, the British unloaded off the north end of Horse Island, splashing ashore through the shallows there and forming up. There was only one way off the island: right down the causeway. Massing his men into a heavy assault column, Baynes went for it, the flank companies of the 100th Foot leading, the 1st Foot tightly behind them. The volunteers on the island withdrew, reforming on the right flank of the militia.

Horse Island could have been a trap, which probably was why Baynes did not land there originally. Brown had ordered the militia to hold their fire until every shot would count against the head and flanks of the close-packed British column. But the strain of facing the rapidly approaching glitter of British bayonets was too gut-wrenching. They let go one straggling burst of musket fire and fled, deaf to Brown's orders and entreaties, abandoning their 6-pounders. Ignoring the fleeing militia, Baynes swung his troops to the left and drove for the western edge of Sackets Harbor.

Immediately he met determined opposition. The volunteers and one small company of local militia under a Captain McNith had held together; now they retired slowly in open order, keeping up a steady fire. Backus brought his second line forward to support them, then gradually fell back into his defenses. The British stormed after them, but were met with a wall of fire that broke up repeated assaults, Backus handling his men and guns with a skill and determination that won Brown's unstinted praise.

The British had no field artillery; the Americans had plenty and knew how to use it. Pleading the lack of wind, Yeo did not take his large ships in close enough to provide fire support. His gunboats' short-range carronades were ineffective against the American log fortifications. What he might have done became obvious when the captain of the 16-gun brig *Prince Regent* put out his sweeps and set his crew to rowing their ship forward into easy range of Fort Tompkins. Once there, its broadsides drove the American artillerymen from most of their guns; some of its shot, passing high over the fort, fell among Navy personnel posted beyond it, setting off a panic. Lieutenant Woolcott Chauncey, the commodore's younger brother in charge of the shipyard, jumped to the conclusion that Fort Tompkins had surrendered and so ordered the naval warehouses burned to keep their contents from capture.

Even with this conflagration roaring behind them, Backus's regulars and volunteers held their line, while other forts began hitting *Prince Regent*. After almost two hours of vain attacks, Baynes told Prevost that the defenses could not be carried. Prevost ordered one more attempt: the troops were pulled back out of American musket range, reformed, resupplied with ammunition, and then, though clearly close to exhaustion, led forward again. Some of the 104th Foot got up against one of the barracks, but then were so deluged with fire that they broke and fled. Baynes ordered a retreat to the Horse Island causeway, and the British stumbled back in considerable confusion.

Brown, meanwhile, after making certain that Backus could hold his position, had gone after his fugitive militia, who by then had run themselves out of breath. He rounded up approximately 300 of them, damned them back into some order, and began advancing toward Prevost's right rear, to cut him off from his boats. British reports give no indication whether this movement hastened Prevost's decision to reembark. Certainly the militia did not attempt to harry the British withdrawal.[21]

It had been a rough morning, but by 9:00 A.M. the British soldiers were back aboard their ships, Prevost beginning a report of how he had driven a "beaten enemy" before him for "upwards of three hours." He had lost 48 officers and men killed and 211 wounded; 18 of the latter were left behind. (Brown gave these wounded proper care and their dead comrades honorable burial.) Officer casualties had been especially heavy. Also, Prevost's reputation was irreparably damaged—ironically, as the result of the most daring and intelligent operation he attempted during the war. Though he had shown courage under fire, his personal and political enemies besplattered him with charges of incompetence and cowardice, to the great hurt of his authority. Specifically he was blamed for not having renewed his attack. (One especially splendiferous story had Prevost ordering his troops to withdraw just as a desperate Brown was seeking to capitulate.) Had he held his ground, it was charged, a few hours or a day or two would have brought favorable winds, allowing Yeo to get his bigger ships into action. Nobody noticed that Prevost already had lost a third of his men, or that those same winds might bring Chauncey's squadron. In fact, though

---

21. At least one American historian, Fletcher Pratt, has converted their deliberate reappearance into a decisive bayonet attack that swept the British from the field.

he probably did not know it, Prevost had barely escaped a worse mauling. Lieutenant Colonel John Tuttle with 450 men of the 9th Infantry Regiment had been on the march from Utica to Sackets Harbor; hearing the firing he had hurried forward, arriving just as the British reembarked.

Of the Americans 23 had been killed, 114 wounded, and some 100 picked up as prisoners. Their major loss was the destruction of much of the shipyard and approximately $500,000 worth of naval stores by frightened Lieutenant Chauncey—who must have been far more frightened when Brown finished with him. This would badly delay Isaac Chauncey's construction program; fortunately the unfinished *General Pike* was only slightly damaged before the fires were gotten under control.

There was no pursuit. Backus had taken a mortal wound during the last British attack, and his dragoons seem to have fallen into confusion until Brown reappeared and took command of the garrison.

Chauncey came back to Sackets Harbor to find the situation very much in hand, repair work being pushed, and Yeo gone up the lake to aid Vincent. For a moment he seems to have considered following the English squadron but "upon mature reflexion" he decided it would be wiser to stay snug at Sackets and protect the *General Pike* "at all hazards" until it could be launched and outfitted. Secretary of the Navy Jones had no objections to this remarkably pacific strategy, and so Chauncey, having encouraged Dearborn to go adventuring on the Niagara frontier, casually abandoned him there.

Yeo promptly made his presence felt at the western end of Ontario, beginning by terrifying Dearborn. As Lewis started back along the lakeshore road with the discouraged "advanced army" on the morning of June 8, a British schooner appeared and took it under fire. Captain Joseph Totten, present as Lewis's engineer officer, rapidly improvised a field furnace for heating shot, a few rounds of which from Towson's guns persuaded the schooner to go elsewhere. The march was then resumed, part of the baggage being transported in bateaux, which hugged the lakeshore. But Lewis or somebody had forgotten to detail a guard for them, and another small British warship appeared and gobbled up a dozen or more. The Canadian militia turned out and, with increasing numbers of Indians, began harassing the American outposts. In what can only have been a spasm of personal fright, Dearborn gave up practically all the territory he had occupied west of the Niagara River, evacuating Chippewa, Queenston, and Fort Erie, to concentrate all available troops around his headquarters at Fort George. Too sick in mind and body to exercise his command, he turned it over temporarily to Lewis, who was ordered to

Sackets Harbor before he could show any indications of knowing what to do with it. Lewis's departure left Boyd the only general with the army—a situation Madison made haste to correct by converting South Carolina congressman David B. Williams, an influential Republican, known as "Thunder and Lightning" from his oratorical flourishes, into a brigadier general and loosing him upon the Army of the North.

Covered by constant irregular operations that ebbed around the Fort George/Newark beachhead, Vincent advanced from Burlington to Forty-Mile Creek, with strong outposts pushed forward to Twelve-Mile Creek and Beaver Dam. On the American side, two new units joined in this squabbling. The Canadian Volunteers, composed of pro-American Canadians under Joseph Willcocks, a former member of the Upper Canada Assembly,[22] proved very useful as guides, scouts, and foragers. By contrast, American regulars nicknamed a force of irregular New York mounted militiamen under a Dr. Cyrenius Chapin "The Forty Thieves."[23]

Boyd decided that the army's reputation and morale could be improved by gaining a little elbow room. Selecting Beaver Dam, then held by Lieutenant James Fitz Gibbon with the 49th Foot's company of habitual disciplinary cases as his target, he obtained Dearborn's approval to dispatch Lieutenant Colonel Charles G. Boerstler against it. Why he picked Boerstler is another of this war's enigmas; Boerstler's one previous performance as a semi-independent commander had been notable only for timidity. However, he had been loudly complaining over not being given sufficient opportunity to distinguish himself, and Boyd may therefore have thought him willing to act decisively. Boyd gave him a strong combat team: Boerstler's own 14th Infantry, reinforced by detachments from the 4th, 6th, and 23d regiments; a company of artillery with two guns; twenty light dragoons; and Chapin's Forty Thieves—approximately 550 men in all. (Chapin claimed to have previously reconnoitered the area; in fact, he had not, but the Army of the North had not yet grasped his capacity for unnecessary lying.)

Boyd's long mercenary service in India had taught him something about irregular warfare. All preparations were kept as secret as possible. Boerstler moved out at dusk on June 23, while a cordon of sentries closed

22. Willcocks was killed in late 1814. This unit's greatest strength seems to have been some 130 officers and men; originally identified only by white cockades and green ribbons in their hats, they later were issued U.S. infantry uniforms.

23. Chapin was a militia colonel, daring, slippery, an unconscionable liar, and possibly psychotic.

off the Fort George/Newark area to keep civilians from carrying warnings of his departure to Vincent's outposts. Reaching Queenston about midnight, his march slowed by muddy roads and two big supply wagons he had brought along, Boerstler followed Boyd's instructions to throw a similar screen around that village while his men caught a few hours' sleep. However, according to received Canadian tradition that appears to be more or less factual, Laura Secord, wife of a Sergeant James Secord of the Lincoln militia, overheard American officers discussing their plans. Sweet-talking a sentry into letting her go into the nearby woods very early the next morning to milk a cow, she slipped away along side trails to reach an Indian camp near Beaver Dam, and was taken to Fitz Gibbon. Directed by two officers of the Indian Department, the warriors— approximately 100 Mohawk and 350 Caughnawaga[24]—set up an ambush in a rough, thickly timbered area a mile and a half east of Beaver Dam. Fitz Gibbon's 46 infantrymen were held in reserve.

Boerstler left Queenston early on the 24th, marching without proper advance or flank guards, even after the Americans detected small groups of Indians hanging on their flanks. Accounts of the following action are hazy. Once he was caught in the ambush, Boerstler first seems to have tried to punch on through, then to extricate himself. A good many of his men had never been in action before; his excited gunners shot too high. Boerstler was wounded and took shelter in a wagon. Even so, the Americans put up a steady fight. Most of the Mohawk got their bellies full and quit. Eventually the Americans broke out into an open wheatfield that offered no cover for the Caughnawaga. A competent commander would have pulled them together and made good his retreat. But then Fitz Gibbon intervened. A limber-jawed west-country Irishman who obviously had kissed the Blarney stone more than once, he came forward with a flag of truce and confidently demanded Boerstler's surrender, stating that the Americans were surrounded and outnumbered; if they did not surrender quickly, it would be impossible for the British to restrain their Indian allies, who were lusting to butcher Boerstler's whole command. There was a little dickering, but Fitz Gibbon was convincing, Boerstler wounded, weak, and very frightened. Quickly caving in, he surrendered 484 officers and men, two guns, and his regimental colors to Fitz Gibbon's superior, a Major P. V. DeHaren, who had just arrived

24. Caughnawaga were a new tribe, Iroquois whom Jesuits had converted to Christianity and resettled near Montreal.

from Twelve-Mile Creek with three companies of English troops. Captain Dominique Ducharme of the Indian Department, who directed the Caughnawaga, put their losses at 15 killed and 25 wounded; the Americans at 56 in both categories.[25] Fitz Gibbon's brashness did not extend to keeping his promise to protect the Americans from the Indians. Most of the American wounded were murdered and the unwounded prisoners robbed—apparently by Mohawk who had suddenly recovered their courage.

While Boerstler's behavior can be taken as an example of the worthlessness of too many of Madison's regular officers, the members of the court of inquiry that examined Boerstler's conduct during this major American defeat furnish even better specimens—they solemnly decreed that he was blameless and his surrender perfectly justified.

Encouraged by this victory, Vincent moved his outposts closer to Fort George, and began raiding across the Niagara River against Dearborn's communications. On July 5 Lieutenant Colonel Thomas Clark with thirty-four Lincoln militiamen and seven regulars surprised Fort Schlosser just after daybreak and got away with considerable supplies of whiskey, tobacco, and salt,[26] as well as one 6-pounder, before the local militia got the sleep out of their eyes.

Even with this warning, American east-bank security continued lackadaisical. Lieutenant Colonel Bisshopp struck Black Rock in the small hours of July 11, burned the blockhouses, barracks, and a schooner; and captured seven large bateaux, which he packed with a tally of 123 barrels of salt, 46 of whiskey, and 11 of flour, besides bales of blankets. During the time needed to load them, however, Porter came raging up from Buffalo and shouted the militia—including Tuscarora tribesmen from their nearby village—into action. These closed in on Black Rock in a wave of sharp-shooting skirmishers. Bisshopp, a highly regarded soldier, received several wounds, one of them mortal; thirteen British were killed, twenty-five wounded. American losses are not recorded, but the British carried off a number of prisoners.

This long run of failures finally was too much. With, for once, the full backing of Madison, the cabinet, and Congress, Armstrong relieved Dearborn of his command; the pottering old soldier was to reestablish

25. For troops supposedly trapped in an ambush, these casualties are surprisingly even, especially since Mohawk losses may not have been included.

26. Salt, which was absolutely necessary for curing pork, was an especially valuable prize.

his health and await further orders. Dearborn left Fort George on July 15. He never understood why.

His departure, however, was no occasion for rejoicing. The inexorable law of seniority brought Wilkinson as his replacement. One disrespect-ful subordinate grumbled that age and fatuity were being replaced by age and imbecility.

NINE

On to Montreal!

Our quarters for this winter will probably be in Montreal.
—Thomas Jefferson to the
Marquis de Lafayette, Nov. 30, 1813

JAMES WILKINSON'S APPOINTMENT PROMPTLY generated a political/military cat fight. The American forces being built up in the Lake Champlain sector were commanded by Major General Wade Hampton, a Virginian who, after some Revolutionary War service as a junior officer of irregular cavalry, had shifted to South Carolina and turned planter, becoming one of the wealthiest men in the United States and a power in the Republican party. He had entered the Army in 1808, but so far had had little opportunity to show any useful qualities beyond a certain talent for administration. In an age of stiff-necked individualists he was conspicuous for his overweening pride, hair-trigger sensitivity, obstinacy, and rigid code of personal honor. He had accepted the command of the Lake Champlain sector on the understanding that he would be directly under the secretary of war, except when it might become necessary for his army's operations to be closely coordinated with Dearborn's—in which case he professed entire willingness to recognize Dearborn's seniority and accept his orders. Wilkinson, however, he regarded as something too corrupt and beneath contempt for a gentleman to deign to notice. He would have nothing to do with Wilkinson, or any of Wilkinson's friends. Wilkinson as frankly hated Hampton; from 1808 onward, their feud had increasingly split the Army's officers into hostile cliques.

Wilkinson's career is an American enigma. The complete solipsist and trickster, a confidence man in uniform, he was without loyalties, yet gifted with a plausibility and charm that successfully bamboozled such intelligent men as John Adams and Thomas Jefferson. For years he was both an American general and a paid agent of the Spanish government, yet he could refer to his sword as the "untarnished companion of my thigh for forty years."

Having no replacement for either of these generals, Secretary Armstrong decided to take over the active direction of operations on the northern frontier himself. He had much confidence in his own military skills and powers of command—and also had political ambitions that a successful campaign would aid mightily. Even so, he rapidly found commanding Wilkinson tantamount to what a later American general would describe as "pushing a wet noodle." Armstrong wanted a concentrated offensive against Kingston; he would consider an expedition down the St. Lawrence against Montreal. Either way, the British line of communications would be shattered. Wilkinson at once reverted to the earlier Dearborn/Chauncey strategy: begin with operations on the Niagara front, *then* make a "lightning" movement against Kingston. Pointing out that victories around Niagara would only nick the lion's tail, Armstrong insisted on Kingston. Wilkinson could pick his own tactics, but Kingston must be the strategic objective.

Wilkinson left Washington on August 11, still unconvinced. Pausing in Albany, he sent Hampton two blandly superior letters full of detailed instructions, perfectly calculated to touch off Hampton's super-quick temper. Hampton ignored them, writing instead to Armstrong to offer his resignation. Wilkinson too wrote Armstrong, demanding that Hampton "be turned out of the service" for his insubordinate conduct in not replying. Armstrong established the rule that all correspondence to and from Hampton should pass through his own office, which he moved into Sackets Harbor on September 5. (Albany would have been a better, more central location as well as a far healthier one: the secretary of war would soon come down with one of the "fevers" that contributed to Sackets Harbor's reputation for being a miserable hole, with unguessable effects on subsequent operations.) For the time being Hampton pledged loyal and ready cooperation, but announced his intention of resigning at the end of the year's campaign.

Wilkinson meanwhile had arrived at Sackets Harbor on August 20, but did nothing much until the 26th, when he called the general officers present—Morgan Lewis, Robert Swartwout, and Jacob Brown[1]—and

---

1. Brown had been appointed a brigadier general in the Regular Army as a reward for his victory at Sackets Harbor.

Isaac Chauncey to a council of war to decide on a plan of operations. It was late in the year for an invasion of Canada, the more so because there had been no preparations for any offensive. Unfortunately the council was altogether unqualified to consider such an operation. Lewis had proved himself a timid incompetent; Swartwout a nonentity. Brown was a fighter, but more the frontier warrior than a trained soldier.[2] And Wilkinson, except for a couple of minor raids on unsuspecting Indian villages in 1791, had never really commanded troops in combat. Chauncey was the one man present who definitely knew what he wanted to do—and that was *not* to risk his beloved ships against Kingston. Consequently they decided to attack Montreal instead, using all available troops in the Lake Ontario area. Covered by a strong feint against Kingston, they would "slip down the Saint Lawrence" and unite with Hampton's division to take Montreal. The British squadron and garrison at Kingston would be "locked up" by Chauncey's blockade: if the garrison attempted to pursue them, it must move overland "without artillery, baggage, or provisions." Orders were issued to procure boats to transport 7,000 men with rations and ammunition for several weeks, and sixty cannon, of which twenty were to be heavy siege guns. This would require at least 300 boats, with a sufficiency of skilled pilots to take them down the river's dangerous rapids. Only fifteen boats were immediately available. The troops at Sackets Harbor and those on the Niagara frontier were to rendezvous on Grenadier Island, where the St. Lawrence flows from Lake Ontario, ready to move out on September 15.

Having so ordered, Wilkinson betook himself to Fort George, ostensibly to hurry the troops there forward, probably to avoid Armstrong. Lewis's contribution was to take a month's leave. Swartwout being of no perceptible use, this left Brown to make all the necessary preparations. Although handicapped by his inexperience in military operations, he went at it energetically, having considerable knowledge of the Ontario/ St. Lawrence area and its resources. In late September, Lewis returned and took over the work, at least in theory.

Wilkinson reached Fort George on September 4 in somewhat damaged condition after a rough voyage. He had Armstrong's orders to shift the Army of the North to Sackets Harbor, leaving Fort George in defensible condition and suitably garrisoned, with Colonel Moses Porter

2. Brown might have picked up a little knowledge of military organization when he served as personal secretary to Alexander Hamilton, then inspector general (and actual commander) of the "provisional army" raised during our Quasi-War with France, 1798–1800.

of the Light Artillery Regiment in command. He also was to replace Captain Nathaniel Leonard, whose failings as the commanding officer at Fort Niagara had become notorious. (Fort George was militarily more or less useless, but its continued possession had political value as a matter of American prestige, and could be a useful token in future diplomatic haggling over a peace treaty.)

Other than outpost bickering, affairs on the Niagara frontier had been at a standstill since the Beaver Dam fiasco, except for Chauncey's and Winfield Scott's aborted thrust at Burlington Heights and their raid on York.[3] (Armstrong, not wanting any more amateur blunderings, had ordered John Boyd to remain on the defensive, except when he could secure Chauncey's cooperation.) For reasons all his own Wilkinson, instead of getting the troops under way as promptly as possible, dawdled at Fort George until October 2. He was indeed somewhat ill, yet it seems likely that he was hoping that something would turn up to prevent his planned offensive. Thus on September 18 he proposed that he sally out and "destroy" Vincent's forces; two days later he called a council of war to discuss the "razing" of Fort George and the withdrawal of all American troops from Canada. In the end he obeyed some of Armstrong's orders, but only in his own careless fashion. He had done nothing to repair Fort George; now he left Scott with 800 men of his 2d Artillery Regiment to look after it, ordered Moses Porter to Sackets Harbor, and left Captain Leonard still making a hash of things at Fort Niagara. Once Fort George was secure, Scott was to follow on to join Wilkinson's offensive. The defense of the Niagara frontier would be entrusted to Brigadier General George McClure's New York militia, supported by Joseph Willcocks' Canadian Volunteers.

Departing on Chauncey's fast dispatch boat, *The Lady of the Lake*,[4] Wilkinson came back to Sackets Harbor on the 4th in such poor health, whether actual or pretended, that he had to be helped ashore. However sick he may have been, he neither resigned his command nor exercised it intelligently, sometimes preparing to carry out the planned offensive against Montreal, then switching to urging a direct assault on Kingston. Meanwhile autumn storms slowed the movement of supplies from Oswego to Sackets Harbor, and pummeled the Army of the North as its boats crept snail-like down the lake.

At Fort George, with Vincent's outposts less than five miles distant,

3. See chapter six.
4. A very "sharp" 89-ton schooner, mounting five guns.

Scott went to work. Neither Dearborn, Lewis, Boyd, nor Wilkinson had done much to repair the damage done by American artillery and English demolition parties in May; the western face of the fort consisted of little more than the stakes Joseph Totten had put out to show where a rampart should be built. Working almost around the clock, officers and men together, the 2d Artillery put Fort George into combat-ready condition in just four days. McClure's brigade had arrived on the frontier on September 27. Once again a good many of his militiamen refused to leave their native state; the rest he brought over to Fort George.

Fortunately, the British had their own troubles. The growing American concentration at Sackets Harbor worried Francis de Rottenburg, governor of Upper Canada, who shifted two regiments (which Armstrong probably overestimated at 1,500 men) from the Burlington/York sector to Kingston, Sir James Yeo delivering them safely, untroubled by Chauncey. Procter's defeat at the Thames River had so unsettled Sir George Prevost that he ordered all Upper Canada west of Kingston evacuated. General John Vincent and other more pugnacious officers finally persuaded him to cancel the order; with winter coming on it would be impossible to move all the supplies, let alone the large number of sick soldiers accumulated at Burlington Heights and York. Also, William H. Harrison was no longer a major threat, and McClure was hardly terrifying. Vincent concentrated his troops at Burlington Heights, ready for an attack from either east or west. Action on the Niagara front dwindled away into occasional hair-pullings between Willcocks' and Cyrenius Chapin's irregulars and Vincent's outposts, to the periodic discomfort of the civilian population. The morale of Vincent's hard-worked, poorly sheltered troops was hardly exemplary. A steady trickle of deserters came into the American lines; others were apprehended, to end in front of a firing squad. McClure's militiamen likewise tended to drift away homeward.

With the Niagara frontier in general and Fort George in particular thus secure, Scott received Wilkinson's orders to move east to the mouth of the Genesee River (modern Rochester) where ships would pick up his regiment. With his departure the only regulars left on the Niagara frontier were a company of the 1st Artillery at Fort Niagara. Hiking hard to catch up with the war, the 2d Artillery reached the Genesee and found only a message from Chauncey: Wilkinson would not spare the necessary shipping.[5] It would be 250 rough and winding miles to Sackets Harbor.

5. Wilkinson had begun moving troops from Sackets Harbor to Grenadier Island, and wanted Chauncey's whole squadron for protection against any possible sortie by Yeo.

(Probably Scott revived a remark he had made in 1810, that serving under Wilkinson was like being married to a prostitute.) Marching on, Scott encountered Armstrong, then en route to Albany, near Utica and obtained permission to ride on ahead and join Wilkinson, while his second-in-command brought along the regiment. (The 2d Artillery ended up garrisoning Sackets Harbor, which Wilkinson had stripped of troops and left almost defenseless.) Riding hard along back roads through sleet and snow, the glory-hungry Scott reached the St. Lawrence at Waddington, 20 miles downstream from Ogdensburg, found that he had outdistanced Wilkinson, and so had to backtrack to meet him.

There had been continual wrangling between Wilkinson and Armstrong, as Wilkinson attempted to evade taking any action and Armstrong sought to fix the responsibility for the delays on Wilkinson. On October 19, learning of Rottenburg's arrival at Kingston, Armstrong gave up and approved Wilkinson's original plan for an advance down the St. Lawrence to Montreal. To save time, the preliminary feint at Kingston would be omitted.

By this time, with winter visibly at hand, it would have been sensible to call off the offensive, spend the winter training troops and completing logistical preparations, and begin active operations in the early spring while Lower Canada still was paralyzed by cold. However, the operation had acquired a momentum of its own; President Monroe and his cabinet were impatient and overconfident (a Virginian of that period could hardly be expected to comprehend Canadian weather), and Armstrong's own reputation and ego were deeply committed. Though he certainly realized that nothing could be expected from Wilkinson, he still insisted on trying. There was always the chance that Wilkinson and Hampton could combine against Montreal, that Prevost might panic, that *something* might be accomplished. At the same time, even before approving the Montreal expedition, he had written Hampton to have his militia brigade begin the construction of winter quarters for 10,000 men some seventy miles upstream from Montreal, so that the combined armies would have shelter in case the campaign, as he later phrased it, ended "with the disgrace of doing nothing" but without serious casualties. Naturally he did not inform Wilkinson of this precaution.[6] He might have relieved Wilkinson, but the next senior officer, Morgan Lewis, was even less promising.

Finally beaten into a corner, Wilkinson asked for formal orders to

6. Adams regards this action (taken on October 16) as "extraordinary" and "not [to] be believed." To the author it seems like a sensible precaution.

attack Montreal. Those given, he began to move out, predicting that he probably would not get to Montreal and that if he did he would be trapped and forced to surrender his army. On October 17 the troops began moving from Sackets Harbor to Grenadier Island, only to be caught in a bad three-day storm that sank fifteen bateaux and damaged a good many more. The last boats straggled in during the first days of November, Boyd's command exhausted from its long trip down the lake. From Grenadier Island the expedition began working into the St. Lawrence on October 1; Wilkinson left with the final elements on the 3rd. Bad weather already had spoiled a considerable part of the rations and ammunition; supplies had been loaded higgledy-piggledy so that medical officers had difficulty finding their chests.

The expedition numbered approximately 7,000 men, organized into four brigades, a "reserve," and an artillery brigade.[7] Lewis had a division consisting of the brigades of Boyd and Leonard Covington.[8] Swartwout's and Brown's brigades were to form a division under Hampton when the two armies united. Alexander Macomb had the reserve; Moses Porter the artillery. Both Wilkinson and Lewis were sick and despondent; the former had been treating his illness for some time with opium. The long line of boats reached French Creek on the 4th. Chauncey had failed to blockade Kingston effectively, or even to screen the mouth of the St. Lawrence. English warships shot up the American campsite until driven off by Porter's guns. They reappeared the next morning, but Porter had prepared hot shot during the night and quickly persuaded them to head back to Kingston. Chauncey appeared too late to either help or hinder.

On the 6th the expedition paused just above Ogdensburg at a place called Hoag's, to prepare to run past the Prescott batteries. Men and ammunition were disembarked and moved down the south bank; during the night the boats were brought downriver. By good luck there was a light fog on the river; the British gunners blazed away mightily but hit practically nothing—no boats were lost and only one man killed. At Hoag's a staff officer appeared to report that Hampton had reached a place called Spears, fifteen miles south of the St. Lawrence, but had been repulsed in attempting to push on. Wilkinson sent him back with word for Hampton to shift farther west and meet him at St. Regis, forty-odd miles on downstream from Ogdensburg.

7. The artillery sometimes was referred to as "the park."
8. Covington entered the Army in 1809 as a lieutenant colonel of light dragoons, but remains a shadowy figure.

The next morning Macomb's "reserve" was moved to the north bank to clear away any British forces that might attempt to fire on the boats.[9] Scott was given command of Macomb's advance guard. Despite its fairly rapid progress, the expedition was already in trouble. Chauncey still had not covered the entrance to the St. Lawrence; the energetic Captain William Mulcaster had gotten into the river with a flotilla of gunboats and some 800 soldiers under Lieutenant Colonel Joseph Morrison, and was aggressively heckling the American rear. And there was no further word of or from Hampton.

Hampton had taken over the Lake Champlain command, with headquarters at Burlington, Vermont, on July 3 to find an ill-supplied, mostly untrained force of approximately 4,000. Shortly after his arrival the Americans lost their naval control of Lake Champlain.[10] Using captured American vessels, a strong British expedition came down from Ile aux Noix and swept the upper end of the lake, destroying or carrying off the stores accumulated at Plattsburg before Hampton could organize any effective opposition. Thereafter, well assisted by Brigadier General George Izard, Hampton began training his command.[11] By the time the campaign opened, his regiments were comparatively well organized, but not yet effective combat units. As Colonel Robert Purdy of the 4th Infantry explained it, his men were mostly recent recruits who had learned a few evolutions, but a spirit of subordination was still foreign to their views. As for their officers, Colonel Henry Atkinson, Hampton's inspector general, groused that they needed far more training than their enlisted men; many were either too ignorant or too lazy to submit correct strength returns for their companies, and some of the returns he did receive were impossible to decipher.[12] Hampton did his best to correct this by forming his officers into awkward squads and drilling them intensively.

Hostile as he was to Wilkinson, Hampton followed his orders, as passed on through Armstrong, to shift his army from Burlington to Cumberland Head on the west shore of Lake Champlain, just north of Platts-

---

9. Macomb's "reserve" (also called the "elite") had Forsyth's riflemen, six or seven companies of the 3d Artillery (serving as infantry), several companies of the 21st Infantry, and two light guns. Total strength was approximately 1,200.

10. See chapter fourteen.

11. Izard was the best-educated officer in the Army, having attended military schools in France, England, and Germany.

12. As an example of American staff organization, Atkinson was actually a captain, but his assignment as inspector general gave him the temporary grade and pay of a colonel.

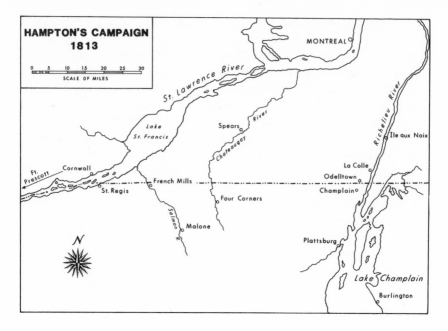

burg. Urged to advance as soon as possible, he arranged with Lieutenant Thomas Macdonough, commander of the American naval forces on Lake Champlain, for an escort, and on September 19, while Wilkinson idled away precious time at Fort George, sailed up the lake to Champlain, just two miles short of the Canadian frontier. Landing around midnight, he at once sent two detachments forward to locate the British frontier defenses. They surprised an outpost at Odelltown, just over the border, but then got lost in the woods and darkness, their reconnaissance dwindling out in some hole-and-corner skirmishing with Indians and Canadian militia.

The next morning Hampton brought his whole force up to Odelltown and looked the situation over. He was on the direct road to Montreal. Prevost would concentrate all available forces to confront any serious threat to that city, and Hampton knew that there was a sizable force of British regulars (actually only 900) at Ile aux Noix on his right flank. He was also very much on his own, with no possible support nearer than Sackets Harbor, and that clearly unready for service. The enemy forces to his front seemed active and confident, and were visibly being reinforced. Also, his subordinates were already complaining of a shortage of water. It had been a droughty summer and the local creeks and wells were practically dry:

horses had to be taken back to the lake for water. After a brief conference with his staff and unit commanders, Hampton decided to shift his offensive to the line of the Chateauguay River, forty-odd miles to the west. Accordingly, he returned to Champlain on the 21st and, after necessary preparations, marched off on the 23d. It was hardly glorious, but it was sensible, and Armstrong approved of it.

Hampton then took position at Four Corners (now Chateaugay), New York, a small crossroads settlement on the Chateauguay River, four miles below the Canadian line. As Prevost complained, this was a "highly judicious" position, forcing the British to keep a large force around Montreal, and also threatening their communications between Montreal and Kingston. Hampton used his time there improving the road back to Plattsburg, bringing up artillery and supplies, and training his troops. Meanwhile, he tried to distract Prevost by sending Colonel Isaac Clark with militia from the Burlington garrison on a raid against illegal traders and British outposts at the northeast corner of Lake Champlain. Clark was quite successful during October 11–12, seizing contraband supplies and surprising Philipsburg, Canada, where he captured a detachment of Canadian militia.[13]

On October 12 Hampton wrote Armstrong a well-reasoned letter. He was anxious because of Wilkinson's delays, which were giving Prevost invaluable time to muster additional troops; and he wanted orders as to where and when he was to meet Wilkinson on the St. Lawrence, noting that he himself would be the best judge of when, depending on the state of the roads and weather, he should leave Four Corners for that rendezvous. Armstrong's reply (dated October 16, received the 18th) was that Wilkinson was almost ready to start; Hampton therefore should advance to the point where the Chateauguay ran into the St. Lawrence. Wilkinson would soon be in touch with him.

Accordingly Hampton began a well-organized advance on October 21 through heavily timbered country; by evening of the next day he had covered twenty-four miles. He then halted for two days to improve the road to his rear and move up supplies and artillery, while his scouts felt out the British dispositions and gathered in British deserters. Indications were that only some 350 militia manned the frontier. Hampton renewed his advance on the 25th, along the north bank of the Chateauguay. Some six miles farther on, near Spears, his advance guard found

13. Americans called Philipsburg "Massequoi Village."

the Canadians holding several lines of abatis [14] and light field fortifications on the far side of a clearing that gave them a good field of fire. The
south bank of the river across from this position was an overgrown hem-
lock swamp, apparently impassable. The British commander, Lieutenant
Colonel Charles-Michel d'Irumberry de Salaberry, was a French Canadian who had served through the Napoleonic Wars with the 60th Foot [15]
and so was experienced in outpost service. He had between 500 and 800
men, a mixture of his Voltigeurs,[16] assorted militia, and a few Indians.
Except for Hampton, de Salaberry, and a few others, it was going to be
pretty much an amateur affair; practically nobody on either side, Izard
included, had ever experienced actual combat.

Hampton decided to outflank this position by crossing Colonel Purdy
over to the south bank that night to bypass the swamp, then recross the
river and swing in on de Salaberry's rear. The next morning Izard with
the rest of Hampton's army would threaten a frontal attack. When Purdy
reported himself in position, Izard would convert his threat into an actual
assault.

That night, after Purdy had vanished through a beating rain into the
woods on the south bank, a courier came to Hampton with Armstrong's
order of October 16, directing the construction of winter quarters for
10,000 men. In his frequently slapdash fashion, Armstrong had not
phrased this message to make it plain that this was a precautionary measure. To make matters worse, Armstrong—sick, probably exhausted from
trying to spur Wilkinson into some action, *and* quite possibly wanting to
distance himself from an operation that seemed more and more likely to
fail—was returning to Washington. Reading this letter quickly brought
Hampton's dark side uppermost. Jumping to the conclusion that the
campaign was at an end, he imagined that he was being sacrificed, and
could "neither feel security nor expect honor." Forthwith, he submitted
his resignation; if he had not already committed Purdy, he would have
countermarched the next morning.

Purdy meanwhile, threshing through a waterlogged forest in the dark

14. Abatis—a row of trees felled with their tops pointed toward the enemy. The
larger branches were sometimes sharpened.

15. The 60th Foot, or Royal Americans, had become an organization of riflemen
and light infantry.

16. The Voltigeurs, properly the Provincial Corps of Light Infantry, was a gray-
uniformed regiment of French-Canadian volunteers activated in April, 1812. De
Salaberry organized and trained it.

and rain, had been misled, probably maliciously, by his civilian guides. Indian scouts watched his movements; when he finally stumbled through to the river the next morning, he found Canadians waiting for him on both banks. His messengers to Hampton, lost or intercepted, never got through. There was a great deal of shouting and shooting, and Purdy's attack stalled. About 2:00 P.M. Hampton finally bestirred himself and ordered his column forward against de Salaberry's defenses. With men and guns enough to punch through and relieve Purdy, he halted within easy musket range of the Canadian front line and began belting out a "rolling platoon" fire in best parade-ground fashion.[17] Entirely unimpressed, the Canadians answered with cheers and bugle calls, possibly on de Salaberry's orders, probably out of sheer French-Canadian exuberancy. To Hampton and Izard this uproar suggested that they were confronted by superior forces. Hampton began worrying that the enemy might be working through the forest to envelop his own left flank, and soon worried himself into ordering a retreat. Accordingly he fell back some three miles, leaving Purdy to get himself out of whatever fix he might be in the best way he could. That Purdy managed to do, after another night in the south bank's swampy woods. Once Purdy was back, Hampton called the usual council of war, which promptly agreed to fall back on Four Corners. Hampton retired slowly, untroubled by de Salaberry who wisely did not attempt to push his unexpected luck.

If Canadian historians sometimes give the impression of considering Chateauguay the equivalent of Waterloo, it was indeed an action that reflects the highest credit on de Salaberry and his men, even as it destroyed any claim Hampton might have to military competence. The casualties were almost ridiculous: de Salaberry had only two men killed, thirteen wounded, and three captured; American losses totaled "barely" fifty, which suggests that the average Canadian was a poor shot, and that Hampton and Izard were faint-hearts indeed.

Once back at Four Corners Hampton nursed his emotional wounds and his wrath, blaming Armstrong for his disappointments. The rains continued, the roads dissolved, supplies ran short, sickness increased. Since no forage could be obtained locally, Hampton had to send his draft horses back to Plattsburg.

In this foul mood and weather, on November 8 Hampton received

17. Companies in each regiment firing in succession at the word of command, from one flank to the other. Effective against troops in the open, it was practically a waste of ammunition here.

Wilkinson's letter from Hoag's, ordering him to join the latter as soon as possible near St. Regis, and also to bring along thirty days' rations for Wilkinson's command. The latter demand, generally overlooked by historians, was completely unreasonable, the more so because this immense amount of foodstuffs would have to be moved by wagon over primitive forest roads. Hampton had neither any such reserve of rations, nor the wagons to move it, as Wilkinson must have very well known.

Wilkinson had continued downriver from Ogdensburg, with Macomb clearing the north bank of British detachments. On November 8 the Americans reached the village of Hamilton (not shown on modern maps), almost eighteen miles beyond Ogdensburg. There Wilkinson held another council of war as to whether the expedition should continue. Undoubtedly to his concealed sorrow, Lewis, Swartwout, Boyd, and Brown voted to attack Montreal; Porter and Covington considered that they were in great danger, but could think of nothing better to do than to keep moving on. Since the expedition was nearing the Long Sault—eight continuous miles of extremely rough rapids that could be run only by daylight—Brown's brigade was landed on the north bank to join Macomb, Brown assuming command of their combined force, now some 2,500 strong. Boyd's brigade was to form the rear guard. Wilkinson then took to his bed, turning the expedition over to Lewis, who was almost disabled by dysentery. During the 10th the boats moved up to the head of the Long Sault, mooring for the night in the lee of Crysler Island, almost abreast of John Crysler's farm on the Canadian bank. Brown meanwhile swept down the northern side of the Long Sault, routing the British garrison out of Fort Matilda at the river's narrowest point. Later, Scott encountered Major James Dennis (of Queenston fame) in a strong position behind Hoople's Creek, just west of Cornwall, but quickly outflanked him and drove him off through the night with considerable loss. Weary, wet, and hungry, Brown's men warmed their camps by the simple expedient of setting fire to the rail fences along the roads, and made "great destruction" among nearby farms' livestock for their suppers.[18]

The morning of November 11, as Lewis slowly got the expedition organized for the descent of the rapids, Wilkinson unexpectedly reassumed the command and immediately began changing Lewis's dispositions, while drenched soldiers stood shivering in a chill rain. About 10:30 A.M. a

18. Some of them reportedly confiscated civilian overcoats, being—according to a Canadian clergyman—"not well provided with camp equipage and still worse with clothes."

courier from Brown reported the north bank clear as far as Cornwall. Wilkinson ordered the movement down the rapids begun, then canceled it when Boyd warned that Mulcaster and Morrison were preparing to attack. Ordering Boyd to drive them back, Wilkinson apparently returned to his bunk; at least he showed no visible interest in the action that ensued.

Gathering up his own brigade and summoning what he could of Covington's and Swartwout's—in all some 2,500 men and six guns—Boyd moved to meet the enemy. In response, Morrison went over to the defensive, taking up a strong position across the narrow western end of Crysler's farm clearing, with his right flank on the St. Lawrence, where Mulcaster's gunboats covered it, and his left on a swampy forest. His regulars and three light guns held the center, with a skirmish line of Voltigeurs and Indians to their front and in the woods on their left. He had taken a major risk in forcing the action, disregarding the excellent chance that he might encounter overwhelming odds. Had Brown and Macomb commanded the rear guard he hardly could have escaped destruction, but Boyd, instead of organizing a coordinated attack with artillery support, pitched his regiments into action, catch-as-catch-can, as they came up.

Struggling across rain-slick gullies and sodden plowed fields, the Americans stumbled into action piecemeal, never achieving any decisive numerical superiority on the firing line. Green troops fired too wildly, mostly for the comforting noise of it: green officers failed to control them; ammunition pouches emptied; nobody had thought to organize an ammunition resupply. Ordered to get around Morrison's left flank, Swartwout somehow flinched before a handful of skirmishers. Boyd forgot his artillery; in the general confusion only two guns seem to have finally been brought into action.[19] About this time Covington took a mortal wound and his brigade began drifting to the rear; Swartwout's followed. Seizing his opportunity, Morrison came forward, threatening to overrun the American guns. At this crisis Wilkinson's adjutant general, Colonel John de Barth Walbach,[20] led a squadron of the 2d Light Dragoons against Morrison's right flank, which had become exposed during his advance. Hindered by the muddy broken ground, pounded by Mulcaster's gunboats, they could not push their three successive charges home, but each time they forced Morrison to halt and refuse his flank. Eighteen out of the 130 of them were killed or wounded, but they bought time for all but one gun,

19. Various accounts mention from two to six guns.

20. Described as a German officer who had served in the French Army before coming to America.

too deeply mired to be extricated. Covered by the 21st and 25th infantry regiments, the Americans gradually fell back to the river. There they embarked and, though neither Wilkinson, Walbach, nor Boyd would later admit giving the order, shifted to the south bank.

Once engaged, Morrison had fought a careful, methodical battle, letting the Americans wear themselves out coming to him, using his regulars' disciplined fire power with maximum effectiveness, and counterattacking when the American lines began to fray away. In itself, this was a fine feat of arms, yet it did not halt or cripple Wilkinson and left Morrison too used up to exploit his tactical success. He reported 23 killed, 148 wounded, and 9 missing—almost one-fifth of his whole force. The Americans had suffered far heavier losses, 102 killed and 237 wounded. Wilkinson admitted no missing or prisoners, but Morrison reported capturing 100 Americans.

The next morning the expedition went down the rapids, the cavalry and artillery marching along the shore, and joined Brown's column near Cornwall. This was, from its location, an excellent chokepoint on the St. Lawrence River, and there was considerable British apprehension lest Wilkinson should "establish" himself there and link up with Hampton. But it was at Cornwall that Colonel Atkinson finally caught up with Wilkinson, after several days of wandering in the wilderness, with Hampton's reply to Wilkinson's letter directing him to proceed to St. Regis.

Hampton (so he had written) would have been happy to meet Wilkinson there, until he realized that the latter was low on provisions and expected Hampton to resupply him. His men could bring no more supplies than they could carry on their own backs, and thus soon would be dependent on Wilkinson's scanty remaining stock for their daily rations.[21] In view of that fact, Hampton had consulted with his senior officers and decided to return to Plattsburg, reorganize, and attempt to open communications with Wilkinson at some other point on the St. Lawrence, which Wilkinson should designate. This was, everything considered, as sensible a course as any.

Wilkinson at once summoned the usual council of war; even Brown and Macomb were now ready to agree that the campaign might as well be

---

21. Wilkinson was never modest or realistic in his demands on others, and during this period seems to have been occasionally under the influence of opium. Even so, the author suspects that Wilkinson's demand for thirty days' rations was intentionally designed to draw a refusal from Hampton (who would have no other honest choice) and thus give Wilkinson an excuse for terminating his own possible exposure to enemy action.

called off. They were almost out of supplies; Prevost was rumored to have concentrated 15,000 men to defend Montreal; the weather would shortly be deadly for their weary, ill-clad men; and nothing was to be expected from either Hampton or Wilkinson. The council's unanimous decision was to withdraw to French Mills (now Covington, New York), a small outpost 50 miles of bad roads distant from Plattsburg and 200 by lake, river, and road from Albany. Even officers only slightly given to cynicism noticed this agreement produced a sudden and remarkable improvement in Wilkinson's health; for the first time since his arrival in New York, he showed decision and energy. On November 13 the expedition accordingly dropped on down the St. Lawrence some fourteen miles from Cornwall, then worked up the Salmon River for seven miles to reach French Mills. There it went into winter quarters, suffering intensely from cold, exposure, sickness, short rations, and incompetent officers. Half of the sick were still in tents at the year's end.

Hampton had taken his column back to Plattsburg. There he proceeded to give most of his officers leaves of absence and betook himself to Washington. The quartermaster service at Plattsburg collapsed; supplies were sold, stolen, or abandoned. Wilkinson took command of both forces, but it was Izard, Macomb, and Atkinson who got the situation around Plattsburg back in hand and reestablished the supply system. There was a good deal of desertion, much encouraged by the British who offered any American soldier who wished to quit the "unnatural war" up to five months' back pay.

Casualties and sufferings aside, the Wilkinson/Hampton campaign with its (as Brown put it) "marching and countermarching most ingloriously" was a fit subject for a comic opera. In sad fact the United States had no general officer capable of either planning, organizing, and coordinating an operation of such scope—or, more to the point, of comprehending that the basic concept simply was not feasible, given the senior officers, troops, and logistical backup available. Kingston was the logical objective, and the Americans had the men and ships, if properly handled, to take it. Yet Armstrong, who at least knew what *should* be done, failed as utterly with Wilkinson and Hampton as he had the year before with Dearborn. Unable to get them to follow their instructions, he ended by merely meddling with their blunderings rather than correcting them. Wilkinson's only concern had been to avoid responsibility and risk: Hampton completely lacked the primary military quality of being willing to fight.

Even with competent American commanders, Montreal, strongly situated behind the junction of the St. Lawrence and Ottawa rivers, was too distant and well defended an objective. Prevost took the American threat seriously, and Wilkinson's quibbling delays gave him plenty of time to prepare. From Prescott eastward to Ile aux Noix, he had approximately 6,000 regulars, around whom he had mustered possibly 12,000 militia of various degrees of effectiveness.[22] In addition, he had a newly arrived rocket company of Royal Marine Artillery and 350 Royal Navy seamen to reinforce his flotilla of light warships on the St. Lawrence. Wilkinson's bateaux would have been helpless against their gunboats.

Moreover, any such offensive, no matter how competently commanded, would have been tripped up by logistical problems. Because of poor roads and the lack of forage for his horses, Hampton could barely feed his 4,000 men at Four Corners. Wilkinson's supplies were almost exhausted when he reached Cornwall. Neither command would have had enough ammunition for extensive combat, such as an actual attack on Montreal would have required. Both commands were increasingly hampered by sickness, which their understrength, poorly equipped medical staffs could hardly alleviate, let alone check. The incompetence and corruption of the Quartermaster General's Department and the greed and inefficiency of the supply contractors left American soldiers freezing and half-starved even at French Mills.

Yet this was not the total of American disgrace for 1813. In order to secure Sackets Harbor, Armstrong had pulled Harrison's troops eastward. Leaving a few companies on the Niagara frontier, Harrison reached that vital base on November 16 with some 1,300 men, a fourth of them sick. The defense of the Niagara frontier remained in Brigadier General McClure's hands, and McClure was becoming dangerously frightened. The terms of service of his militia and volunteers were expiring and he could get few replacements. His repeated pleas for reinforcements got little response from either Albany or Washington. Armstrong, though he had some 12,000 available regulars between Plattsburg and Sackets Harbor, did nothing more than call on Governor Tompkins for New York militia, which did not appear.

By December 10 McClure had only 60 regulars and 40 volunteers at Fort George, with approximately 100 Canadian Volunteers doing outpost duty.[23] Vincent had gradually pushed his outposts closer to the fort, which

22. Prevost reported nearly 13,000; the actual total was at least 9,000 and probably higher.

23. These regulars, from the 24th Infantry Regiment, had been dropped off there by Harrison.

McClure had no hope of holding against a determined assault. In early October, Armstrong had given McClure authority to burn the town of Newark *if that was essential to the defense of Fort George* (the town's buildings would mask attackers from the fire of some of the fort's guns.[24] He was to give the inhabitants ample warning that this might become necessary and "invite" them to evacuate the place. On the 10th McClure decided that his position was untenable. Hastily transferring his garrison to Fort Niagara, he unaccountably burned down Newark and much of Queenston, turning the inhabitants out into the snow with only two hours' advance notice. His excuse was that he intended to deprive the British of all possible shelter for the winter, but he left Fort George and its large stock of supplies and equipment almost intact, taking away only its light guns and dismounting the heavy pieces. It was a rare piece of stupidity and unthinking brutality, and, as McClure apprehensively reported, the British were "much exasperated."

The British command in Upper Canada had just changed, Lieutenant General Sir Gordon Drummond taking over the administration of that province, with Major General Phineas Riall as his subordinate. Both had only limited combat experience and undistinguished records, but both were energetic and ambitious. Together with Prevost they intended to teach Americans that house burnings, while fully sanctioned by the laws of war when applied by the Royal Navy's jolly tars against American "peasants" (the term is Napier's), were "revolting" when His Majesty's loyal Canadian subjects were the sufferers.

McClure had withdrawn to Buffalo, leaving Captain Leonard with approximately 324 regulars (his company of the 1st Artillery, one of the 24th Infantry, and detachments from two other infantry regiments) to hold Fort Niagara. Leonard expected an attack and had drawn up elaborate plans for meeting one, but duty at the fort seems to have been slackly done. McClure reported only 250 men under his immediate command; he was somewhat dazed to find himself disowned by the American government and the Buffalo militia refusing to serve under him.[25] After much argument among New York militia dignitaries, the unhappy task of defending the Niagara frontier was assumed by Major General Amos Hall.

The first British stroke came on the night of December 18. Cana-

24. British accounts usually refer to Newark as "Niagara" or "Niagara-on-the-Lake."

25. He was also having difficulties with Chapin, whom he tried to arrest for treason and mutiny.

dian militia had brought boats by road from Burlington Heights. That night they ferried 562 picked British regulars under Colonel John Murray across the Niagara River some two miles south of Fort Niagara. The attack had been carefully planned and was carried through with skill and drive. While the various accounts differ as to details, it seems that the British surprised an American outpost and forced one of their prisoners to reveal the American countersign, which they used to gain entrance to the fort. The alarm was given only when the British already were pouring through the gate. Their swift bayonet attack overran the place, overwhelming the few hastily formed pockets of resistance. A good many of the 65 Americans killed were sleep-dazed men caught stumbling from their blankets; of the 344 prisoners claimed, only 14 were wounded.[26] Captain Leonard was picked up later at his home some two miles distant, allegedly in an advanced state of intoxication. Possibly 20 Americans escaped; the British lost only 6 killed and 5 wounded.

As soon as the fort was reported taken, Riall crossed behind Murray with 500 regulars and 500 Indians and raged through Lewistown, Manchester (now Niagara Falls), Youngstown, Fort Schlosser, and the Tuscarora village, putting them and every farm building for several miles inland from the river to the torch. There was almost no resistance, although the Canadian Volunteers did halt Riall's movement southward by destroying the bridge over Tonawanda Creek, ten miles north of Buffalo. As usual the Indians collected scalps without any discrimination as to age or sex.

In spite of this indication of British aggressiveness, the Americans were again surprised on the night of December 30 when Riall came back with 1,000 militia and regulars and 400 Indians. The boats used in the first raid had been brought down by sleigh to Chippewa and then floated into Frenchman's Creek. Canadian militiamen ferried Riall's main body across to a point a little north of Black Rock, then took the boats upriver to the vicinity of Fort Erie where they embarked a smaller force under Colonel John Gordon, which was to land south of Black Rock. By then it was almost daylight; Gordon's boats were seen and shot up, several ran aground. Riall's main body, however, drove southward with the Indians fanning out on his left flank. Hall had gotten some 1,200 men together; Riall gave him credit for "considerable obstinacy," but eventually the

26. As usual, the losses reported and claimed do not agree. The garrison morning report for December 15 showed 324 Americans present, 45 absent. How the British managed to kill 45 and capture 344 of the 324 present, especially if some 20 escaped, rather defies the laws of mathematics. Possibly they picked up some stray militiamen.

militia gave way and retreated through Buffalo, a handful of regulars and sailors covering the rout. Riall burned both Buffalo and Black Rock and all dwellings he had missed on his first raid. He reported his losses as 112 killed, wounded, and missing; Hall had 30 killed, 40 wounded, and 69 prisoners. The number of civilians slaughtered was never accurately established. American reinforcements coming into the area found hogs devouring the dead bodies of some of them amid the charred wreckage of their homes. One serious American loss was the destruction of three of Perry's small schooners, which had been pulled up on the beach at Black Rock for the winter.

Prevost followed this with a proclamation, affecting more sorrow than anger that he had been forced to take measures "so little congenial to the British character," but ending with the suggestion that the Americans had better behave themselves in the future, or else!

In fact, American reaction was slight. Some authors have attributed this to an American sense of guilt over American actions at York and Newark, but this seems an academic assumption. There was intense resentment among Americans, especially the New York militia, but there just did not seem much point to complaining over the British version of making war.

TEN

Spaniards and Red Sticks

Retrograde under these circumstances? I will perish first!
—Andrew Jackson

WAR CAME SLOWLY TO THE SOUTHERN United States, where the strategic situation was far more complex than along the Canadian frontier where American and British forces had clashed immediately in 1812. By contrast, except for the Royal Navy's blockade, no British forces threatened the southern states, and England had no nearby land bases. Nevertheless, American armed force had been involved in minor military operations before our declaration of war against England. A considerable part of the coastline—"the Floridas"—was under Spanish rule. Much of the interior was the home territory of large, semi-civilized Indian tribes—Choctaw, Creek, Chickasaw, and Cherokee—some of whom were not wholly reconciled to American rule.

One of the more curious aspects of Jefferson's and Madison's administrations was their unhesitatingly predatory attitude toward the Floridas, even though Spain and the United States were officially at peace. In part, this was precautionary. Spain had been England's ally in the war against Napoleon since 1808, and if war broke out with England the British were likely to use the Floridas as bases for operations against American territory. Moreover, Napoleon had so shattered Spain that her officials in the Floridas lacked the power to enforce the neutrality of their territory or control its Indian tribes. Of the latter, the Seminole, another new people made up of survivors from broken tribes, wandering Creek, and runaway Negro slaves, were particularly careless of international boundaries. But the major power behind this aggression was the insatiable hunger of the citizens of the western states for new land.

In 1810 Madison had managed an "insurrection" by American settlers in West Florida, and taken possession of much of that province.[1] The next year he tried to cook up a similar movement in East Florida, and moved troops across its frontier to occupy Amelia Island (northeast of modern Jacksonville) and the crossings of St. Mary's River (Florida's northeastern boundary) to back up whatever revolt might develop. They remained there through 1812. His plan for 1813 was to secure congressional approval for the complete occupation of both Floridas. Wilkinson at New Orleans was ordered to stand ready to seize the rest of West Florida; Major General Thomas Pinckney[2] was to move south to occupy St. Augustine.

Vaguely aware that he lacked sufficient troops for both this major operation and his current war with England, in October, 1812, Madison already had asked Governor Willie Blount of Tennessee for 1,500 volunteers to "defend the lower country."[3] His circumlocution was perfectly understood by Tennesseans. Major General Andrew Jackson of the Tennessee militia, now converted to a major general of volunteers, left Nashville on January 7 with 2,070 men, 1,400 of these infantry in flatboats, and 670 "dragoons" following Colonel John Coffee across country along the 500-odd-mile old Natchez Trace.[4] The infantry's approximately 2,000-mile trip down the Cumberland River into the Ohio and thence into the Mississippi began during an abnormal cold wave, with both the Cumberland and Ohio full of ice. One boat and three men were lost, but the rest came in to Natchez thirty-nine days later. There Jackson found provisions and staff officers sent by Wilkinson to pay and muster in his troops, and also a very polite order for him to encamp there and await further orders. Wilkinson's explanations were sensible: Natchez was a healthier locality

1. West Florida was the coastal area from the Mississippi River east to the Chattahoochee; East Florida was the modern state, less the Pensacola area. The United States had a certain claim to the first as properly part of the Louisiana Purchase, but none to East Florida.

2. Pinckney was the other major general commissioned in 1812 and so junior only to Dearborn. Though he had served on Gates' staff during the Revolution, his appointment could be justified only as a political measure.

3. Blount issued his call for volunteers on November 14; the men reported to Nashville on December 12.

4. An ancient Indian trail, some 500 miles long, between Nashville and Natchez, passing near the modern cities of Tupelo and Jackson, Mississippi.

than New Orleans, with a better local supply of forage for the Tennesseans' horses; also, its strategic location made it a good base for movements
toward either New Orleans, Mobile, or Pensacola. Unmentioned was the
fact that Wilkinson would prefer not to have 2,067 enthusiastic "Citizen-
Volunteers of Tennessee" whooping it up amid all the opportunities for
ungodly and riotous recreation that New Orleans always offered visitors
from upriver. Moreover, Jackson himself was an explosive commodity, a
rather humorless frontier gentleman with a hair-trigger sense of personal
honor and an extreme proclivity toward instant reckonings, whether formally according to the Code Duello or spontaneously with any weapons
immediately available. During the trials following the collapse of the Burr
Conspiracy in 1806, he had publicly denounced Wilkinson as a "double
traitor."

The various soldiers waited for the command from Washington that
would launch them on the conquest of the Floridas. It never came. For
its own reasons Congress refused to authorize the occupation of East
Florida, though in February it finally approved the seizure of the rest of
West Florida.[5] One of Armstrong's first duties on becoming secretary of
war, therefore, was to order Jackson to discharge his troops, since the
operation for which they were raised had been canceled. Wilkinson hoped
to recruit some of them into his weak regular regiments, but Jackson
marched them home, pledging personally to make good the cost of their
pay and rations, hiring wagons for the sick out of his own pocket, and
walking most of the way so that soldiers could ride his horse. This high-
chinned performance won him vast popularity and the nickname "Old
Hickory" for his personal toughness under hardship. (Once Armstrong
learned the entire facts of the case, he buttered Jackson with praise for
what he might have done, and made good Jackson's emergency expenditures.)

Pinckney was ordered north of St. Mary's River, a shift that he completed in May, leaving East Florida in considerable disorder. Madison,
however, was determined to at least have the rest of West Florida, and so
ordered Wilkinson to occupy it up to the Perdido River. Such an operation was within even Wilkinson's capabilities; the area was defended only
by run-down Fort Charlotte at Mobile, with a garrison of some sixty hungry, sickly Spanish soldiers, and a small outpost on Dauphin Island at
the entrance of Mobile Bay. The nearest support was at Pensacola, and

5. This would bring the U.S. territory east to the Perdido River, Florida's present
western boundary.

the Spanish troops there were in no better condition than the Mobile garrison. At the end of 1813 they had not been paid for almost five years and were on half-rations; their uniforms and equipment were almost worn out.

Collecting a force of approximately 600 men, transports enough to lift them, and five gunboats for escort, Wilkinson sailed from Pass Christian (just west of modern Gulfport) on April 7. Lieutenant Colonel John Bowyer marched south from Fort Stoddart, some forty-five miles north of Mobile, with 400 men to cut the overland communications between Mobile and Pensacola. By luck, the American gunboats intercepted a Spanish supply ship bound for Mobile, and thereafter picked up the surprised handful on Dauphin Island. Once ashore at Mobile, Wilkinson politely informed Fort Charlotte's *comandante* Cayetano Pérez that he was not there as an enemy of Spain, but simply to "relieve" the garrison from duty in territory belonging to the United States. Pérez had no choice but to accede; on the 15th he evacuated the fort and was transported to Pensacola on American vessels. Thereafter, along with generous allowances of rest from such arduous campaigning, Wilkinson established an American outpost on the west bank of the Perdido and ordered construction of a sand-and-log fortification, soon named Fort Bowyer, at the end of Mobile Point, to guard the entrance into Mobile Bay. Then he was summoned to the Canadian frontier, and Brigadier General Thomas Flournoy took over the New Orleans command.[6]

Though furious over this insult to their national honor, the Spanish were no menace. It was among the friendly Creek Indians that sudden, highly dangerous hostilities flared the following July. Guided by their dedicated agent Benjamin Hawkins, the "Beloved Man of Four Nations," whom Washington had appointed in 1796, the Creek were gradually adopting the white man's agricultural methods and had strengthened their internal government.[7] In 1812 their acknowledged territory included western Georgia and much of central and northern Alabama.[8] Though a considerable faction of them resented the pressure to give up their tradi-

6. Properly the Seventh Military District, with headquarters in New Orleans. The Army's administrative/territorial organization, established at the end of 1812, consisted of nine districts, each headed by a brigadier general.

7. The Creek actually were a league of different communities, not all of which had the same origin or spoke the same language. "Beloved Man" was a Creek title of high esteem.

8. Alabama then, together with modern Mississippi, constituted the Mississippi Territory.

tional ways, and others were irritated by trespassing white frontiersmen, they had remained peaceful. Their major problem seemed to be the general scarcity of game in their territory, which had caused some of them to move into Florida and become part of the Seminole. They thus were increasingly dependent on their crops for their food, but the average warrior still considered fieldwork proper only for squaws.

Into this still-placid area during October 1811 came Tecumseh with an escort of northern tribesmen to visit the annual great council of the Creek. Though he called for unity among all Indian tribes, his public speeches were pacific—let red man and white each manage his own affairs and keep the peace. Hawkins and the elder Creek chiefs saw nothing dangerous in his visit.

In private, however, the visitors preached the doctrine of Tecumseh's brother—still at that time the mighty Prophet and not yet the discredited survivor of Tippecanoe—that the Indian must give up the white man's ways, tools, and trinkets and go back to his ancestors' customs. Then the wild game would return in vast numbers, the white man would vanish, and the Indians would once again enjoy their primitive happiness. As a binding "medicine," Tecumseh's party taught a ritual song and the "dance of the Indians of the Lakes." [9] After their departure prophets began to appear in the Creek villages. (It may be that Tecumseh had left a few apostles behind.) These men preached the Prophet's creed: the Creek should destroy the plows, spinning wheels, and even the domestic livestock that Hawkins had introduced, [10] and break off all relations with the white man. And like the Prophet they claimed mystic powers. They could live under water and make their disciples invulnerable; the sun and the Great Spirit talked with them. Some were accomplished magicians and energetic plotters; soon their authority among the Creek came to rival that of the chiefs. Especially among the so-called Upper Creek in central Alabama, the farthest from Hawkins' headquarters, a powerful underground movement grew among the younger men, who met in secret to practice their new rituals.

The more thoughtful leaders of this movement looked for outside help. During the years of peace since the American Revolution the Creek had largely lost their military skills. Possibly only one Creek warrior out of

9. This same doctrine, with its special songs and dance, would reappear in later times of Indian distress. Its last widespread occurrence was the Ghost Dance of 1890, which ended at Wounded Knee.

10. At least one of them proposed to also give up the white man's firearms, but found no converts to that particular idea.

every three owned a firearm, and a good many of these were in poor condition; most Creek would have to depend on bows and arrows and war clubs. Moreover, they had no stores of ammunition. The British traders who still came among them might offer encouragement, but had only limited stocks. (Some of the most influential seem to have hoped to prevent hostilities, which would wreck their business.) British officials in the West Indies were slow to understand the situation; had they moved aggressively to contact and supply the disaffected Creek, the United States might have been hard put to handle the resulting rebellion.

Inevitably, as the tension among the younger warriors swelled, acts of violence erupted. "White" (pro-American) chiefs and subchiefs died, sometimes mysteriously enough for the new prophets to proclaim it evidence of the Great Spirit's anger. There also were occasional killings of white men. However, the elder chiefs had a police system of sorts and acted promptly to apprehend the killers. Not yet sure enough of their strength, the conspirators made no attempts to protect them.

The revolt, when it came, was from typically Indian causes. The Creek had sent Little Warrior, a rising younger chief, north to the Chickasaw on a routine intertribal diplomatic matter. Indians had a great deal of curiosity; having delivered his message, Little Warrior decided to have a look at the big war on the lakes. He and the six warriors escorting him joined Tecumseh and took part in the River Raisin massacre. They also conferred with Procter's staff, one of whom gave them a letter to the Spanish officials at Pensacola, apparently requesting that they assist the Creek with weapons and munitions. Tecumseh also promised to aid a Creek revolt as soon as Fort Meigs had been taken, but warned them not to begin any open hostilities before he arrived. However, the River Raisin slaughter had infected these Creek with a lust to kill. On their way home in early February, they paused just north of the Ohio River to butcher two unsuspecting white families, then went on across Chickasaw territory bragging of their exploits and flaunting scalps and booty they had taken. One would boast that he had grown fat eating white men's flesh.[11]

Reporting to the senior chiefs of the Upper Creek, Little Warrior declared that he brought "talks" (messages) from the British and Tecumseh. They listened, then rebuked him and ordered him from their council. Shortly thereafter they received Hawkins' demand that Little Warrior and his companions be turned over to the American authorities to stand

11. Cannibalism, especially a semi-ritual type during warfare, was occasionally practiced by northern tribes.

trial. The elder chiefs decided it would be simpler to execute them themselves; their police ran the seven down and shot or tomahawked them all.
That rough justice temporarily stunned the conspirators, and the chiefs
concluded that they had squashed any possible rebellion.

The prophets, however, soon redoubled their efforts. By early June of
1813, these had become so obvious, especially in the Alabama town,[12]
that the chiefs felt obliged to order the prophets there either to prove
their assertions of divine favor or else cease from troubling. The Alabama
killed their messenger and sent his scalp through the Upper Creek towns,
which promptly exploded. Of the thirty-four of them, twenty-nine took
up the "red stick" (war club), the traditional Creek sign of war. The old
chiefs had to flee for their lives; their police were killed or driven away.
The remaining "white" towns were assailed, and all possible white man's
artifacts destroyed. The Lower Creek towns along the Georgia frontier
remained at least outwardly peaceable, being under Hawkins' immediate eye.

Many of the chiefs and subchiefs were men of mixed blood, Spanish, French, Scots, and English traders and officials having taken Creek
wives for almost a century. Quite a few of them were well educated and
had grown wealthy, with plantations, orchards, herds, and slaves. But
such possessions might seem of little importance at this time. William
Weatherford, seven-eighths white, wealthy and respected, took up the
red stick.[13] So did Peter McQueen, an influential half-breed. McQueen
somehow had come into possession of the letter to the commandant at
Pensacola which Little Warrior had brought from Malden. With a party
of over 100 warriors he rode down to Pensacola in July to see if it would
help him purchase ammunition. The Spanish governor there found them
itchy visitors, half-pleading, half-threatening. Finally, under the pretext
that he merely wished to give his Creek friends ammunition for hunting
game to feed their hungry families, he provided them with approximately
a half-ton of gunpowder, some lead, and a few blankets, and undoubtedly
felt vast relief when they departed.

Since there were always Americans visiting Pensacola, the news of
McQueen's embassy spread rapidly through the American settlements
north of Mobile. A militia officer, Colonel James Caller, hurriedly gath-

12. The Alabama were a non-Creek member of the league, reputedly the survivors
of an older, more complex culture.

13. There is a claim that he did it only because the prophets' faction held his wife
and child hostage.

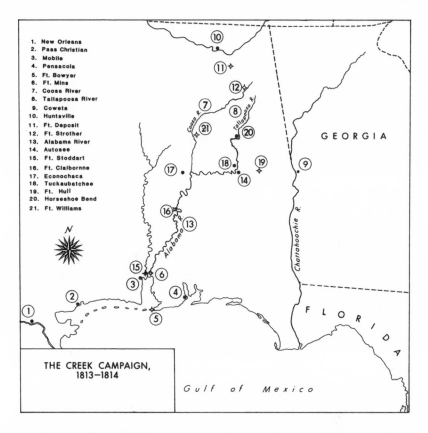

1. New Orleans
2. Pass Christian
3. Mobile
4. Pensacola
5. Ft. Bowyer
6. Ft. Mins
7. Coosa River
8. Tallapoosa River
9. Coweta
10. Huntsville
11. Ft. Deposit
12. Ft. Strother
13. Alabama River
14. Autosee
15. Ft. Stoddart
16. Ft. Claibornne
17. Econochaca
18. Tuckaubatchee
19. Ft. Hull
20. Horseshoe Bend
21. Ft. Williams

N

GEORGIA

Coosa R.

Tallapoosa R.

Chattahoochie R.

Alabama R.

FLORIDA

THE CREEK CAMPAIGN,
1813–1814

Gulf of Mexico

ered some 180 available men, more of a posse than a military organization, and rode to intercept him. It is not certain that McQueen's band
considered themselves at war with the United States, or it may have been
the common Indian carelessness of security when not actually on the
warpath, but whatever the reason, McQueen traveled without scouts.
On July 27 Caller caught his column halted astride Burnt Corn Creek,
some eighty miles north of Pensacola. Fewer than a dozen Red Sticks,
with most of the pack horses carrying the ammunition, were on the near
bank; a larger group had halted in a swampy wood across the creek, and
other warriors were scattered back along the trail. Pouncing suddenly, the
Americans scattered the pack horse drivers and seized the loaded horses.
Then, in the best militia fashion, they halted to argue over the division of
their booty. The Creek rallied in the woods across the stream and opened
fire. Though the Americans outnumbered the Creek, they promptly fled

in disorder. It was some time before the braver men could club together as a rear guard to discourage the pursuit. In this uproar the Creek recovered most of their pack horses, and collected at least two American scalps. Fifteen Americans were wounded. The Red Sticks had two killed and five hurt.

Exultant over his easy victory, McQueen prepared to settle some old scores. Some 553 whites, mixed bloods, friendly Indians, and Negro slaves, including a garrison of 70 Mississippi militiamen, had "forted up" at Fort Mims on the east bank of the Alabama River, approximately thirty-five miles north of Mobile. The fort was an improvised affair, a stockade enclosing Samuel Mims' large fortified house and several smaller buildings. This area, roughly an acre in extent, was divided by a lighter palisade into two enclosures, the larger of which had gates in its eastern and western walls. The garrison commander was a Major Daniel Beasley, who must have been an incompetent lout. Though ordered to build one or two blockhouses to provide flanking fire along the outer faces of the stockade and serve as strong points if the stockade were breached, he did nothing, not even bothering to complete the one blockhouse that he had begun. No sentries were posted, the gates stood open. Eventually drifting sand banked up against the eastern gate.

When slaves tending cattle outside the fort reported seeing Indians in war paint, Beasley sent out a mounted patrol. Red Stick Creek, hiding in the woods along the Mobile road, watched it ride past, its men talking with each other and overlooking tracks the Indians had left at a stream crossing. When another slave made the same report on August 30, Beasley had him tied up and whipped for raising a false alarm. The drummer then struck up his noon "Roast Beef" beat that signaled dinner, and the fort's inhabitants lost all interest in anything outside the stockade.

William Weatherford, now to be known as Red Eagle, had brought warriors to join McQueen, and probably had taken over leadership of the 750-or-so Red Sticks who had collected in the woods near Fort Mims. One story is that he and McQueen had a personal feud with Beasley and one Dixon Bailey, both of them also part white, who was a leader among the refugees in the fort.[14] Red Eagle's plan was simple and sensible. When he gave the signal for the attack, part of the Red Sticks would storm the open gates. Others would get control of the loopholes in the stockade

14. Bailey supposedly had been at Burnt Corn Creek. As an unrelated observation, any one-acre fort with 533 occupants (and quite a few domestic animals) during an Alabama summer must have reeked like the Dogpatch "skunk works."

and fire through them into the fort. The noon drumbeat apparently was the signal; the Red Sticks swarmed in, whooping and shooting. Beasley at least was no coward; sprinting to the east gate, he struggled to close it. It stuck in the sand, and Red Sticks smashed his skull. Their first rush captured the larger enclosure, but Bailey rallied some of the defenders in the smaller one, some of them firing through the loopholes of the interior palisade, others fighting for control of the loopholes in the outer one.

It was a frantic last stand; the Americans held out for at least an hour, inflicting considerable losses, until Red Eagle ordered the houses inside the enclosure set on fire. The flames spread swiftly. In desperation, some Americans cut away several logs of the outer palisade and made a dash for their lives. Favored by the clouds of smoke and the general confusion, some twenty got clear. Bailey was among them, but stumbling from a mortal wound. Most of the blacks were spared, since the Creek also practiced slaveholding. For the rest, there was death and mutilation. It took until September 9 for a party of Americans to gather the courage to visit the burned-out fort and bury the dead. They claimed to have found the bodies of over 100 Red Sticks, which, all in all, seems dubious.[15]

The Red Sticks went home laden with scalps and loot, but they had now to deal with an angry United States. The American strategy was a concentric advance by three columns, totaling at least 10,000 men, Pinckney moving eastward from Georgia, Flournoy from Mobile up the Alabama River, and Jackson southward from Tennessee. Their advance was to be methodical, building roads and forts to secure their communications, devastating the Creek's fields and towns. Their general objective was the fertile "Hickory Ground" where the Coosa and Tallapoosa rivers joined to form the Alabama (the general area of modern Montgomery, Alabama), the center of the Upper Creek towns. As the senior regular officer engaged, Pinckney would command the offensive.

In principle, this strategy was simple; in practice it constantly snagged on assorted difficulties, of which the Red Sticks frequently were the least. Each column would have to advance some 150 miles to reach the Hickory Ground. Pinckney's route was the easiest. Moving out of Georgia through the friendly Lower Creek towns, he could use the relatively good road from Hawkins' headquarter at Coweta (now Columbus, Georgia)

---

15. Numbers here, naturally, are fuzzy. The one certain fact is that Alonzo Chappel's famous painting, *Massacre at Fort Mims*, with its soldiers in immaculate full dress and beauteous ladies in full décolletage, as well as a blockhouse and cannon, is a triumph of the artistic imagination.

to New Orleans for most of his advance. However, Pinckney was also
responsible for the defense of North and South Carolina and Georgia,
and a large part of his regulars were scattered through various coastal
defenses. More important, he was little more than the simulacrum of a
functioning major general; elderly and kindly, he acted only with dig-
nified deliberation. Flournoy could use the Alabama River as a supply
route for his advance but he proved a difficult individual who had rapidly
antagonized the civilian population of Louisiana and had no knack for
handling militia. Jackson's offensive out of Tennessee must follow Indian
trails across the endless ridges of northern Alabama and Georgia.

All three columns would have to bring their own rations. Most of the
friendly Creek were little more than subsistence farmers and would have
little food to spare. This meant locating contractors willing to provide
the requisite beef, pork, flour, and whiskey, and a vast hiring of the boats,
wagons, and pack horses needed to move it. None of the states had an
effective logistic staff to superintend this work, and their contractors were
both inexperienced and unreliable.

Communication between the commanders was difficult from the first.
Because of the British blockade, Pinckney could not send messages to
Flournoy by ship; instead, they must go by courier across the Carolinas
and Tennessee and down the Mississippi to New Orleans.

But the crowning difficulty was the American militia system, with its
elected officers, consequent lack of discipline, and short terms of service, along with the everlasting politicking among senior officers in search
of future political advancement and the two-strange-dogs relationships
between militia from different states.

Even with these handicaps, the military task should have been simple.
Though McQueen had claimed during his visit to Pensacola that there
were 4,800 Red Sticks, it is doubtful that the actual number was even
2,500. (Of course their women and half-grown boys would fight beside
them in defense of their towns. Davy Crockett would tell of seeing a
squaw, seated on the threshold of a burning house, bend a bow with her
feet and put an arrow through a lieutenant at Crockett's side.) The Red
Sticks had neither a strategy of their own nor an acknowledged commander; their prophets continued to promise supernatural help and other
"fooleries," sometimes thwarting their war chiefs. Nor did the Indian
have any concept of a supply system. It was impossible for them to concentrate any large number of warriors at a distance from their home villages, because of the impossibility of feeding them for any length of time.

Consequently each town, or group of towns, had to fight for itself against much larger, better-armed American forces. Usually they remained passively on the defensive, not even attempting to raid the Americans' vulnerable supply trains.

The Tennessee troops were the first in the field, simply because Andrew Jackson commanded them. Though bedridden from wounds received in a public brawl, when the news of Fort Mims came to Nashville, he mustered 2,500 militia and volunteers and rode to the wars, one arm still in a sling. By October 12 he had reached the outlying settlement of Huntsville (now in Alabama), which would be the assembly area for his advance into Creek territory. In his impetuousness, however, he had made only the sketchiest arrangements for supplies; naturally they did not arrive. Sending General Coffee with his mounted men off to the southwest to forage, he took his infantry twenty-odd miles further to the southernmost loop of the Tennessee River. There he built Fort Deposit (near modern Guntersville) as his advanced supply depot, expecting to receive both supplies and Brigadier General John Cocke's division of 2,500 militia from eastern Tennessee. Neither came: the river was too low for cargo craft, and Cocke, deciding to be a conquering hero on his own account, had turned eastward.

Nonetheless, once Coffee returned, Jackson pushed ahead over the mountains some thirty-five miles farther to the upper Coosa River, vowing to "live on acorns" if he had to. This brought him within reach of a few small Creek towns, one of which, Talishatchee, was reputedly hostile. Jackson sent Coffee with his 900 cavalry to deal with it. Surrounding Talishatchee early on November 3, Coffee utterly destroyed the place after what he reported as a stubborn fight, killing an estimated 200 Indians out of a total population of 284. His own losses were only 5 men killed and 41 wounded, a number of them by arrows. Jackson's infantry meanwhile began a small post named Fort Strother, fifteen miles south of modern Gadsden. He still hoped for supplies and Cocke's division, but neither arrived. On November 7 an Indian runner came in from the friendly Creek town of Talladega, about thirty miles farther south, begging help against a large band (reportedly 1,000) of Red Sticks who were besieging the place. Ordering Brigadier General James White, who commanded the nearest element of Cocke's division, to move to Fort Strother to guard the sick and wounded there, Jackson marched the next day, reaching Talladega early on the 9th. En route, he received White's reply that Cocke had emphatically forbidden him to assist Jackson. Luring the

Red Sticks out of a defensive position, Jackson surrounded them; most of them, however, broke out and escaped. Jackson claimed at least 290 Indians killed; his own casualties were 15 killed and 85 wounded.

Thereafter Jackson hung on at Fort Strother, too proud to retreat, hoping always to receive the supplies and reinforcements that would enable him to renew his offensive. Racked by hunger and sickness—Jackson himself suffered from acute dysentery—his men grew resentful. By example, exhortation, and threats, Jackson kept them at the fort, using his volunteers to stop deserting militia, and the militia to check the volunteers when they wavered in their turn. On November 17 sheer starvation finally forced Jackson to give up. Twelve miles out of Fort Strother his homeward-bound division met the first supply convoy. Threatening instant death to the first man who disobeyed, Jackson drove his grumbling troops back to the fort. It was an amazing display of personal determination, but somewhat lacking in common sense, since Fort Strother was approximately 100 miles from the Hickory Ground and so neither a threat to the Red Sticks nor in any danger from them. Jackson could have left a detachment to hold it and taken the greater part of his division back to Fort Deposit and reasonably regular rations until his supply system was properly organized.

Meanwhile the war went on. Cocke had made his bid for eternal glory on November 18 by raiding a small village that was attempting to surrender to Jackson, but otherwise did nothing. On December 12, as Jackson finally allowed the greater part of his division to go home, Cocke at last arrived at Fort Strother with 1,450 "fine looking" troops whose term of service had almost expired.

Georgia had put an "army" of 940 militia, accompanied by more than 300 friendly Lower Creek warriors, into the field under Brigadier General John Floyd. Realizing that he lacked the resources for a sustained offensive, Floyd planned a hit-and-run raid against the large Red Stick town of Autossee on the Tallapoosa River, south of Tallassee. Moving out on November 24 with five days' rations, he reached Autossee unopposed on the 28th, and stormed and burned the town the next day with the loss of 11 men killed and 54 wounded, including Floyd himself. Red Stick killed were estimated, probably generously, at 200. That accomplished, Floyd retired to the Georgia frontier.

Flournoy launched the third attack from Fort Stoddart up the Alabama River with a mixed force of Mississippi militia and volunteers, Choctaw warriors, and the 3d U.S. Infantry Regiment under Brigadier General

Ferdinand L. Claiborne.[16] Eighty-five miles north of Fort Stoddart, Claiborne established an advance base named Fort Claiborne, then pushed on up the river to Econochaca, Red Eagle's town, also known as the "Holy Ground." The prophets had proclaimed the town was protected by an invisible barrier that would destroy any white man attempting to pass through it. After some miscellaneous shooting on December 23 the 3d Infantry went in with the bayonet, and the Red Sticks ran. Only some thirty of them were killed, but the town's capture and destruction was an appreciable wound to the prophets' reputations and Red Stick morale. Claiborne lost only one man, but isolated, far from any source of supply, his militia clamoring that their service soon would be up, he could only fall back to Fort Claiborne. He left Colonel Gilbert Russell there with the 3d Infantry, some 600 strong.

Unfortunately Flournoy's tender ego had been sadly wrenched by being placed under Pinckney. He proceeded to ignore the Creek campaign, at first even refusing to issue supplies to the 3d Infantry. An energetic, capable officer, Russell carried out a series of raids, clearing lower Alabama, largely cutting the Red Sticks off from Pensacola, and training a force of Choctaw and Chickasaw auxiliaries. Pinckney, however, could think of no better mission for him than to build boats, collect supplies, and prepare to move them up the Alabama River to feed the Tennessee and Georgia columns.

At Fort Strother Jackson's command had shrunk to 500 discontented men. The failure, expense, and hardship of his campaign had rather used up Tennessee's military ardor. The only response to Jackson's call for volunteers, or even conscription if necessary, was a letter from Governor Blount advising him to pull his remaining troops back into Tennessee. Jackson flatly refused. In a passionate letter he stormed at Blount's apparent yielding to the "whims of the populace," urged him to do his duty regardless of political consequences, and painted an amazing picture of what would happen should he "retrograde" from Strother. Five thousand Choctaw, Cherokee, and hitherto friendly Creek, Jackson prophesied, would join the Red Sticks. Tennessee's frontier would be "drenched in blood." Mobile would be lost. It was effective propaganda, self-serving and wildly exaggerated, but perfectly sincere. Andrew Jackson utterly believed that ending this Creek uprising, clear through to the seizure of Pensacola, was his own predestined duty.

16. Claiborne's commission was in the militia of the Mississippi Territory.

Blount was also hearing, politely, from Pinckney and, less politely, from Secretary of War Armstrong. Tennessee had pledged to keep 3,500 men in the field until the rebellion was crushed, and Blount was expected to comply. On January 14, 1814, when the Fort Strother garrison had shrunk to 130 men, approximately 800 militia, enlisted for only sixty days, appeared as a stopgap reinforcement. On the 17th Jackson marched south again with every available man, some 930 in all, and over 200 friendly Creek and Cherokee. His objective was a cluster of Red Stick towns in the upper Tallapoosa River, near modern Alexander City. Meanwhile Floyd, in the first coordinated offensive of the campaign, was moving west with some 1,300 Georgia militia and 400 Lower Creek against the Hickory Ground town of Tuckaubatchee, near Montgomery, approximately forty miles south of Jackson's target.

Jackson's force quickly showed itself unsteady and unreliable. It beat off a Red Stick attack on its camp in the small hours of January 22, but Coffee found the nearest Indian encampment too strongly held to risk an attack. The Red Stick attacked again that afternoon and were barely repulsed, three-fourths of Coffee's men refusing to follow him in an attempt to outflank the attackers. Coffee was badly wounded and his faithful handful cut off until their Indian allies rescued them. Jackson claimed a victory and forty-five Red Sticks killed, but started back to Fort Strother the next morning. He handled his retreat with care, but while making a difficult crossing of Enotachopco Creek on January 24 a rearguard squabble stampeded the whole force. Only the courage of a few officers saved it.[17] Jackson regained Fort Strother on the 29th, having lost a total of twenty-four men killed and seventy-one wounded, and concentrated on forming a new army.

Floyd had advanced slowly, building a rough fort at each night's halt. The night of January 26 he camped eight miles south of Tuckaubachee, naming his fortification "Camp Defiance." Red Eagle had collected possibly 1,000 warriors to meet this threat to their heartland. Before first light the next morning he struck shrewdly at Floyd's position[18] and was repulsed only after hard fighting. Thirty-seven Red Stick dead were left

---

17. Just how many Indians were involved in this fighting is anyone's guess. Coffee estimated them at 800 to 1,000, which would indicate no more than 500. The stampede at Enotachopco Creek probably was caused by a small war party; had the Red Sticks been there in strength, Jackson might have gone down in history with Braddock and Custer.

18. Apparently the prophets upset Red Eagle's plan. There is no certainty as to just which prophet or chief—if anyone at all—directed this attack.

on the field; Floyd lost 22 whites and friendly Indians killed and 147 wounded. This was quite enough for the Georgia militia, who announced their intention of going home, whether Floyd came with them or not. Consequently he retired into Georgia, abandoning all his forts except for Fort Hull (five miles southeast of modern Tuskegee, Alabama), where he left Colonel Homer V. Milton with a handful of regulars and volunteers from the militia. Operating with regulars and Indian allies, Milton swept the countryside, while organizing an efficient supply system, preparatory for a methodical advance into the Hickory Ground.

So far, the Red Sticks had held their ground. Except for Autossee and Econochaca, none of their important towns had been destroyed. They probably still had 2,000 warriors under arms; Americans estimated that 1,000 had been killed or disabled, but half that number probably would have been closer to the truth. As their last clash with Floyd had shown, they were developing combat skills. On the other hand, they had very little ammunition and few serviceable firearms left, and were running dangerously short of food.

Though he was too much of a gentleman of the old school to put things so baldly, Pinckney obviously decided that the Georgia militia were (as a later regular said of Arkansas cavalrymen) "dangerous only to cripples and sick women." Reinforcing Milton with more regulars and militia from North and South Carolina, and ordering the 39th Infantry Regiment to join Jackson, he prepared for a final offensive. Milton and Russell were to coordinate their movements with Jackson's.

Much battered by appeals and orders, Governor Blount had rallied to the occasion and ordered out 5,000 Tennessee militia for six months' service. They converged on Fort Strother, griping over their required length of service and all the other awful injustices being inflicted on free American citizens. Their officers frequently encouraged their insubordination. Jackson did not intend to endure any more such unmilitary nonsense. He had always opposed the militia practice of electing their field grade officers, insisting on "Men Capable of Command—who will fight and reduce their soldiers to strict obedience." So far he had had little support, beyond a few friends like Coffee. But now orders were enforced. The 39th was one of the 1813 one-year regiments, raised in Tennessee and never before in action. However, its officers seem to have been above average; its discipline and conduct were an example the militia badly needed. So backed, Jackson rapidly whipped his army into shape. When his second-in-command, the egregious Cocke, actually encouraged a mutiny among his men, Jackson had him arrested. A militia brigadier general suffered the same disposition. And, to the utter astonishment of the entire army, a militia private was shot for mutiny. That done, Jackson marched out to resume his January campaign against the upper Tallapoosa towns. He had approximately 5,000 militia and regulars, with 600 friendly Creek and Cherokee. Sending the 39th and his reserve supplies down the Coosa River in boats to its junction with Cedar Creek, where rapids made further water transport impossible, Jackson moved parallel to the river with his militia, cutting a road as he advanced. At Cedar Creek he built Fort Williams as an advance base, then turned eastward to the Horseshoe Bend of the Tallapoosa,[19] where Red Sticks were reported concentrating. After detaching a garrison for Fort Williams, Jackson had something over 3,000 regulars and militia, his Indian allies, and two light guns.

Undoubtedly overconfident from their earlier success, most of the Red Sticks in the area had fortified themselves at the Horseshoe Bend, a rugged, narrow-necked peninsula about 100 acres in extent, building a concave wall of big horizontal logs, pierced with two levels of loopholes, across the neck of the peninsula.[20] Something over 700 Red Stick warriors manned this breastwork; a roughly equal number of women and children were hidden in caves along the banks of the river. Canoes had been collected to furnish a means of escape if the breastwork were overrun. By a major oversight, no warriors were placed to defend the riverside.

Jackson reached the Bend on March 28. The next morning he moved to surround the Horseshoe. "Determined," as he put it, "to exterminate them," he sent Coffee with his 700 mounted men and the Indian auxiliaries across the river, and brought his infantry and guns against the breastwork. Even at only 200 yards' range the guns (a 6-pounder and a 3-pounder) could not break up the massive logs but, profiting from the diversion they created, the Cherokee allies swam the river and carried off the canoes. Using these, about 200 Indians and white scouts crossed and occupied some high ground in rear of the breastwork, from which they could take its defenders under fire. That accomplished, Jackson ordered the 39th forward.

Resistance was savage. Major Lemuel Montgomery, the first man onto the breastwork, was shot dead; Ensign Samuel Houston, the first across it, was badly wounded; two lieutenants killed. But the regulars stormed

19. Ten miles east of Alexander City.
20. The design of the wall was remarkably clever, permitting the Red Sticks to catch any assault in a crossfire, while making it impossible for American artillery to enfilade it.

across the logs, bayonets and musket butts clearing the way through war clubs and tomahawks until the Red Sticks broke and scattered—to rally, to fight to the death, to be hunted down in the gullies and thickets of the Horseshoe's interior. Mopping up lasted into the night. One clump of Red Sticks defending a log shelter spurned an offer of quarter and were burned out. When it was over, 557 dead were counted; an unknown number had gone into the river, some of them, possibly 200, escaping. Approximately 500 squaws and children were captured. (In what must have been one of the understatements of the century, Jackson's report regretted that "two or three" women and children had been accidently killed.) His own losses showed who had fought and won the battle: the 39th had 20 killed and 52 wounded, the Cherokee and Creek 23 killed and 46 hurt, while the militia, who made up two-thirds of Jackson's forces, suffered 8 killed and 52 wounded.[21]

It had been a notable killing, but the Hickory Ground Red Sticks were still unhurt. Jackson returned to Fort Williams where he spent five days regrouping, then started down the Coosa. On April 15 he met elements of the Georgia column. Milton's methodical advance had reached the area in early April; he had built Fort Decatur near the rivers' junction and accumulated a small reserve of supplies, which was fortunate for Jackson who had used up his own. Both commands then faced lean pickings until Russell worked his way upriver with more rations.

The Americans might be short of salt pork, but they had a surplus of commanding officers. Neither Milton nor Russell would take orders from Jackson, since he was not a regular. As an additional dignitary, Brigadier General Joseph Graham of the Carolina militia was also present. Pinckney solved that problem by coming forward and assuming command in person. The way was now clear for a final roundup of the most fanatical Red Sticks.

The Red Sticks had not waited for Pinckney. A few surrendered. Red Eagle, become once again William Weatherford, walked boldly into Jackson's headquarters and gave himself up, asking only that refugee women and children hiding in the woods be found and fed. Utterly brave himself, Jackson respected courage in an enemy. He stood Weatherford a drink, shook his hand, and let him go. But McQueen and almost all of the leading chiefs and prophets retreated into Spanish territory and stood ready to continue the war. From Lower Creek and British accounts, they could muster at least 1,000 still unbeaten warriors.

21. Some eighty of the wounded died in the wagons or the Fort William hospital.

Their hatred for the United States soon was intensified by the treaty that Jackson, under Armstrong's authority, imposed on the friendly Creek, many of whom had just served with him against the Red Sticks. Jackson stripped his former comrades of at least half of their territory. His strategic justification was that the Creek must be separated from Spanish territory and their Seminole kinsmen, and also from the Choctaw and Chickasaw to the west. The Creek protested vainly. Thereafter a good many of them listened to British agents who had been working out of Pensacola since at least September, 1813. By July, 1814, the British there were furnishing refugee Red Sticks with weapons and clothing.

Taken in its entirety, the Creek campaign had been a collection of bungles and bobbles. Once again logistical difficulties, the uselessness of militia for sustained operations, and the lack of competent generals had resulted in half-successes at great cost. Between Flournoy's pettiness and Pinckney's obtuseness, Russell's strong regiment had been wasted. Had he been reinforced for a drive up the New Orleans/Coweta road, the retreating Red Sticks could have been intercepted. Jackson had displayed energy and pugnacity, but no particular understanding of strategy or logistics. He soon would have a chance to show what, if anything, the campaign had taught him.

American soldiers, 1805–11: uniforms, West Point cadet, engineer private, enlisted men in fatigue dress.—*H. Charles McBarron, Jr.; American Soldier series, Army Historical Program*

American soldiers, 1814: uniforms, general and staff officer, rifle regimental officer, northern frontier.—*H. Charles McBarron, Jr.; American Soldier series, Army Historical Program*

Hull's march to Detroit, 1812, 4th U.S. Infantry Regiment.
—*H. Charles McBarron, Jr.; West Point Museum*

Springfield flintlock musket, model 1795, used by U.S. infantry and artillery during the War of 1812.—*Author's collection*

Regular light dragoons in combat, Mississiniway River, Indiana Territory, 1812.—
Liliane and Fred Funcken, L'uniforme et les armes des soldats des Etats-Unis, II (Tournai: Casterman, 1980)

U.S. naval detachment, Marquesas Islands, 1814.—*Colonel Charles H. Waterhouse, USMCR; Marines in the Frigate Navy, History and Museums Division, U.S. Marine Corps, 1985*

USS *Constitution* captures HMS *Guerrière*, August 19, 1812.—*Engraving by James D. Smillie after Alonzo Chappel, c. 1860; U.S. Naval Historical Center*

Shipbuilding at Sackets Harbor, New York, January 11, 1814.— *Colonel Charles H. Waterhouse, USMCR; Marines in the Frigate Navy, History and Museums Division, U.S. Marine Corps, 1985*

"Remember the River Raisin!" Battle of the Thames, October 5, 1813.—*Ken Riley; National Guard Heritage, National Guard Bureau*

John Hebden (1779–1852),
adjutant of the Canadian
Voltigeurs, Chateauguay, 1813.
—*Public Archives of Canada,
Ottawa*

Swamp ambush, St. Augustine, Florida, September 11, 1812.—*Colonel Charles H. Waterhouse, USMCR; Marines in the Frigate Navy, History and Museums Division, U.S. Marine
Corps, 1985*

"Regulars, by God!" Battle of Chippewa, July 5, 1814.—*H. Charles McBarron, Jr.; West Point Museum*

Rocket detachment, Royal Marine Artillery, 1814: officer (left), sergeant (center), and gunner.—*Eric Manders; Company of Military Historians*

"Our flag was still there." Star-Spangled Banner flying over Fort McHenry, as viewed by Francis Scott Key, 1814.—*Artist's conception by Percy Moran; Peale Museum, Baltimore, Maryland*

Commodore Barney's final stand at Bladensburg, Maryland, August 24, 1814.—*Colonel Charles H. Waterhouse, USMCR; Marines in the Frigate Navy, History and Museums Division, U.S. Marine Corps, 1985*

Battle of North Point, Maryland, September 12, 1814.—*Don A. Troiani; National Guard Heritage, National Guard Bureau*

Major General Alexander Macomb.—*Thomas Sully; West Point Museum*

Bombardment of Stonington, August 9, 1814.—*Painting by G. B. Mitchell; Mystic Seaport Museum*

Attack and capture of the American flotilla on Lake Borgne, December, 1814.—*Oil on canvas by T. L. Hornbrook; Chicago Historical Society and National Gallery of Art; photograph by U.S. Naval Historical Center*

ELEVEN

Regulars, by God!

The British, swear by St. George *and the* Virgin Mary, *they never met such a dd bloody Minded set of fellows as those Yankees are—they march up against double their number of his majesties best troops as at their exercise—that the devils,* even take deliberate aim *and that his Majesties Officers can not take the field on horse back—without being Murdered outright.*

—George Howard [1]

THE MISERY OF GENERAL JAMES WILKINSON'S command at French Mills —riddled by diarrhea, dysentery, pneumonia, typhus, and frostbite— came to an end in late January when John Armstrong ordered him to send Jacob Brown with 2,000 men to Sackets Harbor and move the rest of his command back to Plattsburg. The order was explicit, specifying even Wilkinson's order of march, and leaving him no discretion whatever. This withdrawal shortened the army's supply lines, with consequent improvement in its rations and living conditions. Also a new hospital, excellent for that period, was opened in Burlington for the 450 seriously ill or disabled soldiers then suffering in makeshift accommodations at Malone.

This American withdrawal from French Mills was followed up by Lieutenant Colonel Hercules Scott of the 103d Foot with a picked force of regulars and militia. Scott clashed briefly with the last Americans to leave French Mills; raided into Malone where he paroled those Americans who, too sick to be moved, had been left in the hospital; burned abandoned camps; and picked up some supplies. It was not exactly a heroic exploit, but excellent for British morale. Other parties heckled

1. George Howard Papers, Connecticut Historical Society, p. 116. Howard was an American officer.

American outposts and communications, playing deadly games of tag with American patrols.[2]

Wilkinson had hoped to shift his headquarters to Albany, suggesting that he would be very useful there, training new recruits; Armstrong, probably with malice aforethought, kept him with him with his troops in Plattsburg. Aware that he was likely to be relieved because of his bungling of the Montreal campaign, Wilkinson spent much time planning Napoleonic offensives against Kingston, Prescott, Cornwall, and other posts, all of them requiring soldiers, supplies, and transportation that simply did not exist. But in late March he finally found a target that seemed as helpless as the Spanish garrison at Fort Charlotte. Some five miles beyond the Canadian frontier, where the road north from Champlain through Odelltown to Ile aux Noix and St. Jean crossed the Lacolle River, the British had converted a large stone mill into an outpost. Its garrison numbered only some 180 regulars, militia, and marines; the nearest support would be the garrison of Ile aux Noix, about ten miles of snow-choked road farther north. Accordingly Wilkinson sallied forth from Plattsburg on March 27 with 4,000 men and eleven guns. His officers and men were admonished to "return victorious or not at all." Picked sergeants were designated to shoot down any soldier who broke ranks and ran. Floundering through deep snow, and somehow taking the wrong road, the Americans finally reached Lacolle Mill in the early afternoon of March 30. Moving up to within 150 yards of the building, they opened fire, first with musketry, then with artillery. The garrison shot back, somewhat more effectively; the sturdy building withstood the pounding of American cannon. Alerted by the firing, the Ile aux Noix garrison struggled through the woods to the rescue but was beaten off, apparently by Alexander Macomb's brigade. The shooting went on for over two hours. Though the mill still stood, its weary garrison was almost out of ammunition. But Wilkinson's tiny stock of courage dwindled even faster. It was getting dark; the weather looked threatening; more British reinforcements might be coming. Instead of at least attempting to storm the mill, he ordered a retreat.[3] The Americans went trailing miserably back to Plattsburg. On April 11 Wilkinson received orders relieving him of his command. Macomb took over the Ninth Military District until May 1 when Izard

2. Congressional fiddling with the Army in early 1814 consisted of authorizing three more rifle regiments and consolidating the 1st, 2d, and 3d artillery regiments into a "Corps of Artillery." The two light dragoon regiments were also combined into one.

3. I have found no positive casualty figures for this action.

returned from leave. Like Dearborn, Wilkinson could not comprehend any reason for his relief. In his *Memoirs* he wailed that Armstrong had by "artifices . . . deprived me of my sword in the dawn of the campaign." [4]

The secretary of war, meanwhile, was waging a campaign of his own in Washington. The fortunes of battle and their own obvious incompetence had proven most of the Army's general officers incapable of commanding troops in action. He therefore at last had an opportunity to purge the service, replacing them with men of demonstrated valor and ability. Wilkinson was shelved to await trial; Morgan Lewis and John Boyd were given figurehead rear-area assignments; Wade Hampton resigned, and some judicious heckling irritated William Henry Harrison into doing the same. The two new major generals were George Izard and Jacob Brown, the first selected for his military education and skill as an organizer and disciplinarian, the second for his pugnacity. The new brigadier generals had all been regular colonels: Macomb, Winfield Scott, Edmund P. Gaines, Eleazer W. Ripley, Daniel Bissell, and Thomas A. Smith.[5] When Harrison resigned, Andrew Jackson, originally marked for a brigadier general's commission, was also made a major general. These promotions gave the Army an energetic, competent leadership that would endure to the beginning of the Civil War. Together with the embryonic general staff he had organized in March, 1813, they were Armstrong's major services to the United States.

At the same time, the failure of the 1813 campaign and the ravaging of the Niagara frontier had weakened Armstrong's personal authority. Secretary of State James Monroe's nagging, reinforced by the opinions of other members of the cabinet, finally got Madison to assert himself. Armstrong's orders to the military district commanders must be submitted for the President's (meaning, indirectly, Monroe's) approval. All future strategic plans must be considered by the President and his cabinet. The basic concept of these directives, that Armstrong was the President's executive and not a free agent responsible only to himself, was correct. But the President's and his cabinet's individual and collective unfamiliarity with military matters made them simply a clog on any effective action.

It was a time demanding clear thinking and decisive action. On March

---

4. Wilkinson had requested a court of inquiry to review his Montreal campaign. Being headed by Dearborn and Lewis, it naturally found his conduct spotless.

5. Smith's service was chiefly in the West; in 1815 he commanded the Territories of Missouri and Illinois. Bissell was competent, but had no real chance to distinguish himself. He had entered the Army in 1791 as a cadet.

31, while Wilkinson was making his draggletailed retreat from Canada, the allied armies of Prussia, Austria, Russia, and a half-dozen minor German states, all subsidized by the British treasury, marched into Paris. Napoleon would abdicate on April 6. Thus freed from its major war, England had troops, ships, and even money to expend on lambasting ungrateful, upstart America into a proper state of submission. Sixteen veteran regiments were ordered to Canada;[6] six more were designated for diversionary raids along the eastern and southern coasts of the United States.

Sir James Prevost soon had some 12,000 troops around Montreal, but found his strategic options tightly limited by the usual logistical problems. These difficulties, moreover, were greatly intensified by Commander James Yeo's shipbuilding, which came close to monopolizing the transport service between Montreal and Kingston. Prevost hoped to launch a powerful offensive against Sackets Harbor, but found it impossible to move the necessary supplies to Kingston. In Upper Canada, Sir Gordon Drummond had to subsist on local resources and what small shipments could be filtered through the cargoes of heavy guns and ships' fittings that were consigned to Yeo.[7] Drummond had planned an elaborate winter campaign against Detroit but had been thwarted by an early thaw. Now it was increasingly evident that he would face an American offensive on the Niagara front.

Armstrong still hoped for an offensive against Kingston, combined with a feint at Niagara to split Drummond's forces. Scott had been ordered to Albany to take command of a strong brigade of militia that Tompkins proposed to raise in order to secure the Niagara frontier. Armstrong drew up two sets of orders. One, the contents of which he "leaked" discreetly, directed Brown to recover Fort Niagara and Fort George. The other, carefully kept secret, ordered the capture of Kingston. As in his directions to Hampton the previous year, Armstrong may have failed to make his intentions perfectly clear, or it may very well have been that Brown, lacking both a military education and extensive experience, simply did not recognize Armstrong's obvious intent. Whatever the reason, Brown concluded that he had been given two equally acceptable alternate plans,

6. The 3d, 5th, 6th, 9th, 16th, 27th, 37th, 39th, 57th, 58th, 76th, 81st, 82d, 88th, 90th, and 97th regiments of Foot. The 13th, 89th, and Watteville regiments had arrived during 1813, as well as the 2d Battalion of the 41st Foot.

7. This is one "influence of seapower" that Admiral Alfred T. Mahan somehow overlooked in his studies.

and that he was to select the one more suited to his forces and the existing situation. So believing, he naturally consulted Isaac Chauncey.

Chauncey was once again holed up in Sackets Harbor, feverishly building more and bigger ships to counter recent additions to Yeo's squadron, which he believed now much superior to his own. (Actually that superiority was mostly one of Yeo's clever bluffs, but Chauncey was *not* going to risk his precious ships by putting out to personally determine what Yeo's real strength might be.) He gave Brown his standard sad story on the impossibility of attacking Kingston with the forces they then had available, so Brown gathered his troops and marched for the Niagara front on March 14.

En route, Edmund P. Gaines looked over Brown's orders, immediately understood Armstrong's intentions, and explained them convincingly to Brown. Letting his command go on to Buffalo, Brown made a fast ride back to Sackets Harbor, but found Chauncey absolutely obdurate. He would not stir out of Sackets Harbor until his new ships were ready for action, possibly in July. He was not going to attack Kingston; Brown might as well run along and see what he could do at Niagara. And so Chauncey remained in his den, blockaded by a force scarcely, if at all, stronger than his own. In early May, he came close to losing the guns and equipment for his new frigates when Yeo and Drummond struck at Oswego and Yeo hounded his supply convoys, but none of that moved him to risk a single ship.

The Army had its own preparations to make. Disgusted by the inefficiency of most of his regular regiments, Armstrong had responded to the pleas of some of his more competent officers and authorized the establishment of a "camp of instruction" at Buffalo, where Brown's army was to be properly trained and disciplined before being committed to action. (Izard was to do the same at Plattsburg.) Hitherto such matters had been largely left to the individual regimental commanders, who might or might not be competent. They frequently had very different ideas as to which infantry drill manual to follow, and often no idea at all of military hygiene. Armstrong having designated Winfield Scott to head the Buffalo camp, Brown remained in his official district headquarters at Sackets Harbor. He was an expert hater, and Chauncey provided him infinite opportunity to perfect that talent during the next few months.

Scott's camp of instruction would become something of a legend, which Scott himself—an enfeebled old soldier remembering young days of glory—certainly helped to burnish. He did not, as legend asserts, form his officers into an oversized awkward squad and drill them personally. By now, most of them were competent men, hard-tested by two years of war. Any "butterflies"[8] remaining among them were quickly taught the responsibilities that went with their rank. From his own experience Scott knew that there was nothing wrong with the American soldier: given proper training and leadership he could thrash redcoats and redskins alike. What he gave the "Left Division" (so Brown designated his command) was intense, uniform instruction, based on the excellent French 1791 drill regulations and designed to build a collection of individual regiments into an efficient, tightly coordinated fighting army. Scott put special emphasis on what was then termed "police"—the art of keeping troops healthy. He was insistent that the camp be immaculate and that every known sanitary precaution be strictly maintained.[9] He also saw to the proper preparation of the men's rations, being a sworn foe of underbaked bread and the common American habit of frying everything.

Training was pushed for ten hours a day. Discipline was strict; deserters were apprehended and some were shot. Improvement was immediate and evident. Realizing that they were led by officers who knew what they were doing and how to take care of their men, the soldiers' morale and self-confidence blossomed. Their food was ample and good; their sick rate unusually low. Surgeons marveled that "strict discipline and rigid police" had "exorcised . . . even the demon diarrhoea"! Scott sedulously nursed this feeling with parades, reviews, and maneuvers designed to let every man admire his own growing proficiency. In only one matter was he thwarted; he could not obtain proper blue uniforms for his men. These had been shipped, for once, in plenty of time, but Wilkinson, probably out of spite, and Brown, out of ignorance of the Army's supply system, had diverted them to Plattsburg and Sackets Harbor.[10] In the end Commissary General Callender Irvine had to have 2,000 uniforms hastily made up and sent directly to Buffalo. There being insufficient blue cloth on hand, short gray jackets were substituted.

8. Officers who were constantly flitting off to Washington or state capitals to intrigue for promotion through political influence.

9. Intelligent officers and surgeons of 1814 might be ignorant of microbiology, but they did comprehend the importance of personal cleanliness and the proper management of latrines, garbage pits, and watering points. Scott was unusually insistent on such precautions.

10. See David H. Schneider, "Gray Uniforms on the Niagara," *Military Collector and Historian*, Vol. XXXIII, No. 4 (Winter, 1981), pp. 170–72. Enough blue uniforms seem to have been located here and there to clothe the 21st Infantry.

From late March to late June, Brown seems to have had only one large problem, and that from the western edge of his district. Acting on his own authority, Colonel John Campbell raided across Lake Erie, burning Port Dover and a good many farmhouses, to the accompaniment of extensive looting.[11] Brown had him brought before a court of inquiry, which contented itself with reprimanding him for displaying bad judgment. In contrast to Riall's ravagings of Black Rock and Buffalo, apparently no civilians suffered bodily harm, but Campbell's incursion still was an exercise of needless brutality, considerably condemned by his own troops. It was to produce overwhelming retaliation.

With an efficient little army under organization at Niagara, and Chauncey resolutely refusing to join it in an attack on Kingston, Armstrong looked about for some other mission for it. The Americans still had undisputed control of Lake Erie. Using the fleet there, he proposed on April 30 to land a force of 6,000 to 8,000 men to the west of Fort Erie and move on Burlington. This would be sufficient to overwhelm Drummond. If Prevost shifted troops west from Montreal to reinforce him, the Sackets Harbor garrison and Izard might be able to cut them off. To further strengthen Brown, Armstrong proposed to send him most of the regulars, approximately 900 infantry and two companies of artillery, in the Detroit/St. Louis area.

Madison and his cabinet haggled this proposal. There were two valid objections to it. First, it was unfortunately evident that the 3,000 or so additional volunteers and militia required could not be raised. Second, the Lake Erie squadron was in poor condition and probably unfit for a major operation. Between Chauncey and Yeo, few supplies had been getting through to it. Also, Navy Secretary Jones had somehow developed a mania for recovering Mackinac Island. Madison and the cabinet, possibly influenced as much by a desire to thwart Armstrong as by Jones's arguments, decreed that the Detroit troops must be used for that purpose. Having thus weakened Brown, the cabinet decided that he should forthwith invade Canada and capture Burlington Heights and York. Chauncey promised to be ready by July 1 to support this movement, though Jones thought July 15 a likelier date.

Armstrong thereupon suggested that Brown use the weeks before Chauncey would be ready by taking Fort Erie and establishing a bridgehead across the Chippewa River. Brown was more than willing; moreover

11. This was the worst of a series of raids and counterraids from Sandwich east to Port Dover. See Stanley, *The War of 1812*, pp. 275–81.

he intended to push his offensive as far as possible. On June 21 he therefore sent Chauncey a sharp-edged letter, accusing him of noncooperation and demanding that he be off Fort George by July 10 to join Brown in an attack on that stronghold.

Brown's forces were lean enough. Scott's brigade, composed of the 9th, 11th, 22d, and 25th infantry regiments, had only 1,377 officers and men out of an authorized strength of over 4,000 present for duty on July 1. Ripley's small brigade, made up of the 21st and 23d regiments, numbered 1,028.[12] The four companies of artillery,[13] grouped as a battalion under Major Jacob Hindman, reported 327 officers and men for duty.

With these 2,732 regulars came Peter B. Porter's brigade of volunteers and Indians, which that ambitious gentleman had been struggling for months to raise, in high hopes that he might be given command of the Army. However, New Yorkers were slow to turn out, and Porter had difficulty equipping those who did appear. Disgruntled over being ranked by Scott, of whom he was intensely jealous, and Ripley, he had the further disappointment of being able to bring only 753 Pennsylvania Volunteers to join Brown, along with possibly 600 Indians. The latter were the fighting strength of the Iroquois federation, except for the Mohawk who were, as always, hostile to the United States. Their "commander-in-chief" was Hog-A-Hoa-Qua, known to whites as La Fort. Other chiefs were the famous Red Jacket, Cornplanter, Two Guns, and I-Like-Her.[14]

Once the threat to Montreal had evaporated, Prevost had begun reinforcing Sir Gordon Drummond. Kingston, York, and Burlington Heights were well garrisoned; in addition, Drummond could concentrate approximately 4,000 regulars, plus militia and Indians, as a mobile force. Phineas Riall had some 2,300 of the regulars on the Niagara front, though part of them were tied down as garrisons for Fort George and Fort Niagara, which Drummond insisted be strongly held. One regiment, the unfortunate 8th Foot, which had spent a demoralizing winter in half-

12. Some 745 men were absent—recruiting parties, sick, AWOLs, and deserters. Ripley's brigade had 387 "absents." All six regiments were "northern," two from Massachusetts; one each from Connecticut, New York, Pennsylvania, and Vermont. In addition, there were possibly 100 regular cavalrymen.

13. All from the 2d Artillery Regiment. Company commanders were Captains Thomas Biddle, John Ritchie, Nathan Towson, and Alexander J. Williams.

14. Traditionally the Iroquois war chief had been a Mohawk. Since the Mohawk refused to serve, a special election was necessary to choose one. See W. W. Clayton, *A History of Onondaga Country* (D. Maso and Co., 1878).

ruinous Fort Niagara, had been ordered back to Lower Canada for rest and recuperation.

The British were short of equipment and on the verge of being short of rations. But their major weakness, as yet unrevealed, was the quality of their commanders. Riall was a short, plump, nearsighted Irishman, brave and bustling but without discernible intelligence or military skills. Years before he had seen a little combat in the West Indies, but as a general he had filled only rear-area assignments.[15] Drummond was a more commanding figure but almost equally inexperienced, having seen only brief sideshow campaigns in Holland and Egypt.[16] Both of these officers were quite cockalorum over their recent harrying of the west bank of the Niagara River. Drummond had assured Riall that American soldiers, no matter how numerous, would never have the skill and hardihood to stand against British regulars.

So eager that he would not postpone his offensive for one day even to have it launched on the 4th of July (but not too eager however to neglect a thorough preliminary reconnaissance), Brown passed the Niagara River in the first hours of July 3. Scott, with Hindman, came directly across through dark and rain from Black Rock, about a mile north of Fort Erie. Wading ashore under carbine fire from a British cavalry outpost, Scott stepped into an unexpected hole and almost drowned before he could be retrieved. Undeterred, he got his feet under him again and led his men in. Ripley's crossing, planned to bring him ashore south and west of the fort, was delayed by heavy fog so that he could not land until about sunrise. (As a prelude Ripley engaged Brown in a row over the fact that his brigade was smaller than Scott's; this climaxed with Ripley offering his resignation, and Brown telling him, in effect, to quit acting like a child and get on with the war.)[17]

Porter crossed after Ripley. Meanwhile, to confuse Riall and tie down as many of his troops as possible, a column of New York militia marched north from Buffalo and Black Rock with much martial show, as if to attack Fort Niagara or cross the river from Lewiston against Queenston.[18] By

---

15. He purchased a captain's commission in 1794, and had been on the shelf during 1797–1804 as a half-pay major. His promotions were by purchase or seniority.

16. Drummond had purchased his way up from second lieutenant to lieutenant colonel in less than three years. His promotions thereafter were by seniority.

17. There is evidence that Ripley thought the invasion a suicidal venture.

18. Major John Norton said this demonstration did trouble the British.

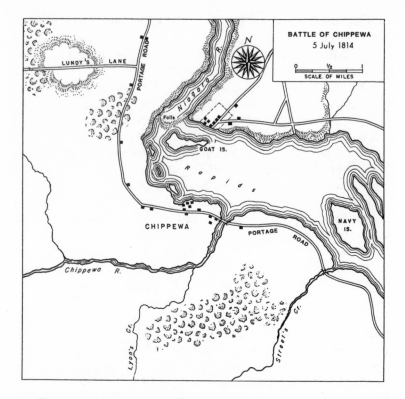

noon Brown had his 3,500 regulars and volunteers and several hundred Indians all ashore and converging on Fort Erie.

Even after two years of war, Fort Erie still was incomplete, being unfinished on the land side and consequently a mere trap once an enemy attack cut in behind it. Even so, Drummond had counted on it to check any American invasion long enough—apparently two or three days—for Riall to mass all his command to oppose it. Fort Erie's commander, Major Thomas Buck, did not share Drummond's rank optimism. He had only 137 soldiers, and an excellent chance of getting them killed very quickly if he attempted any pointless heroics. He fired a few guns "for the honor of the flag," then capitulated at 5:00 P.M.

Early the next morning Brown thrust northward, Scott's brigade leading. Riall had begun collecting troops, among others the 8th Foot, which had reached York only to be told to forget its promised rest and recreation. A Lieutenant Colonel Thomas Pearson, who had been stationed at Chippewa with the flank companies of the 100th Foot, meanwhile had hurried south to check the American advance. The numerous west-to-east streams that drained into the Niagara River gave him a series of delaying positions, at each of which he attempted to check Scott long enough to destroy the bridge. Scott, however, had field guns with his advance guard and had organized a picked force of pioneers.[19] Pearson was blasted out of one position after another before he could seriously damage the bridge; what harm he was able to do, such as tearing up floor boards, was quickly repaired. For sixteen miles this pursuit went fast enough to outdistance Ripley and Porter. Toward evening it reached the Chippewa River, beyond which Riall had thrown up light entrenchments and mustered some 2,100 regulars, militia, and Indians. Wide and swift-flowing, the Chippewa was a major obstacle. After studying Riall's position, Brown, who had come forward to join Scott, decided to outflank it by crossing the river farther to the west. Scott encamped for the night behind Street's Creek, a mile south of the Chippewa. Ripley's brigade and the rest of the artillery halted some distance south of Scott's camp after dark. Porter camped a considerable distance to the rear, and did not close up until the next morning.

Except for a narrow scrape Scott and his staff experienced with a party of Indians,[20] the 5th of July began fairly quietly. Brown and his engineer officers continued their reconnaissance, while Scott treated his brigade to a special, if delayed, 4th of July dinner. During the afternoon, however, Riall's Indians, followed by some Canadian militia, began filtering across the Chippewa and moving into a sizable woods that extended on either side of Street's Creek, to the west of Scott's camp. From this cover they sniped at his outposts and Brown's party. Eventually they became a nuisance and Brown ordered Porter to drive them off. Porter cleared the woods without difficulty. Then, coming out into the open near the Chippewa bridge, he found himself nose-to-nose with Riall, who had decided to sally forth and dispose of Brown's army without further shilly-shallying. Riall sent his light infantry companies against Porter's disordered command; the Indians and Pennsylvanians unhesitatingly launched a mass marathon run for Street's Creek. Witnessing this rout, Brown went spurring back to bring up Scott's brigade. He met it advancing across the Street's Creek bridge.

19. Infantrymen equipped and trained to function as combat engineers.

20. A Canadian farmer's wife, whose house, just north of Street's Creek, Scott had safeguarded, invited them to breakfast. By lucky accident, an aide-de-camp saw the Indians closing in. Possibly the kind lady had invited them, too.

Thick timber and brush along Street's Creek and the Chippewa hid Scott's and Riall's camps from their opposing outposts. Unaware of Riall's advance and Porter's repulse, Scott had decided to top off the day with a dress parade in the open fields along the Niagara River, between Street's Creek and the Chippewa, and he was moving out with that intent when he met Brown. Even with Brown's warning, he doubted that Riall would risk a major attack against the larger American army, but to be on the safe side he hurried Nathan Towson's artillery company forward with its three 12-pounders and brought his infantry on at the double.

Riall already had advanced into the open area. His artillery—two light 24-pounders and a 5½-inch howitzer—at once took the Americans under fire as they debouched from the bridge and deployed into line of battle. According to received tradition, which for once seems largely correct, Riall saw their gray coats and happily concluded that he faced nothing more terrifying than a batch of "Buffalo militia." Then, suddenly aware that *these* Americans were coming into action through his artillery fire with unflinching precision, he blurted, "Those are regulars, by God!"

Towson had quickly gone into position on Scott's right, near the Niagara. At once the British artillery concentrated on him, dismounting one of his guns. In prompt reply Towson's gunners hit a British caisson, which exploded, scattering destruction across the enemy battery position. The swiftly served American 12-pounders soon smothered their heavier, slower-firing opponents, practically putting them out of action.[21]

Amid this artillery duel the opposing infantries formed for battle. Scott had his brigade in line, with the 22d Regiment on the right next to Towson's guns, the 9th and 11th in the center, the 25th on the left in the edge of the wood. Riall, apparently determined to bull his way through Scott's position, came on with his regulars in regimental columns, the 1st and 100th abreast in front, the leg-weary 8th and some militia following. Other militia and Indians began edging into the woods. Meeting a "very heavy" blaze of American musketry, Riall ordered the 8th forward on his right.

That movement was never completed. Holding his center in place, Scott swung the 25th's and 22d's outer flanks forward so that his front formed a shallow U, into which Riall's attack thrust itself. Caught in a murderously accurate crossfire, raked by Towson's guns, the 1st and 100th came on gallantly but were literally knocked to pieces. Scott shouted

21. The light 24-pounder had been designed for use as either field or siege artillery. In practice, it was not too effective in either role.

for a charge, to show Englishmen that Americans could use the bayonet as well as shoot. The English attack collapsed—"mouldered away," Scott reported, "like a rope of sand." Riding recklessly through the fight, Riall got the 8th Foot into a sort of line to cover the rout as his army went tumbling back across the Chippewa. Even so, he might have been completely demolished had not his chief of artillery brought three 6-pounders across the Chippewa and into action to check the American pursuit. Two other 6-pounders also were firing from Riall's entrenchments.

Scott halted his winded brigade, but some of Porter's Indians followed the fleeing British up to the river, picking up prisoners and souvenirs. Ripley's brigade came panting onto the field, just as Riall's rear guard vanished into their entrenchments.

The whole battle had lasted little more than half an hour, but it had changed the war. In that brief time Scott's 1,300 regulars had met and broken Riall's 1,500 British infantry in a stand-up fight in an open field.[22] Riall had lost 148 killed, 221 wounded, and 46 captured or missing for a total of 415, including 33 officers killed or wounded. Scott had 44 killed and 224 wounded; Porter's casualties apparently totaled 54. Losses among the British Indians and militia remain unknown. Riall's clumsy, overconfident tactics, advancing in massed regimental columns against Scott's concave line, undoubtedly were responsible for many of his casualties. On the other hand, had he advanced in line Scott would have held him fixed until Ripley came up, in which case Riall's entire force might well have been pocketed against the Niagara River and destroyed. Scott had taken a calculated risk in leaving a strong position to fight in the open, but his victory there was far more impressive than any mere repulse he could have inflicted on Riall from behind Street's Creek. News of the battle brought a surge of national pride across the United States.[23]

Brown now was ready for a head-on attack on his own, straight across the Chippewa against Riall's entrenchments. Fortunately his brigade commanders and two engineer officers, Major William McRee and Major Eleazer D. Wood, both West Point graduates, dissuaded him. Reverting

22. Riall, naturally, claimed that he had faced "superior numbers," and some British/Canadian writers have wasted considerable energy attempting to prove him right. Riall also had 600 militia and Indians, though these took little part in the main action.

23. The assertion that the gray uniform of the U.S. Military Academy's cadets was adopted in commemoration of that worn here appears to be only a legend. The reasons given in 1816 for authorizing a gray cadet uniform were simply that it wore well and was considerably cheaper than a blue one.

to his original plan, he spent a day accumulating bridging materials, then forced a crossing of the Chippewa, roughly a mile west of Riall's position, on July 7. Riall quickly retired northward to Twenty-Mile Creek without offering any serious opposition. Most of his Indians and a good many of his militia deserted him. On the American side, except for some thirty men—to judge from their names, mostly half-breeds—Porter's Indians likewise went home to celebrate their victory. In their place Porter gradually got New York Volunteers in uncertain numbers and temper. Leaving Porter to cover his communications, Brown took Scott's and Ripley's brigades on to Queenston, where he could cover roads to both the north and west, meanwhile pushing reconnaissance parties up to Fort George and twice trying to lure its garrison out from behind their defenses.

Brown's immediate worry, however, was Chauncey. July 10 passed, as did the 15th, and yet there was no sign of the American squadron, or word from its rotund commander. Brown needed naval support to attack Fort George; he expected the fleet to bring him supplies, siege guns, and reinforcements from Sackets Harbor and Oswego. Chauncey's big frigates were ready, but Chauncey himself had developed a convenient fever that left him deaf alike to appeals from Brown and urgings from Washington. No matter how desperate Brown's situation, his squadron must not suffer the degradation of fetching, carrying, and generally playing second fiddle to a lot of infantrymen. Though supposedly too sick for active service, he absolutely refused to turn the squadron over to his second-in-command. Until he himself was ready to lead them forth, not a ship must stir from Sackets Harbor. Gaines, commanding the Sackets Harbor garrison, tried the risky expedient of forwarding several siege guns in bateaux along the south shore of Lake Ontario, under escort of Major Lodowick Morgan's riflemen, but Yeo quickly chased his makeshift convoy back into harbor.

Meanwhile, brawling slowly intensified along the American line of communication, originally from Queenston back to Fort Erie and across the Niagara to Buffalo, later across the river to Fort Schlosser. Having received reinforcements, Riall edged forward to Twelve-Mile Creek on July 19. The Upper Canada militia turned out sturdily again, even though they were only halfway through their haying season. Reinforced by Riall's light troops, they fought American foraging parties and patrols, which often included Willcock's vengeful Canadian Volunteers. New York volunteers had deep grudges of their own to pay off. The village of St. Davids, two and a half miles west of Queenston, was a center of this irregular warfare. Some exasperated New York cavalry sacked and burned it on July 19; Brown court-martialed the officer responsible. Canadian

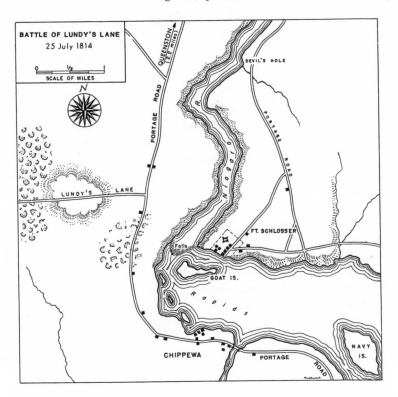

militia moved in again but were chased out on the 22d. Porter thereafter moved on to Chippewa.

Grimly aware that Drummond was concentrating every possible man against him, on July 24 Brown fell back to Chippewa to be nearer his base of supplies. His position east of the Niagara River was practicable only as long as he could retain the initiative. For this, he required Chauncey's support. Lacking it, his position was difficult and potentially dangerous. Drummond would outnumber him two to one; holding both Fort George and Fort Niagara and having control of Lake Ontario, the British could drive south along either or both sides of the Niagara River. Brown's base in the Buffalo/Fort Schlosser area was protected only by the 1st Infantry Regiment[24] and various odds and ends of regulars and volunteers, along with dubious New York militia. Should Drummond launch a major

24. Recently ordered to Brown from western garrisons and now arriving piecemeal. Approximately 500 officers and men were available at this time.

offensive from Fort Niagara, Brown would be forced to attempt a hasty withdrawal to the east bank, at the risk of being caught and destroyed in detail.

As soon as he learned of Brown's withdrawal, Riall followed, marching all night to finally halt at Lundy's Lane, three miles north of Chippewa, about 7:00 A.M. He had approximately 1,000 regulars and militia with him, and had left some 1,600 more under Hercules Scott at Twelve-Mile Creek. About noon Riall called them forward. Drummond had ordered him to maneuver with circumspection, avoiding combat if possible. He was to concentrate his regulars at St. Davids and send his militia and Indians, several hundred of whom had again joined the British, to fix Brown in position. Meanwhile Drummond had collected as many troops as possible—something he could do with comparative rapidity, since Yeo had undisputed control of Lake Ontario and could lift reinforcements forward from Kingston and York—in preparation for a show-down fight with Brown. (Drummond still judged the Americans "undisciplined though confident and numerous.")[25] Disembarking at Fort George early on the 25th, he immediately sent Lieutenant Colonel John G. P. Tucker with approximately 600 men[26] south from Fort Niagara to destroy some batteries the Americans had built at Youngstown to bombard Fort George—an action that Drummond doubtlessly hoped would also distract Brown. Tucker did accomplish the latter, driving a detachment of volunteers out of Youngstown, but hardly with the result Drummond must have anticipated. Then Drummond recalled him.

Brown apparently knew nothing of Riall's presence at Lundy's Lane. (For lack of effective cavalry and officers who knew how to use and lead mounted men, American armies seldom had much knowledge of what went on beyond their infantry outposts.) However, he soon had reports of Tucker's progress. After some hours of cogitation he reacted in his usual aggressive fashion. Rather than attempt to shift troops to the east bank, and thus leave himself too weak to meet any British attack west of the Niagara, he would seize the initiative from Drummond. Accordingly he dispatched Scott's brigade with Towson's artillery company and a few cavalrymen, barely 1,100 officers and men in all, north along the Portage Road toward Queenston.

Scott had been aching for another fight. Quickly getting his men ready,

25. A number of American deserters had come into Riall's lines. Their stories may have given the British an exaggerated idea of Brown's strength and a poor one of its discipline.

26. There were 300 from the 41st Foot, 200 of the 1st, and about 100 Indians.

he marched soon after 5:00 P.M. The road ran though thick timber, ideal for an ambush; Scott's advance guard moved with muskets ready. Soon they glimpsed an occasional Indian ducking from tree to tree west of the road. Scott threw out a flank guard and pushed ahead. Some two miles north of Brown's camp, where a side road ran eastward to Niagara Falls, he flushed a party of British dragoon officers from a locally famous tavern. Its proprietress—a cheerful dame who furnished all comers with drink, food, and information—told Scott that Riall was near Lundy's Lane, a mile farther on, with 800 regulars, 300 militia, and two guns. Eagerly renewing his advance, Scott came out into open country and saw a heavy line of British infantry and guns blocking Portage Road and extending westward along a ridge. Riall was certainly at Lundy's Lane, but in decidedly greater strength than Scott had expected. It was almost 6:00 P.M.

Lundy's Lane was a secondary road that ran west and then northwest from Portage Road, to cross Twelve-Mile Creek at DeCou's Falls and continue on to Burlington. Just west of the Portage Road it went up and along the crest of the isolated hill for approximately a quarter mile before dropping to level land again. This bit of high ground dominated the surrounding area. For almost a mile to the south, where the Americans must deploy, there were open fields; the only cover or concealment was an orchard along Portage Road near its junction with Lundy's Lane. To the east of Portage Road was a belt of open ground about a quarter mile wide, then dense woods and the high, steep banks of the Niagara River.

Coming into the clearing, Scott ordered Towson's guns into battery just west of Portage Road, and sent a line of skirmishers forward through the lengthening shadows to feel out the enemy position. Though he did not know it, he had barely lost a race for the high ground of Lundy's Lane. Riall had been ordered to avoid action if possible. His scouts had reported Scott's advance; from the confidence with which Scott came on, he suspected that Brown's whole army was behind him. At once he ordered a retreat to Queenston, and sent a galloper spurring to intercept Hercules Scott with orders to join him there. Then, with the hill half-evacuated, Drummond came onto the field with a battalion of the 89th Foot and elements of the 1st, 8th, and 41st. Ordering the hill held, he hustled the six British fieldpieces—three 6-pounders, two 24-pounders, and a 5½-inch howitzer—into position on its southern slope. In all, he had almost 1,800 regulars and militia and an uncertain number of Indians.

Scott's skirmishers pushed in some Glengarry Light Infantry and militia that had been covering Riall's front, but it quickly was evident that the Americans were seriously outnumbered and out-gunned. A direct attack would be suicidal; to withdraw would be to risk an attack while they were in the awkward process of changing from line back into march column on Portage Road; also the mere idea of retreating was anathema to Scott and his brigade alike. Sending his adjutant general back to Brown to urge that Porter and Ripley be sent forward, he sent Major Thomas S. Jesup with the 25th Regiment into the woods east of Portage Road to develop the situations there, and held the 9th, 11th, and 22d in line facing Drummond. Pounded relentlessly by the British guns, to which they could reply only by long-range musket volleys, the three regiments stood firm. Towson's gunners did their best, but could not silence their opponents.

Meanwhile Jesup, swinging wide, found a woods road that appeared to lead past Drummond's left flank. Without notifying Scott, he headed down it to fight his own battle. Luck brought him back to Portage Road, just north of its junction with Lundy's Lane and just in time to catch a battalion of "incorporated militia"[27] and a company or two of regulars as they were deploying from march column to cover Drummond's left. Scattering them, he drove ahead, capturing Riall[28] and threatening to break into the British rear. His regiment, however, was too weak for a decisive blow. Drummond finally held him, establishing a new left flank at an angle to his front.

By 9:00 P.M. the 9th, 11th, and 22d had suffered so heavily that they were reformed as a single "battalion"[29] under Major Henry Leavenworth; Jesup had been pushed back; Towson badly hurt. Nevertheless Scott held his ground so grimly that Drummond considered himself outnumbered and would not risk a counterattack. Drummond also had problems. Though joined by Tucker, he had been forced to pull his sedentary militia units out of line. Mostly raw farmers, they had been firing wildly; one unit shot the cockade off their colonel's hat. Stripping them of their ammunition, he sent them to the rear. His Indians had vanished. And Hercules Scott, having countermarched in response to Riall's earlier order, and then again on receiving Drummond's counterorder, was still slogging through the dusty dusk from DeCou's Falls.

Then, as night came down on the smoldering combat, Brown arrived with Ripley, Porter, and Ritchie and Biddle's companies of artillery, approximately 1,200 men in all, including part of the 1st Infantry Regiment,

27. Semi-regulars who had received some training, as compared to the "sedentary" (ordinary) militia.

28. Riall was wounded, then or a little earlier, losing an arm.

29. At that time in the American service, a number of companies from the same or different regiments, virtually synonymous with "regiment."

which had just joined Ripley's brigade. Ripley relieved Scott's battered regiments, which reformed behind him. It was obvious that Drummond's guns dominated the battlefield, so Brown ordered Colonel James Miller of the 21st Regiment to take them. (Miller's reputed reply, "I'll try, sir!" survives as that regiment's motto.)

The attack was carefully planned. Guided by McRee and Wood, who had hurriedly reconnoitered Drummond's position, and Scott, the 21st moved silently from Portage Road up the eastern slope of the hill to a rail fence just twenty yards short of the guns. Meanwhile, to their left, the 1st Regiment made a direct attack on the south face of the hill. They were repulsed, but drew Drummond's full attention, so that the 21st reached the fence undetected. Passing Miller's orders in whispers, its officers got it into line. Fixing bayonets, the 21st rested their musket barrels across the rail fence and took careful aim. Moonlight made the British artillery-men clearly visible. Miller's shout, "Fire!" was echoed by a volley that swept away most of the gunners, and followed by a rush that bayoneted those still standing.

British infantry supporting the battery counterattacked; Miller met them with volleys at twenty yards. Before they could recover from this check, Ripley swung the 23d and 1st against their flanks, holding his fire until within point-blank range. This assault broke Drummond's left wing and center, tumbling it down the hill's steep northern slope. Porter promptly moved up on the 1st Regiment's left and Jesup on the 22d's right, establishing a solid front all along Lundy's Lane. Hindman brought Towson and Ritchie's batteries onto the hilltop; Biddle's two 12-pounders he posted at the junction of the lane and Portage Road. During this move the drivers of one American cannon were shot out of their saddles; the frightened horses bolted into the British lines with it.

It was at about this moment, probably in the brief lull that followed Brown's seizure of the hill, that Hercules Scott's dog-tired column[30] came trailing onto the field from DeCou's Falls. Hit in the neck by a musket ball, Drummond was temporarily out of action, leaving no one in effective command. He had sent staff officers to meet Scott and guide him into position. Ignorant of the sudden change in the situation, they led his column into the center of the new American line, which greeted it with a sudden blast of musketry and artillery fire out of the darkness. Shocked and riddled, the column broke up in confusion, abandoning all or most

30. Seven companies of his own 103d Foot, with elements of the 1st, 8th, and 104th regiments, some 250 to 300 assorted militia, and a Royal Artillery detachment.

of its guns. Some, if not all, of these were soon recovered in a dashing counterattack by the 41st Foot's light infantry company, but their crews had been scattered and it seems unlikely that they ever were in action that night. The disorder spread to other British units, some of which fired into one another.

Finally getting his troops under control, Drummond made three determined attempts to recover the hill, his men surging up the steep slope to within ten or twelve yards of Brown's line before being blasted back. On Brown's left they dislodged Porter's brigade, but the 1st Infantry faced to its left and broke up their attack.

While Ripley's brigade held Lundy's Lane, Winfield Scott had completed the organization of Leavenworth's "battalion" and brought it forward in column. Apparently without either consulting Brown or pausing to coordinate his planned action with Ripley, he thrust it between the 1st and 21st regiments and led it headlong at Drummond's battered line. The British broke, but in the darkness and confusion Ripley's brigade—not knowing that the dimly glimpsed troops surging across their front were Americans—fired into Scott's flank and rear while rallying British units engaged him head-on. Mangled by that crossfire, the battalion collapsed into a stream of fugitives. Scott had had two horses killed under him and been badly bruised by the glancing impact of an almost-spent cannonball. Now, leaving Leavenworth to rally his surviving men, he rode across the field to Jesup's position where he soon was so badly wounded that he had to be carried off the field. Over on the left flank Brown had been shot through the thigh. (By one account, he had also been struck a severe blow in the side by the staff of a Congreve rocket, which barely missed him.)[31] Casualties, thirst, exhaustion, and straggling had thinned the American line to possibly only some 700 men; most of the officers had been wounded. Jesup's regiment was reduced to a single rank, sergeants and lieutenants elbow-to-elbow with privates. Drummond probably had twice as many men still on the field, but in no better condition. One fresh regiment on either side could have quickly settled things, but both commanders had put in every man and gun they could. (Meanwhile, Madison and Jones were wasting 900 regulars at Mackinac and Prairie du Chien.)

Brown finally collapsed from loss of blood. For once in his stormy career his resolution wilted. In this unaccustomed weakness his reactions were more those of a bewildered civilian than a professional soldier: "We

31. Drummond had a "rocket section" of the Royal Marine Artillery. They blazed away during the battle but without notable effect, unless they did nick Brown.

will all go back to camp. We have done all we can." Hindman, coming forward with a resupply of ammunition, was told to withdraw his guns. Their movement to the rear was Ripley's first notice of Brown's intentions, but he then received an order to collect the wounded and follow.

There was some discussion of this surprising decision; to his credit, Porter, though wounded, urged that the Americans hang on to the dearly won hill. Hindman's wagons could have brought water and rations forward; by calling up camp guards and various detachments from Chippewa, several hundred additional men could have been put into line. Had this been done, Drummond probably would have retreated the next morning. But Ripley was a dutiful officer, not overly concerned with glory, and already in Brown's bad graces. Carefully and quietly he got the Americans off the hill and on the road south. Drummond did not stir. Because of losses among the American gun teams, Hindman had had trouble getting his guns away, having to abandon one with a damaged carriage, but carrying off a British 6-pounder in its place. Finding some additional horses, he sent back a detachment to bring off the other captured guns. By the time the detachment reached the hilltop, the American infantry was gone. They encountered British troops, a patrol or possibly a group of stragglers looking for their unit, and some were captured.[32]

Lundy's Lane had been, in the description a Confederate would later give the Battle of Wilson's Creek in 1861, "a mighty mean-fought fight. Both sides whupped." Though only an "affair of outposts" by European standards, it was one of the toughest engagements of the Napoleonic period. Americans had 171 killed, 573 wounded, and 117 missing or captured; the British counted 81, 562, and 233 respectively. Left in possession of the field, Drummond would report a "Great Victory," won against 5,000 Americans, upon whom he claimed to have inflicted at least 1,500 casualties, including several hundred prisoners.

While Drummond had had a *total* of approximately 2,900 regulars and possibly 600 militia against Brown's 1,900 regulars and 300 volun-

32. According to Hercules Scott, the guns remained on the ridge overnight and were not repossessed until the next morning. The story of a final victorious British assault is Cruikshank's invention in *The Battle of Lundy's Lane*. Conscientious historians have troubles with Lundy's Lane: it began in late evening and endured until almost midnight; dust, powder smoke, and darkness obscured most of it. The British had the additional handicap of having the moonlight in their faces, thus blinding them to American movements but revealing theirs to Brown's men. I am infinitely grateful for the help of Donald E. Graves, the authority on the Niagara battles, who "war-gamed" them with me.

teers, he had no overwhelming superiority until Hercules Scott's arrival, which he so mismanaged that he could not make his numbers count. Buffaloed by Winfield Scott's stubborn aggressiveness, he thought himself badly outnumbered, and so used Hercules Scott's column to patch up his line. Had he instead put it in against Porter's unsteady volunteers on Brown's left flank, he probably could have rolled up the entire American line and scored a decisive victory. He may have been suffering from loss of blood and shock, possibly a concussion. Fellow officers thought his conduct during the crucial hilltop struggle aimless and erratic. (He also was suffering from a bad cold, which he considered more trouble than his wound.)

Sometime after midnight Ripley reported to Brown at Chippewa. Brown, possibly out of his head from the effects of his wound and frustration, responded furiously on learning the captured guns had been abandoned. Ripley must move out at dawn to retake the battlefield Brown himself had ordered abandoned. Fantastic as the idea was, Ripley worked through the night reorganizing the exhausted, shaken regiments and marched at 9:00 A.M. with approximately 1,200 men. Most of the officers had been wounded and all, Ripley included, regarded their mission as sheer folly. They found Drummond with clearly superior numbers— approximately 2,200—in line of battle almost a mile south of Lundy's Lane. The two forces considered each other briefly; then Ripley deliberately withdrew. Drummond remained in place. Unable to get a clear idea of Ripley's strength because of the wooded terrain, he apparently still feared that he was considerably outnumbered, and was reluctant to risk another action.

Once Brown had been evacuated to the east bank, Ripley took command. Untroubled by Drummond, he spent most of the day burning Riall's old fortifications along the north bank of Chippewa Creek, the Chippewa bridge, and the light defenses of the American camp. His withdrawal was hampered by the difficulty of moving his wounded; a good deal of camp equipment and rations had to be destroyed to free transportation for them. Drummond used this as a basis for his mendacious claim that Ripley had retreated in great disorder.

The Americans already had strengthened Fort Erie for all-around defense and begun constructing a fortified camp adjacent to it. Ripley went to work improving these defenses, but urged that the army be withdrawn to the east bank. Brown, then in a Buffalo hospital, ordered him to hold the fort. Angry at Ripley for not doing the impossible on July 26, and suspecting his courage, he summoned Gaines from Sackets Harbor to take over the command.

Drummond meanwhile fell back to Queenston, unwilling to risk another battle until he had received enough reinforcements to make up his losses. He also had to organize a supply system to support his advance. His Indians had crept back to Lundy's Lane once Ripley had retired, to scalp and plunder the dead and such unfortunate wounded as had not been gathered in. Exasperated British soldiers shot one of them the next morning for repeatedly tormenting a wounded American, but the Indians were back and so had to be fed.

Both Drummond and his army had been considerably shaken. Veterans of Wellington's army reported the recent fighting rougher than anything they had seen against the French in Spain. This combat fatigue was quickly evident. During the night of August 3 Drummond sent Tucker with 600 regulars across the river to raid Black Rock and Buffalo. Major Morgan, with 240 riflemen and a few volunteers, ambushed them at a stream crossing just north of Black Rock, quickly knocking over 25 Englishmen. The rest broke and fled to their boats.

TWELVE

Bladensburg Races

Strike! Chastise the savages, for such they are! . . . Our demands may be couched in a single word—Submission!

—*Times* (London), 1814

WARNED REPEATEDLY AND EMPHATICALLY by American representatives in Europe[1] concerning the magnitude of England's wrathful preparations, the Madison administration gradually became concerned for the safety of Washington. Only Secretary of War John Armstrong remained uninterested. He could see no reason why the British should attack Washington. After all, it was little more than another slipshod southern village, deep in mud or dust according to the weather, incongruously studded with a few imposing federal buildings. To Armstrong's reasoning, Baltimore would be the logical target of any British invasion. Baltimore was a wealthy seaport and in an unofficial way a major naval base: its shipbuilders were busy with the heavy frigate *Java* and the sloops-of-war *Erie* and *Ontario*, as well as a powerful steam frigate. Moreover, it was the home port of many of America's most effective privateers, and so damned by the British as a "nest of pirates." Rear Admiral Sir George Cockburn had been heard to vow that he intended to burn every house in it. Its capture would bring the Royal Navy prize money galore, as well as joyful revenge.

Meanwhile Armstrong left Washington practically defenseless. Its only protection was Fort Warburton, some twelve miles down the Potomac River from the capital, a newly built work mounting nineteen guns, but

1. American envoys, including John Quincy Adams, Albert Gallatin, and Henry Clay, were negotiating in Ghent with English representatives.

198

with only 80 artillerymen to man them.[2] By contrast, Armstrong had stationed almost 200 regulars in Baltimore's Fort McHenry.

During late June, however, increasing news of formidable British preparations finally made it evident that more active measures should be taken for the protection of the Washington/Baltimore area. Accordingly, a Tenth Military District[3] was created, to have its own commander and military forces. Thereafter politics took over. Armstrong proposed the command go to a veteran artilleryman, Brigadier General Moses Porter, then commanding at Norfolk. Instead, Madison appointed Brigadier General William Winder, recently returned to the United States after a prisoner-of-war exchange. Militarily, his appointment made no sense. Winder's Canadian frontier service had earned him a reputation for personal bravery, activity, and incompetence. (One suffering subordinate grumped that Winder needed to spend a couple of years learning how to command a company.)

Military competence, however, was a consideration outside the routine deliberations of Madison's cabinet. Winder had been an influential Baltimore lawyer, politician, and militia captain—which was why Madison had made him an instant regular lieutenant colonel in 1812—and they hoped that he still would be popular. Moreover, he was a cousin of Governor Levin Winder of Maryland. Maryland would have to provide most of the militia needed to meet the first shock of any British invasion, but Levin Winder was a Federalist and therefore possibly lacking their own dedicated patriotism. William Winder's appointment, they hoped, would ensure his uncle's willing support.

Overridden in this matter, Armstrong largely washed his hands of the defense of the Tenth Military District, resigning it to Madison, Monroe, and Winder. Winder spent the rest of July exploring his command; not until August 1 did he set up headquarters in Washington.

The strategic problem Winder faced was ugly. The Royal Navy had dominated Chesapeake Bay for over a year. Cockburn's expeditions had familiarized its officers with the lower reaches of most of the bay's tributary streams. Barring a considerable period of contrary winds or windless days, the British fleet could shift up and down the bay much more rapidly than American troops could march along the region's sandy roads. So far, it had been capable only of raids against the smaller coastal towns

---

2. Better known by its later name, Fort Washington.
3. Maryland, the District of Columbia, and all Virginia north of the Rappahannock River.

like Havre de Grace and Hampton, but if it were reinforced by an expeditionary force from those 15,000 veterans the Duke of Wellington was
sending from France it could strike Baltimore, Annapolis, or Washington.
By late June such a force was reliably understood to be on its way.

There would be little advance warning of such an invasion. The Royal
Navy controlled both the sea approaches to Chesapeake Bay and much
of the bay itself. Hardly a single Baltimore privateer could slip through
its blockade now; those few that succeeded made haste away from the
Chesapeake. The only American naval force in the lower bay, a flotilla of
thirteen gunboats and one small sloop under that adventurer extraordinary, Commodore Joshua Barney,[4] had waged a lonely hit-and-run battle
through the coastal inlets against Cockburn's swarm of light warships.
There were too many of them, too ably handled. In early June, Barney
was almost trapped; though he finally broke out, he was forced to retreat
up the Patuxent River to Nottingham. From there he could return downstream or march his 400-odd "flotillamen" overland to either Washington or Baltimore as subsequent developments might require. There were
fourteen more gunboats under a Lieutenant Rutter at Baltimore, but they
could only outpost that city's harbor. In consequence Winder depended
on a haphazard assortment of coast watchers to detect the arrival and
strength of any British fleet and to count the men it might put ashore.
Barney had posted observers near the mouth of the Patuxent, and there
were various militia detachments and nervous civilians elsewhere along
the coast. But it would take valuable time for their messengers to reach
Washington, and the dispatches they carried might—or might not—be
an accurate accounting of what was actually happening.

The Tenth Military District was unprepared for serious military operations. Besides the garrisons of Fort McHenry and Fort Warburton, and
39 more men "garrisoning" two forts at Annapolis, there were only some
380 regular infantrymen[5] and 125 light dragoons, in considerable part
recent recruits, and 120 marines around Washington. If there were any
serious fighting, the militia would have to do it, and the militia was
not ready. Except for a number of volunteer militia units in Washington and Baltimore, the Maryland and District of Columbia militia were
poorly equipped and seldom uniformed. Virginia politicians had habitu-

4. Barney served as a privateer and a Navy officer during the Revolution. He refused a U.S. Navy commission in 1797 because of a dispute over seniority, serving in
the French Navy until 1802.

5. From the 12th, 36th, and 38th infantry regiments.

ally neglected their militia; several hundred available men were without weapons. Few militia units had the necessary "camp equipage"—tents, blankets, axes, and cooking utensils—needed for field service, and the quartermaster general had scant local reserves of such articles to issue them. Even gun flints were in short supply.[6]

Winder had all too keen an appreciation of his situation. He knew what needed to be done: organize an effective outpost and courier system to report the appearance of a British invasion fleet; select defensive positions to cover Washington and Baltimore; issue preparatory orders to the major militia organizations; make arrangements for obstructing the roads in front of an invading army by felling trees and destroying bridges. Yet he accomplished none of these things. It may well be that defeat and captivity had cracked something in him. He could not form plans or delegate authority; instead of organizing a useful staff, he attempted to do everything himself, and so rapidly wore himself to a frazzle. He asked that 4,000 militia be called up without delay, pointing out that getting militia properly mustered, equipped, and organized took considerable time, time he would not have once the British landed. Armstrong advised against it; unless there were a clear and present danger, the militia might not respond. (When Maryland summoned 3,000 to duty in late July, only 250 gradually straggled in.) Unmentioned were the established facts that militia held on active service without the stimulus of imminent action soon grew restive and that they quickly began falling sick and dying from various camp diseases.

Meanwhile England's wrath gathered. Admiral Sir John Warren had been replaced as commander of the British naval forces in the North American Station by Vice Admiral Sir Alexander Cochrane, a decidedly grimmer specimen, able, imaginative, arrogant, and exceeding hard-handed—perfectly qualified to be Cockburn's commanding officer. His innate marauding instincts had been whetted by a letter from Sir George Prevost who, angered by Colonel John Campbell's raid on Port Dover and unable at the moment to do any compensatory barn-burning himself, officially requested that the Royal Navy do him a favor of "inflicting that measure of retaliation which shall deter the enemy from the repetition of similar outrages." On July 18 Cochrane happily "required and directed" his squadrons on blockade duty along the American coast "to destroy and lay waste such towns and districts . . . as you may find assailable." They were to continue such "retributory justice" until the United States recog-

6. The best musket flints were good for only about thirty shots.

nized the "impropriety as well as the inhumanity" of its conduct toward "His Majesty's unoffending Canadian subjects." The lives of unarmed American civilians would be spared, but nothing else.[7]

To lengthen and strengthen Cochrane's reach, an expeditionary force made up of the 1st battalions of the 4th and 44th Foot and the 85th Light Infantry, under Major General Robert Ross, sailed from Bordeaux on June 2 after waiting for a week aboard their transports. Reaching Bermuda on July 25, it was reinforced by the 21st Foot and a company of artillery from Gibraltar. Sailing again on August 3 under escort of Cochrane's squadron, it entered Chesapeake Bay during the 16th and 17th and soon was joined by Cockburn's warships.

Ross's mission was simply to "create a diversion on the coasts of the United States in favor of the British army employed in the defense of Upper and Lower Canada." Cochrane was to select the expedition's objectives, subject to Ross's approval, but Ross was not to penetrate any considerable distance inland or occupy any captured objective longer than it might take to destroy or evacuate captured military supplies. In short, British strategy was to be a series of short, powerful raids, designed to divert American forces from the Canadian frontier and inflict the maximum possible destruction on the coastal areas.

Ross's force was organized and equipped for such limited operations in close cooperation with the fleet that would carry its supplies and give it gunfire support. It was almost entirely veteran infantry, Wellington's famous "Invincibles," who had mastered every trick of European wars. Ross has come down to us as a big, cheerful, decent-enough man, a good tactician, brave, well liked by his men. He had led a brigade in Spain under Wellington, but that service had been poor preparation for an independent command. The Iron Duke wanted officers who obeyed orders, kept their mouths shut, and left the necessary thinking to him. Any display of initiative was tantamount to insubordination.

As the expedition gathered in Chesapeake Bay,[8] Cochrane, Ross, and Cockburn debated their next step. The two admirals were all for an immediate dash overland against Washington: Cochrane had a fancy for desperate enterprises; Cockburn's operations had convinced him that the Americans would offer little effective resistance. The capture of Wash-

7. This policy was approved by the British Admiralty. Localities that paid tribute and contributed supplies might have private property spared, but all harbor installations, shipping, and storehouses were to be destroyed.

8. Cochrane and Ross arrived ahead of the transports for consultation with Cockburn, who was operating in the Chesapeake.

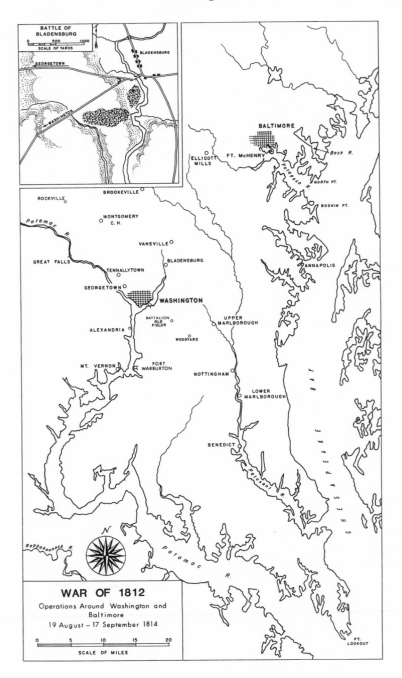

BATTLE OF
BLADENSBURG

500   1000
SCALE OF YARDS

GEORGETOWN

BLADENSBURG

WASHINGTON

ROCKVILLE

BROOKEVILLE

MONTGOMERY
C. H.

Potomac R.

VANSVILLE

GREAT FALLS

TENNALLYTOWN

BLADENSBURG

GEORGETOWN

WASHINGTON

BATTALION
OLD
FIELDS

ALEXANDRIA

WOODYARD

MT. VERNON

FORT
WARBURTON

UPPER
MARLBOROUGH

NOTTINGHAM

LOWER
MARLBOROUGH

BENEDICT

BALTIMORE

ELLICOTT
MILLS

FT. McHENRY

Back R.

Patapsco R.

NORTH PT.

BODKIN PT.

ANNAPOLIS

C H E S A P E A K E   B A Y

Patuxent R.

Rappahannock R.

N

Potomac   R.

PT.
LOOKOUT

WAR OF 1812

Operations Around Washington and
Baltimore
19 August – 17 September 1814

0   5   10   15   20
SCALE OF MILES

ington would disorganize the American government and inflict a major blow to American prestige. Ross was not so sanguine. His soldiers were limp-legged from almost three months packed aboard comfortless transports; some of them still were weak from a "fever" that broke out during the voyage.[9] He had no cavalry to scout his advance, no wagons to haul his supplies. Also, coastal Virginia's abominable summer weather was at its peak of heat and humidity. In case of a major action, Ross would have to depend on rockets—impressive to see and hear but fiendishly inaccurate—rather than dependable field guns. Finally he questioned whether it would be wise to advance while Barney still lurked up the Patuxent River.

The decision was to land the troops. While Ross tested American opposition, the fleet would eradicate Barney. Moving on up the bay, the expedition put into the Patuxent River on August 18; the next day was spent landing the troops at Benedict. On the 20th Cochrane sent Cockburn up the river with an overwhelming force of light craft and armed ships' boats after Barney, who meanwhile had shifted still farther north above a locality with the blunt name of Pig Point. Captain Sir Peter Parker was dispatched up the Chesapeake with his frigate *Menelaus* and several smaller vessels to simulate the leading squadron of an attack on Baltimore, with the intent of frightening the Americans into concentrating troops around that city instead of Washington. To lend emphasis to his feint Parker would shoot up and burn bayside hamlets and farms and otherwise avenge the "injured and unoffending inhabitants of the Canadas." Meanwhile, to further confuse those Yankees and to aid an overland raid on Washington, Captain James A. Gordon had been ordered up the Potomac with two frigates, three bomb ships, a rocket ship, and several small tenders. As for Ross, he waited until the evening's cool before marching his wobbly troops six miles upriver toward Nottingham. He was maintaining strict discipline and respecting private property. Cochrane accompanied him.

On the 21st Ross's advance continued for some twelve miles through wooded country into Nottingham. There was a little shooting there between his advance guard and a hastily departing American outpost; a few stray militiamen, reported as "scouts," were gathered in. Nottingham stood empty; the population had fled; nothing had been done to obstruct the roads.

Word of Cochrane's arrival had not reached Washington until the

---

9. Oddly, most accounts of this campaign consider neither the poor physical condition of the British troops nor their lack of transportation.

morning of August 18. Thereupon the capital of the United States promptly took on the aspect of a half-demolished anthill. Madison frantically mobilized the District of Columbia militia and called on the neighboring states for help. Secretary of State Monroe took a troop of cavalry for escort and rode off toward Benedict to count the enemy's ships and men. By no means a daring scout, he tried to do his counting at three miles' distance and found he had forgotten to fetch a telescope. After two days of cautious sneak-and-peeping he somehow concluded that Ross must have 6,000 men, and proceeded to inflict this, and other, misinformation on Madison, Winder, and anyone else he could catch.

Winder, having failed to do any preliminary planning or provide himself with anything resembling a coherent staff, practically vanished in a whirl of paperwork and frightened politicians "from Thursday the 18th of August until Sunday the 21st," emerging "nearly broken down," but still without any clear idea of what needed to be done. Armstrong could only offer good advice, which unfortunately—since he could not imagine Ross risking an advance on Washington with such an improvised force—did not fit the situation and only left Winder worse confused. One thing Armstrong did: when a group of sensible citizens offered to build defenses at Bladensburg, he sent the only available engineer officer, Colonel Decius Wadsworth, the commissary general of ordnance, to direct them.[10]

The Tenth Military District militia mustered willingly enough. By August 20 Winder had well over 9,000 men under arms, with possibly fifty guns. They were scattered from Baltimore southward through Annapolis and Washington to Fort Warburton, with a dribble or two on down the north bank of the Potomac. The major concentrations were around Baltimore (approximately 5,000 men and thirty guns) and Washington (2,500 and twelve guns). On August 20 most of the militia in Washington were ordered southeastward for some twelve miles to a locality termed "The Woodyard," now Woodyard, Maryland, five miles southwest of Upper Marlboro; it took them almost two days to get there.[11] Winder established his headquarters at the Woodyard the night of August 21. Shortly thereafter a saddle-weary Monroe joined him with his inflated estimate of British strength. Winder accepted it, rather than an emphatic report sent him from Annapolis by veteran Colonel William Beall

10. Time was too short to get much done, but Wadsworth picked the Bladensburg bridge as the critical point and began fortifying it.

11. Most of the regulars in Washington, some militia cavalry, and a detachment of marines from the Navy Yard—approximately 750 men with five guns—had already left for the Woodyard on August 20.

of the Maryland militia, who had actually counted Ross's column and put it at 4,000. Things were uncomfortable at the Woodyard; because of the shortage of camp equipment, a good many militiamen found themselves for the first time in their lives trying to sleep on the bare ground with nothing over them except the sky. What camp kettles they had were seldom full; their quartermasters were providing only half-rations—in part apparently because Washington officials were commandeering their supply wagons to rush the government's archives to safety. The British were spending a quiet night at Nottingham.

Other American forces were on the move. On the 20th Brigadier General Tobias Stansbury's brigade of Maryland militia, officially 1,353 officers and men, had been summoned down from Baltimore to occupy Bladensburg. Stansbury's two regiments, known after their colonels as Schutz's and Ragan's, were drafted[12] units, without uniforms or cohesion and almost without training. Stansbury's principal qualifications were a very loud voice and an admired skill in speaking in profane languages. Then Winder had a second thought. Stansbury had no artillery. If Ross came down on him with 6,000 veterans, it would be either a foot race or a massacre. He called on Baltimore for 950-odd men more—its "Dandy" 5th Maryland Infantry Regiment, made up of uniformed volunteer militia companies; three companies of riflemen; and two companies of artillery with six guns. Lieutenant Colonel Joseph Sterrett led them out through streets crowded with cheering townspeople, but his orders were to halt at Elk Ridge Landing, only five miles south of Baltimore.

Still uncertain of Ross's objective, Winder was attempting to cover both Washington and Baltimore. In that process he was managing to scatter his forces rather than concentrate them, offering Ross an opportunity to defeat them in detail. He had detached approximately 500 militia to cover the land approaches to Fort Warburton in case Gordon's squadron should land troops to attack it from the rear, but he had told the fort's commander, Captain Samuel Dyson, to blow it up if attacked by large numbers of British troops. He also left some 900 militia in Annapolis, and apparently did nothing to expedite the arming of the 700 or so Virginia militia who were waiting south of the Potomac. The one positive action Winder did take, sometime on the morning of the 22d, was at last to order Sterrett to Bladensburg. Sterrett received the dispatch just be-

12. Made up of detachments drafted out of different standing militia regiments and combined into these two provisional regiments. Officers and men were largely strangers to each other.

fore noon. Its contents must have been urgent indeed; the colonel got his command on the road in fifteen minutes and took them south through summer heat and dust along the sandy road with only the briefest halts to catch their breath.

Having destroyed his cockleshell gunboats, Barney was heading for Washington with his flotillamen, hoping to get there before Ross's advance cut him off. And Winder, accompanied by the ubiquitous Monroe, was advancing from the Woodyard toward Nottingham with possibly 2,000 men, too many for a reconnaissance, too few for a fight. What he wanted to do remains unexplained; probably he had no clear idea himself. Riding ahead of his column with a small cavalry escort, he promptly bumped into Ross, then en route to Upper Marlboro. Ross swung his advance guard to meet the Americans. Winder yelled for a retreat and hustled his perplexed soldiers, most of whom never got a clear idea of what all the excitement was about, back to the Woodyard, and then on back to Battalion Old Fields.[13] Barney joined him there. Monroe wrote Madison that the British were "in full march for Washington." As for Ross, once certain that the Americans did not want a fight, he went on to Upper Marlboro.

He found that pretty village also empty except for a Scots doctor named William Beanes, who soon would have a quaint part in American history. During the night Ross decided to risk a dash on Washington, and began organizing his column. Had he moved out promptly the next morning he could have run over Stansbury's isolated command. However, he was conscious that, no matter how pusillanimous the Yankees had seemed so far, he was entering on a tricky, risky venture that could end with the loss of his entire command. He therefore rested his men and readied them for action: four infantry regiments, a battalion of Royal Marines, a company of black "Colonial Marines," a Royal Artillery "rocket brigade," a Royal Marine Artillery "rocket corps," and a 50-man detachment of sappers and miners. To these, Cochrane added 100 Royal Navy gunners and approximately 275 bluejackets to carry and tow reserve supplies and ammunition. With staff and medical personnel this made a total of some 4,370 officers and men, with one 6-pounder and two 3-pounder guns and sixty rocket launchers.[14] It would have to be a slow-moving army of

13. This is now Forestville, at the junction of Pennsylvania Avenue and the Washington Beltway.

14. The "Colonial Marines" (75 officers and men) were organized at Bermuda. The "rocket brigade" and "rocket corps" each numbered 150, "all ranks"; the infantry regiments and marine battalion averaged 700.

invasion, its men loaded with three days' rations and sixty cartridges besides their canteens and packs. Enough horses, probably assorted nags
and screws the fleeing citizens had not thought worth taking with them,
had been picked up to mount 20-odd infantrymen, with saddles and
bridles improvised from blankets and ropes, to serve as scouts. All the
guns and ammunition carts, however, had to be towed by men; sweating
sailors, unaccustomed to marching, took the place of supply wagons. On
the afternoon of August 23 Ross broke camp and headed for Bladensburg. It is notable that he and Cochrane had an excellent knowledge of
the Virginia/Maryland road system.

If you were going to attack Washington from the east you had your
choice of three routes. You could come up the Potomac, working your
way through and across its shoals, a tricky job for heavy ships even if
your pilots knew the river, and then try battering your way past Fort Warburton and whatever other batteries the Americans might have improvised. You could come south from Upper Marlboro through the Woodyard, swing west through Battalion Old Fields, and try to force the East
Branch of the Potomac. The East Branch here was a sluggish, deep,
marshy-banked stream, a quarter mile wide, and practically impassable
unless you had a pontoon bridge train or could surprise one of the two
bridges across it. These were wooden structures, easily burned; also, the
southernmost one led directly into the guns of the Washington Navy Yard.
Or you could drive northwest from Upper Marlboro through Bladensburg.

Bladensburg was a village on a hillside along the east bank of the
East Branch, approximately six miles northeast of the Capitol. Just south
of Bladensburg the East Branch grew shallow and narrow, fordable in
several places. The main roads from Baltimore, Annapolis, and Upper
Marlboro met in Bladensburg to form a single road that crossed the East
Branch on a stout wooden bridge. Just west of the East Branch this road
forked: its left-hand (south) branch, the Washington Pike, ran straight
down to the Capitol and White House; the right fork went looping off to
the north and then the southwest into Georgetown, at that time a separate
village, west of Rock Creek.

By August 20 most American officers and officials had instinctively
comprehended that Bladensburg was the key to Washington. Winder
knew it and most of the time tried to act on that knowledge.

Meanwhile, Tobias Stansbury had reached Bladensburg at 7:00 P.M.
on the 22d. He knew nothing of Ross's whereabouts and apparently not
much more of Winder's. Untroubled, he dropped one regiment west

of the East Branch bridge and took the other through Bladensburg to occupy Lowndes's Hill, which dominated the roads leading into Bladensburg from the east. After an untroubled night he looked the terrain over. Concluding that Lowndes's Hill was the best defensive position available, he called the regiment he had left west of the East Branch forward.

Winder had enjoyed no such quiet night at Battalion Old Fields. In the small hours of the morning a sentry mistook a stray cow, or something, for Ross's army: American outposts therewith blazed away at all Maryland. Several anxious hours passed, with everyone more or less in battle array, before Winder was convinced that it had been a false alarm. Next, after daybreak, President Madison appeared to review Winder's "army" and deliver an inspirational address. (Madison and his cabinet including Secretary of War Armstrong, had been hovering behind Winder since the 21st, and Winder had been consulting them at every opportunity.)

Armstrong offered more advice: as Winder later remembered it, he was to convert the Capitol and adjacent buildings into a fortress and lure Ross into attacking him there. The pertinent point of it, the importance of which Winder did not grasp, was to immediately concentrate his forces. Winder announced that he would concentrate those "within his reach" near Marlboro. Orders went off to Stansbury and Sterrett to move up to within seven miles of Marlboro. Then, recollecting that Ross was somewhere east of Washington, he dispatched Major George Peter, a former regular, with 800 men from Battalion Old Fields to find the British "without running too much risk." The rest of his immediate command (approximately 1,700) was to remain at Battalion Old Fields under Brigadier General Walter Smith of the District of Columbia militia. Having thus further dispersed his command, Winder took a cavalry escort and rode north toward the Bladensburg/Upper Marlboro roads, hoping to meet Stansbury and reconnoiter the area west of Upper Marlboro—and possibly also to call Beall down to join them.

He did not find Stansbury. Just what that thunderous amateur had done remains a question. Apparently he left Bladensburg late and with reluctance; then, about a mile along the road, he met a Captain Moses Tabbs riding at top speed. Tabbs reported that Ross was six miles behind him, heading straight for Bladensburg—and Stansbury. The report was false, but Stansbury at once countermarched to Lowndes's Hill before sending Tabbs back to double-check his story.

Winder's puzzlement was increased when American cavalrymen brought him two of Ross's mounted-infantry scouts they had taken in a three-shots-and-a-gallop squabble. The captives answered, truthfully enough, that Ross still was in Upper Marlboro. Winder could hear firing off to the southeast where Peter was supposed to be probing, and to the east along the Marlboro road where part of his escort apparently had fallen foul of another British patrol. Still seeking Stansbury he started toward Bladensburg, but was overhauled by an anxious courier from General Smith: Ross was advancing up the road toward Battalion Old Fields, and Peter was being forced back.

Leaving two small cavalry detachments to outpost both roads between Bladensburg and Upper Marlboro, so that Stansbury would be warned of a British advance along either of them, Winder spurred his weary horse southward. (One, or possibly both, of these detachments wearied of outpost duty and rode into Bladensburg after dark "for refreshments.") Winder also sent an aide-de-camp to Stansbury with the clearest, most emphatic order he wrote during the entire campaign: Stansbury was to cancel any movement on Upper Marlboro, and take the best defensive position he could find east of Bladensburg. When Sterrett arrived from Elk Ridge Landing, he would be under Stansbury's command. If attacked, Stansbury was to hold out as long as possible. If forced to retreat, he should retire directly on Washington. These orders were confirmed by one of Stansbury's own aides whom he had earlier sent to Winder for orders and information. At Bladensburg, Captain Tabbs returned around 4:00 P.M. to acknowledge that his information was mostly incorrect. Sterrett's dust-choked column staggered in a little later, having trudged forty miles in thirty hours. Stansbury still was worried: he hustled them onto Lowndes's Hill and kept them standing to, without food or sleep. Another stray militia captain wandered in with bad news; Winder was missing, believed captured.

Soon thereafter, about 11:00 P.M., came Monroe. He repeated the rumor of Winder's disappearance, urged Stansbury to sally forth into the night and strike Ross's rear—neither man had the least idea where it might be—and then rode off, leaving Stansbury in something approaching panic.[15] Then Stansbury's pickets suddenly began firing; it was another false alarm, but almost three hours of groping reconnaissance were needed to prove it. Hardly had quiet of sorts been restored when another officer courier arrived from Winder.

Returning to Battalion Old Fields, Winder had ordered his command

---

15. This incredible busybodying was the result of Monroe's conviction of his own superior patriotism and military skills. His misdirected energy has led some careless historians to present him as the soul of the effort to save Washington.

there to fall back across the East Branch. Ross stopped at Battalion Old Fields, but Winder urged his men on until their orderly withdrawal became almost a running rout. Halting on the eastern edge of Washington, Winder spent much of the night making certain that the two bridges were prepared for destruction. His latest message to Stansbury gave his new position, and repeated that Stansbury was to hold at Bladensburg as long as he possibly could.

To frightened Tobias Stansbury, all this added up to just one crucial fact. He, unfortunate Tobias Stansbury, had been left all alone on the east bank of the Potomac to face the full fury of Ross's advance. He had been abandoned, practically betrayed, and was about to be sacrificed. Lacking the least desire to emulate the Spartans at Thermopylae, he roused his groggy command about 3:00 A.M. and headed toward Washington, forgetting to destroy the Bladensburg bridge behind him. Apparently he also temporarily forgot Beall, who would be coming down from Annapolis to join him at Bladensburg.[16] (Finally remembering Beall next morning at 11:00 A.M., he sent a rider to meet him, warning him to detour to the north around Bladensburg by way of an old road Stansbury had heard of but never seen.)

For the rest of the night Stansbury's weary, hungry men alternately moved and stood waiting along the dusty Washington Pike while Stansbury, very proud of having "secured our rear from surprise," looked for a place where they could find water to cook their provisions and refresh themselves. (In his after-action report he would claim that he also was looking for a new defensive position. His real feelings, however, were shown in the message that one of his aides, Major Woodyear, was carrying to Winder: Stansbury's troops were too "exhausted" to fight unless reinforced.) His final halt was "about one and a half miles" west of Bladensburg. During this halt another courier arrived from Winder with a written order reiterating his two previous ones: Stansbury must hold on to Bladensburg. Stansbury shrugged it off, certain that Winder had written it without knowing that Stansbury already had abandoned that position. He consulted his colonels, who agreed that they ought to continue their retreat until they could find a favorable position.

In Washington, confident that Bladensburg was securely held, Winder waited to see what Ross might do. He had word of Captain Gordon's laborious progress up the Potomac, and considered it entirely possible that Ross might strike south from the Woodyard to take Fort Warbur-

16. I have not, so far, discovered just when these orders were dispatched.

ton and link up with Gordon for a joint attack on Washington. These anxieties were infinitely multiplied by the arrival of Major Woodyear to report that Stansbury had abandoned Bladensburg. Thereupon, for the only recorded time during this campaign, Winder publicly lost his temper and addressed Woodyear with something more pungent than the exquisite courtesy to be expected between Maryland gentlemen. Woodyear left like a scalded cat.

Meanwhile, American cavalry left to outpost the roads leading to the two bridges across the lower East Branch kept up a string of reports: Ross had moved out at 4:00 A.M.; he was heading through Battalion Old Fields straight for Washington; he was across the side road that led along the far bank of the East Branch to Bladensburg. Some of these unknown horsemen, militia or regular, had brains and courage enough to cling to Ross's advance even then. Around 10:00 A.M. they reported that Ross had suddenly dropped his feint against the bridges, expertly reversed his order of march, and struck up the road north to Bladensburg.

Monroe departed instantly to offer his "services" to Stansbury. Winder paused to get his troops organized, then followed. There was some ill-recorded fussing; apparently Winder and certainly Secretary of the Navy Jones thought Barney and the marines should stay to protect the Navy Yard. Armstrong advised Barney to go. Barney announced he was going anyway, whether Jones consented or not. Winder left 80 regulars to guard the bridges, and a Colonel George Minor, whose 600-strong Virginia regiment had come in during the night and was still trying to find someone to issue it flints. (Tradition, apparently justified, has it that when he finally found a quartermaster functionary to do so, the count of flints issued did not come out correctly—and the functionary, amid the rumble of battle at Bladensburg, insisted on counting them all over again. Minor marched to the sound of those guns, but came too late.) Behind Winder galloped Madison and his cabinet.

While Winder and Ross raced each other up opposite sides of the East Branch, Tobias Stansbury was experiencing something of conversion. Woodyear had arrived as he was resuming his retreat: even his aide's version of Winder's reaction to the report that he had abandoned Bladensburg had echoes of Canadian frontier Army talk. Stansbury was to resume his position at Bladensburg and prepare to put up the best fight he could. Winder would support him if Ross attacked there. Stansbury's conversion, however, was incomplete: instead of reoccupying Lowndes's Hill, which he could have done easily in the time available, he chose to make his stand west of the East Branch. This was in complete disobedience of Winder's repeated orders, but Stansbury feared Ross more than he did Winder. Lowndes's Hill was a naturally strong position, the best available, but a force defending it must fight with the East Branch at their backs. A retreat through Bladensburg and across that single bridge might be a messy business. Stansbury began posting his troops. Unfortunately he was not a general, merely another flustered politician in a general's uniform.

To his front a hillside sloped gradually to the East Branch, which here ran shallow enough in many places for infantry to ford it easily. Its east bank was largely clear except for Bladensburg's scattered houses and gardens; the west bank was fringed with thickets, especially just south of the bridge where a low-lying area was covered with trees and brush. Along the north side of the Washington Pike, from just west of its junction with the Georgetown Road, a large orchard extended up the slope almost to its bare crest; the fields to either side of the Georgetown Road were open. These two roads joined approximately 200 yards west of the Bladensburg bridge. Some 150 yards farther west, inside the triangular field formed by their junction, Colonel Wadsworth's volunteer diggers had thrown up a battery position, a strongly built earthwork shaped like a shallow U from which heavy guns could sweep the streets of Bladensburg. No one in authority had thought to provide the necessary guns, but to Stansbury this empty emplacement seemed the ideal strong point to anchor his position. He therefore ordered his two Baltimore artillery companies to occupy it. They promptly found themselves in the uncomfortable condition of a small boy trying to walk in daddy's pants and shoes. Built for bigger cannon, the earthwork was higher than their 6-pounders; they had to dig embrasures in it for their guns to fire through.[17] It was hard work, the cannoneers were weary, and none of their officers really understood the business. The embrasures they made allowed them to fire on the bridge and Bladensburg's main street, but they were not cut deep enough for the guns to sweep the slope between their position and the river, or wide enough for them to fire effectively to either flank.

To the right (south) of the guns Stansbury placed the three companies of riflemen under Major William Pinkney, deployed along a fence line and in the brush south of the bridge. To cover the other flank of the guns,

17. Constructed in haste, this was a simple "barbette" battery, a low breastwork the cannon fired over, rather than through embrasures (openings) in it. Wadsworth had placed this battery to sweep the east-bank roads leading to the bridge and not the bridge itself, which he undoubtedly expected would be either destroyed or defended by infantry.

Stansbury took a company apiece from Schutz and Ragan and posted
them around a small mill north of the Georgetown Road. The three
infantry regiments were massed in the orchard, the 5th Maryland on
the right, just off the Washington Pike. They had no field of fire, yet
were close enough to the guns and riflemen to support them readily. But
none of the American units—at best, a scattering of riflemen—were far
enough forward to defend the bridge and the fording places. The Baltimore guns could neither enfilade the river line nor sweep the length of
the bridge. And Stansbury forgot once more to destroy the bridge.

His dispositions were complete before 11:00 A.M. Nothing more was
done to strengthen the position. Gradually the waiting Americans became aware of dust clouds growing on the horizon where roads ran in
from Annapolis and along the far side of the East Branch. About noon
the first spewed out Beall's column, marching itself half-dazed to beat
Ross to Bladensburg. Beall had taken no chances on Stansbury's maybe-
so side road that probably would have ended in somebody's wood lot. His
men passed on down the Washington Pike, to collapse in a position to
Stansbury's right rear.

By noon, the head of Ross's column could be seen approaching Bladensburg; the head of Smith's column was reaching the field from Washington. Preoccupied with watching the approaching British, Stansbury
failed to notice that his infantry was being moved out of the orchard
and back to the crest of the hill. There it was posted in line; the 5th on
the left, next to the Georgetown Road; Schutz's regiment in the center;
Ragan's on the right—perfectly exposed to the enemy's observation and
fire, some 500 yards behind the guns and so out of supporting distance.[18]
Secretary of State Monroe was once again saving the United States. He
had no command authority whatever, yet none of the infantry colonels
thought to challenge his orders to change position.

Any idea Stansbury might have had of correcting the situation was diverted by a meeting with General Smith and the necessity of establishing
which of them was senior. Meanwhile Winder had arrived and checked
Stansbury's dispositions. He failed to correct Monroe's fiddling with the
infantry or order the bridge destroyed. Instead he fiddled with Pinkney's
riflemen shifting one company to the left of the guns, and replacing it
with a company from Smith's leading regiment. His single constructive
action was to also call forward Captain Benjamin Burch's militia artillery

18. The maximum effective range of an infantry musket against troops in formation was 200 yards.

company, posting three of its guns, guarded by a second detached infantry company, on the Georgetown Road to the left of Stansbury's infantry, the remaining two in the Washington Pike to the infantry's right.[19]

In the meantime Smith was posting his brigade along a concave hill line astride the Washington Pike, almost a mile to Stansbury's right rear. To his front were open fields, ending at a steep-banked creek. Any British drive down the Washington Pike would be into the teeth of Barney's guns—two 18-pounders[20] in the road, three 12-pounders just to the south of it, with an improvised battalion of flotillamen and marines on their right. It would also be raked by converging fire from hills to right and left. To the south, beyond Barney's men, was Beall's command. To the north was Magruder's 1st Regiment of "District" militia; to Magruder's left was Major Peter's artillery company with six 6-pounders;[21] beyond Peter was Lieutenant Colonel William Scott's provisional battalion of regulars. Colonel Daniel Brent's 2d District Regiment and two small battalions of Maryland militia[22] formed a second line behind Peter and Scott. Two detached companies were farther north to detect any British advance by the Georgetown Road. Another battalion under Lieutenant Colonel Kramer, some 240 men, were deployed along the creek 400-odd yards to the front. This was a good position, undoubtedly the best available in the little time Smith's brigade had to deploy, but it did not tie in with Stansbury's. The cavalry, which might have been used to establish a linkage, was assembled north of the Georgetown Road to the left rear of Burch's three guns.

Deployed as they were the Americans must fight two separate defensive actions. Neither Stansbury nor Smith could effectively support the other. Winder had no reserve that he could commit to influence the action; in fact, he did not even establish a central command post from which he could try to control his spraddled-out command. Against it, Ross's concentrated force would come surging out of Bladensburg like a red battering ram.

19. Winder afterwards complained concerning local dignitaries who interfered with the deployment. He particularly noted Francis Scott Key, a Washington lawyer and man-about-town who seems to have been AWOL from Peter's company.

20. These guns had come with the marines from the Navy Yard, though Barney's seamen manned most of them here; 18-pounders were properly siege or ships' guns, not field artillery.

21. Peter had commanded Dearborn's experimental horse artillery company in 1808–9, but resigned after Eustis sold its horses.

22. One, Major Henry Waring's battalion, was from Beall's command.

Only one thing was certain: these Americans—militia, regulars, flotil-lamen, and marines—were hard-used men. For four days they had en-dured forced marches, half-rations, comfortless bivouacs, and little sleep. They were half-sick from August heat, dust, salt rations snatched half-cooked or raw. Worse, they had been hurry-scurried back and forth across the countryside by generals who all too obviously did not know what they were doing and were afraid of the enemy to boot. Those redcoats across the East Branch were Wellington's "Invincibles." But, to the honor of the United States, most of them would stand and fight.

Even so, it did not last long—less than an hour by most accounts. The British column had halted while its advance guard probed Bladensburg. (Sensible opponents would have had outposts there, perhaps a small am-bush set and waiting.) When it signaled that the place was clear, Colonel William Thornton launched his "light brigade"—the 85th Light Infan-try Regiment and the light infantry companies of the 4th, 21st, and 44th Foot—against Stansbury. The Baltimore gunners proved surpris-ingly accurate: they broke up Thornton's first push through Bladensburg, silenced a British rocket detachment, and stopped the first rush across the bridge. But the light brigade kept coming, breaking up into open order, working between houses and through gardens, swarming down to the East Branch in a dozen places, and splashing across.

By some oversight the gunners had solid shot, almost useless against small groups of men, but no canister for close-range work. The detached infantry company south of the bridge fired one wild volley and fled. The 100-odd riflemen there fought, but the odds against them were impos-sible. Still desperately loading and firing, they were forced back out of the thickets into the open fields. Flooding through the wooded area south of the bridge, the British light brigade began working up into the orchard and the dead space in front of the Baltimore battery, ignoring the long-range fire of Burch's two guns on the Washington Pike. Unable to defend themselves, with British infantry closing in, the Baltimore artillerymen hastily got five of their guns limbered up and away; the sixth they had to spike and abandon. Together with the two rifle companies, they retreated up the Georgetown Road, the riflemen rallying on the 5th Maryland.

The situation worsened rapidly. While the light brigade filtered through the orchard, its skirmishers sniping at Ragan's and Schutz's exposed regi-ments, the 44th Foot was fording the East Branch at several points north of the bridge, overwhelming and scattering the Americans there. Taking cover behind the mill and a large barn just west of the abandoned battery position, the 44th began forming for an attack to envelop the American left flank. Burch's three guns raked the orchard, then hammered the barn, but could do little damage. More British troops were pouring into Bladensburg. Then the British began showering Schutz and Ragan with rockets. The screeching, flaming flight of these projectiles, their completely erratic ricocheting, always wrung the bowels of raw troops. Apparently none of the dozens of rockets discharged at the two regiments actually hit anyone, but their psychological effect was terrifying.

From his position on the Georgetown Road near the 5th Maryland, Winder could see only a small part of his battle. What he saw he misunderstood. His solution to the British advance was to order the 5th to counterattack. The 5th went down the hill, its right flank under raking fire from the British in the orchard, British firing at it from the front—some 600 men in all, counting Pinkney's two rallied rifle companies. Sterrett halted it just west of the lost battery position, and shot it out with the elements of light brigade to their front, forcing them back toward the bridge. The detached infantry company guarding the guns on the Georgetown Road came down to help; the guns there and on the Pike blazed away in support. But the 44th began to advance past the 5th's left flank; the 5th soon was catching fire from three directions.

Three hundred yards to its right rear, Ragan's and then Schutz's regiments began firing at the orchard, where units of the light brigade were massing for an attack. It was a complete reversal of legendary North American warfare—Americans ranked shoulder-to-shoulder in the open, the British firing deliberately from cover. Then the two drafted regiments collapsed into a running mob. Winder, Stansbury, other officers tried to rally them; some responded, and Winder galloped down toward the 5th. Even as he rode the 85th Light Infantry swarmed out of the orchard and overran the rallied fragments. Ragan was wounded and captured; Stansbury escaped. Downslope, Winder hesitated—ordering Burch and the 5th to withdraw, countermanding those orders, then renewing them. He sent Burch off first, leaving the 5th unsupported. The 5th tried to withdraw in order but lacked the training to do it properly. Suddenly it broke and ran. The 44th Foot came up the hill in pursuit.

Later Winder would claim that he intended to rally Stansbury's brigade in a line with Smith's. Most of the brigade probably was beyond rallying, but the three batteries and the cavalry still were available. There was a half-mile of broken ground between them and Smith's left flank. To Winder, light-headed from lack of sleep and excitement, it looked impassable for guns. He sent them on along the Georgetown Road with orders to retreat "toward the capital." Then he cut across country toward Smith.

Smith's battle already was in full blaze. Down the Washington Pike against him surged most of the light brigade, with the 4th Foot and Ross's one 6-pounder in support. Kramer's men checked them along the creek line, waging a stubborn bushwhacking fight until in danger of being out-flanked. Then they retired on order, firing as they fell back, angling across the field to the south so as not to mask Barney's guns, and rallying on Beall. The light brigade came on again, straight into the buzz saw of Barney's and Peter's expertly served guns. They tried three times; three times the guns stopped them before they got within musket range, even though their rocket troops put down a barrage in support of their third assault.

Thornton swung the light brigade to his left, crossed the creek south of the bridge, and drove for a gap between Beall and Barney's sailors-turned-infantry and marines. Barney ordered a counterattack; there was a murderous short-range fire fight, with the American guns smashing the British right flank. Thornton went down badly wounded; the lieutenant colonel and major of the 85th were hit; the 85th fell apart and was chased back to the creek.

However, Smith's left-flank outposts reported British troops approach-ing from the north. Stansbury's routed troops having fled too rapidly to be overtaken, Colonel Arthur Brooke of the 44th had left the George-town Road and was marching to the sound of the guns. Smith at once shifted Colonel Brent's regiment to his left flank to reinforce the two companies already there. Whether this refused flank could have stood off Brooke can never be known; Winder already had sent aides spurring ahead to order Smith to retreat before he was surrounded. Smith obe-diently pulled his brigade out in almost perfect order. In the bustle, the aides may have missed Barney, who was then reforming his lines after his counterattack; possibly, considering himself a free agent, he may have disregarded their message. Possibly they did not reach Beall, though one of them reported that he did. But Barney shortly found himself alone except for Beall's command, which he accused of "giving a fire or two" and then retreating. Beall would reply that Barney exaggerated. No mat-ter; the 44th, the 4th, and the battered light brigade closed in. Beall was forced off his hill, Barney overwhelmed. Badly wounded, he ordered his survivors to run for it. Ross, Cochrane, and their officers paid him every honor and attention.[23]

23. Barney's report naturally gives the impression that he fought the battle all alone. Probably Peter's faster-firing 6-pounders did as much damage as Barney's heavier guns.

Under orders from Winder, Smith twice halted his retreat and formed to fight again. Each time, Winder changed his mind and ordered the retreat continued. Then came Winder's order to "fall back on the Capitol and there form for battle." Smith still had some 3,000 men—Minor's Virginia regiment had joined him during the retreat—and Peter's guns. Armstrong was there, still hoping to use the federal buildings as strong points. But panic was eating at Winder. Again flinching from the thought of fighting, he ordered a retreat through Georgetown, then on up the Potomac for three miles to Tenleytown. District militiamen fell out of the ranks by hundreds to see to the safety of their families.

Madison and his cabinet had left the battlefield "leaving military movements to military men" (which cynics later interpreted as meaning the British) just before Stansbury's line gave way. He arranged with his cabinet members to rendezvous in Frederick, Maryland, and then crossed the Potomac and headed westward into Virginia. Armstrong and Secretary of the Treasury George W. Campbell rode to Frederick; Secretary Jones and Attorney General Richard Rush went with Madison. The government of the United States had, in effect, collapsed and splattered itself across the countryside.

After crushing Barney, Ross had halted for two hours to rest and reorganize. Short as the fight had been, it had left scars on his command. Some 5,000 to 6,000 Americans had faced 4,000 Englishmen; perhaps a third of each side never fired a shot. Ross reported 64 killed and 185 wounded, which probably did not include those slightly wounded; several British officers privately put their loss at close to 500. Americans claimed only 26 killed and 51 hurt, undoubtedly also an understatement, which does not reflect the complete shattering of Stansbury's brigade. The Americans also lost an undetermined number of guns and two flags.[24]

Resuming his march at 6:00 P.M. with the comparatively fresh 4th Foot leading his column, Ross came into Washington at nightfall. Fires already were blazing at the Navy Yard where Captain Thomas Tingey had touched off its storehouses, shipyard, and vessels and the East Branch bridges. Somebody had set the north end of the "Long Bridge" over the Potomac to Virginia afire. To be doubly safe, Virginians fired its south end. Having unhappy remembrances of British soldiers drunk and beyond all control in captured Spanish towns, Ross took only some 300

24. Ross claimed the capture and destruction of ten guns. The Americans certainly lost eight—one Baltimore gun at Wadsworth's battery position and Barney's five, plus Burch's two guns on the Washington Pike, which seem to have been abandoned by their crews when the light brigade advanced up the Pike against Smith.

men into Washington. Near the Capitol some unidentified Americans fired from a house, killing Ross's horse and two corporals. The snipers got away; the house was burned. The Capitol came next, then the White House. (British Army legend had it that the White House dining room was set for a "victory" banquet, which the British enjoyed before using Madison's furniture for kindling.) A heavy rain that night checked the arson, but all through August 25 details burned other public buildings, including the Washington Arsenal where 12 officers and men were killed and 30 wounded by the accidental explosion of gunpowder cached in a well. Private property was generally spared, much of the looting that occurred being done by local citizens.

Meanwhile at Tenleytown, Winder had reluctantly given the 1,000-or-so men still with him three hours' rest. With Washington flaming through the night behind him, but without making the least effort to see if Ross was pursuing him, he awakened his troops around midnight and fled five miles farther up the River Road. (Monroe was with him, approving his stampede.) The next morning he began to collect what men he could at Montgomery Court House (now Rockville), sixteen miles northwest of Washington.

In Canada, Prevost would grandly proclaim that "as a just retribution, the proud capital at Washington has experienced a similar fate" to that which York had suffered in 1813.

THIRTEEN

Rockets' Red Glare

And the star-spangled banner in triumph shall wave. . . .
—Francis Scott Key

MAJOR GENERAL ROBERT ROSS WAS a sensible soldier. In six days he had marched sixty miles into United States territory, routed a larger American army, and captured the capital of the United States. It was an outstanding feat of arms, and he knew it. But on August 25 he also knew that he was isolated in a hostile countryside, all of those sixty miles from his supporting fleet and any resupply of rations and ammunition. As to what the Americans might be doing he had no idea; his information was limited to what his sentries could see, and this was broken, wooded country. Somehow, possibly from sightings of American stragglers, a rumor was growing of strong American forces concentrating at Georgetown. An effort to regain a lost capital was to be expected—even from Yankees. Meanwhile, a violent two-hour afternoon storm had put an end to such official arson as had not been completed. Also, Ross had his orders: he was not to risk his command by lingering, once he had taken his objective and done all the damage he could.

So, while Winder cowered at Montgomery Court House and Madison was fleeing deeper into Virginia, Ross set about the usual professional preparations for a night withdrawal. Patrols ordered all citizens of Washington to remain indoors during the night; rumors of a renewed offensive the next morning were casually leaked; ample firewood collected. Between 8:00 and 9:00 P.M., with campfires blazing brightly and small details designated to keep them up and simulate normal camp activity around them for a while, the British slipped back into the darkness "by twos and threes," formed up, and marched away in "profound silence." At Bladensburg there was a short halt while the troops recovered the packs they had thrown off at the beginning of their attack. Lacking wagons, Ross perforce had abandoned many of his wounded, including Colonel William Thornton, in an improvised hospital there. The Americans, "however unlike civilized nations they might be" (so Lieutenant George R. Gleig delicately put it), were at least admitted to be merciful to their captives.

Leaving Bladensburg, Ross drove his men on through the darkness. Fatigue gradually eroded their discipline; men began falling out of the ranks. At 7:00 A.M. of the 26th Ross, certain that he had broken contact with any American troops around Georgetown, therefore halted and let his command sleep until noon. After a half-hour of "breakfast," he hustled them on to Upper Marlboro, where they spent the night. From American accounts their march had grown increasingly disorderly, with foraging parties seizing livestock, vehicles, and any convenient loot they could snap up in the process. Also, Ross's column shed stragglers and deserters who looted across the countryside in the hearty old English style. No American troops appeared, but local posses—citizens willing to fight for their hen roosts, if not for their country—began forming. At Marlboro Dr. William Beanes gathered some neighbors and began collecting these marauders. Somehow learning of this flare-up of local resentment, Ross sent a detachment back to seize the doctor, apparently intending to treat him as a guerrilla.[1]

Once back aboard ship, Ross immediately began reestablishing strict discipline and refurbishing his command's arms and equipment. Behind him a shattered United States government was gropingly attempting to reassemble itself. James Madison was sixty-three, in frail health, worn out, and half-dazed by events. Vice President Elbridge Gerry was sixty-nine, ailing, and a complete nonentity.[2] Secretary of War John Armstrong, pursuant to Madison's direction, was in Frederick. But Secretary of State James Monroe was in the area and replete with unexpended zeal. It was

---

1. Some soldiers wounded in the arsenal explosion had to be left in Washington. Others came into the American lines at Baltimore and elsewhere as deserters. An unknown number of stragglers was gathered up by civilians, and there is an odd case of a John Hodges who was tried as a traitor for having arranged the return of some of these when the British threatened to burn Maryland towns if they were not given up.

2. I have not been able to ascertain whether or not he was in Washington at this time. He died November 23.

only natural that Madison should depend on him, especially since he himself had become the object of popular derision and distrust.

Learning of Ross's withdrawal, Winder had left Montgomery Court House late on the morning of the 26th with all the troops he could collect, en route to Baltimore. His going left Washington practically undefended against another threat; Captain James Gordon's squadron finally had worked its way up the Potomac to within striking distance of the capital. Anchoring off Fort Warburton on the evening of the 27th, Gordon had his bomb ships fire a few experimental rounds from their mortars. They missed the fort completely, but Captain Samuel Dyson was even less inclined to heroism than Tobias Stansbury had been four nights earlier on Lowndes's Hill. He at once, to the open-mouthed amazement of the British squadron, evacuated the fort and blew it up behind him. The Potomac thus unblocked, Gordon moved in on Alexandria. Being without defenses the town capitulated: Gordon spent the next three days peeling its citizens of their shipping—twenty-one assorted vessels—and all the flour, cotton, tobacco, wines, and "segars" that could be crammed into it and any spare corners of his warships. Washington he ignored; there would be neither point nor profit in capturing it a second time. Early on August 31 a dispatch vessel from Cochrane brought him orders to rejoin the fleet, and warned him of an American ambuscade farther downriver.

Gordon's presence at Alexandria had practically paralyzed Washington. Citizens talked of surrender. Madison made Monroe acting secretary of war and acting commander of the Tenth Military District. Amid the general panic one gray-headed regular knew what should be done. Colonel Decius Wadsworth rallied some men, found some heavy guns, and began emplacing them to command the river. Monroe, riding forth to survey his new command, ordered their positions changed. (Monroe's three years' service as a junior infantry and staff officer during the Revolution hardly qualified him as an artillerist or military engineer, but he chose to assert himself.) Wadsworth observed something to the effect that he did not take orders from a secretary of state. Monroe brandished his new authority, and Wadsworth, probably unwilling to participate in another military amateur hour, "left the field." Now in full charge, Monroe energetically mustered militia—who promptly announced they would no longer serve under Armstrong. Monroe made no attempt to discourage them in that mutinous opinion; in fact, at least one of their ringleaders was his personal friend.

When Armstrong arrived from Frederick on the 29th, he found the

town roused against him.[3] He and Madison had an unsatisfactory conference, the President urging Armstrong to retire temporarily. Armstrong
left for Baltimore the next morning and from there sent Madison his
resignation. (Monroe continued as acting secretary of war until late September when he finally persuaded the distracted Madison to make his
appointment official, protesting that he never had wanted it but had accepted it only as a patriotic duty after Armstrong's "removal" for "incompetence" and "misconduct." It is a strange story. In later years even
Monroe would have occasional qualms as to whether his conduct *had*
really been inspired only by his personal rectitude and republican virtue.)
For the time being, however, whether acting or official secretary of war,
Monroe could do little. The United States government barely functioned
for weeks after Ross's departure, while its various offices struggled to
reassemble their wits, papers, and personnel and find housing. Many important records had been burned. The fighting men would be on their
own.

Baltimore all too obviously was England's next target. Baltimore was
preparing to meet that threat by an already time-honored American process; it produced a committee. On August 25 this Committee of Vigilance
and Safety called on Samuel Smith, leading citizen, distinguished Revolutionary veteran, and major general of Maryland militia to take command. Some fast back-room politicking with Governor Levin Winder got
Smith selected for active duty as part of the militia quota Madison had
requested from Maryland back in July.[4] Thereupon Smith began gathering troops and fortifying Baltimore. The Committee of Vigilance and
Safety decreed that every able-bodied man would either dig or drill. A
resident French architect, Maximilian Godefroy, recalled former skills
and laid out a very professional line of fortifications along Loudenslager
(or Hampstead) Hill, a curving ridge line that covered the eastern and
northeastern approaches to Baltimore. Black slaves, out-of-work seamen,
and wealthy merchants alike turned out to move the dirt, build the gun
platforms, and emplace the cannon. The mustering militia were somehow
fed, sheltered, and equipped.

3. Madison and Armstrong were, with considerable justice, considered the principal culprits in the failure to take timely measures to defend Washington. Armstrong,
being a "foreigner" among Virginians and the particular target of Monroe's ambitions, became the scapegoat.

4. Maryland's quota had included one militia major general (Smith) and three
brigadier generals. However, Winder had arranged things so that no militia major
generals were actually called to duty.

Impatient with the slow progress of his troops, Winder had left them under Stansbury's command and ridden ahead, eager to establish his headquarters at Baltimore. Somehow, it never occurred to him that he had been tried and found something worse than merely wanting. When a courier met him south of Baltimore with a dispatch from Smith, announcing the latter's assumption of command and requesting a report as to how many men Winder was bringing, he was outraged. He appealed to Armstrong: make me a major general as evidence of the trust the government has in me—that will settle this militia officer's "singular" pretensions. As one of his last official acts, Armstrong told him to leave most of his men with Smith and come back to Washington. Winder appealed to Monroe, and met obfuscation and an offer of the command at Washington and the lower Potomac. Refusing it, Winder finally accepted a command under Smith, but he continued to complain and intrigue, using up his superiors' time, patience, and energy until Monroe finally gave him an overdue squelching.

Smith had the willing support of the Governor Levin Winder, who was intelligent patriot enough to ignore his cousin's wailing, and also that of the Maryland militia's senior officers and Major George Armistead, who commanded Fort McHenry. He also could count on the help of three famous naval officers. Oliver Perry had been in Baltimore with a skeleton crew, waiting to take over the *Java*, once it was launched. Secretary of Navy Jones had had the inspiration (probably out of concern for the ships being built in Baltimore) to order David Porter from Washington and John Rogers from Philadelphia, where Rogers similarly had been assigned the almost-completed *Guerrière*[5] and was commanding the flotilla guarding the Delaware River, to reinforce the Baltimore garrison. Their sailors and marines would furnish skilled gunners and a stiffening for the militia infantrymen. Initially, they were sent south to attempt to trap Gordon before he could get out of the Potomac River, but they would be back, and their hard-won reputations as captains courageous would be an inspiration to Smith's citizens-soldiers. Also, there was Lieutenant Rutter with his gunboats and flotillamen, reinforced by survivors of Barney's force. Since the gunboats now would be used largely as floating batteries, some of their men, too, could serve ashore as artillerymen.[6]

Moreover, Maryland would not have to fight alone. A brigade of Vir-

---

5. These were two of the new heavy frigates authorized during the war.

6. In early July, Barney had put Rutter's strength at fourteen "barges" and 500 men. Probably his actual strength was closer to 400, plus some 50 of Barney's.

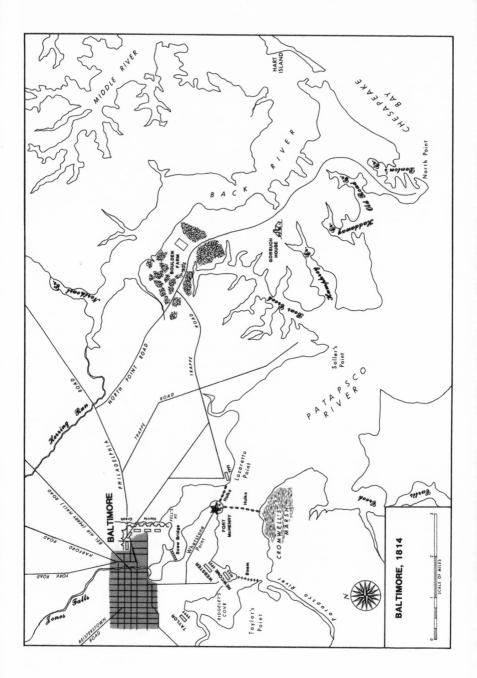

BALTIMORE, 1814

ginia militia had arrived with Winder, and Pennsylvania was mobilizing. Its militia was supposed to concentrate at York to be "regimented" before continuing on to Baltimore, but companies from York and Hanover had already marched on August 28 and 29, reporting to Smith for assignment wherever they might be useful, and companies from Hagerstown, Marietta, and other sleepy, peaceful places had hit the road behind them. A few more regulars trickled in to reinforce Armistead's garrison. (Monroe did try to take nineteen cannon away from the Baltimore defenses to strengthen Washington.)

From the Potomac there were only reports of wasted work and courage. The three sea captains laid their trap for Gordon, but neither Jones nor Monroe gave them proper tools. Porter built a masked battery near the ruins of Fort Warburton where the Potomac ran narrow; Perry roughed out another battery on the bluffs of Indian Head several miles downstream; Roger prepared several fireboats. But Porter had only eleven guns, few if any of them heavier than 12-pounders. Perry had mere 6-pounders, reinforced by an antique 18-pounder he had scratched up somewhere in the backcountry. Almost every one of Gordon's smaller warships carried more and heavier guns than the entire lot. Still, the Americans might have done better had not the impetuous Porter opened fire on the British brig *Fairy*, which was sailing upriver with Cochrane's orders recalling Gordon. That, in contemporary French phrase, "sold the coconut." Gordon thus came ready for action, knowing where Porter was. Even so, it took him four days to silence Porter's guns so that his long convoy of loot-laden prizes could pass in safety. Meanwhile he had to beat off two attacks by Rogers. Then, with his squadron threading its way through the river's tricky shoals and oyster banks, the rocket ship *Erebus* grounded in front of Perry's battery, and there was another lively row until the Americans ran out of ammunition. The next morning Gordon went on unchallenged, somewhat nicked and notched, but with all his ships still serviceable. He had shown skill, courage, and determination, but the odds in men and guns had been overwhelmingly in his favor. He had lost seven men killed and thirty-five wounded; the Americans, eleven and nineteen.

It has been suggested that Ross and Cochrane could easily have taken Baltimore had they attacked immediately after the evacuation of Washington, the troops moving north through Bladensburg to rendezvous with the fleet at the mouth of the Patapsco River. Except for Fort McHenry, which had been sited to protect its harbor's entrance, Baltimore was without fortifications, open and easy of access from the south and west. The best of its militia had been with Stansbury and now were thoroughly scattered. Ross's column probably would outnumber whatever militia could be hurriedly rallied to oppose him.

In fact—barring one of war's unpredictable accidents—Ross and Cochrane could indeed have done it, then or probably any time in the next two weeks. Why they did not really remains a puzzle. Ross finished reembarking on August 30 but held his men aboard ship, "preparing for sea," until the fleet sailed on September 6. It may have been that his command was worse hurt and more disorganized than is generally realized, but probably Ross simply had decided that he had taken chances enough on his dash into Washington, and had no desire to run further unnecessary risks. An overland march against Baltimore would separate him from Cochrane's fleet; he would have to carry his reserve ammunition and several days' rations, or gamble on being able to pick up sufficient food from the country as he marched. He would be isolated in the midst of hostile territory, without cavalry to scout for him and so never certain of the location or strength of American forces. Baltimore was a larger, more important place than Washington and undoubtedly would be more stoutly defended. By now, the Americans would know how weak his command really was and, unmilitary as they might be, they should be able to mass much larger numbers of militia against him. In short, being a sensible professional soldier, Ross expected something resembling professional conduct from his enemy, and so saw risks and dangers where there actually were none.

Cochrane agreed that it would be better for the fleet and expeditionary force to work closely together. The topography of the Baltimore area favored such a joint attack by land and water. They would move against Baltimore and test its defenses. If those appeared weak, they would attempt to take the town. But first they would put its defenders off guard by an apparent withdrawal.

On the 6th Cochrane took the fleet out of the Patuxent River and down Chesapeake Bay to the mouth of the Potomac. (He had two unwanted American passengers: John S. Skinner, the American agent for communication with the British fleet in the Chesapeake[7] and the elegant Francis Scott Key. The two had come with Madison's approbation to seek the release of Dr. Beanes. Ross finally granted their request, as an

7. Skinner handled prisoner exchanges and related matters. Apparently he knew his business, since he brought letters from the captured officers. Probably he conducted the actual negotiations, but Key claimed the credit.

acknowledgement of the excellent care given the wounded he had left at Bladensburg, but kept the three Americans with the fleet until the projected attack on Baltimore was completed.) The fleet's appearance off the Potomac suggested a renewed threat to Alexandria, where Gordon had had to leave large stocks of foodstuffs he did not have cargo space for, and to Washington.

Meanwhile Cochrane and Cockburn were indulging their pyromania: all along the Chesapeake houses and barns went up in flames. Only rarely did their raiding parties pay for their fun. Sir Peter Parker, who had gone northward to threaten Baltimore during Ross's raid on Washington, had looked for something more exciting than destroying waterside villages. Learning that 200 American militia were camped near the mouth of the Sassafras River,[8] he landed after dark on August 30 with 124 sailors and marines to surprise them. His guides, who had probably been impressed, misled him; when he found the militia, they were up and ready. The British attacked headlong, driving the militia from their camp, then found themselves in a closing trap and had to run for it through the American crossfire. They left 13 dead and some of their 28 wounded behind them. Parker was mortally hurt; American casualties are unknown. However, such setbacks were too rare to teach the British caution.

Picking up Gordon as he emerged from the Potomac, Cochrane turned and swept north again on a favoring wind. As he came, alarm guns, beacons, and horsemen spread the news inland along both shores of the Chesapeake. Smith had a "horse telegraph" of dispatch riders to forward the coast watchers' reports,[9] but the fleet moved almost as swiftly as his galloping couriers. By the afternoon of September 11 Cochrane was off the mouth of the Patapsco. A complex of shoals, known to few but local pilots, barred easy passage into the river for large ships. Gordon bucked his heavy frigate *Seahorse* across two shoals, got embedded in another, and had a long, mean job unloading guns and stores to lighten the ship sufficiently to get it back into deeper water. The fleet therefore anchored off North Point. From there, Ross would be approximately fourteen miles away from the eastern edge of Baltimore by a good enough road. Cochrane's lighter ships would have twelve miles of relatively open channel to reach Fort McHenry. Shortly after midnight an ably planned

8. The Sassafras is an east-bank tributary of the Chesapeake, roughly opposite today's Aberdeen Proving Ground.

9. A study of this early warning system would be rewarding. It seems to have been considerably extended and improved after August 25.

and handled landing put some 5,000 men and eight cannon ashore in perfect order. To strengthen Ross's column and make good his losses at Bladensburg, Cochrane had given him a "naval brigade" of almost 1,000 seamen, armed as infantry. The whole force was ashore by 7:00 A.M., sorting itself out for the march on Baltimore.

In Baltimore, General Smith could only wait. As long as Ross's soldiers were aboard ship the British had a choice of tactics: they might land at North Point, or bring their troops up either Back River or the Patapsco in the fleet's light craft and boats for a landing within a few miles of Baltimore. They also might use a portion of their forces to feint, pretending to carry out one of these attacks while committing—once the feint had sufficiently distracted the Americans—their main strength to another. Any American troops stationed out on the peninsula toward North Point thus would be in considerable danger of being cut off by British forces landing in their rear.

Nevertheless, believing that the British would be both overconfident and in a hurry, Smith was willing to take a calculated risk that they would choose what must seem to them the quickest and simplest course of action—for Ross to advance by land from North Point, Cochrane to come up the Patapsco. Smith would have to rely on Fort McHenry and its supporting batteries to stop Cochrane, but Ross's probable line of march—a narrow road through thick woods, broken by occasional farms and laced with swampy creeks and tidal inlets—offered opportunities for an effective delaying action.

A well-handled small force could delay and bleed Ross's advance without allowing itself to be trapped by superior numbers, but such tactics—especially their final phase of slipping away at the last moment—would be a tricky mission for American militia. Smith accordingly chose to risk the best he had, his "City" (or 3d) Brigade, made up of Baltimore citizens who literally would be fighting for their hearths and homes. Its commander was Brigadier General John Stricker,[10] who had been a captain of artillery under Washington; its total strength a bare 3,200—five regiments of infantry, a tiny one of cavalry, a three-company battalion of riflemen, and a company of artillery with six 4-pounders. One of the infantry regiments, the 5th, and the riflemen were veterans of Bladensburg; they had learned something of combat and had reputations to refurbish. The 6th, 27th, and 39th regiments included volunteer militia companies

10. Stricker's selection further injured Winder's infected ego, but it was obvious to everyone else that neither he nor Stansbury was fit for such a mission.

that at least knew parade-ground drill and had a certain cohesion from continued service together.

Moving out in the late afternoon of September 11, Stricker camped for the night along Bread-and-Butter Creek, seven miles east of Baltimore, covered by an outpost line of riflemen two miles beyond. Colonel James Biays's cavalry trotted on into the dusk for another mile to set up a patrol base at the Gorsuch farm. From it Biays sent scouts probing toward North Point. Some hours later, when Ross's troops swarmed methodically ashore, American troopers watched from the edge of the woods that ringed the beachhead. With first light they would count the number of regiments and guns, and couriers would go pounding back to the bivouac at Bread-and-Butter Creek.

Biays's reports made it plain that Ross had indeed staked everything on an advance from North Point, and that there was little chance of any sizable British landing behind Stricker from either the Patapsco or Back River. As an additional precaution Smith had covered Stricker's right flank by posting a small force, Major Randall's "light corps," at Sollers' Point where it could watch both the Patapsco and Bear Creek.

By daybreak Stricker had his men up, fed, and ready to march. Now he moved forward to the position Smith and he already had selected. A mile or so east of Bread-and-Butter Creek the peninsula narrowed suddenly, pinched in between Bear Creek on the south and an unnamed branch of Back River to the north.[11] The woods, known locally as Godly Wood, ended there, replaced by the half-mile-wide clearing of the Boulden farm. Beyond that were more woods, split by the narrow notch where the road went on toward North Point.

Stricker was in position by 9:00 A.M. His first line stood behind the north-south fence along the western edge of Boulden's farm, the 5th Regiment to the right of the road, his artillery astride it, the 27th Regiment (which called itself the "Jefferson Blues") to the left of the guns. Three hundred yards behind that first line he posted the 51st and 39th regiments, the 51st on the right. The 6th Regiment had already taken position across the road just west of Bread-and-Butter Creek as a reserve. This formation was flexible. If Ross drove straight down the road, the 5th and 27th were to resist as long as possible, then retire through the second line and rally on the 6th. The second line, in turn, was to fight while it could, then fall back to join the other regiments behind Bread-and-Butter Creek. Stricker's right flank, anchored on the head of Bear

11. Its width here was between one-half and three-fourths of a mile.

Creek, could not be turned. If the British attempted to envelop his open left flank, he could shift his second line to fill the gap between the 27th and the inlet from Back River. The Americans would be half concealed by the fence and the shadows of Godly Wood behind them; the British must advance across open fields. Their only cover from American fire would be an old cabin south of the road, a straggling row of haystacks north of it.[12] A professional soldier would have had the lot burned immediately—just as Armistead was pulling down houses that might block Fort McHenry's fire. But it was thirty-odd years since John Stricker had been a hard-bitten combat soldier. Now he was a banker, an esteemed figure in Baltimore society, as well as a citizen-soldier. He was going to fight, but the idea of offhandedly destroying a fellow citizen's property just to improve his field of fire probably never occurred to him. At the last moment he did detach a company of the 5th to occupy the cabin, with orders to burn it when they were driven out, but only a few of its men could find places to fire through its windows and chinks in its walls. Meanwhile the company would block much of the 5th Regiment's fire.

Stricker, however, had planned a small-scale delaying action of his own. Just as Smith had sent him to make the British advance on Baltimore as slow and expensive as possible, Stricker wanted some of the drive knocked out of that advance before it came up against his own position. If Ross struck it as he had hit Winder at Bladensburg, headlong and all out, taking his losses in his stride, Stricker's brigade might come apart like Stansbury's had. But if he could give the British advance guard a bloody nose beforehand, Ross probably would advance more cautiously thereafter. Almost three miles farther east was a small, dense pine woods, with another stretch of open ground beyond it—an ideal position for riflemen, whose weapons outranged British muskets. Stricker accordingly ordered Captain William Dyer to take the rifle battalion, some 150 men, forward to the eastern "skirts" of the woods and prepare to "annoy" the enemy.[13] Then it was a matter of waiting.

Ross was a sensible officer. He was not going to plunge forward along the narrow North Point road without proper march security—a strong advance guard and flank guards to probe the woods on either side. But those woods were dense, concealing labyrinths of thorny thickets, bogs,

12. There were also the Boulden farm buildings on the far (east) edge of the clearing, but these were almost a half-mile from Stricker's line and so out of musket range.

13. Dyer was commanding in place of Major William Pinkney, wounded at Bladensburg.

ponds, and tidal inlets through which the flank guards wallowed blas-phemously, occasionally half-drowning themselves or getting lost. Ross's main body had to wait on their inching progress. Stricker, expecting at any moment to hear the distant crackling of Dyer's rifles, waited while two hours crawled by, his waiting broken only by occasional cavalrymen with Biays's reports of Ross's progress.

Then suddenly Dyer came draggletailing back in something of a hurry. He had heard a rumor, source unrecorded, that a British boat expedi-tion had come up Back River and was putting troops ashore behind him. Without pausing to check out that story, he had gathered his battalion and headed for Baltimore. Stricker's remarks, unfortunately, are also un-recorded. He sent the rifle battalion off to his extreme right flank to squat in the bushes between the 5th Regiment and Bear Creek. There they could enfilade a British attack along the road, and also would be iso-lated enough to keep them from spreading their discouragement through his fidgeting brigade. All this left Stricker ready to chew horseshoes and spit nails. And around noon another message from Biays uncorked that bottled-up anger.

Ross's advance guard had reached the Gorsuch farm around 11:00 A.M. Riding just behind it, Ross ordered a halt to rest his men. For him-self and Cockburn, who again was accompanying the troops, Ross re-quested breakfast, which the Gorsuch family served them at a table in their front yard. Lounging along the road, British soldiers dipped into their haversacks for a quick meal of the obdurate sea biscuit and boiled salt pork issued them before they disembarked. The naval brigade how-ever scorned such fare; breaking ranks they went through the Gorsuch barnyard like a swarm of blue locusts, butchering pigs, cattle, and poul-try, completely out of control. By British accounts, Ross, Cockburn, and their staffs found their "Jolly Jacks" antics extremely amusing.

Other Americans besides Robert Gorsuch and his family viewed this "singular behavior" less happily. Ross's advance guard had halted only a short distance beyond the farm. From nearby timber Biays's vedettes had a good view of the entire proceedings. Biays had handled them well. Only three of them had been caught by British patrols, and these, when in-terrogated by Ross himself at Gorsuch's, had lied shrewdly as to Smith's strength and made no mention of Stricker's advance. Now Biays sent back the report that touched off Stricker's ire. The head of Ross's col-umn was halted at Gorsuch's, sailors were running wild while laughing officers had breakfast in the front yard.

To Stricker, this meant an excellent opportunity for a hit-and-run raid that would definitely unsettle British digestions. Quickly assembling a small strike force—two companies of the 5th, seventy volunteers from among the riflemen, one 4-pounder, a small detail of cavalrymen—he sent them off under Major Richard Heath. Unfortunately, Ross had not lingered over his late breakfast.[14] Shortly after noon he resumed his march. A mile or so down the road his advance guard collided with Heath's hurrying column. Mutually surprised, Americans and British promptly had at each other for an enthusiastic bushwhacking brawl through the woods along the road. Increasingly outnumbered, amateurs at such help-yourself fighting against the 85th Foot's veterans, the Americans were gradually outflanked and forced back. They went grudgingly, however, taking their price for ground yielded, stalling the British advance long enough for Ross to become concerned. Conspicuous on his white horse, he galloped forward, as he had done so many times before in European battles, to see the situation for himself. An American rifleman killed him.

Heath somehow broke contact, getting his men out of the woods and away,[15] back to Stricker's line before the British advance guard came cautiously out into the open fields of the Boulden farm—to find itself confronted by Stricker's massed infantry and guns.

Stricker's little diversion had indeed given the British a bloody nose. Colonel Arthur Brooke, who had taken Ross's place, studied the American line and quickly decided against an immediate attack from march column. Mostly well uniformed, the Baltimore regiments looked remarkably like regulars; Stricker's deep formation led the British officers to estimate his strength as at least 6,000 men. Brooke was a brave, skillful officer; his force was too small to waste men attacking superior numbers of Americans in a strong position, especially when these Americans had shown themselves willing and able to fight. He would take his time and fight his battle by the book, bringing his whole force into action to make a victory certain.

The 85th Foot deployed across Stricker's front, to cover the movements of the regiments behind it. The rocket troops, firing from behind the Boulden farm buildings, put down a noisy barrage. Brooke massed

14. American folklore claimed that when Gorsuch ironically suggested that he might be back in time for supper, Ross proclaimed, "I'll sup tonight in Baltimore or hell."

15. His cavalry had proved useless in the woods, and he had not been able to get his gun into action.

his guns to the right of the road[16] and swung his infantry into line of battle: the naval brigade on his left, next to Bear Creek, then the 21st Foot, the battalion of Royal Marines, the 44th Foot, and the 4th. The American 4-pounders hammered this deployment, but were too light to hurt it appreciably. Brooke's planning was excellent. He would use his heaviest guns (two 6-pounders and one howitzer) for counterbattery fire to smother Stricker's artillery, the lighter ones and his rockets to soften Stricker's infantry; the 4th and 44th would envelop the American left flank. The 21st, charging down the road in column, would smash Stricker's right center. Pressed home, these attacks would pocket and destroy most of the American force.

Stricker countered Brooke's movements by bringing his 39th Regiment into line on the left of the 27th and ordering the 51st to form a refused flank, at almost a right angle to the rest of his line, beyond the 39th. To strengthen this new formation he shifted two of his guns to fill the interval between the 39th and 51st. The guns and the 39th moved as ordered; the 51st, Stricker's biggest regiment, promptly collapsed in confusion. Possibly its companies had had too little drill as a regiment, probably its colonel was incompetent. Stricker's staff practically had to herd it into position.

Brooke's plan developed remorselessly. One of the American guns in the road was wrecked; the American infantry battered, its left-flank regiments getting special attention. Once the 4th Foot came into line on the British right, Brooke sent his whole front forward, the 85th deploying as skirmishers to cover the Royal Marines and 44th. American guns slugged at that advance, hitting it, hurting it, but its red ranks closed up and came steadily on, stepping over its dead as if they were not there.

Then the 4th Foot ran into a boggy creek that fed into the Back River inlet, ugly dark water coiling through tall reeds and swamp grass, too wide to jump, too deep to wade. Its advance stalled, officers uncertain, skirmishers probing for a crossing and popping off occasional shots across the stream at the 51st Regiment. The 51st promptly let go one spasmodic volley at the general landscape, and dissolved in instant, utter panic. The 39th's left-flank companies caught the bug-out fever and followed; the 4th Foot found a crossing and came pushing in column through the miry water. But the two 4-pounders' crews did not flinch; half, or better, of the 39th faced half-left and blazed into the 44th's rush. With them Stricker built a new refused flank. What happened then is unclear. The 4th may

16. Brooke had two 6-pounders, two howitzers, and four 3-pounders.

have found its ford difficult going, possibly the officers of its leading companies had been hit or were overexcited. Instead of swinging to its left to
roll up Stricker's line, the 4th plunged straight ahead into the woods, on
the track of the fugitive 51st.[17]

All across the field, meanwhile, Brooke's attack had ground forward,
firing by "half-battalions."[18] The company holding the log cabin in front
of the 5th Regiment fell back, setting it afire as they left. The 5th, 27th,
and 39th were "firing at will," each man picking his own target, but the
odds against them were worse than two to one, and the British still came
on. Stricker eyed the smoke-shrouded, closing gap between his line and
that advance and made hard, swift calculations. Something less than a
hundred yards away, along that line of haystacks, Brooke's line paused
an instant, dressing its ranks for its final drive. Stricker ordered his guns
to the rear, told his regimental commanders to keep fighting until the
British were ready to close with the bayonet, then to pull out and rally
behind Bread-and-Butter Creek.[19] It was a desperately tight business,
but by good judgment and sheer luck the Americans somehow pulled it
off. The British were only some twenty yards distant when they stopped
shooting and ran for it.

It looked like, and undoubtedly was, high confusion. One gun and an
ammunition cart were lost when their horses were killed, but practically
every American who still could run, walk, or stumble along got away. Beyond Bread-and-Butter Creek, where the 6th Regiment waited in line of
battle, most of the fugitives fell in around their flags and officers. Stricker
soon had his brigade, less most of the 51st, ready to fight again.

A driving pursuit probably would have broken the rallying Americans,
but there was no pursuit. Brooke's troops had been roughly handled, his
losses totaling 46 killed and some 300 wounded. At least part of the 4th
Foot had mislaid itself in Godly Wood, and the converging attacks of the
British right and left flanks must have ended with their regiments considerably intermixed. Also the Americans had displayed their uncivilized

17. Whether all the 4th Foot had gotten across the creek by the time the Americans ran is uncertain. Also, in the smoke and general confusion it may have been
uncertain just where the American extreme left flank was.

18. Brooke's regiments had only a single battalion present. Half of each regiment/
battalion would move forward fifteen paces, fire, and then reload while the other
half double-timed fifteen paces beyond it to repeat the process, much like World
War II's "marching fire." It was impressively noisy, but relatively harmless except at
very close range.

19. Stricker issued these orders "about fifteen minutes after four o'clock."

habit of picking off British officers. In revenge, several Americans who had clambered into trees to take better aim, and had not hit the ground running in time to escape, were refused quarter.[20] Their riddled bodies were left hanging amid the branches. Apparently no British patrol even ventured the half-mile from the battlefield to Bread-and-Butter Creek to see if those Yankees were still running. Instead, with two hours' daylight remaining, Brooke went into camp.

Stricker gave his men an hour or so to rest and reorganize, then returned to Baltimore, dropping off details to fell trees across the road behind him. He had lost 24 men killed, 139 wounded, and 50 captured or missing, most of the last being wounded men he had not been able to bring off. Biays's troopers and Randall's "Light Corps," meanwhile, also withdrew along back roads. That night it rained.

ALL THROUGH THAT DAY, WHILE BRITISH and American soldiers had fought along the North Point road, Cochrane had been getting his lighter warships—five bomb ships, the rocket ship *Erebus*, four light frigates, and six brigs and sloops-of-war—through the Patapsco River's shoals. It was slow work, but shortly after dawn of September 13 he was in position to open fire on Fort McHenry, over which flaunted an oversized garrison flag, thirty feet in the hoist, forty-two in the fly, with the then-regulation fifteen stripes and fifteen stars.

Smith, Armistead, the Committee of Vigilance and Safety, and their subordinates had done their best to prepare a fitting reception for the Royal Navy. Merchant vessels had been sunk to block the entrances to the two branches of Baltimore harbor so that only small craft could pass. The entrance to the inner basin of the Northwest Branch was further closed by a boom of heavy timber and chains, as was the mouth of Ridgeley's Cove, at the back end of the Ferry Branch. These booms were locked during the night, so that no vessel could go in or out between sunset and sunrise.

Fort McHenry had been strengthened with additional batteries, and a three-gun battery had been erected on Lazaretto Point, just across the entrance of the Northwest Branch from the fort. On the western shore of the Ferry Branch, at the entrance of Ridgeley's Cove, Colonel Decius Wadsworth had built a large earthwork, baptized Fort Covington. Just north of it was a smaller battery, somewhat extravagantly named Fort Babcock. Both covered the rear of Fort McHenry. From various sources,

20. The British considered such sniping "unfair."

including vessels in Baltimore harbor, a sufficient assortment of guns had been collected to arm these defenses; McHenry alone had fifty-seven. Also there were the gunboats, each with one or two heavy weapons.

Cochrane opened the action with his bomb ships and *Erebus* at a range of some two miles, beyond the reach of Armistead's heaviest guns.[21] Unable to reply, the Americans could only grit their teeth and endure. Fort McHenry had been built to stand up to the broadsides of attacking warships, but the largely amateur American engineers who designed it never envisioned anything like Cochrane's shower of 200-pound mortar bombs, plunging out of the sky at a steep angle to burst above or within the fort's ramparts. None of its buildings, not even its powder magazine, were proof against such projectiles. Both rockets and mortars were inaccurate weapons, but over 400 of the big bombs burst above the fort or fell within it and its outer batteries. One smashed in the magazine's roof but, by the grace of God, did not explode. Many of the rockets fell short. Around 2:00 P.M., thinking the fort must have been considerably damaged, Cochrane moved *Erebus* and three mortar ships forward to increase the accuracy of their fire. That brought them within range of Armistead's batteries.

Fort McHenry had been somewhat knocked about; four artillerymen were dead and fourteen wounded; a bomb fragment had slashed a soldier's wife in two. But only one gun had been disabled and that only temporarily. The four British ships were immediately caught in such an intense, accurate fire that Cochrane had to order a hasty retreat and resume his long-range bombardment.

MEANWHILE, AROUND 10:00 A.M. Brooke had made a tardy appearance, having taken four hours to carefully probe his way forward along the obstructed road from Godly Wood. Emerging at last into open country, he abruptly found himself confronted by the network of entrenchments, redoubts, batteries, and obstacles that covered the crest and eastern slope of Loudenslager Hill. Startled British officers counted over 100 "heavy" cannon, which they assumed to be manned by picked Navy gunners, and estimated that there must be some 22,000 Americans, possibly 5,000 of

---

21. The normal armament of a British bomb ship was either two 13-inch mortars or one 13-inch and one 10-inch. These were tricky weapons and so had a slow rate of fire. The *Erebus* was a heavy sloop-of-war, which carried rocket dischargers in addition to her normal armament; the rocket warheads might be solid shot, canister, or explosive or incendiary shell. These rockets were handled by a detachment of Royal Marine Artillery, under a Lieutenant T. S. Beauchant.

them regulars manning those fortifications. (Smith had approximately 12,000 militia and 600 regulars.) An assault on that ridge line would have two miles of open ground to cross; at the foot of the ridge ran a steep-banked creek that must be forded under fire.

Brooke did his best. A quick reconnaissance revealed that the defenses along the northern edge of Baltimore still were incomplete. Moving to his right, Brooke advanced down the Bel Air Road, only to find that Stricker's brigade and a Virginia brigade under Winder had taken position astride it. Their line was stiffened by several detached redoubts mounting impressive-looking guns. Brooke might break into the American defenses there, but it promised to be a costly business at best, with a strong likelihood of getting swamped thereafter by a massive American counterattack. Shifting back to his left, Brooke feinted a direct assault on the Loudenslager works from the east, possibly hoping to lure some of the garrison out of their defenses. Smith countered by shifting Stricker and Winder eastward into a position from which they could strike Brooke's right flank and rear if he actually attacked. Brooke pulled back and went through the motions of encamping a mile east of the American lines.

Brooke had formed a plan that, considering the few choices he had, was promising. Most of those Americans *were* militia, possibly game enough, but likely to fall into confusion if forced to maneuver under fire. His own men were "old bricks," toughened to all weathers and dangers. They had stormed skillfully defended towns in Spain; their morale, helped by the prospect of looting Baltimore, was excellent. It had been a rainy day; it was going to be a wet, windy, unpleasant night, ideal for a surprise attack with cold steel against green opponents who might not remember (or know how) to keep their powder dry.

Once it was dark enough to conceal British movements, the 21st Foot spread across Brooke's entire front, keeping up camp fires to simulate the outposts of the whole command. The Royal Marines would cover the 21st's left flank. Screened by the camp fires and the rain Brooke massed his remaining troops in one long column—first the 85th Foot, then the naval brigade,[22] the 4th, and the 44th—for an attack down the Philadelphia Road against the northeast angle of the Loudenslager line. Shortly before this main attack got silently under way, a detachment would make a noisy demonstration, with much shouting and shooting, a half-mile to the south to distract the Yankees. Attacking silently, the assaulting column

---

22. The sailors were expected to be handy at the rough hand-to-hand work of clearing the American batteries.

would then bayonet its way through the American defenses and establish a lodgement[23] in the angle of Loudenslager Hill; after dawn, when
they could see clearly what they were about, the British would fight their
way along the American line on both sides of their initial penetration,
peeling the Americans out of their defenses and driving them back into
Baltimore's streets. It would be something of a desperate enterprise, but
Brooke and his fellow officers were certain enough that it would succeed,
if given a degree of help from Cochrane's squadron.

At the southern end of the Loudenslager defenses was a particularly
strong earthwork, called "Rogers' Bastion" by Americans,[24] mounting
twenty heavy guns, a good many of which could lay enfilade fire all along
the east front of the American line. Any of Brooke's troops exposed to
them at first light would be savagely hammered. If the American gunners had noted the direction and range to critical points along their front,
they might even be able to fire effectively through the dark and rain.
Having too few men to risk such possible losses, Brooke therefore called
on Cochrane to destroy or cripple the Rogers' Bastion battery.

Cochrane could not oblige. To get within even extreme range of that
battery his mortar and rocket ships would have to move up to within
comparatively short range of Fort McHenry, the Lazaretto battery, and
the American gunboats guarding the harbor entrance. His continued
bombardment of McHenry having been ineffectual, American gunners
would gleefully proceed to knock those ships to pieces. As an alternative, Cochrane considered sending a boat attack against Rogers' Bastion, putting marines and sailors ashore on the north shore of Baltimore harbor's Northwest Branch to storm the battery from the rear, but
quickly realized that any such expedition would be suicidal during daylight. However, he would do what he could. Communication between his
fleet and Brooke was slow and difficult, but before 11:00 P.M. his messenger reached Brooke with word that, while the admiral could do nothing
against Rogers' Bastion, he would send a boat attack into Ferry Branch
to land in the rear of Fort McHenry. The mortar ships would increase
their rate of fire to cover the landing party's approach upriver, then cease
firing as it closed on its objective.

Along Loudenslager Hill, drenched American sentries peered into the
darkness and saw only the dazzle of the 21st Foot's well-nourished camp-

23. Similar to the modern beachhead or bridgehead.
24. Commodore Rogers commanded this sector of the defense, and his sailors
manned its heavy guns. He wrote his wife that she would split her sides laughing at
the sight of him on horseback.

fires. Afflicted by unjustified optimism, some American brigade commanders—undoubtedly Winder was conspicuous among them—were urging Smith to launch a night attack on what they believed was the British camp. None of them, however, had thought to send out patrols. All unknown to them Brooke's massive column stood patiently in the rain. Ten silent minutes' quick marching, then a sudden rush would bring it storming into the American lines against some 200 sailors and marines and a brigade of utterly raw militia. Off to the south the detachment that was to launch the preliminary diversionary attack likewise awaited Brooke's command. About 11:00 P.M. the slow mortar fire off to the south suddenly swelled into a thunderous pounding. Then, a few minutes before midnight, it stopped. Brooke and his staff listened expectantly.

Captain Charles Napier of the frigate *Euryalus* led Cochrane's boat attack, some twenty barges and launches carrying approximately 300 men. One craft was equipped with rocket launchers; another, described by Americans as a "long schooner," reportedly mounted an 18-pounder gun. Napier led them in through the dark and storm, navigating by experience, instinct, sheer courage, and a brave man's luck. He did not know the harbor's shoals and currents, but he found an opening in the line of hulks across the mouth of Ferry Branch. Fortunately, not all of his subordinates were as skilled or courageous, and by that time only nine boats were still with him. (Some of the missing ones blundered toward the Northwest Branch and were taken for a boat attack on the Lazaretto battery. Major Randall was sent to "dislodge" any landing party, but found none.)

Napier kept on, but took the risk of showing small guiding lights to keep his remaining boats together. They were only 200 yards off Fort Babcock when the seasoned flotillamen who formed its garrison, alerted by the sudden ending of Cochrane's bombardment, detected their approach. Fort Babcock opened with solid shot and grapeshot; Fort Covington and Fort McHenry joined in; the Lazaretto battery and the gunboats began raking the line of the hulks, trying to pen Napier inside Ferry Branch and prevent reinforcements from reaching him. To support Napier, Cochrane resumed dumping mortar and rocket fire on and around Fort McHenry. Amid this raging uproar, Napier fought a canny duel with the American batteries half-encircling him, firing and moving before the American gunners could range on his cannons' muzzle flashes. He had too few men to risk a landing, but for well over an hour he did his best to convince the Americans that he was the spearhead of a major attack. Then, men and ammunition almost exhausted, the American fire as heavy as ever, he fired off the blue rockets that told Cochrane he was retreating. Again British mortars and rocket launchers fell silent. Pulling for their lives, Napier's handful somehow escaped through the raking fire of every American battery that could bring a gun to bear.[25] Once Napier was clear the mortar ships resumed their slow hammering at Fort McHenry. Observers at Loudenslager Hill noted with relief that most of the bombs were either "shorts" or "overs."

Waiting and listening on the Philadelphia Road, Brooke gradually realized that Cochrane's attack was a failure. There had been no diminution in the American fire, and there was no sign of confusion in the American lines. Also, the very length and intensity of Napier's demonstration would have insured that the most rain-soaked and drowsy American militiamen now was thoroughly awake and checking to see if his musket's priming was dry. Brooke's attack might still succeed, but only at the risk of shattering his command. He and Cockburn agreed that Baltimore was not worth that hazard. Sometime after 2:00 A.M. Brooke ordered a retreat to North Point. Silently, efficiently his regiments faced about, got into march order, moved eastward through the dripping night, details from the 21st keeping their screening campfires blazing brightly until just before dawn. American sentries peering eastward at first light saw only empty fields where abandoned fires were smoldering out. And from offshore Francis Scott Key saw the great flag still flaunting above Fort McHenry and was somehow moved for one moment of his ornamental life.

Smith was by no means certain that Brooke was gone for good. The mortar ships were continuing their sullen pummeling of Fort McHenry. It was possible that the British retreat had been only a ruse to draw him out of his entrenchments. But at 7:00 A.M. the mortar fire stopped, and Cochrane's ships began dropping downstream. Accordingly Smith sent Winder and Randall forth in pursuit with Virginia and Pennsylvania troops and his cavalry. If the British withdrawal was genuine, it was too late for an effective pursuit, but even an ineffectual one could be excellent for American morale. And, whether it was genuine or a ruse, Smith did not intend to risk a serious engagement; consequently he entrusted the pursuing force to Winder.

Except for a few stragglers, Winder and Randall saw no Englishmen at all. Only a tiny, reportedly twenty to thirty strong, squadron of regu-

25. Surprisingly, there seems to be no exact statement either as to Napier's strength in boats and men or his losses. Probably they were slight, though Americans claimed to have sunk one of his boats.

lar light dragoons caught up with the 21st's rear guard, near the place where Ross had died. They rode through it, sabers swinging, rallied and charged again down the narrow road against the 21st and canister from two hastily unlimbered British guns, getting in among them before they were beaten off. And a Sergeant Keller and three troopers spurred in a third time through the thickets along the road, cutting their way through the 21st's line and coming back with six prisoners.

Brooke halted and formed to fight, but quickly learned that the dragoons had no infantry support and so resumed his march. He camped that night just short of North Point, and reembarked the next morning. That afternoon Smith could write Monroe that except for a few vessels the British were gone from the Patapsco River, "their destination unknown." They would linger off the coast, finally sail for Jamaica—and then for New Orleans.

It was a mighty stimulation to American pride and self-confidence. (Smith and his militiamen never realized how narrowly they had escaped the desperate assault Brooke had planned.)[26] Combined with the more serious British defeat on Lake Champlain, Baltimore would be a definite factor in persuading England to consider making peace. And Americans had a new song that, however difficult for its average citizen to sing, would ultimately become its official national anthem.[27]

26. He had worries enough over the behavior of two militia regiments he had shifted that night to the Fort Covington area. Encountering a rapidly driven wagon, many officers and men imagined a British *cavalry* attack and fled in all directions.

27. The accepted story of how Key wrote the song contains much fable. See Swanson, *The Perilous Fight*, pp. 496–99.

FOURTEEN

Triumph in the North—Almost

I have told the ministers repeatedly that a naval superiority on the Lakes is a sine qua non *of success in war on the frontier of Canada.*
—Duke of Wellington [1]

SIR GORDON DRUMMOND NOW ONCE MORE had to choose between advancing south from Queenston against the American beachhead around Fort Erie, or shifting his army to the east bank of the Niagara River and moving directly on Black Rock and Buffalo. This latter course would have forced Eleazer Ripley to withdraw hurriedly from Fort Erie, and given Drummond an excellent chance of catching the American forces piecemeal as they attempted to concentrate to defend their base. Nevertheless, he chose to attack Fort Erie.

Drummond's decision was based on several factors. He still considered himself outnumbered, and had learned that he could not take liberties with his opponents. To shift most of his forces to the east bank would expose his own base at Fort George to a counteroffensive by Ripley. Furthermore, an advance up the east bank would involve logistical difficulties, since the troops and supplies for such an offensive would have to be shifted to Fort Niagara, either by ship from Kingston or by bateaux from Fort George. With Isaac Chauncey's squadron once more controlling Lake Ontario, the first method would be impossible, the second risky. (As it turned out, except for one short cruise to the western end of the lake, and inditing top-lofty reproaches to Brown, Chauncey showed no interest in events there. Drummond, however, certainly could not have

1. Stanley, *The War of 1812*, p. 351.

anticipated such forbearance.) Finally, there was the fact that Drummond, though personally brave, was not much of a general. Incapable alike of inspiring his hard-luck little army or of planning and executing a swift and daring maneuver, he seems to have instinctively chosen the simplest course of action, which was following up Brown's retreat to Fort Erie. He did combine this with an attempt to destroy Brown's base at Buffalo—Colonel John Tucker's raid on August 3—but that proved to be sending a boy to do a man's job, and ended with Drummond officially expressing his "indignation" over the "misbehavior" of the troops involved. Apparently it also convinced him that the Americans had strong forces on both sides of the Niagara River.

Even the simplest course of action could be difficult enough on the Niagara frontier. Drummond was able to collect some reinforcements— the 41st Foot from Fort George, and Regiment de Watteville, which had been en route from Kingston[2]—but the 82d Foot, ordered forward from Kingston shortly after the battle of Chippewa, was still struggling along the primitive lakeshore roads.[3] Rations, camp equipment, and even ammunition and a few heavy guns were difficult to obtain: Commodore James Yeo's squadron had preempted, as Sir George Prevost complained, "almost the whole of the summer transport service from Montreal,"[4] just to arm and equip Yeo's new line-of-battle ship, preventing any build-up of army supplies at Kingston. Collecting what supplies he could, Drummond moved into position before Fort Erie on August 4 with slightly over 3,000 men and six siege guns.

The original Fort Erie now was only a projecting knuckle on the new American lines. The average American soldier knew how to use a spade and an axe, and Edmund Gaines,[5] Ripley, and their engineer officers had kept them busy. Fort Erie had been completed for all-around defense and greatly strengthened. The gap between the fort and the Niagara River

2. De Watteville's was a twelve-company mercenary regiment that had been in the British service since 1801. Originally Swiss, it now was made up of men of all nations. Arriving in Canada from Cadiz in May, 1813, it had lost most of two companies to American raiders while on the way up the St. Lawrence to Kingston, but had performed well at Oswego.

3. It took a full month to reach Drummond.

4. Adams, *The War of 1812*, p. 201.

5. Gaines had arrived from Sackets Harbor on August 4 and assumed command. A number of replacements had come in for the 11th, 22d, and 23d infantry regiments as well as detachments of artillery, elements of the 19th Infantry and the 1st and 4th rifle regiments, and the Company of Bombardiers, Sappers, and Miners from West Point.

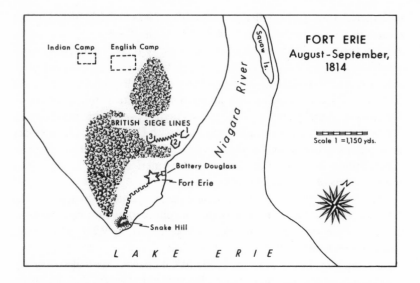

was barred by a seven-foot-high breastwork, ending at the water's edge in a small stone redoubt called "Battery Douglass." To the west of the fort a similar breastwork stretched for some 300 yards to Snake Hill, which was crowned by Battery Towson, another strong redoubt. A short palisade connected Battery Towson with the lakeshore. The total of these defenses was a fortified camp, roughly 700 yards long and 200 deep; its rear along Lake Erie had been left open, but its inland fronts were further protected by a ditch containing a stout palisade, and an abatis of felled trees. American guns—one in Battery Douglass, six in Fort Erie, and six in Battery Towson—were emplaced so as to enfilade the front of the breastworks. In addition, four more pieces were distributed along the front between Snake Hill and Fort Erie and another between the fort and Battery Douglass. Within this defensive perimeter the 2,000 men of Gaines's garrison could live in reasonable comfort.

These defenses were plainly too strong to be stormed out of hand. Drummond brought up his heavy guns and began "opening" conventional siege works, intending to soften up the American defenses by an artillery bombardment before risking an assault. Military engineering, however, had never been a British speciality. Drummond had only two engineer officers, assisted by one "acting corporal" and five privates of the Royal Sappers and Miners, and was further handicapped by a shortage of entrenching tools, felling axes, and sandbags. The average British infantryman was not too handy at such work. It therefore went slowly and often was not well done. The American camp was not even completely invested.

While Drummond's men toiled, the Americans further strengthened and elaborated their defenses. A few of them, fed up with the constant digging and chopping, slipped over the breastwork and deserted to the British. When interrogated, they produced the deserter's usual whining self-justifications and considerable information, most of it incorrect or out of date. Gaines, they said, had only 1,500 "much dispirited" soldiers, and the American defenses between Snake Hill and the lake were incomplete.

Pleased as he was by such stories, Drummond could really take pride in the exploit of a Commander Alexander Dobbs and a detachment of sailors and marines from Yeo's squadron. Three small schooners of the American Lake Erie squadron hovered in the upper reaches of the Niagara River, firing at Drummond's camp and working parties along the riverbank. Though they lacked the firepower to do any great damage, they were a distinct nuisance. Accordingly the British got several large launches up from Lake Ontario, and surprised and captured the *Ohio* (one gun) and *Somers* (two guns) by a boat attack early on August 13. Apparently the American sailors had been overconfident and so kept a careless lookout.

Also on the 13th, Drummond's artillerymen at last completed emplacing their siege guns and opened fire. The result was something between a fizzle and a farce. The guns—Drummond's two light 24-pounders and four naval iron 18- and 24-pounders—quickly proved too light. A good many shots fell short of the fort; those that struck it did no visible damage. Obviously, if the place were to be taken, the poor bloody infantry was going to have to do it. While his guns banged away uselessly through the 14th, Drummond laid his plans for a surprise assault to be launched that night. The main attack would be under Lieutenant Colonel Victor Fischer of de Watteville's regiment with his own regiment, the 8th Foot, the light companies of the 89th and 100th, and a few artillerymen—approximately 1,300 men.[6] Fischer was to move forward through the woods on the British right flank before dark, getting as close to Snake Hill as he could without risking discovery. At 2:00 A.M. he was to advance, the Regiment de Watteville leading, and break into the American position through the supposed gap between Snake Hill and the lake. As

---

6. Both de Watteville and the 8th left details behind as camp or guard detachments.

soon as firing at the western end of the American position indicated that
Fischer was pushing his attack home, two other British columns would
advance. Colonel Hercules Scott with his 103d Foot—650 men—would
attack Battery Douglass, while Lieutenant Colonel William Drummond
of Kelty would lead the flank companies of the 41st and 104th and some
seamen and marines, 250 men in all, directly against Fort Erie. These
two were experienced, capable officers; neither approved of Sir Gordon
Drummond's plan, and both went forward weird-ridden by the premoni-
tion they would not return.[7] To force his men to depend on their bayonets,
Drummond ordered that the attacking troops, except for a few "select
and steady men," take the flints out of their muskets.

There was no chance that the Americans would be surprised. Gaines
and his officers had been expecting a British assault; their outposts were
well forward and alert. When Drummond's siege guns ceased fire shortly
after midnight, the Americans quietly manned their lines. Fischer's advance was immediately detected; the American outposts fired and fell
back. Fischer stumbled against the Snake Hill defenses at 2:30; he had
no clear idea of the terrain and the expected gap did not exist. Elements
of his two leading units, the light companies of de Watteville and the 8th
Foot, managed to get around the lakeshore end of the abatis and palisade by wading well into the water; floundering shoreward they found
themselves facing the leveled muskets of the American reserve. Unable
to fire without their flints, they were badly mauled as they withdrew.
Fischer's scaling ladders quickly proved too short and too few. Nathan
Towson's guns and the 25th Infantry blasted his milling column at point-
blank range, slaughtering his men "like sheep." Entangled in the abatis,
stumbling blindly along the rocky lakeshore, de Watteville's hard-case
mercenaries saw no sense in lingering to get killed. Their retreat quickly
degenerated into panic. Fischer's British units would later claim that they
had attempted to stand firm, but had been "carried away" by the de
Wattevilles' flight. Certainly they did not linger. The whole column fled
back into the woods in such confusion that it could not be rallied and
reformed until after daybreak.

Scott and Drummond of Kelty advanced as soon as they heard Towson's guns. Kelty's weak command was quickly repulsed, but rallied and
charged again. Caught in the blazing crossfire between Fort Erie and

---

7. Scott had served under Wellington in India. Drummond of Kelty, nephew of
the British commander, had a reputation as a cheerfully bloody-minded light infantry
officer.

Battery Douglass, Scott was killed and the 103d Foot driven off. Instead of retreating, however, at least part of that regiment drifted westward. In the dark, misty rain, thick smoke, and uproar, they got across the ditch and into Fort Erie's northeast bastion, overwhelming the American artillerymen there, who already had their hands full repelling Drummond of Kelty's renewed assault. Taking command of the combined force, Kelty attempted to break into the interior of the fort. (American tradition is that he ordered his men to take no prisoners, and he himself killed an artillery lieutenant who had surrendered.) Exit from the captured bastion, however, was blocked by a stone mess hall, held by men of the 19th Infantry. All efforts to storm it failed, Kelty being killed in one attempt. A lieutenant of the Royal Artillery who had accompanied the storming column got one of the American cannon muscled around and began firing at the mess hall. Then something—probably the muzzle blast from his second round—set off the "expense" magazine under the bastion, literally blowing the storming party out of the fort, killing or "dreadfully" mangling some 300 men. Only a few Englishmen escaped through the gauntlet of artillery fire that the American gunners had put down to cover the approaches to the bastion. Total British casualties were 905, 539 of them prisoners or missing. The American loss was only 84.

Drummond blamed his repulse primarily on the "misconduct" of the Regiment de Watteville and proclaimed himself wounded "to the soul" by the "disgraceful and unfortunate conduct" of his troops.[8] In fact, most of his officers and men had shown courage and determination in their attempts to make good his amateur planning. As at Lundy's Lane, he seems to have lost control of his battle. Kelty held the northeast bastion for almost a half-hour, but Drummond either remained ignorant of the situation there or could not decide what to do about it. The accidental explosion that ended the battle put a further dent in British morale; the troops were convinced that the Americans had deliberately set it off, and a rumor spread that other parts of the American defenses were similarly prepared for demolition if the British should occupy them.[9]

While jubilant Americans quickly repaired their defenses, the British had to suffer more than the normal results of a lost battle. The autumn rains began, turning the roads between Drummond's camp and his base at Fort George into sloughs. Already handicapped by a shortage of draft

8. Adams, *The War of 1812*, p. 196.

9. Such mines, termed *fougasses*, were an accepted feature of European military engineering, so these fears were not unreasonable.

animals and wagons, Drummond found it increasingly difficult to bring
supplies and ammunition forward. His men had no tents; the huts they
improvised were not rainproof, and the British camp itself was so poorly
sited that it soon became, in Drummond's own words, a "lake." [10] His
soldiers had to build log platforms to sleep on. Under such conditions
sickness spread rapidly through the sodden British regiments. By September 8 Drummond was writing Prevost that he might have to withdraw.
While the tardy arrival of the 82d Foot made good some of Drummond's
losses, bringing his strength to over 3,000, the weather had delayed the
arrival of another regiment, the 97th, which he had also summoned.
Meanwhile, Drummond's siege guns kept up a desultory bombardment.
On August 29 a chance shot wounded Gaines so badly that he had to
turn the command over to Ripley. Even that hit proved a misfortune for
Drummond.

Jacob Brown still mistrusted Ripley's courage. Though his own wounds
were only half-healed, he left the hospital for Buffalo to resume personal command of the Niagara frontier. Drummond's army was obviously
dwindling from sickness and exposure; British deserters reported preparations for a withdrawal. The Americans had only to wait until Drummond gave up, as he soon must. Drummond, noting increased American activity, was growing apprehensive of an American attack across the
Niagara River farther north against his frayed communications. Properly
handled, such an operation would force him into a hasty retreat to protect
his base. Finally, Brown knew that Major General George Izard was on
the march from Plattsburg with 4,000 regulars, and should reach Sackets
Harbor about the middle of September. But it was not in Brown's character to delay, whether for Izard or the certain erosion of Drummond's
strength by disease and foul weather. Neither did he pause to consider
mounting an operation against Drummond's communications. Drummond was in front of him, and he intended to hit Drummond as soon
as he could and hurt him as badly as he could with the forces he had
immediately available.

Brown's plan, as finally completed, was a hit-and-run sortie to seize
and destroy the British siege guns and "roughly handle" the regiments
on duty in the British lines, withdrawing before Drummond could get
forward with his reserve to support them. Ripley and most of the senior
American officers Brown summoned to a council of war on September 9 considered this an unnecessary risk, but Brown went ahead with his

10. This may have been unavoidable, given the rough terrain in this area.

preparations, raising close to 1,000 militiamen to reinforce Fort Erie's 2,000-man garrison.[11]

The first line of the British siegeworks was approximately 600 yards north of Fort Erie. Beginning with Battery No. 1 (three guns) on the bank above the Niagara River, it ran generally westward for almost a half-mile, ending in Battery No. 3 (two guns) and a strong blockhouse. Battery No. 2 (one gun) had been built some 300 yards to the southwest of No. 1, to which it was connected by some advanced works. The front of these works was protected by an abatis; a second line had been constructed fifty yards to the rear. As previously noted, these lines covered something less than half of the front of the American camp; moreover, Drummond's engineers had not cut back the heavy timber behind and west of Battery No. 3. This fault was compounded by the far more serious failure to maintain a proper outpost system. Drummond's precautions against surprise were, if possible, inferior to those the Americans had taken at Stony Creek the year before. Even after American deserters[12] warned him of Brown's preparations, Drummond did nothing more, merely expressing the hope that Brown would attack since "it will bring us in contact with the enemy at a far cheaper rate than if we were the assailants."[13]

American patrols penetrated the woods west of the British position, and had scouted the vicinity of Battery No. 3 so thoroughly that during September 16 American pioneers were able to open a mile-long trail through the timber from Snake Hill to within 150 yards of the battery, without alerting the troops there. Drummond's Indians should have detected and opposed this infiltration—their camp was only a mile north of Battery No. 3—but there is no evidence they were aware of it. Possibly bad weather and short rations had left them torpid.[14]

Irked by Ripley's caution, Brown entrusted his main attack to Brigadier General Peter B. Porter. Leaving Snake Hill at noon on September 17 with his own volunteers, the militia, and the 23d Infantry Regiment, some 1,600 in all, Porter moved up the new trail, a heavy rainstorm smother-

11. The garrison was all regulars except for Porter's brigade of approximately 220 volunteers. The number of militia Brown brought has never been definitely established.

12. If it is hard to conceive of Americans deserting under such conditions, there always are cowards who will desert even before a probable victory, simply to avoid the risk of battle.

13. Adams, *The War of 1812*, p. 199.

14. Major John Norton, the half-breed Mohawk leader, stated that there were always between 100 and 500 Indians with Drummond.

ing the sound of his advance. At 3:00 P.M. he broke suddenly out of the woods, taking Battery No. 3 from the flank and rear, capturing the blockhouse, and shattering the Regiment de Watteville, which held the left of Drummond's line. At the same time Brigadier General James Miller (recently promoted for valor at Lundy's Lane), moving through a ravine with perhaps 500 men of the 9th, 11th, and 19th regiments, broke the center of the British line. Linking up, Porter and Miller then quickly overran Battery No. 2. While detachments spiked the siege guns and destroyed the captured batteries, they then struck at Battery No. 1. There, however, they met Drummond's reserve, the 1st, 6th, 82d, and 89th regiments. A half-hour's hard fighting could not budge them. Finally, aware that he might be getting too deeply engaged, Brown sent Ripley forward with his regulars to disengage Porter and Miller. Thereafter the Americans regained their lines without trouble.

Both sides had been badly hurt, the Americans losing 511 killed, wounded, and missing; the British 607.[15] American losses in officers were particularly heavy—Ripley, Porter, Miller, and several other senior officers badly wounded, Major Eleazer D. Wood of the Engineers killed. Drummond again claimed a victory over at least 5,000 Americans, but between battle casualties and sickness, he was too weak to maintain his position. Even after the arrival of the 97th Foot, he reported less than 2,000 men still fit for combat. He therefore withdrew during the night of September 21 to Chippewa. Brown had crippled his own army too thoroughly for an effective pursuit, but Drummond's defeat, coupled with similar American successes at Baltimore and Plattsburg, brought a resurgence of American national pride and stiffened the backs of the American negotiators at Ghent.

THE LAKE CHAMPLAIN/RICHELIEU RIVER front had seen little activity during 1813, except for the flow of American foodstuffs into Canada. That summer the British took delivery of some 1,100 head of cattle and 500 horses from Vermont alone.

Initially British naval strength here consisted of three oar-propelled gunboats, manned by soldiers from the garrison of Ile aux Noix, just beyond the mouth of the Richelieu River. The American squadron, organized by Lieutenant Thomas Macdonough at Burlington, Vermont, was far stronger, consisting of two 10-gun sloops, the *Eagle* and the *Growler*,

---

15. The British loss included 115 killed, the American 79. Though more militia than regulars were engaged, only 19 militia were killed, to 60 regulars.

and two tiny gunboats, but Macdonough had great difficulty securing men and competent junior officers. In June, 1813, a reckless lieutenant took the two sloops into the swift-flowing Richelieu after the British gunboats, and found himself trapped in its narrow channel, unable to turn back, and under hot attack by the gunboats and Canadian militia firing from the riverbanks. The *Eagle* was sunk and the *Growler* driven ashore with the loss of 100-odd men, mostly captured. Both vessels were repaired, becoming the *Finch* and *Chubb* in the British squadron.[16] Prevost had no sailors to man them, but managed to obtain a two-week loan of officers and seamen from a Royal Navy sloop-of-war then visiting Quebec. Adding 984 mixed regulars and militia from Ile aux Noix, on July 29 he sent this improvised flotilla raiding up Lake Champlain.

Except for Burlington, where General Wade Hampton was organizing his army, none of the lakeshore towns was garrisoned or fortified. The British came so suddenly that it was impossible to muster militia to defend them. Chazy, Plattsburg, Cumberland Head, Shelburne Bay, and Charlotte were briefly occupied, public property destroyed, and ships and supplies carried off. The raiders made a demonstration against Burlington but did not risk a landing. It was a well-planned and profitable raid, with practically no casualties on either side. Thereafter, both struggled to build up effective squadrons. Because of Chauncey's and Yeo's insatiable requirements, both Americans and British faced a shortage of suitable ships, shipwrights, and sailors.

Macdonough shifted his base to Vergennes, where Otter Creek runs into Lake Champlain thirty miles south of Burlington. This gave him good enough road connections with New York and Boston, and the support of local ironworks. With what workers he had he fitted out the purchased sloops *Preble* (nine guns) and *President* (twelve guns).[17] In March, 1814, Secretary Jones finally answered his pleas for a competent shipbuilder by sending him Noah Brown. Brown swiftly ran up the big, no-frills 26-gun sloop-of-war *Saratoga*. (On April 11 work details began cutting the timber; forty days later she was afloat.) He also converted an available steamboat hull into the schooner *Ticonderoga* (seventeen guns), and built or rebuilt ten gunboats.[18]

16. These ships went through several changes of names. The British first called them *Broke* and *Shannon*. *Eagle* sometimes was known as *Bull Dog*, her first name; as *Finch*, she sometimes was reported as *Tench*.

17. *President* shortly vanishes, either sold as unfit (Pratt, *The Navy*) or captured (Chapelle, *The History of the American Sailing Navy*).

18. Most of the gunboats were seventy-five feet long and fifteen wide, armed with

At Ile aux Noix the British prepared a swarm of gunboats and a 16-gun brig they first named *Niagara*, then *Linnet*. Most of their resources, however, went into the shallow-draft frigate *Confiance* (thirty-six guns), which was intended to be the Lake Champlain equivalent of the *Saint Lawrence*. Such a major undertaking, requiring heavy cables and fittings, proved slow and difficult. (One story had the British placing orders for special cables with American merchants, who were delighted to oblige, at an outrageous price of course. Fortunately some overworked American customs officers intercepted the shipment.)

By the time the Americans learned of the *Confiance*, Noah Brown had returned to New York. Now both he and his brother Adam were ordered to Vergennes with 200 of their expert workmen to build a 20-gun brig, the *Eagle*. In fifty days they had it fully built, rigged, armed, and ready for combat. This American construction program, in turn, worried the British. On May 9 Lieutenant Daniel Pring of the Canadian Provincial Marine probed at the mouth of Otter Creek with *Linnet* and a flock of gunboats, but was chased away by batteries Macdonough had emplaced there and the Vermont militia that rallied to support them. Macdonough still could not get sailors enough to man his ships. Lake service was not popular: it seldom offered a chance for prize money, and "lake fever" and other diseases made it unhealthy duty. Only some 250, few of them able-bodied seamen, could be secured around New York harbor, and competent officers were equally scarce.

On land, George Izard was working diligently at organizing and training his troops. Border outpost and patrol scufflings went on hit-or-miss through spring and summer. In one forgotten skirmish near Odelltown, Captain Benjamin Forsyth, by then a brevet (honorary) lieutenant colonel "for distinguished service," died with his boots on. Pring's excursion led Secretary of War John Armstrong to order Izard to establish a fortified position at the northern end of Lake Champlain to block such sorties. Considering a position there too exposed, Izard selected Plattsburg. He also detailed 400 soldiers to fill up Macdonough's crews; they might have begun as awkward hands, but Macdonough knew how to train and inspire them. During late July he and Armstrong considered an advance toward the St. Lawrence River to threaten the British communications between Montreal and Kingston, and thus divert British forces from the

---

a long 24-pounder gun and an 18-pounder Columbiad. The latter was an American-designed weapon, halfway between a carronade and a gun, for firing explosive shell. Nobody liked them.

Niagara frontier. Moving up to Chazy in early August, Izard began collecting information as to the strength and activities of the British forces in the Montreal area. The result was sobering.

After Napoleon's abdication in April the British government had begun shifting veteran regiments into Canada. Prevost now had approximately 17,000 English troops in the Montreal/Quebec area, and this build-up was continuing—so rapidly, in fact, as to overwhelm Canada's ability to support it. (By August, 1814, two-thirds of Prevost's troops throughout Canada were "at this moment eating beef provided by American contractors, drawn principally from the States of Vermont and New York.")[19] Prevost had hoped to use these troops to overwhelm Sackets Harbor, thereby unhinging the whole American position along the Lake Ontario/Niagara/Lake Erie/Detroit front, but had found it impossible to stock the necessary supplies at Kingston. No logistical build-up would be possible until winter froze the roads between Montreal and Kingston solid enough to support heavy wagon traffic. Consequently, no attack on Sackets Harbor would be possible until the spring of 1815. Being under pressure from both London and Canada to do *something* before autumn made further campaigning impossible, Prevost was preparing a combined land and naval offensive up Lake Champlain.

Such an offensive could be supplied from Montreal by way of the Richelieu River with relative ease. It would have the strategic effect of diverting American attention from the concurrent British attempt to seize eastern and northern Maine[20] and would occupy areas from which Prevost was drawing so much of his food. Also, it should encourage the anti-war New England merchants and lawyers in their burgeoning desire to take the "manly" action of managing a private surrender.[21] And, if the war continued through 1815, possession of the Lake Champlain area would provide both an excellent base for future operations and a potent counter in the peace negotiations. Just which of these strategic objectives really inspired Prevost is uncertain; his general conduct of the campaign rather

19. Adams, *The War of 1812*, p. 202. One British officer reported dickering with a militia officer in full uniform. That defender of American liberty closed the deal with the remark that, while trading with the enemy was forbidden, he could not regard anyone who offered him such a good price for his cattle as really being an enemy!

20. See chapter fifteen.

21. This led to the famous Hartford Convention (December, 1814 to January, 1815) at which representatives of Massachusetts, Connecticut, and Rhode Island (with some from counties in Vermont and New Hampshire) flirted with secession. See Adams, *The War of 1812*, pp. 275–84.

suggests a deep personal uncertainty. He was a sick man, he never had commanded such a large force, and he obviously was remembering what had happened to another British invasion under General John Burgoyne in that same area in 1777. But he had mustered 10,351 officers and men, well provided with artillery, just to the north of Chazy.

Izard emphatically informed Armstrong that such odds were too great. If Armstrong insisted on an advance to the St. Lawrence, he would attempt it, but without any hope of success. Armstrong replied by giving him the most inexplicable orders issued during the entire war: Izard was to march forthwith to Sackets Harbor! Once at Sackets Harbor he was either to attack Kingston or go on to the Niagara frontier and take command of the operations there. Armstrong never bothered to explain this decision. But he had shared in the campaign that bagged Burgoyne, and he knew that Prevost would not be able to advance any great distance into United States territory so long as Macdonough's fleet remained in action. It is possible that he had conceived a major gamble—to tempt the British into a slow advance up Lake Champlain while concentrating his own forces for a decisive attack in the Lake Ontario sector. Victory there would enable the Americans to regroup and, in Armstrong's own phrase, "renew the scene of Saratoga." [22] But, whatever strategic concept or erratic impulse inspired him, his tenure as secretary of war was practically over. He wrote Izard on August 12; on the 23d the British took Washington.

Izard did not argue with Armstrong's orders, amazing as they must have seemed to him. On August 23 he began a well-organized march to Sackets Harbor. To hold the Lake Champlain frontier, he left Brigadier General Alexander Macomb at Plattsburg with some 3,300 men, roughly half of whom were recruits, invalids, mislaid detachments, and militia. However Izard, who had had engineering training in Europe, and Major Joseph G. Totten had carefully fortified a ridge on the south bank of the Saranac River at Plattsburg. Consisting of three mutually supporting redoubts and two heavily built blockhouses, connected by a system of fieldworks, this position commanded the mouth and the north bank of the river and both bridges across it, as well as a considerable sector of Plattsburg Bay. It was well provided with guns; supplies and ammunition had been stocked to enable the troops holding it to stand siege. Izard and Totten had estimated it could hold out for three weeks against both land and naval attack, even if Macdonough were defeated. Macomb was a

22. Ibid., p. 204.

cheerful, competent officer who kept his ego and ambition under control to a degree unusual among his fellow generals, yet was everywhere respected. He called on New York and Vermont for more militia and got an indefinite number, possibly as many as 2,000. (Lacking authority under both federal and state law to *order* his militia into New York, Governor Martin Chittenden of Vermont "invited" them to volunteer. Quite a few responded; at first they found it unsettling to encounter scouting parties of New York militia dragoons, for the New Yorkers wore scarlet jackets!)

Moving out on August 31, Prevost occupied Chazy on September 3; on the 5th he lurched forward to Beekmantown, making good progress, although Macomb's outposts wrecked bridges and felled trees across the road as they retired. From Beekmantown, Prevost sent one brigade along a road that followed the lakeshore south around Plattsburg Bay and into Plattsburg; two brigades took a direct road some two miles inland. It was an impressive host, but somewhat brittle. Victorious veterans always have been, in an old Scots phrase, "kittle cattle" to handle. Wellington's veterans considered themselves "Invincibles" but now they were somewhat sulky. Instead of enjoying their hard-won victories back home in England or amid the comforts of occupied France, they had been hustled overseas into a third-rate little squabble in a howling wilderness! They did not much like Sir George Prevost, either; under Wellington, who had an eye only for essentials, uniform regulations had been generally disregarded, especially by the officers. Now Sir George was ordering them to shape up!

Prevost also had his honest problems. His big army had a big appetite. Unless his fleet gained control of Lake Champlain so that supplies could be brought forward by water, he could not push much farther southward. The autumn rains would ruin the roads and swell the Richelieu River rapids. He might capture Plattsburg, but if he intended to hold it through the winter he must take it soon enough to accumulate reserves of food and fuel to last until spring.

Even so, the British came on in style. The inland column, apparently advancing without any effective reconnaissance, was ambushed by Major John Wool with some 250 regulars and Brigadier General Benjamin Mooer with 700 New York militia. Despite heavy American fire the British neither deployed nor halted, taking their losses and coming on in march column. The militia went away hurriedly; Wool's regulars retired gradually, skirmishing as they went. Reinforced by a detachment of regular artillerymen with two field guns, they made another stand, but soon were forced to withdraw. Macomb had sent another detachment to harass the lakeshore column but soon recalled it, fearing that the advance of the inland column would cut it off. Macdonough's gunboats took over its mission, keeping up a brisk fire against the British on the shore road. Retreating through Plattsburg with the British at their heels, the American advance parties crossed to the south bank of the Saranac River, details taking up the flooring from both bridges as they crossed.

Checked, the British took up positions in and around that portion of Plattsburg village north of the river. Prevost has been blamed for not attacking immediately and simply destroying Macomb's smaller command. He seems to have considered such an attempt, but the objections of Major General Frederick Robinson, who commanded the leading British brigade, and a closer look at Macomb's position soon checked that impulse. After all, Prevost could remember the bloody nose he had gotten the year before when he tried to rush far less formidable defenses at Sackets Harbor. In addition, there was Macdonough's squadron swinging at anchor out in Plattsburg Bay, free to stand in and add its fire power to Macomb's against any British attack. Prevost decided to await the arrival of his fleet.

His fleet was not ready. The *Confiance* had been launched only in late August, and there was vast trouble equipping and manning her. Captain George Downie, whom Yeo had just detached to take command of the Lake Champlain squadron, finally got her under way on September 7, but it took two more days to tow the *Confiance* up the Richelieu from Ile aux Noix and into Lake Champlain. Downie picked up the rest of his squadron at Chazy and headed up the lake, battered by Prevost's increasingly imperious summons, which came to verge on insult. Angered, Downie rushed his preparations, filling out the *Confiance*'s crew with soldiers. Carpenters and artificers labored to complete the ship as she sailed.

Prevost had sound reasons for his urgency. He could not hold his position indefinitely. September 9 had turned wet and windy, an omen of harsher weather to come. (To add insult to his anxiety, that night some fifty Americans under Captain George McGlassin slipped across the Saranac and destroyed an annoying British rocket battery.) However, the British had located a good ford across the Saranac, approximately a mile upstream from the upper bridge. Prevost's plan was simple: when Downie attacked Macdonough, Major General Thomas Brisbane's brigade of over 3,500 men would make a limited attack at both bridges to pin down Macomb's forces. Meanwhile, Robinson, with 2,500 men, would force his way across the ford and then attack eastward along the south bank. Major General Manley Power's brigade, 3,500 strong, would fol-

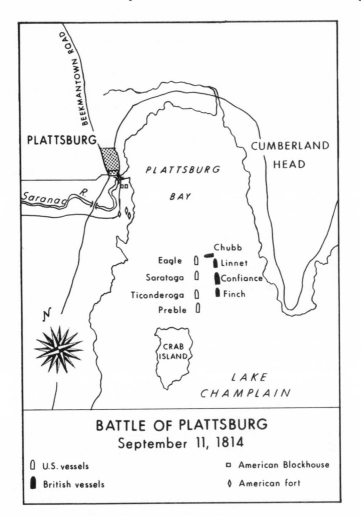

BATTLE OF PLATTSBURG
September 11, 1814

☐ U.S. vessels   ▫ American Blockhouse

◼ British vessels   ◊ American fort

low Robinson. As Robinson advanced, Brisbane would convert his feint
into a real attack. Everything waited on Downie.

Macomb meanwhile strengthened and extended his defenses. More
militia came in and took up position along the south bank of the Saranac
behind light field fortifications. Macdonough had completed his preparations after a thorough study of both fleets and Plattsburg Bay. Somehow,
he had secured reliable information on Downie's armament. Like Perry
on Lake Erie, he was handicapped by the U.S. Navy Department's insis-

tence on arming sloops-of-war with short-range carronades, whereas the British ships carried mostly long guns, which would give them every advantage in a battle on the open lake. Macdonough therefore chose a position that would make Downie come to him and fight at carronade range. His ships were anchored in line just inside the entrance to Plattsburg Bay in the order (from north to south) *Eagle*, *Saratoga*, *Ticonderoga*, and *Preble*, with his ten gunboats behind the intervals in this line. *Preble* was near the shoals at the north end of Crab Island, *Eagle* close to those fringing Cumberland Head, the promontory that formed the eastern shore of Plattsburg Bay. This left Downie no maneuver room. As a final precaution Macdonough had put out extra anchors, their cables hanging loose under water so as to be out of danger of being cut by enemy gunfire; with these, if a ship's starboard (right side) guns were disabled, its captain could spin it like a top and bring his port side weapons into action.

Downie came around Cumberland Head at 7:00 A.M. on September 11, which had dawned bright and clear. After reconnoitering Macdonough's dispositions from a small boat, he summoned his captains and gave his orders. Considering *Confiance* practically the equal of the whole American squadron, he would take it in and engage *Saratoga* at close range. Once *Saratoga* was knocked out, the rest of the American squadron could be rapidly mopped up. *Linnet* and *Chubb* would attack *Eagle*; *Finch* and the gunboats would engage *Ticonderoga* and *Preble*. Drums rumbling, crews cheering, the British swept into Plattsburg Bay.

Downie's luck was out. As his ships came around Cumberland Head, straight into the raking fire of what long guns Macdonough had, the wind fell off into random gusts, slowing their headway to a crawl. Before it could fire a round, *Confiance* had its wheel and two anchors shot away; unable to close with *Saratoga*, Downie dropped anchor some 300 yards away. His first broadside killed or wounded forty of *Saratoga*'s seamen; *Saratoga*'s answering broadsides shortly thereafter killed Downie.

At the tail of the line *Finch* and Downie's gunboats attacked *Ticonderoga*, but were beaten off and turned on the smaller *Preble*. In less than an hour the little American sloop was so badly crippled that she had to cut loose from her anchors and retreat across the bay to the protection of Macomb's guns. However, she had hurt *Finch* badly; poorly handled, *Finch* drifted onto the shoals north of Crab Island where a 2-gun battery, manned by invalid soldiers, started knocking her apart.[23] The British gunboats then turned on *Ticonderoga*, which again fought them off.

23. Macomb's hospital was on Crab Island.

The battle at the head of the line had become a short-range slugging contest that shattered ships and men. First victim was *Chubb*; caught in the blast of *Saratoga*'s and *Eagle*'s batteries, she was swiftly reduced to a drifting hulk and had to surrender. *Eagle* and *Linnet* pounded each other, but *Eagle* also suffered badly from the hammering of *Confiance*'s forward guns. With most of his starboard guns knocked out, *Eagle*'s captain hauled up his anchors, worked his way to the rear of *Saratoga*, and then brought his port guns into action against *Confiance*. This, however, left *Linnet* free to open a raking fire on *Saratoga*. Both *Confiance* and *Saratoga* were badly smashed, but *Confiance* still had a few guns in action, as did *Linnet*. At 10:30 *Saratoga*'s last starboard gun was disabled. It seemed a crisis, but Macdonough methodically turned *Saratoga* to bring her port-side guns into action. *Confiance*'s one surviving lieutenant tried desperately to match that maneuver but his ship was too badly hurt; his ill-assorted crew refused to make the effort. *Confiance* struck, then *Linnet*, which Pring had fought until she was practically sinking under him. Unfortunately, the English gunboats, most of them battered, were able to get away, thanks to the pusillanimity of the American gunboat commanders, who had hung back out of danger throughout the action.

Once he had seen Downie actually engaged, Prevost ordered his troops forward. Apparently things went sluggishly. Some regiments still were at breakfast, others were slow to form up. Robinson got moving around 10:00 A.M., but somehow his guides missed the side road to the ford and led him off to the northwest. Behind him a major artillery duel raged across the Saranac, the Americans giving as good as they got and possibly a little better. Brisbane made a tentative thrust at the upper bridge and was stopped in his tracks. Belatedly discovering his error, Robinson countermarched, locating the ford an hour later. His light infantry drove the militia there back and he began getting his brigade across the Saranac. However, the woods around him still were swarming with militiamen, some of them in a pugnacious mood as word of Macdonough's victory passed down the American line. Before Robinson could attempt to renew his advance, an aide-de-camp overtook him with Prevost's order to withdraw.

Prevost's reasoning was sensible: with his fleet destroyed he would not be able to hold Plattsburg even if he did capture it—and capturing it promised to be a bloody business and a useless waste of good men. Supposedly Brisbane protested, claiming that he could defeat Macomb in just another twenty minutes—which sounds as if the general were posturing for posterity as a cruelly thwarted hero. During the past hour he had not even dented Macomb's outpost line.

The artillery exchange dwindled away into the late afternoon. Once it was dark Prevost withdrew, abandoning his sick and wounded and large amounts of supplies and ammunition. Too weak to risk a pursuit in force—there was always the chance Prevost might turn on him suddenly with greatly superior numbers—Macomb sent out only a detachment of light troops to shadow the retreating British, and these soon turned back because of furious rains and increasing cold. Prevost's army stumbled on into Canada in growing disorder. Wellington's soldiers always had grown sullen and careless during retreats; now lacking Wellington's "iron fist" to keep them in order, they straggled, deserted, and turned insubordinate. (Only the Swiss mercenary Regiment de Meuron expressed any pride over the affair, claiming that they had "seized the lower town at the point of the bayonet and held for six days, repulsing all counterattacks. When the British Army withdrew before sixty thousand Americans, Captain Mattley's company of chasseurs were the last to leave the blazing town, covering the retreat.") [24] It was a sorry end to great hopes, and also to Sir George Prevost's career. [25] "A lamentable event to the civilized world," wept the London *Times*. [26]

Decisive as it was on land and water, Plattsburg had not been an especially costly affair. Macomb had 37 men killed and 62 wounded; Prevost admitted to 35 killed, 47 wounded, 72 captured, and 234 deserters—all of which seems rather understated. Macdonough reported 52 killed and 58 wounded; the British 57 and 72 respectively. Yet Macdonough's victory literally shattered any hope the British might have of success on Lake Champlain in 1814; they would have to build a new fleet before they came again, and it would need to be a far stronger one, because Downie's captured ships were added to Macdonough's squadron.

The British disputed furiously over their disaster. Prevost blamed Downie's squadron and, by inference, the Royal Navy: it had been tardy and some of its officers had not served well. Yeo responded by bringing official charges of misconduct against Prevost: he had forced Downie into action prematurely (here Yeo conveniently forgot his own failure to allow the Lake Champlain squadron sufficient supplies) and had failed to sup-

24. Jean-René Bory, *Les Suisses au Service Étranger* (Noyon: Courier de la Côte, 1965), p. 134. Unfortunately, this whole book is full of such matamore stuff.

25. Prevost was recalled in early 1815, but died of dropsy and exhaustion from his journey from Montreal to Halifax, much of which had to be made on foot.

26. Adams, *The War of 1812*, p. 338.

port him. Prevost, Yeo claimed, should have stormed Macomb's position without waiting for Downie's appearance; thereafter, he could have used his artillery to drive Macdonough out of Plattsburg Bay into the open lake where Downie's long guns would have given the British squadron a "fair chance." Prevost retorted that Macdonough's anchorage was out of effective artillery range. The captain of the *Linnet* confused matters by inventing a yarn that Macomb was ready to surrender if attacked in force. None of the disputants brought up the point that Prevost might have advanced down the *east* side of the lake against Burlington, which would have forced both Macdonough and Macomb to evacuate their Plattsburg stronghold.[27]

Marching an average of fourteen miles a day over bad roads, Izard meanwhile had brought his command into Sackets Harbor on September 17. There he found an appeal, dated September 10, from Brown, who that same day was assaulting Drummond's siege lines at Fort Erie, asking for support. Chauncey was willing to transport Izard's troops up Lake Erie, but bad weather delayed that movement until September 21.[28] Six days later, however, Izard had his troops at Batavia, thirty-five miles east of Buffalo and, his commission as major general being prior to Brown's, assumed command of the Niagara frontier.

This concentration of Brown's and Izard's divisions gave the latter an army of approximately 5,500 regulars and 800 volunteers and militia. Drummond had only some 2,500 troops, many of them decidedly dispirited, defending the north bank of Chippewa Creek. After careful preparation Izard advanced from Fort Erie on October 13—and almost immediately halted. An express rider from Sackets Harbor had brought word that the 112-gun *Saint Lawrence* had joined Yeo's squadron, and that Chauncey had fled into Sackets Harbor and was frantically strengthening its defenses.

Brown wanted a sudden, all-out effort to destroy Drummond before he could be reinforced. Izard, while allowing that he might "give Drummond a good deal of trouble," felt the risk of being overwhelmed by British

27. The only reason given against this movement was that most of the American smuggling of foodstuffs went on east of Lake Champlain, and that an offensive there would have interrupted its flow.

28. Chauncey's ready cooperation in this case may have been based on his knowledge that Armstrong had also given Izard the option of attacking Kingston, a development Chauncey was anxious to avoid. On the other hand, Chauncey definitely would have wanted to prevent the destruction of Brown's army, which would have left the British free to concentrate against Sackets Harbor.

reinforcements was too great. Even Bissell's success in a smart engagement at Cook's Mills on October 19 did not inspire him. Two days later at Brown's request, he sent Brown's division off to Sackets Harbor, since it was certain that the British would attack that vital base as soon as they could begin operations the next spring. He then evacuated and destroyed Fort Erie, and put his own division into winter quarters around Buffalo. That done, he politely informed Monroe that his health would not permit him to endure another northern winter.[29]

The result—aside from a first-class row with Brown, in which the latter ranked Izard with Chauncey as several sorts of poltroon and an outstanding menace to the United States—was twofold. American possession of Fort Erie had forced Prevost to maintain a considerable force on the Niagara frontier, thereby placing a severe strain on his logistical system and, during 1814 at least, using up large numbers of British troops. It had also been a useful negotiating point for the American peace commission at Ghent. Izard casually threw away both of these advantages. Drummond was able to move part of his command back to the relative comfort of Kingston and to put the rest into winter quarters. More supplies were thus made available for the straitened garrisons at Burlington Heights and posts farther west, and Prevost could expedite his preparations for an early 1815 offensive from Kingston against Sackets Harbor.

In sad fact, Chauncey, and especially Izard, had given up too soon. Line-of-battle ships were generally clumsy affairs, and the *Saint Lawrence*, built hurriedly from green timber, certainly was no shining example of the shipbuilder's art. Yeo wanted to test her sailing qualities before risking her in action. Chauncey might have kept the lake long enough to learn whether the *Saint Lawrence* had enough speed and maneuverability to be really dangerous. Izard should have known that Prevost could not organize and launch a rescue operation overnight. Unfortunately for the United States, the two were much alike—organizers and administrators, not fighting men.

29. Izard offered his resignation, but was refused. Apparently he got no farther south than Buffalo.

FIFTEEN

War's Fringes, East and West

[Americans] were already known to be impervious to any noble sentiment, but it is only of late that we find them insensible of the shame of defeat, destitute even of the brutish quality of being beaten into a sense of their unworthiness and their incapacity.

—*Morning Post* (London) [1]

THE ONE NEW ASPECT OF Vice Admiral Alexander Cochrane's intensified smash, loot, burn, and run maraudings along the Atlantic coast during 1814 was their extension to the New England states, which so far had not even been effectively blockaded. Undoubtedly the British purpose was twofold: to increase the pressure on the United States government, and to encourage New Englanders' pacifist/secessionist tendencies by demonstrating that the United States could not protect them. With that went the possibility of more prize money and a little excitement. The Royal Navy, enthusiastically seconded by swift Canadian privateers out of Nova Scotia and New Brunswick, went joyfully to work.[2]

The first British stroke was against New London, Connecticut, where

1. Adams, *The War of 1812*, p. 325. The *Morning Post* was then the most authoritative London newspaper.

2. Liverpool, Nova Scotia, was particularly active in this, "Liverpool Privateers" becoming a nautical byword. Canadian descendents of Loyalist refugees who had been forced out of the United States after the Revolution naturally sought revenge. This, however, did not prevent their continuing mutually profitable commercial relations with New England merchants, who would send ships to sea to be captured by prearrangement, the two parties splitting the profits from selling the cargoes to eager Englishmen.

several privateers were being built. Guided by an American renegade, Captain Richard Coote slipped into the Thames River with 136 sailors and marines early on April 8, torched twenty-seven assorted vessels, and got clean away. (The blockading squadron put together a $1,000 reward for his guide; Cochrane later added an equal sum in the hope of encouraging other traitors to offer their services.)[3]

On June 13 another boat expedition penetrated clear to the head of Buzzards Bay and burned shipping and a textile factory at Wareham, Massachusetts. The militia turned out, but the British escaped unscathed by seizing civilians as hostages and sheltering behind them until out of danger.

That same night the British 20-gun brig *Nimrod* sent her boats into New Bedford harbor to attack Fairhaven. The garrison of Fort Phoenix on the east side of the harbor detected their approach and opened fire. At this moment, according to local legend, a mail carrier chanced to come galloping across the Acushnet River bridge just north of the fort, lustily blowing his post horn and sounding like a whole squadron of cavalry to the rescue! Whatever their reason, the raiders hastily pulled back to *Nimrod*, which headed out to sea.

This constant coastal harassment, however, soon became only an accompaniment to the major British campaign against Maine. That operation, unlike other British offensives launched out of eastern Canada, had a definite territorial objective; the British intended to seize and hold all of the Passamaquoddy Islands and all of Maine east and north of the Penobscot River. Possession of the latter territory would give the British free use of the St. John River and a secure overland route between Halifax and Quebec that would be invaluable in winter when the St. Lawrence was frozen.[4] All of this, and also the fact that the to-be-conquered territories would include vast tracts of valuable timber, had hearty Canadian support. In fact, the New Brunswick authorities had been foremost in urging such action. The operation appeared ideally suited for the British forces available—a series of limited amphibious operations against small, mostly unfortified coastal and river settlements. Their troops and war-

3. Reportedly this renegade offered his services with the understanding that he would be rewarded only if the raid was successful.

4. In view of the American appetite for Canada, the British were justified in planning for future wars with the United States. Their failure to secure this territory embarrassed them greatly during the *Trent* affair of 1861 when the reinforcements they rushed to Canada that winter were able to reach Quebec only after the United States cheerfully offered to let them cross Maine.

ships could work closely together, bringing overwhelming numbers and fire power against isolated American garrisons.

Maine was then a somewhat neglected (and increasingly resentful) part of Massachusetts. Though Massachusetts militia were considered among the best organized, armed, and equipped in the United States, those in the thinly populated Maine districts quickly proved an exception. When the British made a minor raid on June 21 against Thomaston and St. George, some fifty miles southwest of the mouth of the Penobscot River, apparently to test American readiness, the militia mustered but showed no inclination to be inhospitable. The few regulars formerly stationed at Fort St. George's—actually only a few old guns behind a crescent-shaped breastwork—having been transferred the year before, the British experienced no great difficulty overwhelming its single elderly custodian. Spiking the guns and seizing four cargo vessels, they left without suffering a single casualty.

On July 11 a much stronger expedition under Commodore Sir Thomas Hardy, who had been Admiral Horatio Nelson's flag captain until Nelson's death at Trafalgar, moved to seize the Passamaquoddy Islands. The principal town, Eastport on Moose Island, was defended by Fort Sullivan, another small battery, open from the rear. Its commander, Major Perly Putnam, had 86 regular infantrymen, possibly 250 militia, and six guns. Hardy could put ashore at least 600 men of the 102d Regiment of Foot; his ships included the line-of-battle ship *Ramillies*. Any impulse Putnam may have felt toward a heroic last ditch stand was squelched by the blunt threat that such action would result in Eastport's destruction. Hardy gave the civil population seven days either to swear allegiance to King George III or get out. A third of them did choose to give up their homes and livelihoods and go. The rest, whether willingly or resentfully, continued business as usual, but as new citizens of New Brunswick.

Hardy's conqueror's career, however, promptly took a pratfall. Dropping south to join the blockading squadron off New London, he was ordered to destroy the small port of Stonington, Connecticut. The official reason for this mission seems to have been an unfounded report that "Fulton's torpedoes" were being manufactured there. Since the Royal Navy did not possess such weapons, it considered them, unlike its rockets, to be infernal, illegal, and immoral.[5] Accordingly Hardy swooped down

5. According to the August, 1964, *Bulletin of the Stonington Historical Society*, Vol. I, No. 4, several Yankees had used various infernal machines against the blockading squadron, leaving its officers and men somewhat jumpy.

upon Stonington on August 9 with *Ramillies*, the frigate *Pactolus*, the brig *Dispatch*, and the rocket ship *Terror*[6] and gave its citizens one hour to get out of town. The noncombatants fled, but the men, using two 18-pounders and one 6-pounder assigned the town, fought back, while militia poured in from neighboring communities. The offshore waters being shallow, *Ramillies* could not get within effective range of Stonington; *Pactolus* grounded while trying to work in closer. These ships therefore sent in their largest boats, armed with carronades and rocket launchers, to accompany *Dispatch*, while *Terror* furnished long-range fire support. After an odd three-day squabble, once interrupted when the Americans ran out of ammunition, Hardy pulled away, *Dispatch* with rigging badly cut up, holed at her waterline, two guns knocked out, and fourteen men killed or wounded. Several of the ships' boats were hit when the British attempted a landing; the Americans buried four bodies that washed ashore from them.[7] Only one or two Americans were wounded, and Stonington suffered remarkably little damage; there, as at Baltimore, the British rockets proved ineffective.

Hailed as an important American victory, Stonington did inspire a stouter resistance to British marauding. Six months earlier Commodore Stephen Decatur, blockaded in the Thames River with *United States*, *Macedonian*, and *Hornet*, had caused a great deal of resentment in and around New London by claiming that his attempts to slip out to sea had been betrayed by persons unknown burning "blue lights" at the harbor's entrance.[8] Now Colonel Henry Atkinson, ordered from Plattsburg to organize the 37th Infantry Regiment at New London, found its citizens and those of Groton across the Connecticut River eager to join with his soldiers in strengthening the harbor defenses. Cochrane did score one typical victory. By a close blockade he starved Nantucket Island into submission, forcing its inhabitants to declare themselves absolutely neutral and to publicly pledge not to pay taxes to the United States as long as the

6. *Pactolus* is variously described as mounting thirty-eight to forty-four guns, *Dispatch* as having eighteen to twenty-two. Apparently *Nimrod* joined Hardy during the action.

7. American accounts, probably optimistic, put the total British loss at twenty-one killed and fifty wounded.

8. Decatur implied that antiwar members of the community were responsible. Nothing ever was proved, but "blue-light Federalist" became a standard insult. The British undoubtedly did have an effective intelligence system along the American coast; Hardy was able to identify individual Americans who opposed the sale of food-stuffs to his squadron, sending them warnings to be "more guarded in their conduct."

war lasted. In return, he graciously permitted them to import food and fuel from the mainland and to fish in the shoal areas around the island.

Meanwhile Lieutenant General Sir John Sherbrooke, governor general of New Brunswick, had organized the major offensive against Maine, employing three veteran regiments totaling some 2,500 men that had recently arrived from Gibraltar and a squadron of two line-of-battle ships, three frigates, two sloops-of-war, a brig, and a schooner. His original intent was to begin by seizing the port of Machias, but news that the American sloop-of-war *Adams*[9] had taken refuge in the Penobscot River caused him to change objectives. *Adams*, after taking nine prizes, had struck a reef and suffered severe damage. Her captain Charles Morris nursed her up the Penobscot to Hampden, five miles below Bangor. There he took out *Adams'* guns to lighten her, and began hasty repairs.

Coming up to the mouth of the Penobscot on September 1, Sherbrooke found it guarded by Fort Madison, another open work with a popgun battery of four 4-pounders and a garrison of fifty regulars. Unable to offer any effective resistance to Sherbrooke's fleet the American commander sensibly fired a few rounds at the leading British ship, then spiked his guns and withdrew before the British could land infantry behind him to cut off his escape. Sherbrooke promptly organized a force of some 700 picked infantrymen with two light guns to move up the Penobscot in ships' boats in pursuit of the *Adams*. To prevent American reinforcements from the Rockland/Bath/Portland area from intercepting this expedition, he dispatched a regiment to occupy Belfast, across the Penobscot from Fort Madison, thus cutting the west-bank road to Bangor—as it turned out, probably the war's most unnecessary precaution.

Learning of Sherbrooke's arrival, Morris emplaced some of the *Adams'* guns to command the river and east-bank road, and called on the local militia commander, Major General John Blake, for support. Blake should have been able to muster well over 1,000 militia, but barely 600 responded, many of them without weapons.[10] In any event, their numbers proved inconsequential; Blake had not the least idea what to do with them, the situation in general, or himself for that matter. Morris had some 200 sailors and marines, only 150 of whom had muskets, and the regulars

9. See chapter five.

10. Militia were supposed to possess their own weapons. Some evaded the requirement; others, who did own weapons and equipment, preferred to report without them, hoping to be issued government arms, which they then would try to take home with them.

from Fort Madison. The night of September 2–3 was filled with cold rain; the next morning blind with fog. The British infantry had landed a few miles below Hampden; now they felt their way slowly up the east bank, the ships' boats keeping abreast of them. Their scouts stumbled onto an American outpost; a few muskets went off, and both sides began blazing blindly into the mist. Thereupon the British risked a bayonet charge and the militia ran for their lives. Keeping his men together, Morris spiked his guns and set *Adams* afire, then withdrew without much difficulty to the west bank.

The British pushed on to Bangor, where they enacted a slightly re-fined version of the capture of Hampden. No civilians seem to have been seriously injured, but there was plenty of drunkenness, roughhousing, and looting. (The next day Blake rode in and humbly made his formal submission.) After cleaning out Bangor the British returned downriver, pausing at Hampden to burn the local meetinghouse and get in a little more looting; they also seized or burned every ship they could find along either bank, and confiscated personal firearms and ammunition.[11] This jaunt cost the British exactly 1 man killed, 8 wounded, and 1 missing; the Americans lost 13 killed and wounded, plus between 200 and 300, apparently all militia, taken prisoner.

Sherbrooke subsequently evacuated Belfast and turned back to Machias. Completely isolated, the fifty-man garrison of Fort O'Brien there managed to evade converging English sea and land attacks and escape westward through the woods. Sherbrooke thereafter organized all Maine up to the Penobscot as part of New Brunswick; all males of over sixteen years of age were required to take an oath of allegiance. Not many refused.[12]

The United States government, then in complete disorganization, had no troops to spare for operations in Maine. Massachusetts reputedly could put 70,000 militia into the field. Its Governor Caleb Strong went through the motions of calling up a contingent, but insisted that they must remain state troops under the command of a Massachusetts major general, though he did attempt to get the federal government to pay and supply this state force. However, Strong and his fellow extreme Federalists, mostly well-to-do merchants, lawyers, and politicians, had no concern with the "new states" beyond the Appalachian Mountains and were frankly ready to surrender part or all of them, plus territory along the Great Lakes and even a slice of Maine, if only England would be graciously pleased to allow Massachusetts citizens to fish for cod on the Grand Banks and peddle Yankee notions through the seaports of the world. And if the Royal Navy continued to impress seamen from their ships—well, that *would* be regrettable, but really nothing more than another necessary business expense. Consequently, Strong did not venture any attempt to regain eastern Maine, thereby undoubtedly saving his militia from public humiliation.

As a further weakening of American military capabilities in this area, Connecticut then reclaimed the brigade of militia it had placed under fed-

11. As an example of how profitable this excursion was, the Bangor authorities were forced to provide a $30,000 bond for the delivery of seven vessels then under construction there.

12. Naturally, British rule did not penetrate deeply into the thinly settled interior.

eral command for coast defense. This may have been in part because its federal commander, Brigadier General Thomas H. Cushing, had shown himself a pompous incompetent during the Stonington affair.[13] The net result of such actions was the serious deterioration of the United States' overall strategic position: the northeastern states were not only left practically defenseless, but in the hands of politicians who considered President Madison a worse menace than King George III. At the same time the build-up of British forces in Canada continued steadily, reaching a total of approximately 27,000 by the end of 1814.

Despite the rigorous British blockade of the American coast, privateers continued to slip in and out, piloted by men who knew every trick of local tides, reefs, currents, and weather. One of the most famous, Captain Samuel C. Reid's brig *General Armstrong*, was in the harbor of Fayal in the Azores when a British squadron arrived on September 26. Deliberately disregarding the neutrality of the port, the British commander attempted to take her by a massive boat attack, which failed with the loss of about 200 officers and men to 9 Americans.[14] Thereafter, unable to escape to sea, Reid scuttled his brig and occupied a ruined castle ashore; the English commander finally decided that going after him would be too great a violation of Portuguese neutrality.

The *Prince de Neufchatel*, caught in a calm near Nantucket, routed a boat attack from the British frigate *Endymion*, killing, wounding, and capturing over seventy Englishmen. Such bloody affairs, even when the British won, left their warships crippled. In addition to the hazards of wind and weather, there was also a constant dribble of casualties from accidents and skirmishes with American coastal patrols and inshore shipping. Meanwhile American privateers went on raiding from the West Indies to Canton, while British merchants showered the Royal Navy with accusations of sloth, stupidity, and inefficiency. And then, in the last days of 1814, Captain Charles Stewart took *Constitution* out of Boston and headed southeast for the Azores.

IN THE WEST THROUGH 1814 AND 1815, except for occasional clashes between militia and Kickapoo in northern Illinois[15] the war was largely a

---

13. Cushing had been the Army's adjutant general, but had been too sickly to discharge those duties satisfactorily.

14. Officially, only 34 killed and 86 wounded; unofficial reports went as high as 210 and 140 respectively. The action, fine as it was, has been much exaggerated by American writers.

15. Though driven away in 1812, the Kickapoo returned in 1813, rebuilt their

contest for possession of Fort Mackinac and Prairie du Chien, the control centers for the fur trade with the Sioux, Fox, Ojibwa, Sac, Kickapoo, and Winnebago. These tribes had become almost completely dependent on the white man's guns and gunpowder for their hunting and his kettles, hatchets, knives, and blankets for their daily existence. Out of that stark necessity, they had to ally themselves with whatever nation controlled the supply of such essentials.

For western Americans the recapture of Fort Mackinac and Prairie du Chien thus was something more than a matter of self-respect. It was a chance to detach those powerful northwestern tribes from their long-time British alliance, expel the North West Company from American territory, and expand their own trading, possibly even northward toward Hudson Bay. Naturally they and their congressmen had belabored the Madison administration with demands that it insure their future prosperity by launching large-scale offensives against both posts. Oliver Perry's and William H. Harrison's victories in 1813 had cleared the way for such action, though their own combined attempt had failed because of bad weather. By 1814 the westerners had gained the support of Secretary of the Navy William Jones, possibly because he thought Fort Mackinac a suitable target for his underemployed Lake Erie squadron. An expedition accordingly was organized at Detroit, and Brigadier General Duncan McArthur established Fort Gratoit (now Port Huron, Michigan) at the southern tip of Lake Huron as a new advanced base. Governor William Clark prepared to recover Prairie du Chien.

Important as these operations were to westerners, however, they were a serious diversion of the Regular Army's all-too-scanty combat strength from more important missions. Had the regulars so employed been added to Brown's little Left Division as Armstrong intended, 1814 could have seen decisive American successes in the Niagara/Burlington/York area. Such a victory would have cut the flow of British supplies and trade goods to their western posts to a mere trickle. A successful stroke against Kingston, possible if Chauncey could be somehow stimulated or—better yet—replaced, would have been even more effective. Given competent leadership, there was militia enough in the western states and territories to deal with Prairie du Chien. More than that, the Lake Erie squad-

---

"Kickapoo Town" (near modern Bloomington, Illinois), and resumed raiding. Americans again drove them out. In 1814 Illinois offered a $50 bounty for the scalp of any Indian, regardless of age or sex, who entered an American settlement with "murderous intent."

ron alone could have broken up the British supply system across Lake
Huron and kept Fort Mackinac under rigorous blockade. But Madison
and his cabinet chose to squander almost 1,000 regulars by dibs and dabs
in mismanaged wilderness squabbles.

These were peripheral, small-scale operations but the British found
them a grim challenge. England had large, if indefinite, strategic objectives in the Great Lakes area. The most ambitious was a drastic modifica-
tion of the United States' northern frontier, under the pretext of setting
up an Indian state as a buffer between the United States and Canada.
Its boundaries were to be generally the Ohio, Mississippi, and Missouri
rivers; its creation would have stripped the United States of most of the
present states of Ohio, Indiana, Illinois, Wisconsin, Michigan, and Minnesota.[16] Since this territory would include the headwaters of the Mississippi River, England also would demand free navigation for British vessels throughout its length. Americans would be denied the right to have
either warships or fortified bases on any of the lakes. England naturally
would retain Fort Mackinac and Fort Niagara, the last with a five-mile
radius of territory surrounding it, and possibly also a strip of territory
running along the east bank of the Niagara River to Buffalo. (These demands, British diplomats were currently assuring American representatives in the drawn-out peace negotiations at Ghent, were actually proof
of Great Britain's moderation; because they were designed only to ensure
peaceful future relations between the two nations, the national honor of
the United States would take no shame from accepting them, without
delay or argument.)

The achievement of such imperial designs, however, depended heavily
on the willingness of the northwestern tribes to support the few soldiers
that Sir George Prevost was able to spare for the defense of his frontier
outposts, and that willingness, in turn, depended on the British ability to
keep the tribes supplied with trade goods and gifts. Their major supply
route to their western posts was blocked by the American control of Lake
Erie and the Detroit/Fort Malden area. The North West Company's network of canoe routes through the waterways north of Lake Ontario and
Lake Erie could handle little more than an essential minimum of supplies for both English and Indians. The British therefore labored through
1813 to improve and extend this secondary system. One new route ran

16. Purposely the British left its boundaries somewhat indefinite, hinting that they
could be enlarged should the Americans be reluctant to submit. The approximately
100,000 Americans then residing in this area would have to shift for themselves.

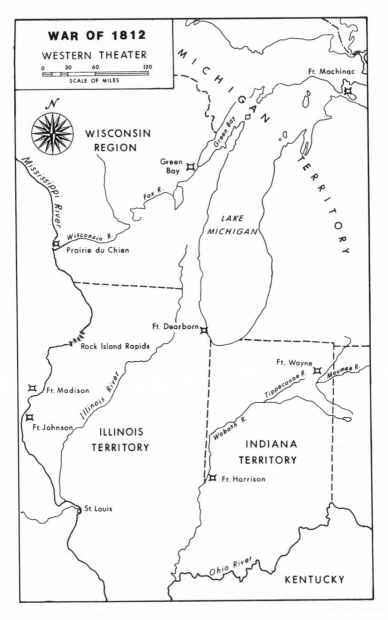

WAR OF 1812

WESTERN THEATER

0   30   60   120
SCALE OF MILES

N

WISCONSIN
REGION

MICHIGAN

Ft. Machinac

Green Bay

Green
Bay

Fox R.

LAKE
MICHIGAN

TERRITORY

Mississippi River

Wisconsin R.

Prairie du Chien

Ft. Dearborn

Rock Island Rapids

Illinois River

Ft. Madison

Ft. Johnson

ILLINOIS
TERRITORY

Ft. Wayne

Tippecanoe R.

Maumee R.

Wabash R.

INDIANA
TERRITORY

Ft. Harrison

St. Louis

Ohio River

KENTUCKY

from York northward to Lake Simcoe and thence westward by canoe or cart to new bases at Nottawasaga and Penetanguishene on Georgian Bay, where North West Company vessels picked up cargoes for Fort Mackinac and the smaller posts beyond. Even with their best efforts, however, existence was difficult at those frontier stations during the winter of 1813–14. Fort Mackinac's garrison had to survive on locally procured fish and Indian corn, but they managed not only to strengthen the fort's defenses, but also to build a redoubt on the high ground behind it where Captain Charles Roberts had emplaced his 6-pounder in 1812. In May, Lieutenant Colonel Robert McDouall, with supplies and ninety-odd men of the Royal Newfoundland Regiment, arrived to take command. Though aware of the likelihood of an American attack on Fort Mackinac, he promptly found himself involved with operations some 400 miles to the southwest at Prairie du Chien.

Governor William Clark had thrust up the Mississippi River in May with a considerable force of regulars and militia, scattering the Sac warriors who attempted to halt him at the Rock Island rapids.[17] Finding Prairie du Chien undefended—too badly outnumbered to risk a stand, its tiny garrison of Canadian volunteers had withdrawn—Clark laid out a small fort and returned to St. Louis, leaving Lieutenant Joseph Perkins and sixty-five men of the 24th Infantry Regiment to complete its construction. To support Perkins, he also left the *Governor Clark*, an improvised river gunboat with an eighty-man crew.[18]

An active, imaginative officer, McDouall quickly grasped—aided no doubt by the excited urgings of the British fur traders at Mackinac—the effect that American possession of Prairie du Chien might have on the northwest tribes. Disregarding the risk of weakening his own garrison, he organized an expedition to "dislodge" Clark whom he thought still at Prairie du Chien. The backbone of this British force was 63 men of the "Mississippi Volunteers," newly raised by two leading traders from among their employees and associates. A good many Indians from the northwestern tribes were at Mackinac at this time; some 130 of them volunteered to go along but, apparently having some reservations as to the

17. Between modern Rock Island, Illinois, and Davenport, Iowa. With a fall of twenty-two feet, these rapids were a major obstacle to early river travel.

18. From various accounts, the *Governor Clark* was propelled by thirty-two oars, had planking thick enough to stop musket balls, and mounted fourteen cannon, probably swivels (miniature cannon with one- to two-inch bore, throwing approximately one-and-a-half-pound shot).

martial qualities of their white comrades, requested that an army officer be placed in command of the expedition and that one of their "Father's big guns" be attached to it. McDouall, who may have had his own reservations, obliged by assigning Captain William McKay of the Michigan Fencibles,[19] whom he made an acting lieutenant colonel; he also detailed a Sergeant James Keating with a 3-pounder gun from his small detachment of regular artillerymen. Finally he added a sergeant, a corporal, and twelve "smart fellows" from the Michigan Fencibles. The Mississippi Volunteers were armed, equipped, and clothed out of stores available at Mackinac; their weapons may have included some captured from the Americans in 1812. Uniforms must have been sketchy: Thomas Anderson, a trader-turned-captain, described his as "a red coat . . . a couple of epaulettes and an old rusty sword with a red cock feather adorning my round hat."[20]

Leaving Fort Mackinac on June 28, McKay moved by way of Lake Superior, Green Bay, and the Fox and Wisconsin rivers, picking up additional volunteers as he went. The British had a minor post at Green Bay, and he may have gathered in Prairie du Chien's former garrison. When he reached Prairie du Chien on July 17, his command was approximately 650 strong, mostly Indians.

McKay's arrival took Lieutenant Perkins by surprise. The fort he was building, already named Fort Shelby, was still unfinished. Instead of attacking at once, however, McKay merely demanded Perkins' unconditional surrender. Perkins refused, and a good deal of wild shooting followed. Sergeant Keating's 3-pounder was ineffective against the two American blockhouses, but he did land several hits on *Governor Clark.*[21] Either the gunboat or its crew's courage thereupon developed a leak; the gunboat fled downstream, going, McKay reported, remarkably fast. Thus abandoned, Perkins held out until the 20th, when it appeared that McKay was ready to attempt an assault. After some dickering, Perkins agreed to surrender the fort and his arms on condition that his garrison be allowed free passage by boat to St. Louis. Considering his hopeless position, it was not a bad bargain. Both sides being deplorable marksmen, there had

19. This unit had been raised locally during 1813 from unemployed voyageurs and small traders to supplement the sixty-four veterans then garrisoning the fort.

20. *Michigan Pioneer and Historical Collections*, Vol. XXIII (1895), p. 510.

21. Perkins reportedly had six cannon, caliber uncertain, but these either were not mounted or he did not use them effectively. Apparently he was able to get a messenger away to request help.

been few, if any, casualties. Though suffering from the mumps, McKay kept his Indians under control, enabling the Americans to get away safely. He then had the fort completed, and modestly renamed it Fort McKay.

Meanwhile downriver, learning that Fort Shelby was under attack, Major John Campbell had hastily collected some 120 regulars and rangers and pushed up the Mississippi in six keelboats to its relief. While working his way up through the Rock Island rapids on July 22 he was ambushed by approximately 400 Sac, Fox, and Kickapoo and came close to being overwhelmed. Rescue came unexpectedly, *Governor Clark* lurching downstream into the midst of the brawl.[22] Campbell disengaged his mauled command, with at least 35 of them killed or wounded, and retired to St. Louis.

The American expedition against Fort Mackinac had begun in much disputing over who was to command the land forces involved. Lieutenant Colonel George Croghan, the hero of Fort Stephenson, finally was designated and assigned something over 700 men, including five companies of regulars, a regiment of Ohio militia, and a few regular artillerymen, to be supported by the squadron's marines.[23] The squadron consisted of the brigs *Lawrence*, *Niagara*, and *Caledonia* and the little schooner-rigged gunboats *Scorpion* and *Tigress*. Its commander was Captain Arthur Sinclair, otherwise unknown to fame.

Sailing from Detroit on July 3, Sinclair began by wasting two weeks looking for the new British supply bases on Georgian Bay. The weather was foggy, and Sinclair had only the foggiest notion of their location. He found nothing and so turned north to St. Joseph's Island, where he discovered only the empty base the British had abandoned in 1812 after they secured Fort Mackinac. Burning it by way of consolation, he scored his first success when he captured a North West Company supply vessel loaded with flour. McDouall of course had learned of this expedition; its wanderings gave him time to transfer two companies of militia from St. Joseph's Island and Sault Ste. Marie to Mackinac.

Arriving off Mackinac on July 26, the Americans quickly found that the best nearby anchorages were dominated by the fort's guns. Attempting to bombard the fort the next morning, they discovered that *Niagara*'s and *Lawrence*'s 32-pounders could not be elevated sufficiently to hit the fort. After too much consideration Croghan decided to land on the north

22. This is the most picturesque account. Another version implies that the gunboat caught up with Campbell after he had fought his own way clear.

23. The regulars were drawn from the 17th, 19th, and 25th infantry regiments, and so were unused to acting as one unit.

shore of the island to find and occupy a position dominating the fort, thereby forcing McDouall either to stand a siege or come out and attack him. His plan was vague enough; his execution of it proved that a hero in a besieged blockhouse could be a blockhead outside it. Without any attempt at deceiving McDouall by a pretended withdrawal or by feints at landing at several places, he came ashore on August 4 in broad daylight, after the squadron had bombarded the landing site heavily to flush out any Indians who might be lurking there. (Apparently none were.)

Thus given ample warning, McDouall decided to meet the Americans halfway. Leaving only 25 militiamen (plus a few gunners and his sick and disabled) in Fort Mackinac and 25 more in the hilltop redoubt, he took up a strong position along the south side of a clearing, astride the trail from the north shore to the fort. Here he had his men build breastworks and emplace two guns (a 6-pounder and a 3-pounder) to cover the trail. Thick woods covered both flanks. To hold his position, McDouall had some 150 infantry—a mix of Royal Newfoundland Fencibles, Michigan Fencibles, and probably a few of the 10th Royal Veterans—and 50 militia. Approximately 350 Indians took position in the timber on either flank.

Coming uphill into the clearing the Americans were caught by British artillery fire, and tumbled back into the trees. Croghan brought two 6-pounders forward and hurriedly reconnoitered the British position. Considering it too strong to rush, he ordered his leading troops, the Ohio militia, to move through the woods to envelop McDouall's right (east) flank. As the regulars came up, he sent them to the right to attempt to work around McDouall's left. While these movements proceeded at a crawl because of the difficult terrain, some frightened subordinate warned McDouall that the American squadron was landing more troops behind him. McDouall withdrew to meet this supposed threat—which suggests what Croghan might have accomplished, had he used a feint or secondary attack to confuse his opponent. During these shifts, however, the regulars were more or less accidently ambushed by a party of Indians, and their commanding officer, Major Andrew H. Holmes, and several others were killed. The rest retreated. McDouall rapidly learned that there were no Americans behind him and hustled his men back to their original position. Croghan gave up, pulled back to the shore, and reembarked. His losses had been quite heavy for so brief an action, nineteen killed or died of wounds, forty-five wounded, two missing. McDouall apparently had only one or two casualties.

Seeking some compensatory success, Sinclair thereafter did find and destroy the British base at Nottawasaga, with the British supply schooner

Nancy. He then took his three brigs and Croghan's troops back to Detroit, leaving *Tigress* and *Scorpion* to blockade Mackinac Island. The two little gunboats did this quite effectively for a time; McDouall had to put his soldiers on reduced rations, and even kill some of his horses to keep his Indians fed. The British finally managed to capture *Tigress* by an overwhelming boat attack, and then used it, still flying American colors, to surprise and take *Scorpion.* Their capture gave the British control of upper Lake Huron and a secure line of communications for such supplies as were available for the western posts.

In August the Americans made one last effort to recover Prairie du Chien. Major Zachary Taylor moved up the Mississippi with 350 regulars and militia in eight armed river boats. Warned well in advance by his Indian allies, Captain Anderson, who then commanded Fort McKay, decided to meet him at the Rock Island rapids. Possibly more than 1,000 Sac, Sioux, and Winnebago, under the famous Sac leader Black Hawk and other chiefs, mustered there around 30 Mississippi Volunteers and Sergeant Keating with his 3-pounder and several swivels. A brave, bull-headed officer who never bothered to reconnoiter an enemy position, Taylor attempted to force his way through on September 5, but found the odds too great and Keating's fire too accurate. He therefore fell back to the junction of the Des Moines and Mississippi rivers, where he erected a temporary work, called Fort Johnson, and attempted to check the exultant Indians' raiding. With winter imminent, in October he burned the fort and retired to St. Louis. The British at Prairie du Chien, now commanded by a Captain Andrew Bulger, spent an uncomfortable, hungry winter amid crowds of discontented Indians who resented the meagerness of the Indian Department's distributions. The Michigan Fencibles and Mississippi Volunteers turned semi-mutinous; Bulger quarreled with the officers of the Indian Department, but they did cooperate in considering an offensive against St. Louis for 1815.

The only American successes in the West during 1814 were in several raids out of their bridgehead in the Fort Malden/Sandwich area. Some of these were mere plundering expeditions by Canadians who had sided with the Americans; loyal Canadians considered them renegades and traitors, and frequently hanged those they captured, and outlawed those who remained uncaught. McArthur led the final and greatest one in October and November, advancing up the Thames River through Moraviantown with 800 mounted men to Oxford. He there swung southward to Port Dover on Lake Erie and rapidly then back to Detroit. This dash tied down considerable British forces, and should have furnished a valuable diversion, had General George Izard had the fortitude to move decisively against the British on the Niagara frontier.[24] As an independent operation it is an odd little preview of Sherman's 1864 march across Georgia: McArthur carried off horses and destroyed almost all of the flour mills in western Upper Canada, leaving the area too stripped of resources to support any British operations against Detroit during the coming winter. At least one Canadian source listed the whole affair as the "Expulsion of McArthur's Brigands."[25]

24. See chapter fourteen.
25. From the Stormont, Dundas, and Glengarry Highlanders 1st Battalion Association's publicity for a 1972 tour of France and Scotland.

SIXTEEN

The Confusions of Andrew Jackson

Will you only say to me, Raise a few hundred militia . . . and with such a regular force as can be conveniently collected, make a descent upon Pensacola and reduce it.
—Andrew Jackson to Secretary of War John Armstrong, July, 1814 [1]

SIR ALEXANDER COCHRANE, "Vice-Admiral and Commander-in-Chief of the Fleet on the North America and Jamaica Stations," was a grim, gray fighting man who, as Canadian voyageurs would put it, never saw a small wolf. Skilled and aggressive, he led his men in danger and hardship, and kept their loyalty—and his appetite for prize money was as outstanding as his military skills. As the campaigning along the Canadian frontier guttered out in general stalemate, he prepared to carry the war into the southern United States.

New Orleans was the biggest of Cochrane's wolves. In peace, it was the commercial outlet and trading center of the western United States. And now New Orleans' warehouses were packed with two years' accumulation of sugar, tobacco, cotton, hemp, and lead, which, with the ships tied up in its harbor, would have a contemporary value of at least $20 million.[2] The loss of this hoard would be a grievous wound to America's economy; its capture would enrich Cochrane and his subordinates astoundingly. Inspired by such a combination, Cochrane had for months urged the British government to mount an expedition against New Orleans. Having some two centuries' experience at being mousetrapped into costly, sometimes humiliating, amphibious operations because of sanguine reports

1. Adams, *The War of 1812*, p. 289.
2. Fortescue, *History of the British Army*, Vol. X, pp. 150–51.

from overly optimistic admirals (most recently at Buenos Aires in 1806), the British Army was less enthusiastic. However, the British government could see the value of having New Orleans in its hands. Initially it planned to send out a very strong expedition [3] under Lieutenant General Sir Rowland Hill, Wellington's ablest subordinate. Major General Robert Ross, who was just then preparing for his stroke at Washington, was sent orders to head for Negril Bay, at the western tip of Jamaica, to join Hill's force, once he had finished with the Chesapeake Bay area. However, the general deterioration of England's relations with Russia and Prussia and the revival of pro-Napoleonic feeling in France soon made it evident that troops earmarked for Hill might soon be needed in Europe.

About this same time another rosily optimistic report came from Cochrane: the American forces along the Gulf of Mexico were weak, and Americans were becoming unpopular. (This was reasonably true, the incompetent General Thomas Flournoy still being in command when Cochrane wrote.) If 3,000 British soldiers were landed in Mobile, the Creek and other southeastern tribes would rally to them, as would the French and Spanish inhabitants of the Mississippi Valley, eager to throw off the yoke of American rule.

The British government thereupon decided to put the land forces for the New Orleans operations under Ross. He was to be reinforced by another brigade, some 2,150 men under Major General John Keane, consisting of the 93d Highlanders from the Cape of Good Hope and two West India regiments from Jamaica and Guadeloupe made up of black enlisted men with white officers. The objectives assigned Ross and Cochrane were the seizure of the mouth of the Mississippi River, so as to cut the American "back-settlements" off from the Gulf of Mexico, and then to "occupy some important and valuable possession by the restoration of which we may improve the conditions of peace, or which may entitle us to exact its cession as the price of peace." [4] The operation was to begin on November 20: otherwise Ross and Cochrane were allowed complete freedom of action in planning their operations. If the French and Spanish inhabitants, generally termed "Creoles," wished to revolt against the United States, they were to be supplied with arms and clothing. "With their favor and cooperation . . . we may expect to rescue the whole province of Louisiana from the United States." [5]

3. With Ross's command, 40,000 men.
4. Adams, *The War of 1812*, p. 285.
5. Ibid.

Meanwhile, the report of Ross's raid on Washington had created such proud pleasure in England that the government was moved to dispatch yet another brigade of 2,200 men, under Major General John Lambert, as an additional reinforcement.

The next report from Ross's command, announcing his death, reached London on October 17, 1814. Major General Sir Edward M. Packenham was hurriedly designated as Ross's replacement. It was a peculiar choice, often ascribed to the fact that Packenham was the Duke of Wellington's brother-in-law. He had served in Spain with the duke, first as his adjutant general, then as a division commander. Very brave, a hard hitter, cheerful, and well liked everywhere, he had not the slightest experience in independent command. Also, the duke seems to have thought him something of a blockhead.

Accompanied by Major General Samuel Gibbs and provided with an adequate staff that included two experts, Colonel Alexander Dickson, Royal Artillery, and Lieutenant Colonel John Fox Burgoyne,[6] Royal Engineers, he was sent off on the fast frigate *Statira* on November 1, with instructions to join Cochrane at Negril Bay and take command of the land forces concentrating there. Thereafter he would follow the orders originally issued for Ross, taking particular care to protect peaceful civilians and prevent slave revolts.

Statira reached Negril Bay on December 13, just as the convoy carrying Lambert's brigade appeared. The captain commanding its naval escort had word that Cochrane had left Negril Bay with Keane's brigade and Ross's former command about two weeks previously (actually on November 27).[7] Leaving Lambert to replenish his water casks and follow, Packenham sailed at once in pursuit of his army. Nine days later he finally sighted the Louisiana coast, low mud banks sheathed in mirages and haze.

American preparations had been something quite different. Andrew Jackson had been given command of the Seventh Military District (Louisiana, Tennessee, the Mississippi Territory, and West Florida) on May 28. There being no visible English threat at the time, he remained at newly built Fort Jackson (twelve miles northeast of modern Montgomery, Alabama), supervising the final mop-ups of his Creek campaign and planning the seizure of Pensacola from its Spanish garrison as an appropriate finale to it.

6. Son of "Gentleman Johnny" Burgoyne of Saratoga fame.
7. Keane's brigade had arrived on November 25, to find Ross's former command already there.

Like most westerners, Jackson wanted Florida. The facts that it was a Spanish possession and that the United States was not at war with Spain were trifles to be disregarded by free Americans. The frontier did have honest historical grudges against Spain, but it also seems that many westerners, like Sir Frances Drake, regarded "spoiling the Dons" as a natural Christian activity. So Jackson urged Armstrong to allow an attack on Pensacola, and meanwhile did his best to pick a fight by bombarding Don Matteo Manrique, its commandant, with impossible demands for the return of Red Stick chiefs who had escaped into Spanish territory. Once the Creek treaty was signed, Jackson moved into his district headquarters at Mobile on August 22 and began serious preparations. The fact that the United States already had one war on its hands did not trouble him at all.[8]

Armstrong had assigned five regular infantry regiments, the 2d, 3d, 7th, 39th, and 44th, and 350 regular artillerymen to the Seventh Military District. The infantry regiments averaged less than half-strength, having a total of some 2,030 men, and the artillerymen were largely scattered through the district's forts, but by 1814 American standards this was a respectable force.

The American naval units based at New Orleans were an improvised lot. There were five gunboats with two small tenders (supply vessels) stationed on Lake Borgne.[9] At New Orleans the schooner *Carolina* and the merchant ship *Louisiana* were being converted into warships. *Carolina*, mounting twelve 12-pound carronades and three 9-pound long guns, was ready enough; *Louisiana*, rated as a 16-gun sloop-of-war, was neither completely armed nor manned. Work also had begun early in 1814 on a powerful "block ship," the *Tchifonta*, a shallow-draft cross between a sloop-of-war and a frigate, mounting twenty-two long 32-pounders and 42-pounder carronades, for river and harbor defense. In midsummer, however, Navy Secretary William Jones decided that New Orleans was in no danger and ordered construction stopped. The naval station commander was Commodore Daniel T. Patterson, hard-working if somewhat limited in imagination. Jackson found him a willing partner.

Jackson's bloody-minded intentions toward Pensacola were further stimulated by the activities of a Lieutenant Colonel Edward Nicholls who

8. Though the Pensacola garrison was weak, there were considerable Spanish forces, including some ships of the line, based on Cuba.

9. British reports mention other gunboats operating in the Mississippi River. More research is needed.

had turned up there on July 23 with a small force of Royal Marines, seized the nearby Fort San Carlos de Barrancas (usually termed "Fort Barrancas"), and installed himself as an uninvited guest. Since he was accompanied by a squadron of four sloops-of-war under Captain Sir William Percy, the Spaniards could not control his activities. He ranged the Florida coast, collecting refugee Red Sticks; clothing, arming, and organizing them; issuing proclamations urging Louisianians to join him in freeing their native soil; and giving out thunderous plans of campaign. These pictured the British using Pensacola as a base to seize Mobile and the mouth of the Mississippi, then striking from Mobile through the Mississippi backwoods for 200-odd miles to Baton Rouge to block the Mississippi River above New Orleans and so starve it into surrender.

Jackson swallowed Nicholls' "plan" hook, line, and sinker. After all, it differed from his own idea of the best way to take New Orleans only in that he thought Walnut Hills (now Vicksburg) a better objective than Baton Rouge. Accustomed to moving mounted riflemen across rough country, Jackson did not pause to consider where a British army, consisting mostly of infantry, could find the horses, wagons, and supplies necessary for such a march, or how they could move the heavy artillery they would need to block the river.[10]

How much of Nicholls' plans were optimistic ignorance and blarney, and how much the sort of deceptive cover plan[11] that "perfidious Albion" has frequently used successfully, is impossible to determine. Certainly Nicholls' noisy activity must have camouflaged some intensive intelligence collecting. Cochrane would have little trouble finding the weak point in the defenses of New Orleans.

To add to the confusion, on September 3 Captain Charles Lockyer's sloop-of-war *Sophie* dropped anchor in Barataria Bay, forty-five miles south of New Orleans, the headquarters of the Laffite brothers' community of pirates and smugglers,[12] with an invitation from Nicholls to enter the British service and have their sins forgiven. This was reinforced by a letter from Captain Percy, threatening destruction unless the Baratarians

10. Some sources had the British planning to create a gunboat flotilla in the river above New Orleans.

11. An apparent plan of campaign, revealed to the enemy by calculated intelligence leaks and ostensible preparations, to cover a commander's real intentions.

12. They had assumed the role of privateers in the service of the Republic of Cartagena, a portion of Colombia in revolt against Spanish rule, but had attacked American and British ships and killed an American customs officer.

joined England in its "just and unprovoked" war. Jean Laffite, the free-booters' acknowledged leader, put the British off with soft words. He and many of his men were French; and one of his brothers was currently in a New Orleans jail for smuggling. Through his many influential friends in New Orleans, Jean passed the British letters to Governor William C. C. Claiborne and offered the services of the Baratarians for the city's defense. Claiborne had been vainly attempting to halt their smuggling for years; Laffite's proffers crossed an attack that the exasperated governor had launched against Barataria with the *Carolina* and the 7th Infantry Regiment on September 16. There was no resistance, the Baratarians abandoning ships and settlement and scattering into the bushes and bayous.

Meanwhile Percy had gathered his squadron—*Hermes* (twenty-two guns), *Carron* (twenty), *Sophie* (eighteen), and *Childers* (eighteen)—and headed for Mobile, apparently to test the American defenses. The first of these was Fort Bowyer, a semicircular coast-defense battery at the bay's entrance, held by 160 men of the 2d Infantry Regiment under Lieutenant Colonel William Lawrence. It mounted twenty guns, some of them demonstrable antiques; reportedly only eight were definitely more dangerous to an enemy than to their cannoneers. Landing 60 marines and 120 Indians with a howitzer behind the fort on September 15, Percy led his ships into the maze of sand bars around the bay's entrance. *Carron* and *Childers* could not get within range, but Percy brought *Hermes* up to within musket-shot of the fort, and Lockyer worked *Sophie* almost as close. An hour's determined pounding ended with *Hermes* aground and out of action, *Sophie* damaged, and 31 Englishmen dead and 40 wounded. Lawrence had three guns dismounted, 4 men killed, and 5 hurt. Unable to free *Hermes*, Percy set her afire, picked up his landing party, and retired to Pensacola.

Insisting that the capture of Pensacola was essential to the defense of Mobile and New Orleans, Jackson had ignored both Claiborne's pleas to personally check the defenses of New Orleans and the orders of James Monroe, the new secretary of war, to leave Pensacola alone and prepare to meet a major British invasion. Reliable warnings as to its strength had come from Europe and the West Indies. Jackson, on his own authority, already had summoned Tennessee's whole 2,500-man militia quota, called out Mississippi militia, and enlisted friendly Indians. Monroe now called on Tennessee for 5,000 additional men, and on Georgia and Kentucky for 2,500 each to reinforce Jackson. Weapons were another matter; only on November 2 did Monroe think to order 4,000 stands of arms [13] sent to New Orleans from Pittsburgh. They were shipped during November 11–15, but by flatboats instead of a steamer, apparently to save the contractor the extra freight charges. Somewhat tardily Jackson was clamoring for weapons, claiming that half of those carried by his militia were unserviceable.

Brigadier General John Coffee joined Jackson on October 25 with 2,800 Tennessee mounted riflemen. Preparations completed, on November 3 Jackson marched on Pensacola with approximately 4,000 men. Reaching the town on the 6th, he demanded its surrender. Neither Manrique nor Nicholls had the strength to defend the place, but the British fired on Jackson's flag of truce, then retired to Fort Barrancas leaving the Spanish to face Jackson's wrath. Next morning Jackson's regulars stormed the town, losing 7 killed and 11 wounded. Having upheld Spain's honor, Manrique capitulated.[14] Before Jackson could move against Fort Barrancas, the British there, short of food and water, blew the place up and took to their ships. Fearing that they might strike behind him to seize Mobile, Jackson hastily countermarched. The expedition had been a waste of time and men, though the cheap victory raised American morale. Nicholls soon established a new base, British Fort,[15] on the Apalachicola River, some 150 miles east of Pensacola, and remained a nuisance to Georgia and West Florida until the war's end.

Mobile secure, Jackson dispatched a Major Uriah Blue with 1,000 mounted riflemen and friendly Indians toward the Apalachicola River to hunt down English detachments and refugee Red Sticks. Having thus sent a fifth of his forces off on a wild-goose chase—Blue accomplished nothing useful—Jackson finally left for New Orleans on November 22, after further scattering his little army. Still certain that Mobile would be the British objective, he posted the 3d and 39th infantry regiments and some militia there, packed the 2d Infantry Regiment into hastily strengthened Fort Bowyer, ordered the 44th Infantry Regiment to New Orleans, and sent Coffee with 1,200 mounted riflemen to Baton Rouge. The 7th Infantry Regiment and some regular artillerymen were at New Orleans. Two days earlier 2,500 Tennessee militia—semi-uniformed in "dark blue or nut-brown homespun" or buckskin hunting shirts and trousers—under Major General William Carroll had left Nashville by boat; Major General John Thomas and as many Kentucky militia were

13. A musket complete with sling, ramrod, and bayonet.
14. Spanish losses were four killed and six wounded.
15. Also Fort Nicholls; later Negro Fort.

following, but the former would need a month, the latter six weeks, to reach New Orleans.

Jackson himself was in poor health and traveled slowly, reaching New Orleans only on December 2. Worn and ill though he was, however, he could draw on that innate, furious courage with which he met every crisis. His mere appearance brought order and hope to the squabbling, apprehensive city. However, he spent most of the next two weeks leisurely reconnoitering its surroundings.

Several routes led to New Orleans from the Gulf of Mexico, and Jackson and Cochrane both considered them. Cochrane, having the initiative, could select whichever one seemed best suited to his purposes. Jackson must prepare to defend them all.

Some seventy miles northwest along the coast from the mouth of the Mississippi River is the Lafourche River—actually a narrow side channel of the Mississippi, which it rejoins north of New Orleans. Twenty miles farther east is Barataria Bay, then the Laffite brothers' stronghold. From it a string of lakes, streams, and trails led to the Mississippi opposite New Orleans, a route the Baratarians had developed to bring their booty to the New Orleans markets without troubling United States customs officials. Neither of these routes would take large ships; both were at an unhandy distance in the stormy winter season.

The Mississippi River was the only practical route for large ships sailing to and from New Orleans, but an advance upriver would have to contend with the river's current and shifting channels, properly known only by local pilots, for approximately 100 miles. Some 30 miles upstream was strongly built Fort St. Philip; roughly 45 miles farther were some new batteries Jackson had ordered built on the east bank at the great river loop known as English Turn.[16] Just above these on the west bank was new Fort St. Leon, which commanded the river for 3 miles downstream and 2 miles above it.

Between the Mississippi's mouth and Lake Borgne, several bayous meandered inland through the swamps, their headwaters close to English Turn. However, these were shallow and easily guarded and obstructed.

An advance across Lake Borgne into Lake Pontchartrain would put the British north of New Orleans, but would have to get past the forts guarding the two channels between the lakes, Fort Petite Coquilles (also called Fort Rigolets or Fort Coquilles), on Pas Rigolets, the larger, eastern

16. From the old story that an English sea captain turned back there when some wandering Frenchmen told him gaudy lies about a big French stronghold a little way farther upriver.

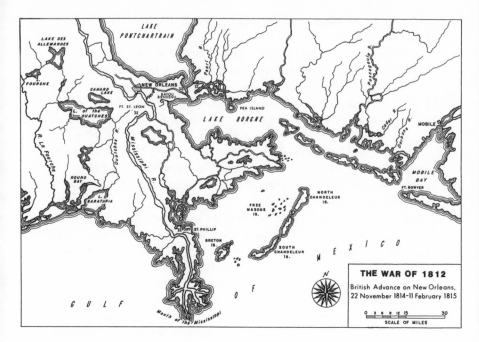

THE WAR OF 1812

British Advance on New Orleans,
22 November 1814-11 February 1815

SCALE OF MILES

channel; and the queerly named Fort at Chef Menteur on Chef Menteur
Pas, the western one.[17] Surprise therefore would be next to impossible:
Jackson would have ample time to shift his forces and improvise a defensive line. Moreover, the British would be able to use only their smallest
vessels, Lake Borgne being shallow and laced with shoals.

There remained an approach across Lake Borgne itself into one of the
many bayous feeding into it from headwaters that groped westward almost
to the Mississippi. Except for a narrow rim of reasonably firm plantation country along the edge of the river, the terrain between them was all
swamp and waterlogged cypress and palmetto woods. One British officer
described it succinctly as an accumulation of mud. Any movement across
Lake Borgne would have to be made in small boats. The bayous were a
network of channels, full of dead ends, many of them known only to a few
fishermen or trappers.

Jackson's planning was handicapped by several factors. To begin with,
as late as December 10 he still was convinced that any British attack

17. There is considerable confusion concerning these forts. Fort Petite Coquilles
seems to have been three-quarters of a mile west of the present Fort Pike State Park;
Fort at Chef Menteur is modern Fort Macomb.

would be directed at Fort Bowyer and Mobile. When Lieutenant Thomas Ap Catesby Jones, commanding the gunboat flotilla on Lake Borgne, reported sighting a British squadron off the lake's entrance the next day, Jackson persisted in regarding their appearance as a "faint." Having no knowledge of naval warfare, he was certain that Jones's "Gun Boats on the Lakes will prevent the British from approaching in that quarter." [18] And, if the British really intended to attack New Orleans, he was certain that they would either come up the Mississippi or through Lake Pontchartrain, probably the latter. He accordingly strengthened the defenses of these two approaches. As for the others, since it would be impossible to find men, guns, and time enough to fortify them, Jackson had to content himself by using detachments of local militia to block bayous and creeks with tangles of felled trees, and to establish a chain of coastal outposts. Most of this work seems to have been done more or less thoroughly, but Major General Jacques de Villere of the Louisiana militia failed completely to block those channels of Bayou Bienvenue that extended from Lake Borgne into his plantation.[19] This failure was known to local Spanish fishermen who used those waterways.

Alexander Cochrane had a very different estimate of the situation, undoubtedly based on considerable information concerning the New Orleans area. To him Lake Borgne offered the best opportunity for a sudden surprise attack, straight at the city, bypassing Jackson's prepared defenses. He had overwhelming naval superiority and knew how to use it. The delay that would be imposed by having to shift Keane's troops into small boats to cross the shallow lake and get them through the swamps on its western shore could be overcome by careful planning and driving execution of those plans. Having no idea of when Packenham might appear, he could not wait for him; in any case, Packenham would have little knowledge of the existing situation. Since Jackson had not yet concentrated his forces at New Orleans [20] it was essential to strike before he did. To divert Jackson's attention he would send a small squadron into the Mississippi River to tap at the American defenses there.

Lieutenant Catesby Jones had more valor than common sense. All five

18. James, *The Life of Andrew Jackson*, p. 208.

19. This lapse remains unexplained, since de Villere served loyally. Possibly, since this was his usual route to Lake Borgne, the general had thriftily sought to avoid the cost of clearing away obstructions after the war.

20. Cochrane had sailed, with Keane, a day before the rest of the expedition left Jamaica. En route he paused off Apalachicola and Pensacola, obviously to pick up the latest intelligence.

of his little vessels together were hardly a threat to the lightest warship in Cochrane's fleet, but they were Jackson's principal source of information as to what that fleet might be doing. Jones's mission therefore demanded careful patrolling, fast delivery of information, and no showy heroics. In fact it would have been far more sensible to use a few fast fishing boats for such outpost work, while holding his gunboats in reserve. Instead, Jones paraded his whole flotilla around the entrance to Lake Borgne when Cochrane came over the horizon on December 11. With Cochrane as his enemy, this was asking for trouble. On the night of the 12th, as soon as the rest of his fleet had closed up, the admiral armed and sent off his ships' barges and large boats [21]—forty-five in all, carrying 1,200 sailors and marines and forty-three guns—under Captain Lockyer to dispose of Jones. Jones had retired into Lake Borgne; tardily apprehensive, he headed deeper into the lake, but the wind failed. Knowing he could not outrow the lighter British craft, he formed his gunboats in line in a channel between two islands [22] to make whatever fight he could with his 183 men and twenty-three guns. Catching up early on December 14 after a thirty-six-hour row, Lockyer attacked straight up the channel, concentrating on Jones's own gunboat. Jones beat off two attacks, sinking two barges; both he and Lockyer were wounded. A third British rush was successful; swarming onto the gunboat's deck, English sailors turned its weapons on the nearest American gunboat, overwhelmed it, and so carried each of the other three, then seized the tenders. It had been a rough affair, bravely waged on both sides. Seventeen Englishmen were dead and 77 wounded; the Americans had only 6 killed and 35 wounded, but the rest were prisoners and their gunboats added to Cochrane's fleet.

Jackson was inspecting the Lake Pontchartrain defenses on December 15 when he received word of the flotilla's destruction. At once he dispatched couriers to call in Coffee from Baton Rouge and to hurry Carroll and Thomas forward. Next day he declared martial law and proceeded to rule New Orleans with a high and heavy hand. This evidence of determination and defiance appealed to the volatile Creoles. Their morale swelled still more when Coffee appeared on the 20th after a forced march of 135 miles in three days, which had left a third of his "Dirty Shirts" straggling along his line of march. Carroll's flatboats came into the river

21. Some of these barges would have been almost as large as the American gunboats.

22. These were the aptly named Malheureux Islands near Lake Borgne's northern shore.

docks the next day. Capable beyond the average of militia generals, he had given his men whatever drill and instruction was possible on his big flatboats. Overtaking a shipment of muskets and ammunition bound for New Orleans, he also had the blacksmiths among his men get them all into order, and make up 50,000 buck-and-ball cartridges. This was doubly fortunate, since a good many of his men had been without weapons.

The loss of the gunboats left Jackson without any effective means of watching British operations on Lake Borgne. Oddly, neither he nor Patterson thought of taking the obvious action of quickly commissioning several small, fast boats to replace them, even though such craft, and daring men to handle them, were available. Jackson did send a flag of truce to learn the fate of Jones and his sailors. During the resulting parley, British officers pumped the American emissaries (whom they detained until after the fighting ended) as to the strength of Jackson's forces. Some inspired liar among them put it at between 16,000 and 20,000. Unfortunately, having no further information as to British movements, Jackson lapsed into the easy belief that, as he wrote a friend on December 23, they were doing nothing of importance.

Quite to the contrary, eradicating American gunboats had not in the least distracted Cochrane from his primary duties. He had to discover a good landing place. Meanwhile, since Lake Borgne was too shallow for any but the lightest ships, it would be necessary to find some advanced base where Keane's troops could be collected from the transports and warships and readied for that operation. Accordingly Captain Robert Spencer of the Navy and Lieutenant John Peddie, the Army's "deputy assistant-quarter-master-general,"[23] were dispatched to reconnoiter Bayou Bienvenue, at the northwestern corner of Lake Borgne. As another indication of the workings of British espionage, they were given an "intelligent" guide.

Meanwhile Pea Island, off the mouth of the Pearl River, was selected as the staging area, and ships' boats and small craft began ferrying the troops there across the thirty miles of water from the lake's entrance where most of the fleet had had to anchor. What with wet weather and tricky navigation it was a difficult business, but soldiers and sailors were in high spirits and worked heartily together despite hardships. Between December 16 and 19 all the troops except the 1st West India Regiment were ashore and had run up rough huts for shelter against cold and rain.

---

23. In present American times, an officer of the G-3 (Plans and Operations) staff section.

Peddie and Spencer found a tiny settlement of Spanish fishermen just inside the mouth of that tangle of creeks generally known as Bayou Bienvenue.[24] Happy to accept English pay, these Spaniards guided the two Englishmen along waterways through the swamps into the narrow Canal Villere, which ran westward through General de Villere's plantation to within 1,000 yards of the Mississippi. On the night of December 18, disguised in fishermen's smocks, Peddie and Spencer capped their reconnaissance by strolling over to the river and taking a drink of its water. They were within eight miles of New Orleans. They also quizzed their guides as to the number of American troops around New Orleans. Less than 5,000 men, the Spaniards said.

Keane and Cochrane were ready to move as soon as the two officers returned. The fleet's boats could lift only approximately 2,000 men at one time, but they were the most reliable means of transport across the shallow lake. During December 21, the 21st and 44th regiments were embarked on gunboats and schooners, the 93d Foot and a detachment of Royal Artillery joining them the next morning. At 9:00 A.M. on the 22d Colonel William Thornton's "Advance"—the 85th and 95th, with a rocket brigade and a company of Royal Sappers and Miners—and the 4th Foot clambered into the fleet's boats. That completed at 11:30, the whole expedition (except for the 5th West India Regiment) shoved off. At sunset, south of the channels leading into Lake Pontchartrain, the water had become so shallow that, in the failing light, most of the small vessels had to anchor to avoid running aground. The boats, however, kept on through the bitterly cold darkness, reaching the mouth of Bayou Bienvenue about midnight. There Spaniards met them with the warning that an American outpost, a sergeant and eight men, had been established in their village the day before. While the Advance waited in anxious silence, two boats carrying a detachment of the 95th slipped past the village (the Americans probably were observing the ancient militia custom of sleeping soundly on duty) and landed it behind them. The picket was quickly bagged.

Cochrane and Keane had accompanied the boat expedition; now they interrogated at least one of the prisoners as to the strength and disposition of Jackson's forces. This was something beyond militiamen's comprehension: they had seen quite a few soldiers recently and, like most inex-

---

24. Contemporary sources have a corresponding tangle of names for these islands and waterways, the British using Bayou Catalan for Bienvenue and Pine Island for Pea Island.

perienced observers, greatly overestimated their numbers. Also, they may have had a revengeful desire to give their lordly questioners something to worry about. Whatever the reason, one prisoner insisted that Jackson had 4,000 men at English Turn and 12,000 to 15,000 around New Orleans. By sheer luck, these figures matched roughly with those Cochrane had gotten from Jackson's flag-of-truce party.

The landing went on with smooth efficiency. Cochrane set up an advanced headquarters near the fishermen's village, hoisting a large red flag on a pole nearby to mark the entrance to Bayou Bienvenue. The troops continued up the bayou under Peddie's guidance, turning into Bayou Mazant, which soon narrowed so that the boats had to go single file. The water level proved a foot lower than during Peddie's reconnaissance—probably the tide was out—so Keane decided to land the troops at the junction of Bayou Mazant and Canal Villere. The boats were packed into the bayou bow to stern, and the troops clambered from one to the next, a slow and awkward business. For almost a mile, the Sappers and Miners had to hack a trail along the bank of the canal through dense seven-foot stands of tough, sharp-edged reeds, and improvise temporary bridges over numerous creeks that fed into the canal. Next came over a mile of dense cypress woods, full of stagnant pools and thick brush. As soon as the Advance finished landing, around 10:00 A.M., Thornton sent a detachment ahead to take position in the woods and cover the toiling engineers. The 4th Foot and rocket troops finished landing around noon and the whole force then pushed forward to the western edge of the woods, while sailors extricated the emptied boats from the bayou and went back for their next load.

Whether from the Spaniards or their prisoners, the British had learned that a company of Louisiana militia was stationed in the buildings of the Villere plantation. Deploying several companies, Thornton surrounded the buildings in one quick rush, gathering in thirty prisoners; one of them was Major René de Villere, commander of the various outposts along Bayou Bienvenue. Humiliated over his failure, de Villere promptly made a desperate break for freedom and escaped.

As aggressive as at Bladensburg, Thornton urged an immediate advance on New Orleans—while Jackson was still unaware of their presence. His troops—the 85th were light infantry, the 95th green-uniformed riflemen—could reach the city in two hours, catching the American forces in detail. Keane chose not to risk it. He had barely 2,000 men, without artillery, between what might be greatly superior American forces at New Orleans and English Turn. The 21st, 44th, and 93d regiments,

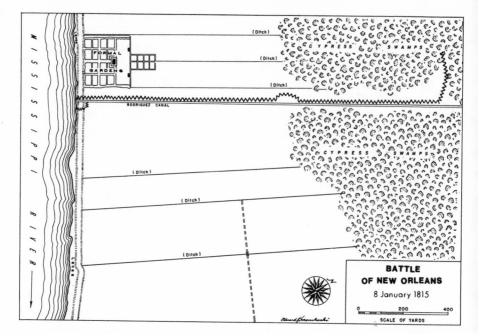

BATTLE
OF NEW ORLEANS
8 January 1815

0   200   400

SCALE OF YARDS

approximately 2,500 men, were scheduled to arrive by midnight; Keane chose to wait for them before resuming his advance. He posted Thornton facing toward New Orleans, the 4th toward English Turn, put out strong outposts; and prepared to sit tight. Not until around 3:00 P.M. did the British see any Americans. Then a small cavalry patrol probed Thornton's outposts, lost two horses, and "quickly retired."

During that wait, British officers examined their new field of operations. There was the Mississippi River, 1,000 yards wide and running fast from recent rains, between four-foot-high levees along either bank. The main road to New Orleans paralleled the inner side of the levee. Then came a belt of cleared land from 1,000 to 1,500 yards wide, flat but broken by high, stout fences between the various plantations. There was a scattering of planters' houses, some of them quite large and all of them with a surrounding clutter of outbuildings, slaves' quarters, orchards, and gardens. From most of them a "wet" ditch like Canal Villere ran off through the woods into the bayous. The principal plantation crop was sugarcane, which had been harvested, leaving the fields littered with "cane trash."[25]

25. The refuse left after the cane has been pressed.

From the edge of cultivation the land sloped downhill through the belt of swampy woodlands. A practical-minded artillery officer noted that the main road was a dirt affair that even a little rain would turn into deep mud.

The British landing had not been a perfect secret. During the morning of December 23 some of Jackson's militia outposts reported glimpses of British vessels that seemed to be headed for one of the bayous leading inland toward English Turn. Jackson therefore sent his chief of engineers, Major A. Lacarrière Latour, to investigate. (Latour was a somewhat mysterious Frenchman, a trained military engineer, and apparently a veteran of considerable service, also possibly once part of Napoleon's intelligence network.) He left Jackson's headquarters at 11:00 P.M., about the time Thornton's advance guard was moving into the woods behind the Villeré plantation. En route he met panicked civilians all a-babble about redcoats at the Villeré house. Sending back one of his staff to alert Jackson, he rode as close as he could to Keane's position, counted between 1,600 and 1,800 men, noted their dispositions, and spurred back to New Orleans. Even before he arrived at about 2:00 P.M. several other messengers of disaster, including a disheveled Major de Villeré, had come panting to Jackson's headquarters.

Briefly, Jackson exploded—then quietly and quickly gave his orders. Major Thomas Hinds' recently arrived squadron of Mississippi Dragoons were to scout Keane's position; the 7th Infantry would take up a blocking position below New Orleans while other troops concentrated for a counterattack. Orders given, Jackson snatched a short nap. Now that he knew where his enemy was, "I will smash them, so help me God!" [26]

It was an oddly assorted little force Jackson had summoned. There were the 7th and 44th infantry regiments and a detachment of regular artillery with two 6-pounders. Commodore Patterson cleared *Carolina* for action and provided a company of marines. From New Orleans, Jackson drew its battalion of volunteer militia, another of "free men of color," and a rifle company.[27] Coffee's brigade of mounted riflemen and eighteen Choctaw warriors completed the assemblage. Hinds' Mississippi Dragoons were back from their reconnaissance with word that there now were 2,000 British at the Villeré plantation, preparing to encamp for the

26. James, *The Life of Andrew Jackson*, p. 222.
27. The volunteer militia (approximately 300) were mostly French, tiny separate companies with ornate uniforms and names. The "free men of color" (some 200) were mulatto refugees from the Haitian slave revolt, some of them as light-skinned as any Creole. The rifle company ("Beale's Rifles," approximately 60) consisted of American residents.

night. Jackson reported his own strength at no more than 1,500, but approximately 2,100 seems a more accurate figure. He left Carroll's brigade and three newly raised regiments of Louisiana militia under Governor Claiborne to watch the Lake Pontchartrain approaches to New Orleans.

Jackson's plan was for the *Carolina* to drop downstream and begin bombarding the British camp at 7:30 P.M. He would advance along the river at 8:00 [28] with the marines and the 6-pounders on the levee and the road bordering it, the 7th Infantry, the 44th, and the volunteer militia formed on their left in that order. Guided by local planters, Coffee would move along the edge of the woods to envelop the British right flank. It was a chill, moonlit night with thickening fog over the river. This fog hid the approach of the *Carolina* as Patterson maneuvered her close in to the east bank opposite the British camp, unseen by their sentries. At 7:30 sharp, aiming at the campfires, he blasted it with grape and roundshot. It was a complete surprise, but Thornton quickly got the 85th and 95th in behind the levee; while Keane shifted the 4th to the shelter of some nearby buildings. The rocket company attempted to reply to the *Carolina*, but could not find suitable positions.

At 8:00 Jackson jumped off, but his advance quickly became ragged. Having to get over a series of stout fences and water-filled ditches, the regulars and militia fell behind the marines and guns; then the militia, unfamiliar with such vulgar exertions, lagged behind the regulars. When the regulars struck the British outposts and the shooting began, excited militia fired wildly in the general direction of the enemy, and rather nicked the regulars. The British outposts were driven in, but Thornton hustled his two regiments into line and counterattacked. The marines gave way, leaving the guns exposed; the 7th stopped Thornton; Jackson rallied the marines, and staff officers brought the militia forward into the line. Both sides slammed at each other through the fog and thickening powder smoke for almost an hour; then Jackson broke contact and withdrew. His reports would offer "heavy smoke" and "thick fog" as an excuse, but a careful reading makes it obvious that the militia had fallen into confusion. Again, casualties told the tale: 884 regulars had 15 killed and 43 wounded; 560 militia only 17 wounded.

Jackson's disengagement was made easier by Coffee's advance. Dismounting and turning their horses loose,[29] Coffee's riflemen drove deep

---

28. This delay must have been necessary to allow Coffee to get into position. An immediate attack should have been more effective.

29. Most of them were later recovered, but others were picked up by the British. It is possible that some were used during the Waterloo campaign.

into the British right rear, throwing Thornton's right flank into confusion. For some reason, possibly because he feared an attack on his rear by American forces reported at English Turn, Keane still kept the 4th in reserve. Only the innate cohesion of veteran troops kept the British from breaking: clubbing up around their officers, they stood stubbornly against the riflemen's rush. Coffee's loose attack formation fragmented around such tough little knots. All intermixed, unable to clearly tell friend from foe until literally hand to hand, Americans and British fought it out with bayonet,[30] gun butt, sword, knife, and fist until Thornton finally patched a line together behind an old abandoned levee that ran parallel with the new one some 300 yards farther inland. Forted up between the two, which protected them from *Carolina*'s fire, they beat off Coffee's disorganized brigade. At the same time 200 of the 93d Foot came out of the woods into Coffee's rear, followed by parts of the 21st and 44th. In danger of being trapped, Coffee made his way back to the levee, where he rejoined Jackson shortly after midnight.

It had been a lively affair. Had Jackson had with him the regular regiments he left in useless idleness at Mobile, it could have been a decided American victory. He simply had expected too much from utterly raw militia. Even so he had won a psychological victory. Casualties were not far from even—American: 24 killed, 115 wounded, 74 missing; British: 46 killed, 167 wounded, 64 missing.[31] The suddenness and fury of Jackson's assault, however, had convinced Keane that he had been assailed by 5,000 Americans. The *Carolina*, which Patterson had shifted over to the west bank, kept firing at any movement in the British camp. Giving up all thoughts of an immediate advance, the British concentrated on getting troops, guns, and supplies ashore.

Once Coffee had rejoined him with word that the British were being reinforced, Jackson also dismissed any idea of further offensive action. Leaving a screen of cavalry to watch the British, he retired approximately two miles to a defensive position his engineers had selected behind the so-called Rodriquez Canal, a one-time millrace running from the woods to the river—a distance of only some 1,000 yards. Here, approximately five miles below New Orleans, the army immediately began to dig in, half resting, half working, while Jackson scoured New Orleans and the surrounding area for entrenching tools and laborers. Planters sent their slaves.

30. Coffee's men would have been handicapped by their lack of bayonets. By contrast the British 95th Regiment, though riflemen, had a special sword bayonet.

31. Most of the "missing" on both sides had actually been taken prisoner.

By Christmas Day the position was defensible. Her outfitting finally completed, the *Louisiana* came down the river and anchored abreast of the British outpost line, to join *Carolina* in bedeviling the enemy. From January 2, 1815, through the 6th, having completed their breastwork, the Americans extended their defenses into the woods and swamp on their left for some 500 yards, building a palisade of loopholed logs, with a wooden platform behind it to keep its defenders out of the mire. Its final 100 yards bent abruptly to the rear to block any British flanking attack. On their right they built a small redoubt atop the levee in front of their breastwork to give them enfilade fire along its front. Across the Mississippi, Patterson began emplacing heavy guns to fire into the flank of any British advance on the east bank. Not content with these measures, Jackson had Latour construct a second line of defenses on the east bank, a mile and a half behind the Rodriquez line. Employing as many as 900 blacks, Latour finished this and began a third line a mile behind the second.

A British engineer officer who inspected the American defenses after the war reported that the canal was about 8 feet deep and 15 feet wide for some 650 yards in from the Mississippi. The remaining 350 yards measured only 4 and 10 feet respectively. The Americans had made no effort to deepen or widen it, and had left it full of brambles. Their breastwork had been made by scraping up earth on the far side of the canal; the inner side was revetted with planks, held in place by posts. In his preparations Jackson almost ignored the west bank of the Mississippi. Having practically no knowledge, except for an occasional sighting by one of his coastal outposts, of what the British fleet might be doing, he continued to be apprehensive of a second British landing, this one in his rear near the southern end of Lake Pontchartrain. He therefore kept Claiborne's three Louisiana militia regiments in that area, and ordered the garrisons of the forts guarding the passages between Lake Borgne and Pontchartrain to defend their posts "to the last extremity."

Packenham finally caught up with his army on Christmas Day, after seventy chilly hours in the *Statira*'s gig. Apparently he and his staff were somewhat appalled at the situation that greeted them. However, no major movements could be undertaken until *Carolina* was put out of action. The troops had so far gotten two 9-pounders, four 6-pounders, and two 5½-inch howitzers ashore; the next morning before daylight Colonel Dickson moved these up to the levee, opened some camouflaged embrasures in it, and made arrangements for heating the 9-pounder shot. During that same night an American detachment had either infiltrated up from

English Turn or slipped across the river and cut the levee not far from Packenham's headquarters; much labor was needed to plug the gap and stop the flooding.

At 7:45 A.M. on December 27, Dickson put his guns into battery and opened fire on *Carolina*. Though the range was long—at least 800 yards—for 9-pounders, British gunnery was excellent; *Carolina* soon caught fire and blew up. The guns then shifted to *Louisiana*, which had begun warping upstream, but the distance was too great to damage her. A number of horses had been picked up and, after considerable fussing, Dickson secured enough of them for some of his guns. The rest were used to mount staff officers and orderlies, but none were spared for the dismounted squadron of the 14th Light Dragoons attached to the Army which could have been useful for reconnoitering the American position. Consequently, when the Army advanced on the 28th, it blundered into Jackson's entrenched line, of which it seemingly had no knowledge. Its leading elements were shot up in a crossfire from Jackson's batteries and *Louisiana*, which killed or wounded some sixty men and wrecked two guns. After a personal reconnaissance on foot close up to the American position, Packenham decided it was too strong to rush, and apparently impossible to outflank. He therefore ordered his troops to fall back approximately 2,000 yards and construct huts. There would be no attack until heavy guns could be brought from the fleet, still anchored off the entrance to Lake Borgne, to support it.

It took immense labor to get 18-pounder guns and 24-pounder carronades forward, especially since the Army's siege train equipment had not yet arrived. Parties of sailors somehow delivered the massive weapons with their clumsy, small-wheeled ship's carriages, moving them seventy-five miles by open boats and boggy roads. Men of the two West Indies regiments detailed to help them proved "unmanned" and torpid. Sent off in light tropical uniforms, they were dying by dozens in the hard frosts and cold rains.

Sufficient heavy artillery having been brought up, Packenham ordered battery positions constructed and armed during the night of December 31. These would have to be built within 800 yards of the American line, which meant that the American outposts would have to be forced back after dark, battery positions constructed, and the heavy guns and ammunition moved into them before daylight. Lacking adequate engineer equipment and artillery sling carts and traveling carriages for moving heavy guns, Burgoyne and Dickson had to substitute human muscle, ingenuity, and determination. Two 18-pounders were placed to deal with

Louisiana if she appeared, two more to pound the right of the American line. To their right were three 5½-inch mortars, a rocket battery, and another battery mounting three 6-pounders, two 9-pounders, and two 5½-inch howitzers, all of which were to concentrate on the center of the American line, especially its gun emplacements. Approximately 700 yards in from the Mississippi was the "great" battery: six 18-pounders and four 24-pounder carronades, manned by sailors, to first silence the American left-flank guns and then try to break down the breastwork. Beyond this was another rocket battery. The emplacements around the guns consisted of single rows of sugar barrels, loosely filled with dirt, with more dirt thrown up against them on the outside. The platforms for the heavy guns were uneven, but it was the best that could have been done in the eight hours available. (This work, even if carefully conducted, would have produced considerable noise. That, combined with the driving in of his outposts, should have warned Jackson that the British were preparing a major attack. Yet there seems to have been no American reaction, neither reinforced patrols nor artillery fire.) Dickson's major worry was the shortage of ammunition, the 18-pounders averaging only sixty rounds per gun, the carronades forty, and the mortars thirty, with no prospect of an immediate resupply.

During the last hours of darkness the infantry moved forward and took shelter in ditches and fence lines, to wait for the guns to clear their way. As soon as the guns had sufficiently breached the American line, Gibbs's 2d Brigade—4th, 21st, 44th, and 1st West India regiments—was to rush it in column of battalions without firing,[32] its attack to be preceded by a firing party of 100 men, shooting to make surviving Americans keep their heads down, and 300 carrying fascines to fill up the Rodriquez Canal in front of the breach. That done, this detachment would deploy to either flank along the canal and continue sniping. Keane's 3d Brigade would feint an advance nearer the river, but, since any advance it might make would be exposed to Patterson's battery on the west bank and possibly to the *Louisiana*, would do so discreetly unless an unexpected opportunity appeared for carrying the American lines. On the extreme right Captain Robert Renny of the 21st Foot, lieutenant colonel by brevet for valor, with 200 men would move through the edge of the woods in a feint to threaten Jackson's left.

Jackson had twelve guns along his line to answer Dickson's twenty: one

---

32. On December 26, Packenham reorganized his army into two brigades. Keane had the 3d Brigade (85th, 93d, 95th, and 5th West India regiments).

32-pounder, three 24-pounders, one 18-pounder, three 12-pounders, three 6-pounders, and a 6-inch mortar. West of the Mississippi, Patterson had one 24-pounder and two long 12's that could fire into the left flank of the British guns. American battery positions were strongly built, their walls revetted with cotton bales, plastered over with mud; gun crews were regular artillerymen, sailors from the *Carolina*, militia (some of them veterans of the great wars), and a few Baratarians whose services Jean Laffite finally had persuaded Jackson to accept. By one account this first morning of 1815 found the Americans preparing to hold a review.

It was a foggy morning. At 9:00 A.M., finally able to see their targets, the British gunners opened with a crash; showers of rockets and mortar shells deluged the rear of the American line, momentarily sparking vast confusion. This however soon steadied; for over three hours the opposing artillerymen fought their roaring duel. By then, the British central battery of light guns and howitzers had been silenced, with several pieces disabled; the great battery's 18- and 24-pounders were almost out of ammunition; the American breastwork showed no serious damage. With thirteen artillerymen dead and an equal number wounded, Dickson had to order "cease firing," and swallow his ire when the Americans, thinking they had silenced all the British guns, began cheering. Being a fair-minded man, he would admit that the heavier American guns were smashing the British hogshead defenses, and that it was proving impossible to work the carronades effectively on their wobbly platforms. Even with sufficient ammunition, he concluded, he would have had to cease fire in another hour or two.

That afternoon it began to rain. By the time it was dark enough to begin withdrawing the guns, the fields and roads were boggy, the mud around the great battery knee-deep. Exhausted working parties began dissolving into the night until Packenham learned of the trouble, went to the spot, and called up details from every regiment until all ten heavy guns were back within the British outpost line before dawn. During this withdrawal Renny reported himself still in the woods, somewhere near the American left flank, and requested orders. Just how close he actually got to the left end of the American line is uncertain; he did find the body of an engineer lieutenant missing since December 30 when his scouting party was driven off while attempting to locate it.

The Americans had not come through the day unhurt: three guns were somewhat damaged, two artillery caissons blown up by rockets, and thirty-four men killed or wounded. They went hurriedly to work repairing and improving their defenses, meanwhile keeping the English position under artillery fire. Patterson's heavy guns on the west bank used hot shot in a systematic effort to set fire to all the buildings in the English-held area, hoping to destroy Packenham's reserves of supplies and ammunition. Warned of this on the 3d by a deserter from the 44th Infantry, Packenham had had the munitions distributed in small lots across a cleared field near the woods. Repairs to the American defenses included the removal of the cotton bales, some of which had caught fire during the artillery battle.[33] Brigadier General David Morgan's Louisiana militia, which had hovered on the east bank near English Turn without profit, and the guns from the batteries there were moved across the river.[34]

Packenham and Cochrane agreed on new tactics. Another attack would be postponed until the arrival of Lambert's 1st Brigade, the 7th and 43d regiments. Meanwhile, Cochrane suggested that the Canal Villere would be enlarged and extended through the levee into the Mississippi, enabling sizable ships' boats to reach the river from Lake Borgne. Using these, a strong force would be sent across the Mississippi to take Patterson's batteries from the rear. Once this attack had succeeded, Packenham would launch a heavy frontal attack against Jackson's line. Both attacks were to be made in the early morning when fog would conceal the advancing British columns. Dickson emplaced additional guns along the river, to support the west-bank attack and to halt American warships that might attempt to intercept its crossing.

Despite American artillery fire, preparations for this attack went rapidly. On January 4 Lambert's 1st Brigade began arriving, less one boat lost with a midshipman, 4 seamen, and 17 soldiers of the 7th Fusiliers[35] drowned. That same day a determined reconnaissance failed to find any route through the woods into the American left rear, though armed boats exploring a northern branch of Bayou Bienvenue broke up an American scouting party and captured its interpreter, who told them of the arrival of the Kentucky militia brigade. Apparently he did not mention that only 700 out of 2,368 Kentuckians were armed.

By January 7 forty-two boats had been collected in the new canal. Once more Colonel Thornton was given the honor of leading the initial attack, to consist of his own 85th Foot, reduced to some 300 men, together with

33. See George Stimpson, *A Book About American History* (New York: Harper and Brothers, 1950), pp. 220–22.

34. An English officer reported this as of January 2, but it must have happened several days earlier.

35. The 7th Regiment of Foot was ordinarily known as Royal Fusiliers.

200 marines, 200 seamen, and the 5th West India Regiment, with two 9-pounders and two howitzers. He was to cross during the night, seize Patterson's batteries, use their guns and his own fieldpieces to enfilade Jackson's line, and push on up the river to create as much alarm as possible in New Orleans.

On the east bank, the 2d and 3d brigades were to move up to the British outpost line before daylight. The 2d, reinforced by most of the 95th Foot, roughly 2,200 strong, was to deliver the main attack, advancing in column along the edge of the woods where it would be out of sight of Patterson's batteries. The 44th Foot, carrying fascines and ladders, would be the head of its column; its light infantry companies and 100 men from the 1st West India Regiment would move through the outskirts of the wood, to cover its right flank.

The 3d Brigade (1,200) was to await the results of Thornton's attack before advancing, but Renny, with the light companies of the 7th, 43d, and 93d, and 100 men of the 1st West India, was to attack along the riverbank to seize the advanced redoubt on the right of the American line and spike its guns to prevent their firing into the left flank of the 2d Brigade. Lambert's 1st Brigade (1,200) with the dismounted light dragoons formed the reserve. Guns were to be massed between the 3d and 2d brigades to support the assault.

It was an excellent plan in concept, but its tight scheduling left no time for the hitches inevitably caused by the innate perversity that afflicts most night operations. The sides of the canal collapsed in places, hindering the movement of the boats. Then the cut through the levee proved too shallow. Only the most exhausting efforts by sailors working waist-deep in mud got the bigger boats into the river. Checking on the operation shortly after 5:00 A.M., Packenham learned that only the 85th, the marines, and part of the sailors were yet embarked. Realizing that this delay would keep Thornton from carrying the American west-bank position before the 2d Brigade attacked, he almost canceled the crossing, but then decided to let Thornton go with what men he already had in the boats, leaving his artillery and the 5th West India Regiment behind. Thornton's troubles were not over. The Mississippi was running fast and full, his oarsmen were already weary from their night's labors. His boats were carried downstream, so that he finally got to shore considerably below his intended landing point.

Packenham's main attack likewise had its troubles. In the darkness and fog the artillery had difficulty finding and preparing its positions; worst of all, the 44th Foot failed to pick up the ladders and fascines it was supposed to carry. Once Gibbs discovered this error the regiment went back to pick them up, but time was running out.

Deserters had warned Jackson of an impending attack, but it was late on January 7 before he suspected that Packenham would also advance on the west bank. Because of his failure to have scout boats on Lake Borgne and his whacking overestimate of Packenham's strength—at least 12,000 he thought—he remained apprehensive of a flanking move through Lake Pontchartrain, and insisted on keeping Claiborne's militia, some 2,500, in that sector. Morgan had 450 militia on the west bank, with one 12-pounder and two 6-pounders; Patterson had emplaced thirteen guns there to fire across the river, but these could not be shifted to fire to their right flank in the time available. Latour's black laborers had begun a defensive line approximately a mile south of Jackson's breastwork; only the section next to the river had been completed. When Morgan called for reinforcements late on the 7th, Jackson sent 400 Kentuckians, only 250 of whom could be armed. Since there was no ferry available except at New Orleans, it was 4:00 A.M. on the 8th before possibly 170 Kentuckians, tired and hungry, reached Morgan, the rest straggling along the way. On the east bank Jackson had 3,500 men in line, and 1,000 partially armed Kentuckians in reserve.[36]

Close to 6:00 A.M. January 8, 1815, Packenham ordered the attack. It was almost dawn, but winter mist still clung to the ground, partially shrouding the advance. Dickson's guns opened through it, and Gibbs' column lurched forward. The 44th had finally gathered up ladders and fascines, but, too late to regain the column's head, came straggling up along its left flank. Its commander, Lieutenant Colonel Thomas Mullens, lost control, and would be accused of heading to the rear somewhat prematurely. And then the fog broke.

American artillery raked and buffeted Gibbs' column, shredding it before it got within musket range. Few if any of the 44th got their fascines into the canal. Then American infantry opened fire. Gibbs rode to the head of his column, shouting his men forward, then pitched from his saddle with a mortal wound. Some of the 21st Foot, following their Major Wilkinson, scrambled and wallowed across the canal; a handful lived to

36. Figures here are even more disputed than usual. Including Hinds' dragoons, other small mounted units, and sailors from *Louisiana*, Jackson must have had close to 5,500 men available on the east bank. Thomas being ill, Brigadier General John Adair commanded the Kentuckians.

claw their way up the slippery face of the breastwork. Wilkinson fell dying inside it, acclaimed by his enemies. But most of the 2d Brigade was now a milling mass, halted and firing wildly. The light infantry and West Indians on their right were shot to pieces, their commander killed.

At the last minute, when he was aware that Thornton's attack would be delayed, Packenham had changed Keane's orders: Renny would go in as planned, but the 93d would attack to the left of Gibbs. It was a mistake, and a bad one. Moving swiftly forward along the river where some fog still clung to shield him from Patterson's guns, Renny stormed the redoubt and broke in between it and the main line. But there was no 93d to exploit his success. The whole right flank of the American line concentrated its fire against his forlorn hope. Renny died there; some of his men got away.

Keane took the 93d angling across the field. They were Highlanders, though in trews and blue bonnets in place of Highland dress: this was their first real battle. Swinging them half-left, Keane led them against Jackson's center, into a cross-raking blaze of artillery and musket fire. Here the ditch was deep, and there were no fascines. Keane took a ball in his neck, the 93d's colonel was killed; three out of four men went down. The rest halted, but stood firing—"like a brick wall," one American remembered.[37]

Ordering Lambert to throw in the reserve, Packenham had gone spurring to the 2d Brigade. By personal example he started a rally, then was hit in the thigh and had his horse killed under him. His aide-de-camp extricated him and gave him his own horse. As Packenham swung into its saddle, he was hit again, mortally.

Lambert came forward, but found only confused streams of men retreating through a steady American fire. Seeing no sense in throwing the last solid regiments away, he took up a defensive position to meet any American sortie, rallied the 2d Brigade, and put his men under cover. By 8:30 it was all over on the east bank.

It was then that Thornton finally struck. Morgan had put the newly arrived Kentuckians and 100 Louisiana militia into an improvised advance line, approximately a mile south of Latour's partially completed works, and occupied the latter with his remaining 350 Louisianians and three guns. Thornton hit with his usual force and skill, enveloping the open right (west) flank of each position in turn. The Americans fought surprisingly well, despite language problems and Morgan's ineptness. Both

37. Elting, *Military Uniforms in America*, Vol. II: *Years of Growth, 1796–1851*, p. 70.

Thornton and the senior naval officer were badly wounded. Patterson spiked his guns before retreating, but the British advance continued for a mile upriver above Jackson's line. In frustrated fury, Jackson dispatched a mere 400 men under a General Jean Humbert[38] to cross at New Orleans and reinforce Morgan. The troops refused to take orders from a foreigner. The next morning promised to be one of much tribulation; if the British continued their advance, Jackson would have little choice except to evacuate his present position.

Lambert, however, with the whole responsibility for a riddled army, sent Dickson across the river to examine the situation there. Dickson found the sailors scattered to plunder, and the position one that would require 2,000 men to hold. Lambert therefore ordered the force withdrawn to the east bank. Before going it disabled thirteen iron guns, and brought back three "brass" (bronze) pieces, one of which had been captured by the Americans at Yorktown in 1781.

The day ended in heavy rain, making it impossible to withdraw four 18-pounders and four 24-pound carronades that had been put into battery close to the American line. These were therefore wrecked, and the army retired into its former camp. It took time to reckon the losses— for the British 291 killed, 1,262 wounded, 484 missing/prisoners; for Jackson 13 killed, 39 wounded, and 19 missing, mostly on the west bank.

Though New Orleans has come down in American tradition as a victory for the Kentucky rifle, it was the American artillery that did most to crush the British attack. Next was the smooth-bore musket with which regulars and most of the Louisiana, Kentucky, and Tennessee militia were armed. Coffee's riflemen, being on the far left flank, were not heavily engaged. In fact, the musket's higher rate of fire made it superior to the rifle for such fighting.

While the battle was thus lost and won, Cochrane's feint up the Mississippi with a sloop-of-war, a brig, a schooner, and two mortar ships, reached Fort St. Philip.

The key to the Mississippi, Fort St. Philip,[39] was expertly sited on its east bank at Plaquemines Bend. Here sailing vessels, already bucking the Mississippi's four-mile-an-hour current, would have to tack to follow the river's curve, thus becoming almost stationary targets. Any troops landed

38. One of Napoleon's discards, then living in New Orleans, serving as a volunteer.

39. First built by Spanish military engineers during 1792–95; strengthened by Americans during 1808–10.

to support a naval attack would find themselves enmeshed in a roadless tangle of swamps and bayous.

The British spent the 9th reconnoitering. On the 10th their mortars opened fire from a range of almost 4,000 yards, sometimes launching a "bomb" every two minutes. The fort had only one piece, a 13-inch mortar, that could reply at that distance—and its ammunition quickly proved defective. Therefore the garrison had to stand and take the pounding until the 17th, when at last a resupply reached them from New Orleans. They began firing that evening; on the 18th the British withdrew. Two Americans had been killed and seven wounded but the fort had sustained very little damage, most of the 1,000-odd British mortar shells having fallen short of or beyond it, to the discomfort only of alligators, catfish, and turtles.

On the east bank, meanwhile, January 9 had been a day of white flags and twelve-hour truce for burial of the dead. The Americans, Dickson noted, were very civil.

Like England's other 1814 offensives, this had been a hastily mounted, shoestring affair. Cochrane's planning had been brilliant, but his preparations overconfident and incomplete. Had he provided enough small boats to land 3,000 to 3,500 men on December 23, instead of 2,000, Jackson might well have been crushed immediately. As for Jackson, the topography of the New Orleans area and his decisiveness and pugnacity saved him from his strategic incompetence and tactical awkwardness. "A battle you win cancels all your other mistakes."[40]

40. The remark is Niccolò Machiavelli's. See Edward M. Earle, ed., *Makers of Modern Strategy* (Princeton, N.J.: Princeton University Press, 1944), p. 17.

SEVENTEEN

The Last Shots

*We have retired from the combat with the stripes yet bleeding on our backs—
with the recent defeats at Plattsburg and on Lake Champlain unavenged.*
—*Times* (London), December 30, 1814 [1]

IN WASHINGTON IT WAS A WINTER OF DISCONTENT, almost of despair. President Madison was still a shaken man, distracted by New England's threatened defection. Lacking any national leadership, much of the nation remained apathetic to the impending danger of invasion. Congress fumbled noisily with the crucial problems of raising the necessary money and manpower to continue the war. Federalist congressmen were interested only in thwarting the administration, whatever the result; most Republicans were too thoroughly wedded to their party doctrine to recognize the emergency confronting them—and Madison did nothing effective to rally them. The new secretary of the treasury, Alexander J. Dallas, could get no cooperation. When Secretary of War Monroe proposed to bring the Army up to strength with men drafted from the militia for two years' service, a proposal he had violently opposed when Armstrong had considered it a year before, Federalists and Republicans combined to shout it down as an "odious" threat to American liberty that should be resisted, by force of arms if necessary.

In the end Congress did nothing much—and made a dog's breakfast of what it did. The Navy was authorized to build twenty small sloops-of-war, the details of how they would be paid for being omitted. The states

1. Adams, *The War of 1812*, p. 346.

were authorized to raise and "keep in pay" their own armies at the expense of the United States; the President might call up to 40,000 of such troops into the federal service—if the states would release them. Nothing was done for the Regular Army; in fact, the formation of state armies would make it impossible for regular units to secure recruits, since the state service, like the militia, was certain to be better paid and far less risky. There was much orating to the effect that each separate state, with whatever help it might get from its neighbors, would be fully competent to defeat any enemy.

In January the government could not pay Andrew Jackson's troops at New Orleans; for several months it had been unable to give new recruits their enlistment bounties. In February the Regular Army had 32,360 enlisted men, including those in the hospitals and absent without leave, out of an authorized strength of 62,000. Along the Canadian frontier, from Plattsburg west through Sackets Harbor and Buffalo to Fort Malden and St. Louis, there were possibly 9,000 regulars. Morale in some units weakened under increasing deficiencies in pay, clothing, and supplies. The prospect they faced was grimmer than ever before.

Hoping for victory in 1815, England had continued to stuff troops into Canada until winter closed the St. Lawrence River—by January there were almost 30,000 of them. The Duke of Wellington had declined the American command, but Lieutenant General Sir George Murray, who had been Wellington's quartermaster general,[2] had arrived to replace Sir George Prevost. Though Murray's last experience as a unit commander had been as a lieutenant in Holland in 1793–95, he undoubtedly was England's ablest staff officer and a man of proven energy and intelligence.

The Royal Navy was matching this army build-up. Commodore James Yeo had those two line-of-battle ships, *Wolfe* and *Canada*, each of 120 guns, and another frigate under construction. The British were planning a naval base on Lake Huron, where they already had built three small schooner-rigged gunboats, and had begun new gunboats on Lake Champlain. Moreover, they were building a new naval base near Port Dover on Lake Erie, with the intent of regaining control of that body of water.

This preparation, far more massive than any before in North America, had one major weakness: it badly overloaded Canada's transportation system, a problem further complicated by the conflicting requirements of Yeo's fleet and the Army. At times it resembled an attempt to get an im-

2. In modern terms, he had been Wellington's G-3 / operations officer.

perial gallon of rum into a one-quart canteen. The mass of those British troops were infantry, with some artillery and a very thin sprinkling of cavalry and engineers. They brought no supply train troops with them; English armies always had depended on contractors or local inhabitants to move their supplies, but what resources Canada had were already over-strained.

Seeking some means of both strengthening their supply services and reducing the overall volume of supplies consumed, British officers rec-ommended that the Select Embodied Militia of Lower Canada be con-verted to transportation units, and that all other militiamen on active duty be sent home to their farms. Much Canadian reaction was definitely um-brageous. Why should their battle-tested veterans be reduced to menial fetching and carrying for a lot of redcoat Johnnies-come-lately who still had everything to learn about North American campaigning—and had not shown any particular ability to terrify Yankees during 1814?

Any large-scale British offensive out of Canada must necessarily be tied to those lakes and rivers the Royal Navy controlled. The larger the army involved, the more dependent on supply ships it would be, the more restricted its radius of operation. This hard fact ruled out Lake Cham-plain and Lake Erie: months of hard labor would be needed to rebuild the British squadron on either lake, especially distant Erie. Also, it was dubi-ous that either men or material for such work could be spared from Yeo's perpetual Ontario construction program. Yeo did control Lake Ontario, but his superiority was an uncertain thing; he could not match the Ameri-can shipbuilders now swarming in Sackets Harbor. Moreover even James Madison might finally lose patience with Chauncey's timid fuddling and replace him with a commander such as Perry, Macdonough, or Rogers. In that case the planned British offensive against Sackets Harbor could meet unpredictable troubles. Yeo was admittedly a clever, efficient ad-ministrator, but many Englishmen had serious doubts as to his pugnacity when confronted by an equal American fleet, especially one eager to fight and led by an officer who knew how.

A further problem to English operations in Lower Canada was the changing attitude of its Indian tribes. The war's increasingly professional aspect and bloody stand-up battles were decidedly not their accustomed type of hostilities. More important, in July, 1814, their American relatives had sent emissaries to them, suggesting that it now was very much a white man's war, and that the Indians on either side could expect nothing from it except hardship and a growing casualty list. The Canadian tribes had harkened willingly, to the considerable annoyance of British commanders, and the number of warriors with the British forces had dwindled steadily thereafter.[3]

Out of all these uncertainties, however, the Americans could feel certain that Murray would attempt a massive offensive against Sackets Harbor, while launching minor offensives in the Lake Champlain and Niagara sectors to pin down the American forces there. His great numerical superiority would make such secondary operations possible without weakening his attack on Sackets Harbor. Victory there would soon give him control of Lake Ontario, unhinging the whole American northern front and opening New York—along with Tennessee, Kentucky, and Ohio, one of the last states actually supporting the war—to invasion.

All that, however, was something months away. The clear and present danger was at New Orleans. Not all Americans feared a British victory there; extreme Federalists actually cherished the hope that such a development would force Madison to resign and the United States to make peace on terms satisfactory to both England and New England. News from Louisiana, however, came sporadically and slowly. Jackson had fought his battle on January 8; it was February 4 before his report reached Washington.

Meanwhile, practically unnoticed amid the pointless clamor in Congress, the anxiety over New Orleans, and the Federalist plotting at Hartford, Georgia was begging for help. On or about New Year's Day, Sir George Cockburn had occupied Cumberland Island, just off the southern extremity of Georgia's coastline, apparently as a diversionary action to draw American forces from the defense of New Orleans. On January 13 the British thrust up St. Mary's River, seized the fort at its mouth,[4] stripped the town of St. Mary's of its shipping, and emptied its stores and warehouses, all without meeting any appreciable resistance or suffering a single casualty. Thereafter Cockburn combined duty with profit and pleasure by giving Georgia's coastal districts the same dosage of arson and plundering he previously had inflicted on the Chesapeake Bay area. (Had the war continued, he would have been reinforced for an attack on Savannah—a venture that promised a truly lavish haul of prize money!) His operations began too late to assist the British attack on New Orleans, but they did pin down Georgia's militia and—again, had the war continued—probably would have seriously hampered American attempts to

3. This changing attitude might have been responsible for the unusual inertia of the Indians with Drummond during his siege at Fort Erie.

4. Very little is known concerning this fort, which seems to have been known variously as Fort Gunn or Fort St. Tammany.

defend Mobile and Pensacola. Moreover, his welcoming and employment of fugitive slaves stirred fears of a black revolt across Georgia. In fact, Lieutenant Colonel Charles Napier, whose 102d Foot still was serving with Cockburn, though lamenting having to take part in this "plundering and ruining the peasantry," was seriously suggesting that a bloody slave rebellion like the Haitian holocaust of 1791–1804 would be just the proper thing to bring the Yankees to submission!

At New Orleans, General John Lambert and Admiral Cochrane considered the shattered state of their forces. One-third of their infantry and three out of four major generals were casualties. Since the fleet had been unable to get past Fort St. Philip, American warships still controlled the Mississippi. Supplies of food and ammunition were dangerously low, and a protracted period of bad weather (not unlikely at this time of year) could ruin their long, tenuous supply line. Finally, their tactical situation was little better than a trap. Lambert decided to get out while he could.

The British withdrawal was handled with decision and skill. Working parties built nine miles of temporary road back through the swamps to the landing place, corduroying the miry soil with bundles of rushes, and building sixteen light bridges over the creeks and gullies. It was a filthy, exhausting detail; naturally, in keeping with immemorial military concepts of therapeutic treatment, the 44th Foot got it. Between January 8 and 18 the wounded, sick, reserve supplies and ammunition, and the heavier field guns were gradually evacuated. In the midst of this delicate operation the 40th Regiment of Foot, some 850 strong, suddenly appeared from a newly arrived convoy, to be told to turn around and get back aboard its transport.[5]

All this went on unknown to the Americans, who remained splendidly uncertain of what the British might intend to do next. Both Jackson and Patterson inexplicably failed to maintain contact with the enemy, contenting themselves with periodically bombarding the British position. Mostly this proved a mere nuisance, though an especially heavy shelling during the night of January 16–17 caused several casualties, including one unfortunate lieutenant who had both legs "taken off" by an American cannonball while asleep in his tent. The Americans reestablished and extended their defenses on the west bank of the Mississippi and got five gunboats into action on the river, where they accomplished nothing useful. The one

5. The 40th had come with a convoy that had brought a siege train, which would have been very useful had it arrived in December; naval and engineer supplies; and rations. The last were most welcome, since the expedition had food left for only six days.

recorded American raid into the British lines came out of the woods close to General Lambert's quarters late on January 13, but only to carry away several slaves who had huts nearby. (Obviously some patriotic Louisianians had launched a private expedition to recover their human property.) Patterson even failed to support those combative junior officers who had improvised four small gunboats on Lake Pontchartrain and begun raiding the British shipping on Lake Borgne as early as January 4. Their major catch was a schooner carrying fourteen seamen and forty officers and men of the 14th Light Dragoons. When one of them finally was trapped in turn, Cochrane invited him to dinner.

Meanwhile, their impedimentia cleared away, the British began moving off their combat units. The useless 1st and 5th West India regiments went first, then the marines were sent back to their ships, followed by the light dragoons. At dusk on the 18th, once a party of American prisoners had been sent off, the remaining guns were taken away one by one, a quarter of an hour apart, camouflaged with cane stalks and leaves. The artillery drivers led their horses instead of riding them; the cannoneers strolled after them as scattered individuals. Eight pieces—four 18-pounders and four 32-pounder carronades—that had been emplaced on the levee to keep off Patterson's ships were spiked and abandoned, since it would have been impossible to remove them without alerting the Americans. A surgeon was detailed to remain with eighty soldiers too badly wounded to be evacuated.

With darkness the infantry withdrew, leaving their camp fires burning. The last outposts followed before 3:00 A.M., replacing their sentries with uniformed dummies. It was a difficult march, the passage of the guns having cut up the improvised road, which was further damaged by a short rainstorm and an unexpectedly high tide washing in through the swamp. The last regiments frequently found the mire waist-deep, and boats had to be worked in to assist them. Compounding the confusion, fugitive slaves, men, women, and children mixed in with the floundering soldiers. But by noon of the 19th the whole army, numbering some 4,700 officers and men, had reached the embarkation point and encamped. The rear guard had wrecked the bridges, and gunboats and pickets covered all the approaches to their new position. The fleet's boats and small craft shuttled back and forth across Lake Borgne and out to the waiting transports.

It took until January 28 for the whole army to reembark. Surveying its battered condition, Lambert decided to land it on Dauphin Island, on the west side of the entrance to Mobile Bay, for reorganization. This

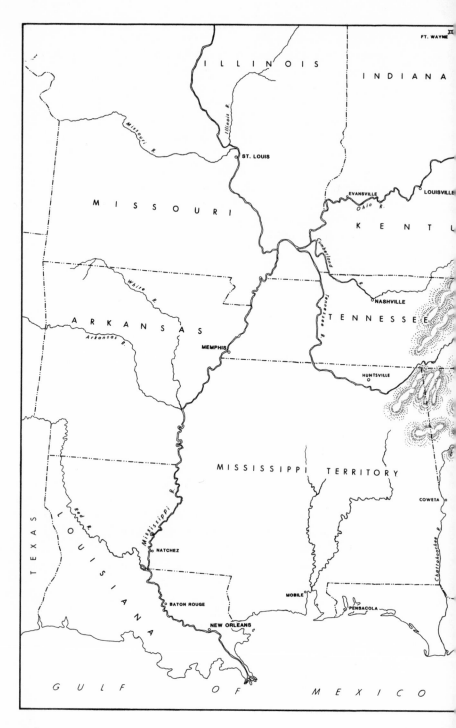

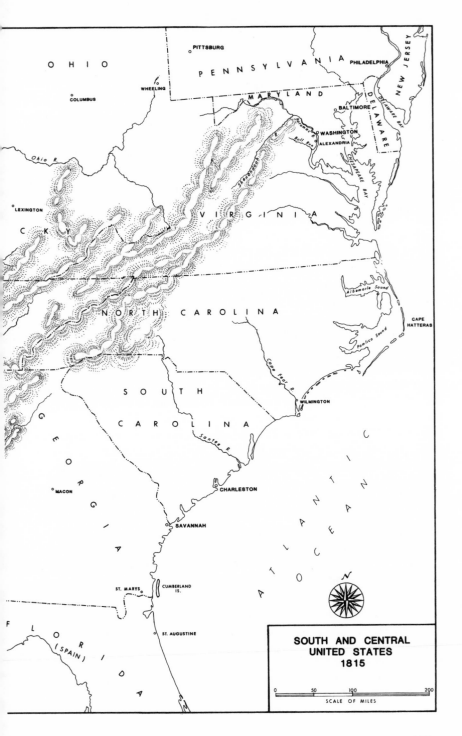

SOUTH AND CENTRAL
UNITED STATES
1815

0   50   100   200
SCALE OF MILES

would require the capture of Fort Bowyer, to permit the heavier English ships to anchor safely within the bay. That accomplished, he would decide whether to attempt an attack on Mobile.

Unfortunately for Lambert's calculations, the Gulf Coast's winter weather had not yet finished with the British. Early on the 29th a raging storm pounced on its huddled ships, pinning them at their anchorages. The battleship *Plantagenet* got away with woeful dispatches for England, but by the next morning it was practically impossible for a small boat to get from one ship to another. A week of heaving, rolling, wallowing misery followed, with torn sails and wrenched rigging, until the storm finally blew itself out on February 5. A safe haven for refitting then being really necessary, the fleet sailed for Dauphin Island on the 6th.

This expert British withdrawal had caught Jackson flat-footed. Surveying their camp the morning of the 19th, he remained uncertain as to whether they were really gone until, so an old story has it, an officer who had made war under Napoleon pointed out a crow perched on one of the redcoat "sentries." Jackson took proper care of the abandoned British wounded, but he did not pursue Lambert nor did he trouble his reembarkation, though his frontier riflemen and Choctaw warriors should have been especially qualified for such work. If the British attacked Mobile, he expected the forces he had left there to defeat them; if they had withdrawn merely to regroup for another assault on New Orleans, he would be ready for them. Meanwhile his major problem was simply holding his army together. Victory and rumors of peace had all New Orleans avidly speculating on the renewal of international trade: the Louisiana militia wanted to go home and began deserting when not allowed to.[6] Fevers ravaged the unacclimated Tennessee and Kentucky troops, killing them by dozens. And, because Jackson insisted on keeping his forces on war footing and maintaining martial law, local lawyers and politicians labored assiduously to undermine his authority, to the point of encouraging mutiny among his Louisiana troops.

Infuriated by such conduct, Jackson responded with arrests and courts-martial. A number of annoying prominent citizens, including the French consul and a federal judge, were banished from New Orleans. This summary treatment increased the resentment among both Creoles and the American mercantile element. Had the British come again, Jackson might not have been able to muster enough troops to meet them.

---

6. Some of them were responding to appeals from their hungry families, the local authorities having done nothing to care for militiamen's dependents.

Meanwhile Cochrane and Lambert came down on Fort Bowyer. Believing it to be the key to the coast between Mobile and New Orleans, Jackson had strengthened it until "ten thousand men cannot take it."[7] Unfortunately, to Andrew Jackson, innocent as he was of either training or experience in conventional warfare, such "strengthening" was merely a matter of stuffing more men and guns into that hopelessly isolated position. Lieutenant Colonel William Lawrence's garrison now totaled 370 officers and men,[8] roughly one-fifth of the regular troops in Jackson's entire command, with twenty-two guns, including three 32-pounders. The nearest American troops were around Mobile, thirty miles to the north by ship and more than twice that distance by primitive roads along the east shore of Mobile Bay. Though the Mobile garrison included approximately 1,000 regulars—the 3d and 39th infantry regiments and some artillerymen—its militia contingent was of dubious quality, some 200 Tennesseans being on trial for mutiny. (Jackson soon had their 6 ringleaders shot.) Even more dubious was the commander Jackson had left in Mobile—Brigadier General James Winchester, still quite pleased with his performance at the River Raisin and nowise educated by his experiences. (Monroe had sent Brigadier General Edmund P. Gaines, barely recovered from his Fort Erie wound, posthaste southward to give Jackson a competent subordinate, but Gaines arrived too late for the fighting.)

British intelligence on Fort Bowyer was excellent—a cramped coast defense battery, built of timber and rammed sand, without bombproofs, its guns mounted to fire over its ramparts, so that the heads and chests of their crews were exposed.[9] It would be very vulnerable to regular siege operations. Accordingly on February 8, Lambert put a brigade—the 4th, 21st, and 44th regiments, approximately 1,000 men—ashore east of Fort Bowyer, thereby cutting it off from reinforcement by land. Moving up behind a series of sand dunes, the British were able to get within 200 yards of the fort before coming under American artillery fire. This, directed by an observer high on the fort's flagpole, was unexpectedly accurate, but the British began digging their siegeworks close to the fort that night.

7. James, *The Life of Andrew Jackson*, p. 198.

8. This total included 327 from the 2d Infantry Regiment, most, or all, of that organization.

9. Senior British artillery and engineer officers together described it as a small semicircular sea battery, its rear fortified for all-around defense, surrounded by a deep ditch at the bottom of which was a strong palisade. Fort Bowyer would have been a tough nut for infantry to crack without heavy artillery support, but the British had the time, means, and trained officers to conduct a methodical siege.

Making out the dark figures of the diggers against the white sand, American gunners killed eight or ten men, but the British kept digging. During the 9th their zigzag approaches were close enough to the fort for them to open an effective musket fire against the exposed American gunners and force the flagpole observer to quit his perch. The Americans responded by stacking sandbags on their parapet to shelter their gunners, but the entrenched British offered few good targets.

Meanwhile, reinforced by 200 sailors, all available engineer troops, and Royal Marine artillerymen, the British gunners readied their batteries: four 18-pounders, two 8-inch howitzers, two 6-pounders, three 5½-inch and three 4.4-inch mortars, and a hundred 12-pounder rockets. Their elaborate fire plan called for the use of shrapnel and explosive and incendiary shell against the crowded interior at the fort. The approaches were pushed to within thirty yards of the fort's ditch and preparations made to run mines under its walls if it resisted the artillery bombardment. Finally the 85th Foot was brought across from Dauphin Island to reinforce the besiegers. Everything being in readiness for the bombardment to commence at 10:00 A.M. on February 11, Lambert summoned the fort to surrender, offering to let the women and children of the garrison come out in safety before opening fire.

Lawrence had not risked a sortie to interfere with the British preparations, probably because his garrison was so heavily outnumbered. (The British main body was just across the channel on Dauphin Island, being reequipped for future operations.) In addition to his garrison the fort held twenty women and sixteen children; an artillery bombardment would turn its crowded interior into a slaughterhouse.[10] After some parleying, he accepted Lambert's terms but requested that the actual surrender be postponed until the 12th, since many of his men had gotten drunk and out of hand. Thereafter traditional military etiquette took over: hostages were exchanged, the British flag hoisted over the fort, and its gate occupied by a company of British infantry. The next morning the garrison marched out with the honors of war and laid down their arms and the 2d Infantry's colors. American losses, if any, had been trifling; the British had only some twenty-five casualties.

Meanwhile Winchester had busied himself with preparations to re-

10. The fort may have been short of water. Colonel Alexander Dickson, commanding the British artillery, noted that the Americans were "very dirty." He also thought they looked "like Spaniards," which was about as derogatory as he could get without employing profanity.

enact the River Raisin, sending a force, reported by the British as 1,000 men, to relieve Fort Bowyer. Done promptly, this might have enabled Lawrence to break out and save most of his command, but the relief force did not sail from Mobile until the 11th. Landing on the east side of Mobile Bay some twelve miles north of the fort the next morning, they had the luck to capture some stray English sailors, from whom they learned that Fort Bowyer had surrendered and that English warships had entered Mobile Bay. A return by water thus being highly risky, the Americans had to abandon their vessels and hurriedly hike back to Mobile, with the prospect of soon having to face a heavy British attack. However, on February 13 a British dispatch ship arrived off Mobile Bay with notice that England and the United States had signed a peace treaty at Ghent on Christmas Eve, December 24.

ENGLAND HAD STRAINED EVERY RESOURCE she had to bring down Napoleon, but his defeat had brought no peace to Europe. Russia and Prussia had proved singularly lacking in gratitude for the money and supplies England had lavished on them to keep their forces in the field through defeat and victory. They now were preparing to gobble up as much of Europe as possible, answering England's protests with open defiance and boasts of their military strength. A new alliance, made up of England, Austria, France, Holland, and the smaller German states, was forming against Russia and Prussia, but France was increasingly restive under the bumbling Bourbon dynasty the victors had reimposed on her. From Elba, Napoleon watched Europe fester and squirm with old hatreds and new enmities, pondering the time for his last bid for empire. Everywhere, like forest fire smoldering through the crevices of a rocky hillside, there was the unhappy sensing that the great wars had only paused, not ended. Within England itself there was trouble enough—a population wearied by twenty years of almost uninterrupted war, high taxes, and increasing industrial unrest.

To England the American war was a secondary theater, a minor colonial squabble, something to be mopped up as soon as possible to free ships and men for whatever new crises Europe might develop. Through 1814 she therefore had committed large numbers of veteran troops and much of the Royal Navy for that purpose. Such a major effort should have brought the United States down, and in fact did leave it with its capital in ruins and its government reduced to near impotency. Yet, somehow, these British offensives failed: Fort Erie, Baltimore, and Plattsburg all

ended with mauled British armies in full retreat. And all this time American privateers were gutting British commerce from the English Channel
to the China Sea.

It was both humiliating and embarrassing. Foreign diplomats offered
sardonic condolences or cocked quizzical eyebrows when English military capabilities became a subject of discussion; news of the British defeat
at Plattsburg sparked impromptu public celebrations in Paris.

With former allies and old enemies increasingly uncertain, England
dared not risk further weakening her forces in Europe. The Duke of
Wellington not only would not go to America, but bluntly advised his
government to make peace without further haggling. Thus thwarted, the
British government abruptly decided to cut its losses. (As some French
minister had said during the Seven Years' War, when your house is on
fire you do not worry about your barn.) And so the sturdy American
negotiators at Ghent, who had fought one another over their own sec-
tional interests almost as doggedly as they had opposed the British diplomats, had their reward for the stubbornness with which they had resisted
British threats and blandishments alike. Their treaty was simply a bald
agreement to quit fighting and revert to the *status quo ante bellum*—accept
the prewar boundaries and settle other outstanding disputes by negotia-
tion. It was none too soon for England: on March 1, 1815, Napoleon was
back in France, sweeping triumphantly northward to Paris. Lambert's
soldiers, homeward bound, would see his tricolor flag flying along the
French coast, and some of them would conclude with wry professional
approval that the "Great Man" had regained his empire.

The Treaty of Ghent had been signed by the British and American
negotiators on December 24, 1814. The British government ratified it
on the 28th. But messages passed slowly through the Atlantic's winter storms; the British sloop-of-war *Favorite* that sailed from London on
January 2, 1815, with the official dispatches did not reach New York until
February 11. Meanwhile the war continued. Even after Madison proclaimed the treaty on February 18, both sides had had difficulty in getting
orders to cease hostilities to all their forces. At Prairie du Chien Captain
Andrew Bulger had been sending out strong war parties to threaten St.
Louis and keep the Americans on the defensive. His reports gloated that
they "have taken more scalps within the last six weeks than they did during the whole of the preceding spring and summer." [11] American rangers

11. Robert S. Allen, "Canadians on the Upper Mississippi," *Military Collector and
Historian*, Vol. XXXI, No. 3 (Fall, 1979).

hunted those will-o'-the-wisp killers. Eventually runners found and re-called rangers and Indians alike, or they came into camp to replenish supplies and learned the war had ended.

Bulger then had the disagreeable duty of explaining to his Indian allies that he must turn Prairie du Chien back to the Americans. It was sad news to the tribes and Canadian traders alike. Bulger tried to temper it by distributing whatever supplies his troops would not need for their return to Mackinac among the Indians at Prairie du Chien, and expressed his own feelings by burning his fort behind him. Canadian soldiers, traders, and officials resisted giving up Fort Mackinac, delaying its evacuation as long as possible. The Americans, however, countered by retaining Fort Malden until the Canadians finally, unhappily complied with the peace treaty.

Ships at sea were even more difficult to contact than Indian war parties. American privateers, now bigger, swifter, farther-ranging, and more capably commanded than ever, had achieved their greatest successes during the last six months of the war. They would learn of the war's ending only through visits to neutral ports or by speaking a friendly or neutral ship at sea, and even then it was well to be cautious. British warships sent to hunt them might not yet have learned that the war was over.

The United States Navy had one last flare of action. Perry's and Porter's raiding squadrons were not yet ready, but *Constitution* had evaded the blockade and sailed for the Bermudas. Commodore Stephen Decatur's squadron—the fast heavy frigate *President*, the new sloop-of-war *Peacock* (twenty-two guns), the smaller sloop-of-war *Hornet* (eighteen), and the storeship *Tom Bowline*[12]—had orders to break out from New York harbor, rendezvous at the isolated Tristan da Cunha islands in the South Atlantic, and thereafter ravage England's vital Indian ocean shipping.

Decatur went first, running out to sea on January 14 amid the snow squalls of a western gale. His pilot missed the channel and ran *President* onto the harbor bar; after two rough hours the *President* got over it, but with her hull damaged and leaky. The delay brought four blockading British ships down on her; the swiftest, the heavy frigate *Endymion* (50 guns), overhauled *President*, shooting to wreck her rigging. Decatur beat *Endymion* off, but *President* was too badly hurt to escape before the other British ships closed in. Stunned and bleeding from two wounds, Decatur

12. Decatur had been transferred from the *United States*, which still was blockaded at New London. *Tom Bowline* was a merchant schooner, re-rigged as a brig, mounting twelve light guns and very fast.

had to strike his colors. Two days later another gale dismasted both *Endymion* and *President*, which had to be escorted out of danger. The blockade thus weakened, the other American ships had no trouble escaping on January 22. All of this, added to the dispatch of frigates to pursue *Constitution*, left the British so weak in the New York/New England sector that a final swarm of privateers broke out and went their freebooting ways.

Reaching the rendezvous, *Hornet* encountered the British sloop-of-war *Penguin* of approximately equal force and reduced it to wreckage in twenty-five minutes. Shortly thereafter *Peacock* and *Tom Bowline* appeared. The American captains, Lewis Warrington of *Peacock* and James Biddle of *Hornet*, waited for Decatur until April 13; then *Peacock* and *Hornet* replenished their supplies from *Tom Bowline* and set off around the Cape of Good Hope. *Tom Bowline* went home with the survivors of *Penguin*'s crew as cargo. During April 27–28 in thick weather the two sloops closed in on a ship they took to be a large Indiaman [13]—and discovered in the very nick of time that their intended prize was actually the line-of-battle ship *Cornwallis* (seventy-four guns). Newly built at Bombay of teakwood, *Cornwallis* was still clean-bottomed and unusually fast and handy for a vessel of her class. Being one of the swiftest warships afloat, *Peacock* raced clear. *Hornet* was almost caught, but Biddle was a skilled seaman and *Cornwallis*'s gunners proved cross-eyed and thirteen-thumbed. By jettisoning his anchors, boats, much of his stores and ballast, and all but one of his guns, Biddle lightened *Hornet* enough to outrun the battleship. Lacking weapons and supplies, however, he had to cut his cruise short and return.

Meanwhile, Captain Charles Stewart with *Constitution* had found the West Indies a barren hunting ground, so thoroughly had American privateers raked it. British merchantmen huddled in fortified seaports until the Royal Navy could organize them into heavily escorted convoys. Picking up only one small prize, he turned eastward and then south toward the Madeira Islands, gathering in a fat Indiaman en route. On the afternoon of February 20 he sighted two British warships, which proved to be the heavy corvette *Cyane* of thirty-two guns and the sloop-of-war *Levant* of twenty-one.[14] The two British captains planned to engage *Constitution*

13. Indiamen were properly large vessels belonging to the British East India Company. Since they carried valuable cargoes they were heavily armed and strongly manned, and made very profitable prizes. The term, however, came to cover any large ship in the Far East trade.

14. *Cyane* was an odd ship that had undergone several alterations, giving her the appearance of a small frigate.

after sundown, intending to outmaneuver and cripple her in the dusk and cannon smoke,[15] but *Constitution* was too powerful a ship and too expertly handled. Stewart took them both and brought them into Porto Praya in the Cape Verde Islands for refitting. There, on March 10, he was almost trapped by three British frigates. Having no hope that the Portuguese authorities would or could enforce the neutrality of their harbor, Stewart got to sea instantly with his three ships, the British in hot pursuit. First *Cyane*, then *Levant*, could not keep up; certain that the British would concentrate on *Constitution*, Stewart signaled each in turn to attempt to escape separately. *Cyane* succeeded, but when little *Levant* swerved away all three English frigates followed her, forcing her back into Porto Praya harbor where they battered her until her prize crew surrendered—probably the most remarkable display of bashfulness in the whole history of the Royal Navy.

It was *Peacock*, half the world away from the United States, that fired the last shot. Warrington had taken and burned three big Indiamen and was in the Strait of Sunda between Sumatra and Java on June 30 when he met the East India Company brig *Nautilus* of fourteen guns.[16] The British ship hailed, stating that the war was over. Suspecting trickery, Warrington ordered *Nautilus*'s captain to haul down his colors in proof of his assertion, or take the consequences. The Englishmen refused to perform that act of submission; *Peacock* promptly smashed *Nautilus* with one broadside.[17] Naturally Warrington's conduct has been much deplored, but—utterly alone on hostile seas—there was no reason why he should trust his enemy or spare him humiliation.

The War of 1812 left few statistics and most of those questionable. Official Army records show 528,274 Americans as having served, but this must represent the number of enlistments and not of actual soldiers; a considerable number of men served several short enlistments and were counted each time. Total Army deaths are reported as 1,950—clearly an

15. A similar fight in December, 1939, ended in a British victory when three British cruisers crippled the German pocket battleship *Graf Spee*.

16. The "Honorable Company" (also called "John Company") had its own army and navy.

17. Having been taken after both nations had ratified the peace treaty, *Nautilus* was later returned. As an example of the self-sufficiency of a well-handled sailing vessel, Warrington returned to New York on November 2, 1815, after nine months at sea with *Peacock* in good condition, her crew healthy and fed, paid, and clothed with money and goods taken from prizes.

understatement, especially since there are no figures on deaths by disease—and "wounds not mortal" as 4,000. Again there is no data on men taken prisoner or missing in action.[18]

It had been an amateurs' war indeed. Fortunately for the United States, some of its amateurs had learned their trade before it ended.

18. *Army Almanac* (Washington, D.C.: Government Printing Office, 1950), p. 411.

EPILOGUE

God looks after little children, idiots, drunken sailors, and the United States of America.

—Old proverb

MADISON'S SELF-CONGRATULATORY PROCLAMATION that the peace treaty was "highly honorable to the United States, and terminates, with particular felicity, a campaign signalized by the most brilliant successes" [1] was tall talk indeed from a President who, after deliberately pushing an unprepared nation into a war of conquest against a major power, had recently been a bewildered fugitive in the Virginia backcountry while his capital was torched behind him. He had achieved none of the objectives for which America went to war. Yet, so great was American relief at the war's ending, especially when Jackson's victory at New Orleans capped the treaty, that the nation felt a swelling sense of triumph. In hard fact, the United States had achieved no more than what westerners later would call a "Mexican standoff": we had gotten out of the war with our scalp, shirt, and weapons all reasonably intact, and should have considered ourselves undeservedly lucky to have managed that much. But, as the veterans went home with scars and memories, as the politicians who had misused and neglected them won reelection as architects of victory, as renegade Americans who had fed their enemies flaunted their tainted wealth, a sense of national unity and destiny did bud and grow. The blundering War of 1812 would be remembered as a victorious "Second War of Independence." Legends like that of Jackson's frontier sharpshooters leveling their long Kentucky rifles across a breastwork of cotton bales at New Orleans would be taken whole into American history.

1. Engelman, *The Peace of Christmas Eve*, p. 290.

In cold fact the United States survived only because handfuls of American soldiers and sailors, ill-supported and finally almost abandoned by their central government, ignored and often betrayed by their fellow countrymen, somehow made head against all odds until England at last wearied. But for them, all the skill and determination of the American negotiators would have been useless—mere words, a fitting target for British mockery.

It is well that the American Armed Forces of today remember these men. Such times may come again: the United States government shattered by a surprise nuclear attack, communications out, a panicked public swayed by fainthearts and traitors screaming for surrender. In such broken-backed war, commanders of the breed of Brown, Scott, Macomb, and Jackson will grip whatever forces they can rally and lash out against every target they can reach, taking an overconfident enemy by surprise. God send us such, in place of overly housebroken Winders and Dearborns who will huddle, anxiously waiting for orders that will never come, or come too late.

The War of 1812 did have certain solid results. The power of the great Indian tribes of the Old Northwest was completely broken, and English fur traders were largely thereafter penned within Canada's frontiers. Responsible citizens came to acknowledge the folly of the nation's dependence on militia for defense, and the need for an efficient Army that would be something better than a scattering of detachments along our far frontiers. Men such as John C. Calhoun, Winfield Scott,[2] and Sylvanus Thayer[3] would build one. When war came with Mexico in 1846 the Army and Navy of the United States were first-class services, ably commanded and capable of large-scale foreign service.

There was one further result. England had learned that the United States could be a prickly proposition; the United States realized that England could not be bullied out of her possessions in the Western Hemisphere. This knowledge did not run too deep among their respective populations: for generations many Americans would view England as a natural and hereditary enemy. Nevertheless, a certain mutual respect developed between the better statesmen and fighting men of the two nations. There would be repeated crises through the nineteenth century, accom-

---

2. One of Scott's greatest strengths was his ability to learn. His reckless aggressiveness of 1812–14 would show again in the daring of his strategy in 1846–47, but his tactics would be very careful of his men's lives.

3. The "Father of West Point."

panied by shouts for war, but these would be quietly solved. Thus Winfield Scott would be active along the Canadian border calming popular turbulence during Canada's Patriots' Rebellion of 1837–38; cooperating with a former opponent of 1813, Sir John Harvey, then lieutenant governor of New Brunswick, to defang the informal "Aroostook War" that had developed between the lumbermen of that province and those of Maine, and finally in 1859 deftly quieting a potential explosion between American and British forces on San Juan Island.[4] From such beginnings came eventual reconciliation and the long unfortified frontier between Canada and the United States.

4. On the Pacific coast, between Vancouver Island and the entrance to Puget Sound.

ESSAY ON SOURCES

AMONG THE NORTH AMERICAN CONTINENT'S many wars, the War of 1812 has remained something of an unwanted orphan stepson. To British historians it has been the sad tale of a minor nuisance that steadily festered into an intolerable string of missed opportunities, useless victories, and unexpected defeats—something best somehow ended and then forgotten. Some Americans have seen it as a war of barefaced aggression, incompetently directed, and too often stained by cowardice, stupidity, and treason—something of a national disgrace, redeemed only by half-mythical deeds of valor. Only the Canadians, who saw it as a successful war to maintain their independence, could write of it with pride.

GENERAL HISTORIES

There has been no better general history than Henry Adams' *The War of 1812* (Washington, D.C.: The Infantry Journal, 1944)—actually an extract from his famous *The History of the United States of America During the Administrations of Jefferson and Madison*. Though a century of continued use has found some errors and omissions in its descriptions of military operations, this book remains an example of honest and careful history. Adams' own unusual career had familiarized him with the inner workings of both the United States and British governments, the hard interrelationships of military power and diplomacy, and the ways in which piddling domestic politics can trip up crucial measures of national policy. He regarded men and history with a cool, impartial irony. In contrast, Benson J. Lossing's *The Pictorial Field Book of the War of 1812* (New York: Harper and Brothers, 1868) is more patriotic than exact, but still worth reading for its nuggets of accepted folklore and occasional factual interludes, such as Major Thomas Jesup's account of his 1814 regimental training. More modern histories include J. C. A. Stagg's *Mr. Madison's War*

331

(Princeton, N.J.: Princeton University Press, 1983); Francis F. Beime's *The War of 1812* (New York: E. P. Dutton, 1949); and Glenn Tucker's *Poltroons and Patriots* (New York: Bobs-Merrill, 1954). The last contains interesting items, such as the celebrations among the "better classes" in New England in 1814 over Napoleon's abdication, heedless of the fact that England could then turn greater strength against the United States. However, Tucker overstrains himself trying to make Monroe the war's primary hero. Specific works on the development of the U.S. Army and this nation's military policy include Lawrence D. Cress's *Citizens in Arms* (Chapel Hill: University of North Carolina Press, 1982), a sober, detailed study of regular forces and militia in America up to 1812; James R. Jacobs' *The Beginnings of the U.S. Army, 1783–1812* (Princeton, N.J.: Princeton University Press, 1947), and Richard H. Kohn's *Eagle and Sword* (New York: The Free Press, 1975). John K. Mahon's *The American Militia: Decade of Decision, 1789–1800* (Gainesville: University of Florida Press, 1960) is a definitive work. *History of the United States Army* by Russell F. Weigley (New York: Macmillan, 1967) is handy as a quick reference for legislative/organizational matters, but its coverage of military operations for this period is riddled with errors. William A. Ganoe's mistakenly revered *The History of the United States Army* (New York: D. Appleton-Century, 1924) also can be used as a chronological record of changes in organization, weapons, and clothing, but shows no comprehension of the interrelationship between the Army and American society; it also is saturated with whiny self-pity. More detailed information on soldiers' lives is in John R. Elting's *American Army Life* (New York: Scribner's, 1982) and *Military Uniforms in America: Years of Growth, 1796–1851* (San Rafael, Calif.: Presidio Press, 1977) and in Detmar H. Finke's "U.S. Infantry Uniforms, Winter 1812–1813," *Military Collector and Historian*, Vol. II, No. 1 (March, 1950).

There is excellent coverage of the forts that had such an important function in this war as bases, and frontier strong points in Emanuel R. Lewis's *Seacoast Fortifications of the United States* (Washington, D.C.: Smithsonian Institution Press, 1970) and Robert B. Roberts' *Encyclopedia of Historic Forts* (New York: Macmillan, 1988). *American Forts, Yesterday and Today* (New York: E. P. Dutton, 1965) by Bruce Grant is also useful.

The difficulties inflicted on would-be conquerors by North American topography are well described by Henry Adams in the first chapter of his *The History of the United States of America During the Administrations of Jefferson and Madison* (abridged edition, Chicago, Ill.: University of Chicago Press, 1967), which can startle the modern reader with its portrayal of Thomas Jefferson in 1801, happy to have covered the 100 miles from Monticello to Washington without accident and noting that of the eight rivers he had crossed "five have neither bridges or boats." *Sugar Creek* (New Haven, Conn.: Yale University Press, 1986), by John M. Faragher, and R. Carlyle Buley's *The Old Northwest* (Bloomington, Ind.: Indiana University Press, 1951) are excellent sources for the topography and living conditions in the modern Middle West—then mostly frontier. The title for Glenn A. Steppler's master's thesis (McGill University, 1974) accurately describes its picture of the tribulations of Canadian logistical operations—"A Duty Troublesome Beyond Measure."

Among useful works on special aspects of this war George W. Cullum's *Campaigns of the War of 1812* (New York: J. Miller, 1879) covers the work of the U.S. Corps of Engineers, such as the construction and defense of Fort Meigs. Russell J. Wheeler's "Vengeance on the Frontier: Some Aspects of Retaliation in the War of 1812" (Master's thesis, University of South Florida, 1972) studies the wolf-eat-wolf struggle growing out of the employment of Indians and undisciplined troops.

Miscellaneous references are plentiful and useful, beginning with J. C. Fredericksen's *Free Trade and Sailors' Rights: A Bibliography of the War of 1812* (Westport, Conn.: Greenwood Press, 1985) and Alvin M. Josephy, Jr.'s *The Indian Heritage of America* (New York: Alfred A. Knopf, 1970). Secretary of War John Armstrong left his two-volume *Notices of the War of 1812* (New York: Wiley and Putnam, 1840), which is more of a self-justifying diatribe than good history, but yet notable for sharp and bloody-minded insights. His *Hints to Young Generals by an Old Soldier* (Kingston, N.Y.: J. Bull, 1812) was probably the first book on military strategy written by an American.

An unusually able depiction of American diplomatic activity throughout the war, the various effects of our fluctuating military situation on the endeavors of our stubborn negotiators, and the degree to which the delicate European military/political situation shackled British military operations against the United States is provided by Fred L. Engelman's *The Peace of Christmas Eve* (London: Rupert Hart-Davis, 1962). That European situation, with all its double-dealing and implicit threats of new wars, is well described in *The Congress of Vienna* (New York: Barnes and Noble, 1966) by Charles Webster.

Everything considered, the War of 1812 still awaits a British/Canadian historian capable of matching Henry Adams. Sir John W. Fortescue's many-volumed *History of the British Army* (London: Macmillan, 1899–1930) rather hurries past it. The best English work to date is Reginald

Horsman's concise and impartial *The War of 1812* (London: Eyre and Spottiswoode, 1969). Among Canadian authors, Ernest Cruikshank's *The Battle of Lundy's Lane: A Historical Study* (Welland, Ont.: Lundy's Lane Historical Society, 1893) and other works have proven quite unreliable. J. Mackay Hitsman's *The Incredible War of 1812* (Toronto: University of Toronto Press, 1965) concerns itself too exclusively with Canadian affairs. George F. G. Stanley's *The War of 1812* (Ottawa: Canadian War Museum, 1983) also is written out of an intense dedication to Canada and its people, but gives a full description of both British and Canadian activities and is especially valuable for its presentation of Canada's resources and military preparedness in 1812. Unfortunately, Stanley concerns himself almost entirely with the war along the Canadian/American frontier; his coverage of other campaigns—such as the British capture of Washington—is not of equal quality. William W. Wood has edited *Select British Documents of the Canadian War of 1812* in three volumes (Toronto: 1920–28). There are a number of personal histories of the war (probably more than have so far been discovered in the United States). The letters written by Sergeant James Commins, 8th Foot, edited by Norman C. Lord as "The War on the Canadian Frontier, 1812–14," *Journal of the Society for Army Historical Research*, Vol. XVIII, No. 72 (1939) is an old-soldier story, much of it apparently written with the help of something more inspiring than a pint of bitters. (The stout sergeant's estimates of American strengths and casualties were astronomical; Lord has not seriously deflated them.) Far more enlightening and interesting is the unpublished memoir of Lieutenant John Le Couteur, 104th Foot, recently unearthed by Robert Graves. Le Conteur, a cheerful, adventuresome officer, went through the hardest fighting of the northern theater: having had to watch Indians scalping the American wounded at Beaver Dams, he did agree with Sergeant Commins in detesting their red brethren and allies as a literally savage lot. The story of the Indians serving with British troops on the Niagara frontier is contained in the generally observant memoir of Major John Norton, their able half-breed leader in Carl F. Klinck and J. J. Talman, *The Journal of Major John Norton*. Toronto: The Champlain Society, 1990.

WAR IN THE WEST

An essential minority report on the opening operations in the west is the *Revolutionary Services and Civil Life of General William Hull*, together with *The History of the Campaign of 1812, and the Surrender of the Post of Detroit* (New York: D. Appleton, 1848) prepared from Hull's papers by his daughter, Mrs. Maria Campbell, and his grandson, James F. Clarke. This book contains a wealth of information on both wars, including the construction of Oliver Perry's squadron on Lake Erie. It also is notable for Hull's remark when he saw that all the witnesses against him during his stacked court-martial had been promoted since the fall of Detroit (in which all of them had participated): "my expedition was more prolific of promotion than any other unsuccessful military enterprise I ever heard of." Another necessary source is Keith R. Widder's *Reveille Till Taps* (Fort Mackinac, Mich.: Mackinac Island State Park Commission, 1972), a history of Fort Mackinac, that combines nicely with Brian Dunnigan's *The British Army at Mackinac* (Fort Mackinac, Mich.: Mackinac Island State Park Commission, 1980). Bernard De Voto's *The Course of Empire* (Boston: Houghton Mifflin, 1952) has a full account of the naval explorations and fur-trading ventures that had Americans and Englishmen at loggerheads even before the official hostilities began.

Robert B. McAfee's *History of the Late War in the Western Country* (Bowling Green, Ohio: Historical Publications Company, 1912) is a detailed study of both the major campaigns and many minor clashes and scalp-liftings. *Recollections of the War of 1812: Three Eyewitness Accounts* (Toronto: Baxter Publishing Company, 1964) from the Canadian Heritage Series is useful, as is Alex R. Gilpin's *The War of 1812 in the Old Northwest* (East Lansing: Michigan University Press, 1958).

WAR IN THE NORTH

Henry Adams and George F. G. Stanley remain the principal authorities for this theater, Stanley's *The War of 1812* (Ottawa: Canadian War Museum, 1983) being supplemented by his *Conflicts and Social Notes* (Ottawa: Parks Canada, 1976), which concentrates on operations large and small along the St. Lawrence River. Louis L. Babcock's *The War of 1812 on the Niagara Frontier* (Buffalo, N.Y.: Buffalo Historical Society, 1927) and Pierre Berton's *Flames Across the Border* (Boston: Little, Brown, 1981) are routine works.

Canadian sources are quite variable. The once-esteemed Ernest Cruikshank's *The Battle of Lundy's Lane: A Historical Study* (Welland, Ont.: Lundy's Lane Historical Society, 1893) and other publications are now recognized as biased and unreliable. John K. S. F. Richardson's *A Full and Detailed Narrative of the Operations of the Right Division of the Army of Upper Canada During the American War of 1812* (Brockville, Ont.: A. C. Casselman, 1842) is—as might be expected for that period—somewhat chauvinistic, but also useful. Major R. L. Rogers' *History of the Lincoln and Welland Regiment* (private printing, 1954) briefly covers the operations of Canadian militia along the Niagara frontier; *Recollections of the War of 1812: Three Eyewitness Accounts* (Toronto: Baxter Publishing Company, 1964) from the Canadian Heritage Series is an excellent source. Donald E. Graves' "Joseph Willcocks and the Canadian Volunteers" (Master's thesis, Carleton University, 1982) tells of those Canadians who served with the American Army, in literal peril of their necks. Graves also is the author of the meticulously researched "Where Right and Glory Leads: The Battle of Lundy's Lane, 25 July 1814" (unpublished), which is the definitive history of that campaign.

Useful biographies and memoirs include Charles W. Elliott's excellent *Winfield Scott: The Soldier and the Man* (New York: Macmillan, 1937) and Roger L. Nichols' *General Henry Atkinson* (Norman: University of Oklahoma Press, 1965). James Wilkinson, being a treacherous scoundrel, naturally has two good biographies: *The Admirable Trumpeter* (Garden City, N.Y.: Doubleday, Doran, 1941) by Thomas R. Hay and M. R. Werner, and James J. Jacob's *Tarnished Warrior* (New York: Macmillan, 1938). To these should be added the *Public Papers*, 3 vols. (Albany: B. J. Lyon, 1898–1902) of Daniel D. Tompkins, New York's sorely tried governor.

Brian L. Dunnigan's *Glorious Old Relic* (Youngstown, N.Y.: Old Fort Niagara Association, 1987) is the history of that key fortress. The more-or-less Swiss mercenary regiments in the British service have two histories: Jean-René Bory's *Les Suisses au Service Étranger* (Noyon: Courier de la Côte, 1965) and Vicomte Grouval's *Les Corps de Troupe de l'Émigration Française*, Vol. I. (Paris: La Sabretache, 1957). Both, especially Bory's, are splendidly mendacious.

To conclude I am much indebted to Patrick A. Wilder for surprising new facts on the battle of Sackets Harbor. His forthcoming book will be the first detailed, carefully researched account of that engagement.

WAR ON THE LAKES AND HIGH SEAS

Henry Adams' descriptions of these naval actions are excellent—and have served as a basis for many subsequent works. The most prestigious history, of course, is Alfred T. Mahan's *Seapower in Its Relation to the War of 1812* (Boston: Little, Brown, 1905). Good general histories include Dudley W. Knox's *A History of the United States Navy* (New York: G. P. Putnam's Sons, 1948); Edward L. Beach's *The United States Navy: 200*

Years (New York: Henry Holt, 1986); E. B. Potter's *The Naval Academy Illustrated History of the United States Navy* (New York: Thomas Y. Crowell, 1971); and Fletcher Pratt's *The Navy* (Garden City, N.Y.: Garden City Publishing Co., 1941). Pratt is the most entertaining of the lot, but all—especially Mahan, Potter, and Pratt—have the disadvantage of being written entirely from the Navy's point of view, with only a flawed knowledge of the interrelated land operations. Fortunately *The Age of Fighting Sail* (Garden City, N.Y.: Doubleday, 1956) by Cecil S. Forester is both impartial and thoroughly integrated with military and diplomatic events, stressing the British dependence on American foodstuffs.

The one essential reference for an understanding of naval warfare during this period is Howard I. Chapelle's *The History of the American Sailing Navy* (New York: Bonanza Books, 1949)—a veritable mother lode of information on ship design, construction, handling, operations, and development.

Also highly useful are Peter Padfield's *Guns at Sea* (New York: Saint Martin's Press, 1974), a history of naval gunnery; the U.S. Navy's *Dictionary of American Naval Fighting Ships* (Washington, D.C.: U.S. Division of Naval History, 1959–81); and William S. Dudley's *The Naval War of 1812: A Documentary History* (Washington, D.C.: Naval Historical Center, 1985).

The decisive battle of Lake Erie is described in both Robert J. Dodge's *The Battle of Lake Erie* (Pretoria, Ohio: Gray Printing Company, 1967) and Alex R. Gilpin's *The War of 1812 in the Old Northwest* (East Lansing: Michigan State University, 1958). Both it and the battle of Lake Champlain are featured in Marvin H. Albert's *Broadsides and Boarders* (New York: Appleton-Century-Crofts, 1957); Charles G. Muller's *The Proudest Day* (New York: John Day, 1960) is a spirited account of American operations on Lake Champlain.

Among British sources Reginald Horsman's *The War of 1812* (London: Eyre and Spottiswoode, 1969) has an account of the Royal Navy's maraudings along the American East Coast. *War in the Eastern Seas* (London: George Allen and Unwin, 1954) by C. Northcote Parkinson notes the activities of American privateers and warships in the Indian Ocean.

WASHINGTON AND BALTIMORE

Neil H. Swanson's *The Perilous Fight* (New York: Farrar and Rinehart, 1945) is the best single book on this British raid, full of color and detail, and fun to read. Wilfred M. Burton's *The Road to Washington* (Boston: Gorham Press, 1919) is acceptable. However, Henry Adams remains the best authority.

On the British side, the *Narrative of the Campaigns of the British Army at Washington and New Orleans in the Years 1814–1815* (London, 1821) by Lieutenant John R. Gleig (later chaplain general of the British Army) is lively and interesting but not always reliable. Charles W. C. Oman's *Wellington's Army, 1809–1814* (London: Edward Arnold, 1913) provides a splendid picture of the veteran soldiers who took Washington.

Readers interested in the Fort McHenry flag should use *The History of the United States Flag* (New York: Harper and Brothers, 1961) by Milo Quaife, Melvin Weig, and Roy Appleman.

WAR IN THE SOUTH

Because Jackson's self-willed personality dominated operations in this theater, Marquis James's *Andrew Jackson, The Border Captain* (New York: Bobbs-Merrill, 1933) or his *The Life of Andrew Jackson* (Garden City, N.Y.: Garden City Publishing Co., 1940) is essential reading. The best of Jackson's biographies, it somehow blends a large dose of hero worship with a realistic appreciation of his difficult character. Its accounts of American military operations are factual, but unfortunately the author seldom comprehends British movements or the military "big picture." Jonathan Daniels' *The Devil's Backbone* (New York: McGraw-Hill, 1962) is a colorful picture of life along the old Natchez Trace, between Natchez and Nashville, with Jackson and James Wilkinson as two of the principal characters. James Jacobs' biography of Wilkinson, *Tarnished Warrior* (New York: Macmillan, 1938), also is useful.

Books on Jackson's campaigning include Robert B. McAfee's detailed *History of the Late War in the Western Country* (Bowling Green, Ohio: Historical Publications Company, 1912) and *Struggle for the Gulf Borderlands* (Gainesville: University Presses of Florida, 1981) by Frank L. Owsley, Jr. *Historical Memoir of the War in West Florida and Louisiana* (Gainesville: University Presses of Florida, 1964) is a revival of the account of Arsene L. C. Latour, Jackson's somewhat mysterious chief of engineers and, as such, an eyewitness. In his *The Amphibious Campaign for West Florida and Louisiana* (Tuskaloosa: University of Alabama Press, 1969), Wilbert S. Brown endeavors to justify Jackson's strategic blunderings. Other works are Robin Reilly's *The British at the Gates* (New York: G. P. Putnam's

Sons, 1974) and Fairfax Downey's *Indian Wars of the U.S. Army, 1776–1865* (Garden City, N.Y.: Doubleday, 1963).

English sources are especially plentiful and reliable, beginning with Gleig's handle-with-care *Narrative* and A. B. Ellis's *The History of the First West India Regiment* (London, 1885). S. P. G. Ward's *Wellington's Headquarters* (New York: Oxford University Press, 1957) outlines General Edward Packenham's earlier service and also demonstrates how service under Wellington destroyed his subordinates' initiative. Extremely useful are *Life and Correspondence of Field Marshal Sir John Burgoyne, Bart.*, Vol. I (London: Richard Bentley and Son, 1873), edited by George Wrottesley, and "Artillery Services in North America in 1814 and 1815," *Journal of the Society for Army Historical Research*, Vol. VIII, Nos. 32, 33, and 34, (1929), edited by J. H. Leslie. The latter especially contains the details of the British Army's daily activities through most of the New Orleans campaign.

REFERENCES

Adams, Henry. *The War of 1812*. Washington, D.C.: The Infantry Journal, 1944.

Armstrong, John. *Hints to Young Generals by an Old Soldier*. Kingston, N.Y.: J. Bull, 1812.

———. *Notices of the War of 1812*. 2 Vols. New York: Wiley and Putnam, 1840.

Babcock, Louis L. *The War of 1812 on the Niagara Frontier*. Buffalo, N.Y.: Buffalo Historical Society, 1927.

Beach, Edward L. *The United States Navy: 200 Years*. New York: Henry Holt, 1986.

Berton, Pierre. *Flames Across the Border*. Boston: Little, Brown, 1981.

Bory, Jean-René. *Les Suisses au Service Étranger*. Noyon: Courier de la Côte, 1965.

Brown, Wilbert S. *The Amphibious Campaign for West Florida and Louisiana*. Tuskaloosa: University of Alabama Press, 1969.

Burton, Wilfred M. *The Road to Washington*. Boston: Gorham Press, 1919.

Canadian Heritage Series. *Recollections of the War of 1812: Three Eyewitness Accounts*. Toronto: Baxter Publishing Company, 1964.

Chapelle, Howard I. *The History of the American Sailing Navy*. New York: Bonanza Books, 1949.

Clarke, James F. *History of the Campaign of 1812 and Surrender of the Post of Detroit*. New York: D. Appleton, 1847.

Cress, Lawrence D. *Citizens in Arms*. Chapel Hill: University of North Carolina Press, 1982.

Cruikshank, Ernest. *The Battle of Lundy's Lane: A Historical Study*. Welland, Ont.: Lundy's Lane Historical Society, 1893.

Cullum, George W. *Campaigns of the War of 1812*. New York: J. Miller, 1979.

Daniels, Jonathan. *The Devil's Backbone*. New York: McGraw-Hill, 1962.

Dempsey, Janet. *Washington's Last Cantonment*. Monroe, N.Y.: Library Research Associates, 1987.

DeVoto, Bernard. *The Course of Empire*. Boston: Houghton Mifflin Company, 1952.

Dickson, Alexander. "Artillery Services in North America in 1814 and 1815." *Journal of the Society for Army Historical Research*, Vol. VIII (July and October, 1929).

Dodge, Robert J. *The Battle of Lake Erie*. Pretoria, Ohio: Gray Printing Company, 1967.

Downey, Fairfax. *Indian Wars of the U.S. Army, 1776–1865*. Garden City, N.Y.: Doubleday, 1963.

Dudley, William S. *The Naval War of 1812: A Documentary History*. Washington, D.C.: Naval Historical Center, 1985.

Dunnigan, Brian L. *The British Army at Mackinac*. Fort Mackinac, Mich.: Mackinac Island State Park Commission, 1980.

———. *Glorious Old Relic*. Youngstown, N.Y.: Old Fort Niagara Association, 1987.

Elliott, Charles W. *Winfield Scott: The Soldier and the Man*. New York: Macmillan, 1937.

Ellis, A. B. *The History of the First West India Regiment*. London, 1885.

Elting, John R. *American Army Life*. New York: Scribner's, 1982.

———, ed. *Military Uniforms in America*. Vol II: *Years of Growth, 1796–1851*. San Rafael, Calif.: Presidio Press, 1977.

Emmons, George F. *The Navy of the United States*. Washington, D.C.: Gideon, 1850.

Engelman, Fred L. *The Peace of Christmas Eve*. London: Rupert Hart-Davis, 1962.

Faragher, John M. *Sugar Creek*. New Haven, Conn.: Yale University Press, 1986.

Finke, Detmar H. "U.S. Infantry Uniforms, Winter 1812–1813." *Military Collector and Historian*, Vol. II, No. 1 (March, 1950), pp. 5–6.

Fortescue, Sir John W. *History of the British Army*. 13 vols. London: Macmillan, 1899–1930.

Fredericksen, J. C. *Free Trade and Sailors' Rights: A Bibliography of the War of 1812*. Westport, Conn.: Greenwood Press, 1985.

Gilpin, Alex R. *The War of 1812 in the Old Northwest*. East Lansing: Michigan State University, 1958.

Gleig, John R. *Narrative of the Campaigns of the British Army at Washington and New Orleans in the Years 1814–1815*. London, 1821.

Grant, Bruce. *American Forts, Yesterday and Today*. New York: E. P. Dutton, 1965.

Graves, Donald E. "Joseph Willcocks and the Canadian Volunteers." Master's thesis, Carleton University, 1982.

———. Personal communications on the 1814 Niagara campaign.

———. "Where Right and Glory Leads: The Battle of Lundy's Lane, 25 July 1814." Unpublished manuscript.

Grouval, Vicomte. *Les Corps de Troupe de l'Émigration Française*, Vol. I. Paris: La Sabretache, 1957.

Hay, Thomas R., and M. R. Werner. *The Admirable Trumpeter*. Garden City, N.Y.: Doubleday, Doran, 1941.

Hitsman, J. Mackay. *The Incredible War of 1812*. Toronto: University of Toronto Press, 1965.

Horsman, Reginald. *The War of 1812*. London: Eyre and Spottiswoode, 1969.

Jacobs, James R. *The Beginnings of the U.S. Army, 1783–1812*. Princeton, N.J.: Princeton University Press, 1947.

———. *Tarnished Warrior*. New York: Macmillan, 1938.

James, Marquis. *The Life of Andrew Jackson*. Garden City, N.Y.: Garden City Publishing Co., 1940.

Josephy, Alvin M., Jr. *The Indian Heritage of America*. New York: Alfred A. Knopf, 1970.

Knox, Dudley W. *A History of the United States Navy*. New York: G. P. Putnam's Sons, 1948.

Kohn, Richard H. *Eagle and Sword*. New York: The Free Press, 1975.

Latour, Arsene L. C. *Historical Memoir of the War in West Florida and Louisiana.* Gainesville: University of Florida Press, 1964.

Leslie, J. H., ed. "Artillery Services in North America in 1814 and 1815." *Journal of the Society for Army Historical Research*, Vol. VIII, Nos. 32, 33, and 34 (1929).

Lewis, Emanuel R. *Seacoast Fortifications of the United States.* Washington, D.C.: Smithsonian Institution Press, 1970.

Lord, Norman C. "The War on the Canadian Frontier, 1812–14." *Journal of the Society for Army Historical Research*, Vol. XVIII, No. 72 (1939).

Lossing, Benson J. *The Pictorial Field Book of the War of 1812.* New York: Harper and Brothers, 1869.

McAfee, Robert B. *History of the Late War in the Western Country.* Bowling Green, Ohio: Historical Publications Company, 1912.

Mahan, Alfred T. *Seapower in Its Relation to the War of 1812.* Boston: Little, Brown, 1905.

Mahon, John K. *The American Militia: Decade of Decision, 1789–1800.* Gainesville: University of Florida Press, 1960.

Nichols, Roger L. *General Henry Atkinson.* Norman: Oklahoma University Press, 1965.

Oman, Charles W. C. *Wellington's Army, 1809–1814.* London: Edward Arnold, 1913.

Owsley, Frank L., Jr. *Struggle for the Gulf Borderlands.* Gainesville, University of Florida Press, 1981.

Padfield, Peter. *Guns at Sea.* New York: Saint Martin's Press, 1974.

Parkinson, C. Northcote. *War in the Eastern Seas, 1793–1815.* London: George Allen and Unwin, 1954.

Polley, Jane, ed. *American Folklore and Legends.* Pleasantville, N.Y.: The Reader's Digest Association, 1978.

Potter, E. B. *The Naval Academy Illustrated History of the United States Navy.* New York: Thomas Y. Crowell, 1971.

Pratt, Fletcher. *The Navy.* Garden City, N.Y.: Garden City Publishing Co., 1941.

———. *Preble's Boys.* New York: William Sloane Associates, 1950.

Purcha, Francis P. *Broadaxe and Bayonet.* Madison: State Historical Society of Wisconsin, 1953.

Quaife, Milo; Melvin Weig; and Roy Appleman. *The History of the United States Flag.* New York: Harper and Brothers, 1961.

Reilly, Robin. *The British at the Gates.* New York: G. P. Putnam's Sons, 1974.

Richardson, John K. S. F. *A Full and Detailed Narrative of the Operations of the Right Division of the Army of Upper Canada During the American War of 1812.* Brockville, Ont., 1842.

Roberts, Robert B. *Encyclopedia of Historic Forts.* New York: Macmillan, 1988.

Rogers, R. L. *History of the Lincoln and Welland Regiment.* Private Printing by Lincoln and Welland Regiment, 1954.

Stagg, J. C. A. *Mr. Madison's War.* Princeton, N.J.: Princeton University Press, 1983.

Stanley, George F. C. *Conflicts and Social Notes.* Ottawa: Parks Canada, 1976.

———. *The War of 1812.* Ottawa: Canadian War Museum, 1983.

Steppler, Glenn A. "A Duty Troublesome Beyond Measure." Master's thesis, McGill University, 1974.

Swanson, Neil H. *The Perilous Fight.* New York: Farrar and Rinehart, 1945.

Tompkins, Daniel D. *Public Papers.* 3 vols. Albany: B. J. Lyon, 1898–1902.

Tucker, Glenn. *Dawn Like Thunder.* New York: Bobs-Merrill, 1963.

U.S. Navy. *Dictionary of American Naval Fighting Ships.* Washington, D.C.: U.S. Division of Naval History, 1959–81.

U.S. Public Works Administration, Kentucky. *Military History of Kentucky.* Frankfort, Ky.: U.S. Public Works Administration, 1939.

Ward, S. P. G. *Wellington's Headquarters.* New York: Oxford University Press, 1957.

Weigley, Russell F. *History of the United States Army.* New York: Macmillan, 1967.

Wheeler, Russell J. *Vengeance on the Frontier: Some Aspects of Retaliation in the War of 1812.* Master's thesis, University of South Florida, 1972.

White, Leonard D. *The Jeffersonians.* New York: Macmillan, 1951.

Widder, Keith R. *Reveille Till Taps: Soldier Life at Fort Mackinac, 1780–1895.* Fort Mackinac, Mich.: Mackinac Island State Park Commission, 1972.

Wilder, Patrick A. Personal communications.

Williams, T. Harry. *Americans at War.* Baton Rouge: Louisiana State University Press, 1960.

———. *History of American Wars.* New York: Alfred A. Knopf, 1981.

Wrottesley, George, ed. *Life and Correspondence of Field Marshal Sir John Burgoyne, Bart.* Vol. I. London: Richard Bentley and Son, 1873.

INDEX

Other titles of interest

**THE CAMPAIGN OF 1812
IN RUSSIA**
Carl von Clausewitz
New foreword by Sir Michael Howard
272 pp., 15 maps
80650-9 $13.95

**JOURNAL OF THE WATERLOO
CAMPAIGN**
General Cavalié Mercer
New afterword by
Philip J. Haythornthwaite
. 416 pp.
80651-7 $15.95

**GREAT DOCUMENTS IN
AMERICAN INDIAN HISTORY**
Edited by Wayne Moquin with
Charles Van Doren
New foreword by Dee Brown
458 pp., 20 illus. & 5 maps
80659-2 $16.95

**BATTLES OF THE
REVOLUTIONARY WAR
1775-1781**
W. J. Wood
Introd. by John S. D. Eisenhower
363 pp., 40 illus., 30 maps and
diagrams
80617-7 $13.95

THE BLACK PHALANX
African American Soldiers in the
War of Independence, the War
of 1812, and the Civil War
Joseph T. Wilson
New introd. by Dudley Taylor Cornish
534 pp., 64 illus.
80550-2 $16.95

**THE DEFEAT OF IMPERIAL
GERMANY, 1917-1918**
Rod Paschall
Introd. by John S.D. Eisenhower
288 pp., 61 photos, 14 maps
80585-5 $13.95

INVINCIBLE GENERALS
Philip J. Haythornthwaite
240 pp., 160 illus.,
29 maps and plans
80577-4 $16.95

**THE MILITARY MAXIMS OF
NAPOLEON**
Edited by William E. Cairnes
Introduction and commentary by
David G. Chandler
253 pp., 10 illus.
80618-5 $13.95

**MONTCALM AND WOLFE
The French and Indian War**
Francis Parkman
Foreword by C. Vann Woodward
674 pp., 116 illus., 9 maps
80621-5 $18.95

**THE SPIRIT OF 'SEVENTY-SIX
The Story of the American
Revolution as told by Participants**
Edited by Henry Steele Commager
and Richard B. Morris
1,436 pp., 47 illus., 28 maps
80620-7 $27.95

THE WAR OF 1812
John K. Mahon
476 pp., 35 illus.
80429-8 $15.95

**AMERICA'S WARS AND
MILITARY ENCOUNTERS
From Colonial Times to the Present**
Edwin P. Hoyt
535 pp. 80338-0 $14.95

Available at your bookstore

OR ORDER DIRECTLY FROM

DA CAPO PRESS, INC.

1-800-321-0050